HOW CONTEMPORARY NOVELISTS REWRITE STORIES FROM THE BIBLE

The Interpretation of Scripture in Literature

HOW CONTEMPORARY NOVELISTS REWRITE STORIES FROM THE BIBLE

The Interpretation of Scripture in Literature

Anthony C. Swindell

With a Foreword by
Terence Wright

The Edwin Mellen Press
Lewiston•Queenston•Lampeter

Library of Congress Cataloging-in-Publication Data

Swindell, Anthony C., 1950-
  How contemporary novelists rewrite stories from the Bible : the interpretation of
scripture in literature / Anthony C. Swindell ; with a foreword by Terence Wright.
    p. cm.
  Includes bibliographical references and index.
  ISBN-13: 978-0-7734-4764-6 (alk. paper)
  ISBN-10: 0-7734-4764-4 (alk. paper)
  1. Bible--In literature. 2. Bible and literature. 3. Bible--Hermeneutics. I. Title.
  PN56.B5S85 2009
  809'.93522--dc22
                                    2009013479

hors série.

A CIP catalog record for this book is available from the British Library.

Front cover: Color reproduction of *The Body of Abel Found by Adam and Eve* by artist William
Blake, Image ID N05888. © Tate, London 2008

          The Edwin Mellen Press   The Edwin Mellen Press
               Box 450   Box 67
          Lewiston, New York   Queenston, Ontario
          USA 14092-0450   CANADA L0S 1L0

                        The Edwin Mellen Press, Ltd.
                        Lampeter, Ceredigion, Wales
                        UNITED KINGDOM SA48 8LT

                     Printed in the United States of America

Dedication

To my wife, Angela

CONTENTS

FOREWORD

The Bible, as David Lyle Jeffrey says at the beginning of his invaluable *Dictionary of Biblical Tradition in English Literature,* 'is a book like no other book. It presents ... itself as revelation, the enduring Word of God' but 'men and women for more than three millennia have been "writing out" these hallowed words', often with significant differences, in the attempt to make sense of them in very different historical contexts, 'reading into' the text layer upon layer of additional meanings.[1] Faith communities of all kinds have attempted to impose limits upon this interpretive process (some more than others) but individual readers and writers have always managed to find something 'in' the text, to which they respond in new and often highly creative ways. This ongoing process is the subject of Anthony Swindell's wide-ranging and comprehensive study. Even Swindell cannot, of course, include the whole range of attempts to rework the Bible, itself a collection of very different texts, but he does provide an extremely useful survey of the interest in this subject over the last three decades and a representative sample of the kinds of creative reworking of the Bible to be found in Western Literature from Milton to David Maine (though his focus is mainly on the modern period). Such has been the prevalence of rewritten biblical stories in recent years, in fact, that it sometimes appears as if the Bible is the first port of call for any novelist suffering from writer's block.

In an age of specialisation most evident in the academic world, not only between disciplines but within them (biblical critics often forced to specialise on one or two texts and rarely talking to other kinds of theologian, let alone to literary critics) the breadth of vision Swindell offers is refreshing. He also throws up interesting

---

1   David Lyle Jeffrey (ed.), *A Dictionary of Biblical Tradition in English Literature* (Grand Rapids, Michigan: William Eerdmans, 1992), p. xiii.

connections between writers who themselves are often unaware of others working on similar interpretative questions, albeit from different perspectives. Swindell's eight 'theorists' and fourteen 'reception theorists', for example, make very few cross-references to each other. And yet, as he is able to demonstrate, they can be seen to partake in an 'unfolding hermeneutical process' sharing similar interests in the creative response to the Bible of writers not bound by the same rather rigid conventions of academic biblical criticism.

There are, as Swindell acknowledges, significant differences between the approaches adopted by the critics studied, from J.D. Levenson seeking in his writers fidelity to the theology of the original text to Marina Warner bidding farewell to all earlier 'myths' about the Virgin Mary, from Susan Haskins attempting to uncover the historical Mary Magdalene to Ricardo Quinones recognising that there is no possibility of recovering the 'original' Cain. There is a similar distance between the conservative approach of the Anglican theologian David Brown and the radical speculation of the Jewish literary critic George Steiner. Common to all these theorists and critics, however, is a recognition of the importance of art in the full understanding of the Bible.

Literary texts in particular, as Swindell shows, respond to elements of the biblical texts that 'orthodox' readings tend to ignore or repress, asking questions of which authoritarian communities disapprove (using 'authoritarian' in the Bakhtinian sense of 'monological', attempting to impose a single closed meaning upon texts inherently 'dialogical', open to intertextual discussion with other texts). Bakhtin's own experience of the Russian Orthodox church was such that he failed to recognise the openness of the Bible itself to this kind of intertextuality. Yvonne Sherwood, whose study of the differing responses to the Book of Jonah is one of the most interesting books discussed here, uses the terms 'mainstream' and 'backwater' for these two opposed tendencies though this runs the risk of accepting the past privileging of the former as irreversible.

What readers of Swindell's book will discover, however, is that the literary rewriting of the Bible presents a powerful challenge to the past (and present) dominance of 'mainstream', authoritarian or fundamentalist attempts to close its interpretation. They will also find their own understanding of the Bible, whatever that is, considerably broadened by the range of readings exemplified here. They will also find suggestions for future reading sufficient to last for a very long time. If they had regarded the Bible (in its traditional black binding) as a dull, dutiful book, they will discover from the many examples of its reworking offered here that this is far from the case.

Professor Terence Wright
University of Newcastle
The School of English Literature, Language and Linguistics

ACKNOWLEDGEMENTS

The author gratefully acknowledges the wise guidance and assistance of Professor J.K. Elliott throughout the period which led up to the writing of this book. During the earlier part of that period, the guidance and assistance of Dr (now Professor) Hugh Pyper are also gratefully acknowledged.

The author wishes to thank the staff of The Brotherton Library at the University of Leeds and the staff of the Library at the University of Wales, Aberystwyth, for their kind help and co-operation. He wishes to thank the University of Wales, Aberystwyth, for permission to use library facilities. He also wishes to thank the staff of St Deiniol's Library, Hawarden, and the staff of Jersey Library for their kind assistance.

Thanks are due to Cambridge University Press for their kind permission to quote from W.W. Robson's summary of *Maud* (Chapter 7), to Indiana University Press for kind permission to cite Francis Utley's words about reception-history in Chapter 1 and Jorn Donner's description of Bergman's film *The Seventh Seal* in Appendix A. The paragraph from Bruce Merry: *Anatomy of the Spy Thriller* quoted in Chapter 2 is reprinted by kind permission of Gill & Macmillan, Dublin. The lines from the Kafka short story *The City Coat of Arms* (Chapter 6) from *The Collected Short Stories of Kafka*, published by Vintage Classics, are reprinted by permission of the Random House Group Ltd. (London) and Schocken Books, a division of Random House Inc. (New York). Thanks are due to Yale University Press for kind permission to cite Louis L. Martz's presentation of the Robert Southwell poem (Chapter 6) and to Princeton University Press for kind permission to quote the passage from Unamuno's *El Otro* (Chapter 5). The reproduction on the cover of Blake's painting, *The Body of Abel Found by Adam and Eve*, is by courtesy of the Tate Gallery. Especial thanks are due to Dr Yvonne Sherwood for permission to quote the private correspondence about her study of the Jonah story, *A Biblical Text and its Afterlives.*

Chapter 1

INTRODUCTION

This work is an examination of fourteen monographs written by fourteen different authors over a period of thirty years on the subject of the treatment of specific biblical stories in literature, art and theology, mainly in that order of priority. The period covered is 1972 to 2002 and the fourteen reception-histories examined are believed to represent the bulk of all such works published in English during that time.[1] The topics covered by our authors, J.D. Levenson, James Pritchard, Marina Warner, Ricardo Quinones, Susan Haskins, Norman Cohn, Richard Trexler, Margarita Stocker, Pamela Norris, Ann Wroe, Janet Howe Gaines, Tina Pippin, Yvonne Sherwood and Kim Paffenroth, are, respectively, the stories of Job, Solomon and Sheba, The Virgin Mary, Cain and Abel, Mary Magdalene, Noah's Flood, The Magi, Judith, Eve, Pilate, Jezebel, The Apocalypse, Jonah, and Judas.

As a totality, the fourteen works handle a significant proportion of the repertoire or *doxa* of stories basic to the Judaeo-Christian tradition.[2] There is no precise way of gauging the size of the repertoire of stories which constitutes this pool, but specific historical lists often seem to consist of between forty and fifty biblical stories.

---

1 The two works of which I am aware which are not included in the list are Geoffrey Ashe: *The Virgin* (London: RKP, 1973) which is referred to in the discussion of Marina Warner: *Alone of All Her Sex* (Chapter 2, p. 42) and the collection of essays edited by Raymond-Jean Frontain and Jan Wojcik: *The David Myth in Western Literature* (Indiana: Purdue University Press, 1980), which is more of a loose collection of disparate monographs. There are other works which restrict themselves largely to one historical period in literature, such as Brian Murdoch: *Adam's Grace: Fall and Redemption in Medieval Literature* (Woodbridge: D.S. Brewer, 2000) and Philip Almond: *Adam and Eve in Seventeenth-Century Thought* (Cambridge: Cambridge University Press, 1999).

2 The term *doxa* is borrowed from Mieke Bal's analysis of cultural stories treated in visual art (see below, p. 13). We acknowledge that the term 'Judaeo-Christian', despite its usefulness, is not free of the connotations of supersessionism, a topic to which we return at intervals.

For example, Pierre du Bourget lists twenty-eight Old Testament and twelve New Testament subjects of catacomb art.[3] M.R. James quotes Prudentius as recording twenty-four Old Testament and twenty-four New Testament themes current in early mural painting in basilicas.[4] The York cycle of Mystery Plays consists of forty-nine plays.[5] A mid-fourteenth-century Veronese compendium-painting, however, depicts just thirty biblical stories, with the Old Testament in this example reduced to just three episodes.[6] Needless to say, the content of these lists varies considerably and they tend to exclude certain mercurial biblical stories which achieve great prominence at particular historical moments, for example those of Joshua and Susanna.

The second chapter of our study surveys the fourteen reception-histories as a phenomenon, looking at the premises of the various authors, the way they select their material and the use they make of that material, particularly the 'reading' of creative works which can sustain a multiplicity of interpretations.

Reception-history in mainstream theology or in biblical hermeneutics has tended to connote the history of the formal theological exegesis of biblical texts, of the kind that can be found in traditional commentaries, such as Luther's Commentary on Romans. However, a recent biblical commentary series[7] has itself added the treatment of biblical texts (or their allusive use) in the arts to its account of the reception-history of particular texts, in harness with the theological tradition.

The works considered here were written before this development got underway and their authors often seem to be conscious of themselves as pioneers, although

3   Pierre du Bourget: *Early Christian Painting* (London: Weidenfeld & Nicolson, 1965), pp. 19–20.
4   M.R. James: *The Apocalypse in Art* (The 1927 Schweich Lectures, London: British Academy, 1931), p. 32. He cites the *Dittochaeum*, xlix.
5   J.S. Purvis (ed.): *The York Cycle of Mystery Plays* (London: SPCK, 1971), pp. 5–6.
6   Paolo Marini and Gianni Peretti: *Castelvecchio Museum* (Venice: Marsilo Editori, 2003), p. 29.
7   The *Blackwell Biblical Commentaries*, 'the first to be devoted primarily to the reception-history of the Bible'. (Series editor's Preface, p. ix, in Mark Edwards: *John* (Oxford: Blackwell, 2004)).

their awareness of what has been happening in the field of academic biblical studies varies considerably from author to author. The fourteen authors also do little or nothing to acknowledge each other as participants in a similar enterprise, although there are signs of a formula developing after the appearance of the first example in our study, Marina Warner's *Alone of All Her Sex* in 1976.[8]

In Britain, the idea of a panoramic survey of the treatment of a literary theme goes back at least to W.B. Stanford's *The Ulysses Theme*[9] (1954) and devotional or semi-devotional accounts of the development (particularly in the visual arts) of some biblical themes stretch back into the mid-nineteenth-century, where Anna Jameson's *Legends of the Madonna*[10] stands out as an early landmark in the history of the genre. In the early twentieth-century there is also Rowland Prothero's highly discursive, but in its time very popular, *The Psalms in Human Life*, which, although it is not about the reception-history of a biblical *story*, can be said to be part of the general background.[11] But there is something decisively new and innovatory about *Alone of All Her Sex* both as a publishing phenomenon and in terms of its approach to its subject, in this case the history of 'The Myth and Cult of the Virgin Mary'.

The fact that another book on the same subject was published in the very same year, although with a very different approach, Geoffrey Ashe's *The Virgin*,[12] does suggest that something was in the air at the time and, in that sense, the succeeding authors can be seen as belonging to a more widespread or diffuse background than the simple publication sequence of their respective essays. Whether that background can be characterised as post-modernistic pluralism or secularisation or

---

8   Marina Warner: *Alone of all Her Sex* (London: Weidenfeld and Nicholson, 1976).
9   W.B. Stanford: *The Ulysses Theme* (Oxford: Blackwell, 1954).
10   Anna Bronwell Jameson: *Legends of the Madonna* (London: Longman, Brown, Green and Longmans, 1852).
11   Rowland E. Prothero: *The Psalms in Human Life* (London: John Murray, 1903). The work reached its fourth edition in 1913 and a fifth impression appeared in 1949.
12   Geoffrey Ashe: *The Virgin* (London: RKP, 1976).

something else will be one of the underlying concerns of this study. In any event, the fourteen writers differ greatly in their attitude to the future viability of the narratives which underpin their accounts.

Before turning in Chapter 2 to a survey of the fourteen works, we will attempt to draw a sketch of developments in hermeneutics which may provide a framework for understanding the phenomenon under consideration.

Chapter 2 will then examine the fourteen works in turn. This chapter is inevitably somewhat unwieldy, because it has to lay the ground for the various forms of critical analysis which form the rest of the thesis. Chapter 3 will look at the work of a number of recent theorists, whose concerns are closely related to the field of 'rewritten Scripture', and also at the ideas of George Steiner, whose notion of transcendence is very relevant to our discussion. Chapter 4 will examine the extent to which theology can be said to be present, whether explicit or implicit, in the fourteen reception-histories. Chapter 5, entitled *Vox Dei*, will explore the range of theological discourse within a selection of the major rewritten biblical stories treated by our fourteen writers and also some significant works they omit to discuss. Chapter 6, entitled *Variations on a Theme*, will review a number of the more minor works discussed by the fourteen, as well, again, as some they ignore.

Chapter 7 will take the term The Other, a concept which is prominent in several of the fourteen reception-histories, in order to explore the relationship between religious and postmodernist senses. Chapter 8 will analyse the fourteen studies as literary structures. Chapter 9 will consider the evidence of conflations and convergences between biblical stories and also amongst the rewritten examples, in order to discuss the significance of these features. It will also look at the notion of contamination. Chapter 10 will examine the range of each of the fourteen studies, comparing the extent of their coverage of their respective material.

Chapter 11 will explore the notion of 'Nodal Points' amongst the fourteen studies, in the sense of particular literary or iconographic works which seem to be determinative for the overall direction of the reception-historian's reading of *all* the material under consideration. Chapter 12 will make comparisons between the fourteen and three non-biblical reception-histories, beginning with Stanford's *The Ulysses Theme*, mentioned above. Chapter 13 will explore notions of closure and resistance to closure, attitudes to newly-published apocryphal material, and also notions of canons, both literary and theological. Chapter 14, the final chapter, will attempt to draw conclusions; to suggest the hermeneutical value of what has been learned from this study; and to consider its value for Biblical Studies as a whole.

The Publishing Background

The material which forms the background to the study of the reception-history of biblical stories in its wider sense became familiar to various sorts of specialist audience throughout the first seventy years of the twentieth-century. In 1903, E.K. Chambers had published his two-volume *The Medieval Stage*,[13] bringing the contents of the English mystery plays to prominence, many of the texts themselves having appeared under the auspices of the Early English Text Society in the 1890s. Didron's *Christian Iconography*[14] had appeared in English back in 1854 and was to lead to a rich harvest of specialised monographs, of which F. Harrison's *The Painted Glass of York*[15] (1927) is a typical example. A work already mentioned, Anna Bronwell Jameson's *Legends of the Madonna*, had appeared in 1852. Although concerned predominantly with the background to the iconographic tradition, it could be said to be the forerunner of reception-history monographs dealing with a single biblical story or theme.

---

13 E.K. Chambers: *The Medieval Stage* (Oxford: Oxford University Press, 1903), 2 vols.
14 Adolph Napoleon Didron: *Christian Iconography*, trans E.J. Millington (New York: Frederick Ungar, 1851), 2 vols.
15 F. Harrison: *The Painted Glass of York* (London: SPCK, 1927).

6

In the 1950s and 1960s refinements in academic studies both of literary and iconographic subjects found their outworking in such publishing successes as M.D. Anderson's *The Imagery of British Churches* (1955)[16] and Murray Ruston's *Biblical Drama in England* (1968)[17]. Meanwhile, more specialised works opened up further vistas. Milton's *Paradise Lost* was widely recognized as an inspired reworking of the opening chapters of Genesis, but it took J.M. Evans to unveil the luxuriant tradition in Jewish and Christian exegesis, Old English poetry and later literature, which lay behind this seminal piece of writing.[18] Five years later, in 1973, Eric Smith was emboldened to trace the links from *Genesis B* through *The Faerie Queene* and *Paradise Lost* and onwards to *The Lord of the Flies* in his treatment of the Fall Theme in literature, *Some Versions of the Fall,*[19] a book which in places exemplifies the hazardous territory associated with identifying rewritten biblical stories where the text gives no specific pointers.

In another part of the wood, F.W. Dillistone had, in 1960, considered treatments of the passion story in the fiction of Mauriac, Melville, Kazantzakis and Faulkner in a book, *The Novelist and the Passion Story*, which became the model for a certain kind of theological appropriation of modern fiction.[20] The topic of the Jesus-figure in fiction later became the subject of a much larger and more literary study, covering a wider range of authors, in Theodore Ziolkowski's *Fictional Transfigurations of Jesus* (1971).[21]

Two stories from the Hebrew scriptures received attention in two separate books published in 1969 by Schocken Books, Shalom Spiegl's *The Last Trial*[22]

---

16   M.D. Anderson: *The Imagery of British Churches* (London: Murray, 1955).

17   Murray Roston: *Biblical Drama in England* (London: Faber, 1968).

18   J.M. Evans: *Paradise Lost and the Genesis Tradition* (Oxford: Oxford UP, 1968).

19   Eric Smith: *Some Versions of the Fall* (London: Croom Helm, 1973).

20   F.W. Dillistone: *The Novelist and the Passion Story* (London: Collins, 1960).

21   Theodore Ziolkowski: *Fictional Transfigurations of Jesus* (Princeton NJ: Princeton University Press, 1971).

22   Shalom Spiegl: *The Last Trial* (New York: Schocken Books, 1969).

(mainly on the medieval Jewish legends of the Akedah) and the collection of essays edited by Nahum Glatzer, *The Dimensions of Job*,[23] covering elements of the Jewish and Christian exegetical tradition and also some philosophers, including Kierkegaard, but ignoring the literary and iconographic tradition. A further book by a Jewish writer, this time Sol Liptzin, covered a range of literary treatments of biblical stories, from Lilith to Belshazzar, including works often overlooked.[24]

Marina Warner's *Alone of All Her Sex* appeared in 1976. It drew on the accumulated academic work done on the theme of the Virgin Mary in theology, literature and art. It had many more illustrations than previous works on biblical themes. But most significantly it marshalled its diverse material in the service of an argument which was simultaneously sensitive to its central subject matter in relation to cultural history and sceptical about religion. Warner herself seemed conscious of writing at the time of a watershed in the public attitude to the sacred and, in particular, to one specific sacred story.

Like those who followed her, Warner drew on a long list of often specialist academic monographs to create a sweeping narrative of her subject's life, almost from cradle to grave, for she was concerned not just to map out the origins and growth of the cult of the Virgin Mary, but also to argue from a feminist perspective that the myth had run its course. Warner's valedictory style seems to have been imitated, or endorsed, by some of the other writers who are the subject of this study, covering topics as diverse as Eve and Pontius Pilate, but, as will become evident, there are others who take a very different approach. What all fourteen authors have in common is the concept of the biblical story as the vehicle for a cultural tour from which a theological or humanistic message, whether strong or weak, emerges. Sometimes this overall decoding seems to take place in contradistinction to the process of mapping out fluctuations in meaning through time. Sometimes it seems

---

23   Nahum Glatzer (ed.): *The Dimensions of Job* (New York: Schocken Books, 1969).
24   Sol Liptzin: *Biblical Themes in World Literature* (Hoboken NJ, Ktav Publishing, 1985).

to be ironically acknowledged as just another example of the endless cavalcade of meanings. Thus Stocker finds in Judith a powerful myth capable of subverting all dehumanising influences at all times, whereas Trexler's Magi[25] seem to float on a sea of endlessly pliable meaning.

Alone of All Her Sex revealed the wealth of material waiting to be harvested in the service of an overarching account of the Life of the Virgin in religion, literature and art. The subject was one also with an enormous emotive charge, touching as it did on the whole question of modern womanhood and tackling head-on topics which some of her readership must have previously regarded as taboo. The fact that the author displayed a considerable degree of historical and aesthetic sensibility in her treatment of topics such as Mary as the Queen of Heaven put her in a different league from previous iconoclasts. But the book, whatever its authorial point of view, was also a fascinating journey across a swathe of cultural history, addressed to a general readership which, perhaps for the first time, could both be interested in the topic and relish the author's detachment from religious commitment.

Later authors in our survey may have missed out on the religious frisson effect enjoyed by Warner as a pioneer in the field and, in any case, their subject matter is not always as highly charged. An alternative strategy, already present in Warner, is to treat the reception-history of the biblical story as a highway into more general cultural history or as a sort of thread linking major writers, say from Chaucer to Samuel Beckett. Although this strategy is demonstrably present in several of the works, it tends to be overridden by arguments about the rise and fall of myths and about the cultural status of the reception-history's central topic. Ricardo Quinones sees Cain as supreme amidst the vast repertoire of Western myth; Pamela Norris contends that the story of Adam and Eve is the primary site for the Christian definition of sexuality for two thousand years; Susan Haskins sees the story of Mary Magdalene as the 'hidden history of womanhood; Margarita Stocker

---

25   Richard C. Trexler: *The Journey of the Magi* (Princeton, Princeton University Press, 1997).

celebrates Judith as the ultimate counter-cultural myth; Norman Cohn regards the Noah story as the litmus test of cultural change and continuity; Ann Wroe connects Pilate with the villain archetype in literature; Janet Gaines treats Jezebel as the platform for a mythographic rescue-operation; Tina Pippin sees the Apocalypse as ineradicably the most misogynist of texts; Yvonne Sherwood treats Jonah as the passport to an alternative reading of the Bible; and Kim Paffenroth treats Judas as a sort of case history of role reversal.[26]

The common factor seems to be that biblical authority as a topic has been replaced by claims about the influence of the respective biblical stories as transmitted through literary and iconographic variants. Advances in printing techniques allow the inclusion, in several of these books, of large numbers of photographic illustrations of works of art, sometimes in colour, perhaps subliminally reinforcing the sense of breaking through to a new dimension in the understanding of the stories which form the basis of discussion.

The Hermeneutical Background

The works we are considering span the years 1972 to 2002 in terms of their dates of publication. What was happening in biblical studies and in the philosophy of language during these years?

Before the Second World War, form criticism had dominated biblical studies. It was the study of the prehistory of the text, concerned to identify underlying segments of tradition, both those which belonged to an oral tradition and those which originated in lost early texts. The object was to reconstruct the process of development, or tradition history, and also to assign the components of the final text to a literary genre. There was a concern also to reconstruct the original life-setting of the component parts, for example locating parts of the Psalms in a

---

26   These authors form the main subject of the survey in Chapter 2 and this book as a whole.

specific, though conjectural, liturgical context. In the case of the gospels, form criticism led to an emphasis on small units of tradition and on the community as the agent of shaping the material, rather than on the work of the evangelists.[27]

Redaction criticism, which became current in the 1950s and 1960s, returned attention to the biblical writers as editors and shapers of the material and was particularly influential in the study of the gospels, since it allowed comparisons to be made amongst the Synoptics and between them and the Fourth Gospel. Interest grew in the different theological perspectives of the individual gospel writers.[28]

Canonical criticism, associated particularly with the name of Brevard Childs,[29] moved the emphasis again, this time to the final form of the canonical text. This approach took account of the importance of the finished text as sacred writing for the community of faith and as a result began to draw attention to the way successive communities of faith interpreted that text for their time. Canonical criticism also treated individual books of the Bible as part of the larger whole, the canon being a 'fait accompli' for the purposes of historical hermeneutics. In a wider context, canonical criticism can be seen as part of a philosophical shift from interest in locating meaning 'behind' the text to locating meaning 'ahead of' the text, an approach which is really the driving force of reception-history. It suggests that a text's meaning emerges through its use.

In literary criticism, the post-Second World War period saw the rise of the school of Wimsatt and Beardsley,[30] which attacked the location of meaning in what could be imputed to be the author's original intention (the 'Intentionalist

27 This summary is drawn mainly from the entry, 'Biblical Criticism' in Paul J. Achtemeier (ed.): *Harper's Bible Dictionary* (San Francisco: Harper & Row, 1985), pp. 129–33.

28 See Joachim Rohde: *Rediscovering the Teaching of the Evangelists*, trans. Dorothea M. Barton (London: SCM Press, 1968).

29 See Brevard Childs: *Biblical Theology in Crisis* (Philadelphia: Westminster Press, 1970) and *Exodus: A Commentary* (London: SCM Press, 1974).

30 See William K. Wimsatt, Jr: *The Verbal Icon, Studies in the Meaning of Poetry* (Lexington: Kentucky University Press, 1954).

Fallacy'). The attack was firstly on the grounds that the author's intention was frequently unclear or unknown, secondly that it might change, and thirdly (and most significantly) that later readings might discover richer meanings than those of which the author was consciously aware.[31] The author may also have projected a fictive author within the text and in any case might himself or herself be considered an unstable entity. To all of this were added uncertainties over the stability of texts and over which version might be preferred when there were competing variants of a text.

Roland Barthes[32] became famous as the one to proclaim the death of the Author, although his seminal work *S/Z*[33] seems to be as much about the multivocal character of language as about the rebutting of authorial intention. Others indeed argued that the key issue in hermeneutics was not the author but the question of the closure of representation. Jacques Derrida[34] was more willing than some of his followers to take account of the author as one source of meaning amongst others, but at the same time he argued not just for the instability of the text but for the instability or waywardness of language itself.

In all of this the Reader emerged as of central importance to the creation of meaning. According to Alison Jack, 'For Fish and other postmodernists, interpretation is not the art of construing but of constructing.'[35] For Wolfgang Iser, similarly, meaning occurs as a product of the interplay between the text and

---

31 The origins of this approach go back to Schleiermacher. See David Jasper: *A Short Introduction to Hermeneutics* (Louisville: Westminster John Knox Press, 2004), pp. 83–6.
32 Roland Barthes, author of *Mythologies* and *S/Z* and other works.
33 Roland Barthes: *S/Z* trans. Richard Miller (Oxford: Blackwell, 1990/1998). The work seeks to deconstruct Balzac's short story *Sarrasine*.
34 Jacques Derrida: *Of Grammatology*, trans. G.V. Spivak (Baltimore and London: John Hopkins UP, 1976) and *Positions* (London: Athlone, 1981).
35 Alison Jack: *Texts Reading Texts, Sacred and Secular* (Sheffield: Sheffield University Press, 1999), p. 28.

12

the reader.[36] The text has its implied reader, a construct of the text, and also an empirical reader, who herself/himself may be changed in the course of the reading. Important in Iser's schema was the identification of gaps within the text which licensed the reader to add to what he found there.[37] Mieke Bal has countered robustly that gap-filling is an inadequate notion, since the terms *gap* and *gap-filling* 'fail to account for repression and elimination, and end up accounting only for supplementation'.[38] Nevertheless, the notion of gap-filling has had an immense influence on the development of reception-history as a field of research.[39]

Reception-history as a phenomenon or as a concept meshes quite comfortably with the developments described above, since it is the record of successive readings of a text. However, even if one may assume a degree of stability in the text which is held to be the subject of the reception-history (being, for example, the biblical text as received in the Vulgate or King James version), there remain the questions both of the stability of treatments of the text (a working example might be Unamuno's two approaches to the story of Cain and Abel) and, more importantly, of how the readings themselves are read. There are further complexities generated by the multiplicity of readings of the readings, for example the many ways in which Byron's *Cain* and Conrad's *The Secret Sharer* (understood to be versions of the Cain and Abel story) have been read.

The purpose of this study is to examine how the literary and iconographic readings are themselves read by our various authors, comparing their final text with their source material (for example in the Mystery Plays) and also with rival

---

36 'Authors play games with readers and the text is the playground.' (Wolfgang Iser: 'The Play of the Text', p. 327, in Sanford Budick and Wolfgang Iser: *Languages of the Unsayable, The Play of Negativity in Literature and Literary Theory* (Stanford, California: Stanford University Press, 1987/1996). See also note 42.

37 See entry on 'Phenomenology' in Jeremy Hawthorn: *A Glossary of Contemporary Literary Theory* (London: Arnold, 2000/2003), p. 263.

38 Mieke Bal: *A Mieke Bal Reader* (Chicago: University of Chicago Press, 2006), p. 425.

39 The tenacity of gap-filling as a concept can be illustrated by its pervasive use in works such as Philip Almond's *Adam and Eve in Seventeenth-Century Thought* (1999), mentioned above.

interpretations of the same material. The fact that what we call the 'base text' or 'urtext' is in each case a sacred story carries its own resonances in terms both of that story's relationship with the history of its canonical interpretation and also of our modern reception-history authors' relationship with a sacred story in the context of an era of religious scepticism. If, as Harold Bloom argues,[40] all readings are misreadings, divisible into strong and weak misreadings, then we will also be dealing with the strength of sacred stories relative to later readings, as well as with the way in which hermeneutical gaps are filled (or exposed) by later readings and the questions of repression and elimination highlighted by Mieke Bal.

In his *Canon and Creativity*,[41] Robert Alter welcomed Harold Bloom's argument, in *The Western Canon*[42] and elsewhere for the canon not as an instrument of ideological coercion, but as the repository of those literary works which had won their place in the pantheon through their originality and strangeness. But he found Bloom's picture of a Darwinian clash of authorial wills less convincing, arguing for pleasurable playfulness and continuity as the means by which later works inserted themselves in the canon. Alter's book argues for the 'double canonicity' of the Hebrew Bible as both the basis of a system of beliefs and the fountainhead of a (sometimes Quixotic) literary tradition. Examples discussed include variations on the Tower of Babel story by Kafka (reminiscent of Kierkegaard's versions of Genesis 22 in *Fear and Trembling*) and also the experiment conducted by James Joyce in *Ulysses*, fusing biblical themes with the Homeric epic.

It was Eric Auerbach in *Mimesis*[43] who had developed the idea of the lacunae in the biblical text as pregnant sources of meaning, contrasting the depth he found in Genesis 22 with the flatness of the Homeric narrative. More recent scholars have

---

40   See Harold Bloom: *The Anxiety of Influence* (Oxford: Oxford University Press, 1973/1997).

41   Robert Alter: *Canon and Creativity* (New Haven: Yale University Press, 2000).

42   Harold Bloom: *The Western Canon* (London: Macmillan, 1995).

43   Eric Auerbach: *Mimesis, The Representation of Reality in Western Literature*, trans Willard R Trask (Princeton NJ: Princeton University Press, 1968. First published Berne: 1946).

14

tended to find hermeneutical gaps in all literature (as with Iser)[44] and to esteem Homer more highly.[45]

Although Frank Kermode celebrated the gaps in the biblical text as the agent in bringing alive for the reader such figures as Judas (one of the subjects of the fourteen reception-histories we will study), he did so without resort to a contrast with Homer.[46] More recently, as we have noted, Mieke Bal has argued that gap-filling is an inadequate hermeneutical concept and needs to be supplemented by a form of ethical criticism which brings into the frame rewritings which offer a cultural critique of the urtext.[47] Bal is also the originator of the term 'ideo-stories', as a description of culturally important stories which are open to constant adaptation.[48]

A quite different avenue of development, not pursued in this book, deserves mention. This is what can loosely be described as The Bible As Literature. An early exponent was Matthew Arnold, for whom the discovery of the Bible as a

---

44   See, for example, Wolfgang Iser: 'The Play of the Text' in Sanford Budick and Wolfgang Iser (eds).: *Languages of the Unsayable* (Stanford, California: Stanford University Press, 1987, pp. 325–39. In this essay, Iser argues that reading is a form of play and that there is no meaning before play. The structure of a piece of writing creates 'play spaces' by its very nature, where the 'split signifier' opens up a gap between what is ostensibly present and what is denoted as absent.

45   There is a discussion of the influence of Auerbach on Herbert Schneidau, Robert Alter and Harold Bloom by Gabriel Josipovici, who believes that the contrast between Homer and the Bible has been overstated. See Gabriel Josipovici: *The Book of God* (New Haven: Yale University Press, 1988), pp. 26, 300–1. Gregory J. Riley challenges the equation of 'Homeric' with 'pagan' in the context of early Christian literature in his essay 'Mimesis of Classical Ideals in the Second Christian Century' in Dennis R. Macdonald (ed.): *Mimesis and Intertextuality in Antiquity and Christianity* (Harrisburg PA: Trinity Press, 2001), pp. 91–103. The writer Roberto Calasso, as a modern champion of Homer, is discussed in A.S. Byatt: *On Histories and Stories, Selected Essays* (London: Chatto & Windus, 2000), pp. 125–8.

46   Frank Kermode: *The Genesis of Secrecy* (Cambridge Mass: Harvard University Press, 1979), pp. 84–96.

47   See Mieke Bal: *Religious Canon and Literary Identity* in Mieke Bal (ed.): *The Mieke Bal Reader* (Chicago: Chicago University Press, 2006), p. 415–37. Bal's chief intertext for a reading of part of Thomas Mann's *Joseph and his Brethren* is the passage from the Koran dealing with Potiphar's wife.

48   'Usually one knows of them vaguely; they are part of the *doxa* or stock of cultural commonplaces. This status makes them ideal as 'ideo-stories,' ready to be semantically filled.' See Mieke Bal: *Looking In, The Art of Viewing* (Amsterdam: G& B Arts, 2001), p. 189, note 7.

work of literature was of a piece with the rejection of supernaturalism. In 1970, T.R. Henn's *The Bible As Literature*[49] looked in a more neutral way at the literary qualities of the biblical text. This book was a study of the influence of the style and rhetoric of the AV on English literature. Chapter 14, entitled 'Imitatio', came closest to reception-history, paying particular attention to Dryden's *Absalom and Achitophel*, a sermon by Donne and George Moore's *The Brook Kerith*. In 1987 *The Literary Guide to the Bible* appeared, under the editorship of Robert Alter and Frank Kermode, adding considerably to general appreciation of the Bible's intrinsic literary qualities.[50] More recent works have taken further the influence of the Bible as literature, ranging from contextual studies such as that of the historian, Christopher Hill, in *The English Bible and the Seventeenth-Century Revolution* (1993)[51] to magisterial assaults on the whole field of the Bible in the English language, of which David Daniell's *The Bible in English* (2003)[52] and David S. Katz's *God's Last Words* (2004)[53] are the most recent examples. David Norton's two-volume *A History of the Bible as Literature* (1993)[54] was another major survey of the field, giving particular emphasis to the nuances of the boundary between religion and literature.

There have also been numerous studies of the influence of the Bible on specific authors, of which important examples are Robertson and Huppe: *Piers Plowman and Scriptural Tradition* (1951),[55] showing us how steeped in medieval scriptural

---

49 T.R. Henn: *The Bible as Literature* (London: Lutterworth, 1970).

50 Alter, Robert and Frank Kermode: *The Literary Guide to the Bible* (London: Collins, 1987).

51 Christopher Hill: *The English Bible and the Seventeenth-Century Revolution* (London: Penguin, 1993).

52 David Daniell: *The Bible in English* (New Haven: Yale University Press, 2003).

53 David S. Katz: *God's Last Words, Reading the English Bible from the Reformation to Fundamentalism* (New Haven: Yale University Press, 2004).

54 David Norton: *A History of the Bible as Literature* (Cambridge: Cambridge University Press, 1993), 2 vols.

55 D.W. Robertson, Jr and Bernard F Huppé: *Piers Plowman and Scriptural Tradition* (Princeton NJ: Princeton University Press, 1951).

exegesis Langland's work was, and J.M. Evans: *Paradise Lost and the Genesis Tradition* (1968),[56] locating many elements of Milton's masterpiece in a hinterland which included rabbinic exegesis and such Old English texts as *Genesis B*. Also relevant are David C. Fowler's *The Bible in Early English Literature* (1977),[57] and *The Bible in Middle English Literature* (1984),[58] which made vast tracts of the literary reception-history of the Bible available to a non-specialist audience. Finally, there is David Lyle Jeffrey's *The People of the Book* (1996),[59] with its defence of the 'broken-hearted' reader against the 'hard-hearted' reader and its insistence on the central importance of the concept of 'narratives of repentance' in the culture sustained by the Bible. Jeffrey attacks what he sees as postmodern hermeneutical narcissism.

But whether or not the postmodernists are narcissistic, it is within their arguments that we discover much of the impetus behind the spate of reception-histories which are the subject of this study. Postmodernism has brought with it a repertoire of themes which can be gathered together under the heading of The Hermeneutics of Suspicion. Marx, Nietzsche and Freud have been seen as 'the crucial proponents of suspicion in modern thought,' observes Denis Donoghue in a passage where he weighs up the prospects offered by elements in the thought of Josopovici which support an alternative hermeneutic of trust.[60] But the literary antecedents to the Hermeneutics of Suspicion go back further. As early as Laurence Sterne,[61] sophisticated writers had played with the idea of unreliable narrators,

---

56 J.M. Evans, ibid.

57 David C. Fowler: *The Bible in Early English Literature* (London: Sheldon Press, 1977).

58 David C. Fowler: *The Bible in Middle English Literature* (London and Seattle: University of Washington Press, 1984).

59 David Lyle Jeffrey: *The People of the Book* (New York: Eerdmans, 1996).

60 See Dennis Donoghue: *Adam's Curse, Reflections on Religion and Literature* (Indiana: University of Notre Dame Press, 2001, p. 3.

61 Laurence Sterne's novel *Tristram Shandy* appeared in 1759 and broke with many of the conventions of the English novel, including that of the reliable narrator.

even though the recent phase in hermeneutics has brought with it new levels of instability to the text.

There are implied authors and readers, unreliable authors and witnesses, hidden or suppressed voices. Most influential of all has been the systematic application of these notions under the umbrella of specific reformist agendas, notably feminism, anti-racism and anti-colonialism.[62] For Christian texts the argument has revolved particularly around the issues of the patriarchal assumptions or androcentricity now thought by feminists and others to be inherent in many, if not all, biblical texts and the anti-semitism (in its weakest form, supersessionism) which for some is detectable in Christian literature of nearly all eras.

The general heading for these revisionist approaches could be described as ideological criticism. From a feminist perspective, androcentrism is not merely present in the text but has been internalised by readers, both male and female. Indeed, for some post-structuralists, there is no text but only readers and therefore androcentric reading is a product of culture. For Stanley Fish[63] the key to hermeneutics is the interpreting community. The latter move, of course, makes ancient texts more congenial than does the approach which sets out to purge them of error.

The remedy for the ills of ideologically oppressive readings, according to the school of Judith Fetterley,[64] as reported in *The Postmodern Bible*, is the creation of resistant strategies for reading. Such strategies include the collapsing of the subject-object dichotomy and the refusal to privilege early readers over later. They

---

62   The umbrella term, 'Ideological Criticism,' might be applied to these approaches. It is worth remembering at the same time Northrop Frye's observation that the Bible itself is 'a violently partisan work.' See Northrop Frye: *The Great Code, The Bible and Literature* (London: RKP, 1982), p. 40.

63   Stanley Fish: *Is There A Text In This Class? The Authority of Interpretive Communities* (Cambridge Mass: Harvard University Press, 1980).

64   See The Bible and Culture Collective: *The Postmodern Bible* (New Haven: Yale University Press, 1995), pp. 36–7.

18

also include the perception that hermeneutical power is political power[65] and the acceptance that gender-neutral or politically neutral criticism is not possible.[66]

Two further outcomes of these academic developments are theoretical interest in the analysis of popular reading practices, an approach associated with the influence of Hans Jauss, and in writing the reception-histories of specific texts. *The Postmodern Bible*, written by a collective in true postmodern fashion,[67] comments that, whereas literary studies have attended to the reception-history of such works as *Moby Dick* and *Uncle Tom's Cabin*, 'As long as biblical reader-response critics concentrate on the implied reader and narratee in the biblical texts, they will continue to neglect the reception of biblical texts by flesh-and-blood readers'.[68] Whilst agreeing with that argument, our response would be that the novelists, dramatists, poets and visual artists who rewrite biblical stories are themselves flesh-and-blood-readers.

This problem had been discussed in slightly different terms by Robert Carroll in an essay[69] in a Festschrift published three years earlier than *The Postmodern Bible*, in 1992. He argued that the Rezeptionsgeschichte of the Bible had hardly yet been written, in spite of works like the three-volume *Cambridge History of the Bible*. The reason was that the subject was much larger than many scholars imagine. 'It is larger because it includes a vast amount of reading done outside the confines of the academies and the religious institutions revering the Bible as sacred.' Carroll goes on to discuss a variety of retellings of biblical stories, including Bulgakov's *The Master and Margarita* as a modern version of the story of Jesus (see below), Poe's poem *The Raven* as a modern midrash on Jeremiah 8:22 and an allusion to the Song of Solomon in *Krapp's Last Tape*.

---

65   Ibid., p. 58.
66   Ibid., pp. 61–6.
67   Ibid., pp. 35–6.
68   Ibid., pp. 36 and 67.
69   Robert Carroll (ed.): *Text as Pretext* (Sheffield: Sheffield Academic Press, 1992), pp. 61–85.

Similarly, John F. Sawyer, introducing his book on Isaiah in the History of Christianity, *The Fifth Gospel,*[70] is conscious that mainstream biblical hermeneutics has largely ignored the vast territory represented by the influence of the Bible over literature, music and art. The new *Blackwell Biblical Commentary* series, of which he is co-editor, is a further attempt to fill the gap left by conventional commentaries. That series sets out deliberately to avoid the sense that there is or can be a normative reading of a biblical text, although its chief editor, John F. Sawyer, points out that the individual reader will evaluate different readings according to his or her hermeneutical stance and according to the consensus of the interpretative community to which he or she belongs.[71]

However, for those who are engaged in reformist programmes and other exercises which re-contextualise the reception-history of a biblical story, it may not be enough to produce a catalogue of variants or treatments of a biblical theme, no matter how erudite or 'pluralistic' the setting in which it is done. The contest over whether the reading of a text can in any way be neutral will be evident in our study in, for example, the application of feminist reading strategies to the reception-histories of the stories of Eve, Judith and the Virgin Mary. Also the isolation of one story, such as that of Judas, from a much denser mass of gospel-originated material, may have the effect of inviting the application of a master-narrative as a strategy for handling the subject either pre- or post-factum. This master-narrative need not be ideologically driven. It could be based, for example, on orientating the 'reception-history' towards seeing all the material flowing towards and then out of a work by Shakespeare or Milton. Or it might engage itself in a claim that one particular story with its reception-history is the key to the western mind.

---

70 John F. Sawyer: *The Fifth Gospel, Isaiah in the History of Christianity* (Cambridge: Cambridge University Press, 1996, pp. 1–20).

71 John F. Sawyer: *The Role of Reception Theory, Reader-Response Criticism and/or Impact History in the Study of the Bible: Definition and Evaluation* (BBC Website article on www. bbibcomm.net, downloaded 26.2.06), p. 13.

The most recent developments in the hermeneutics of texts which rewrite earlier texts have emphasized the sense of the appropriated version 'writing back' to the original, a phrase which encapsulates the shift in authority from past to present which is characteristic of postmodernism. In this book we will tend to use the term 'urtext' to refer to the original biblical story and 'rewriting' to refer to the appropriated version. However, as Julie Sanders has shown in her recent study *Adaptation and Appropriation*,[72] there exists a multitude of terms for the sourcetext and the appropriative text, including 'hypotext' for the former and 'hypertext' for the latter (in the theories of Gérard Genette), as well as 'source and re-vision' and 'pretext and text'. She herself favours a combination of musical terminology ('riffs' and 'variations') and the language of genetic adaptation to describe the way in which a text survives and mutates into other texts. Of particular significance for our study is her argument that a novel like Jean Rhys's *Wide Sargasso Sea*, which is a postcolonialist feminist rereading of Charlotte Brontë's *Jane Eyre*, effectively supplants the sourcetext, making it virtually impossible to read the latter in a way which is uninfluenced by the newer work.[73]

In the fourteen main examples which we will examine all of these issues will emerge, as well as others which are the outcome of identifying and comparing the members of a literary genre. There are still traces in our fourteen works of a more innocent age in which a cultural tour could be undertaken for its own sake or for its educative value. This approach has never been better expressed than in Francis Lee Utley's introduction to his account of the Noah legend:

> The Noah story, used sensibly can bring the man who wants to know something of culture change, and of the permanence of culture, to a number of contrasting cultures: the despotic and canalised polytheism of Babylonia, the ruder but more consistent monotheism which the Hebrews learned in the Wilderness and the Promised land, the dedicated devotion of the early

---

72 Julie Sanders: *Adaptation and Appropriation* (Abingdon: Routledge, 2006). See Appendix C.
73 Ibid., pp. 98, 100–7.

Christians who still had some hope for a millenium, the feudalism and formalism of their medieval followers, the humanism of the Renaissance and the humanitarianism of more recent centuries...We can witness the change of supernatural sanctions from the mad dogs of Babylonia to the wrathful god of the Old Testament to the gentle God of André Obey ... the change from the hierarchic world of the past to the present world of social change and protest.[74]

Whether the biblical stories in our fourteen case studies are 'used sensibly' is an interesting question. It is unlikely that the fourteen authors would agree on a definition of 'sensibly' and most of them would probably object to the latent paternalism in such a notion. Despite this, they each impose their own personal sort of order on the material and tend to adopt a stance which belongs to either an academic discipline or some other tradition which has its own particular ideas about what is sensible. As practitioners in the art of the cultural tour, they share in Francis Lee Utley's delight in the quirky and in the sense of great vistas opening out over the human endeavour. But they also belong to a world where religion is much more suspect and where gender studies and other hard-nosed critical approaches make cultural tourism suspect as well.

Several of our authors are heavily committed the use of ideological critiques which owe no or little loyalty to the sense of the biblical urtext or its afterlife as the conduit of the sacred. David Lyle Jeffrey in *The People of the Book*, contends that the biblical stories as 'narratives of repentance' offer resistance to the paradigm-driven theorists of post-modernism and sees literary history as the record of the blunting of the text.[75] One of the major questions we shall have to address is that of how far the mainly literary reception-histories we are considering are indeed the record of such blunting and how far they reveal post-biblical literary texts which are ethically or theologically challenging. But we will also have to bear in mind

---

74 Francis Lee Utley, essay in Raphael Patai, Francis Lee Utley, Dov Noy: *Studies in Biblical and Jewish Folklore* (Bloomington: Indiana University Press, 1960), p. 86.

75 Jeffrey, ibid., Chapter 10.

the strong tendency in postmodern hermeneutics to see all texts as polysemous and therefore potentially available to a wide range of readings. One of the theorists discussed in Chapter 3, Nicholas Boyle, exploits this development in the service of a 'Catholic' reading of certain literary texts. Further on in this book we will return to the questions posed by the ambiguity of literary texts and also to the sense in which the reception-history of a biblical story becomes a dialogue between two sorts of canon, the theological and the literary. We will also consider whether the concept of 'The Other' (particularly in the thought of Emmanuel Levinas) offers a way of recovering theological treasure from the wreck threatened by the ideological critiques ranged at biblical stories and their reception-histories.

Chapter 2

A SURVEY OF THE PRINCIPAL TEXTS

The Chosen Examples

In this section we will survey the fourteen principal texts in chronological order of publication. It would be possible to construct a 'prehistory' which would include F.W. Dillistone's *The Novelist and the Passion Story* (1960)[1] and Theodore Ziolkowski's *Fictional Transfigurations of Jesus* (1971).[2] However, although there will be occasion to refer to these works elsewhere, they fall outside the scope of this book; first of all, chronologically; secondly, in that they are less than panoramic treatments of their subjects, concentrating mainly on twentieth-century literary appropriations of their biblical stories; and, thirdly, in that they avoid reference to the visual arts. They also pre-date the postmodernist climate which took hold around 1972 and which our fourteen authors mostly seem sharply conscious of, whatever their own particular stance. Although three[3] of our fourteen examples do concentrate on twentieth-century fiction, their inclusion can be justified on the grounds that they fall within the chronological parameters dictated by the rest, that they are incipiently or thoroughly postmodernist in approach, and that the fourteen works discussed here are, as far as can be determined, the bulk of substantial, culturally-orientated, reception-histories of individual biblical stories published in English during the period 1972 to 2002.

---

1   F.W. Dillistone: *The Novelist and the Passion Story* (London, Collins, 1960).

2   Theodore Ziolkowski: *Fictional Transfigurations of Jesus* (Princeton NJ: Princeton University Press, 1971). Both this work and that by F.W. Dillistone were earlier mentioned on p. 6.

3   The three are Levenson, Paffenroth and Gaines.

It is notable that, during the discrete thirty-year period covered in this study, there seem to have been no examples of imaginative reception-histories dealing with the life of Christ, despite the production of volumes on the theological tradition, such as Jaroslav Pelikan's *Jesus Through the Centuries*.[4] It is almost as though the subject had become taboo or too difficult to handle, with even primary texts rare.[5] Instead, we have works on the Virgin Mary, the Magi, Mary Magdalene and even Pontius Pilate and Judas, alongside those on stories derived from the Hebrew Scriptures. The principle of selection seems to be related to authorial interest, the absence of comparable previous essays on the theme, the existence of radical retellings or treatments of the subject, and (obviously) marketability as perceived by the publisher.

The question as to whether the fourteen writers consider themselves to be contributors to a genre is hard to answer. There is a clear influence of Warner on Haskins, for example, and at least two of the authors seem to belong loosely to a school of rehabilitation for biblical villains (Paffenroth and Gaines), but otherwise one is drawn to the conclusion that the movement which we have identified is one in process of gradual, almost unconscious formation, rather than one which the fourteen authors deliberately joined.

By 'movement' we refer not so much to a common set of conclusions (there is none), but to a common perception of the importance of the aesthetic reception-history of various biblical stories and a desire to trace developments in the literary and often iconographic treatment of the subject. In some cases the reading is driven by an ideological or reformist paradigm, such as feminism; in other cases,

---

4   Jaroslav Pelikan: *Jesus Through the Centuries* (London and New Haven: Yale University Press, 1985).

5   José Saramago's *The Gospel According to Jesus Christ* (1991, English trans. 1993) is discussed in my article, 'Against the Grain and with the Grain', *Theology*, Nov/Dec 2008, but direct treatments are not as common as one might suppose. Even *Jesus Christ Superstar* essentially centres on rewriting Judas. The novels of Kazantzakis predate the postmodernist period by two decades.

the hermeneutics of suspicion seems to be the driver; in yet others the motivation seems to be a general wish to demonstrate and analyse radical hermeneutical upheavals in the reception-history.

The authors range from those who see their material in valedictory terms, as part of a dying religious culture, and those who seem to be dealing with an ongoing tradition stretching into the future. Although it may seem slightly episodic, I have decided to set out a separate description and critique of each of the fourteen 'reception-histories' in the rest of this survey-chapter, in order to provide the basis for the forms of analysis which appear in later chapters. The fourteen are discussed in chronological order of publication, in order to avoid lumping them together thematically and in order also that the sense may emerge, however tentatively, of an unfolding hermeneutical process.

Clearly the approach has necessarily to be selective, as an exhaustive survey might possibly find enough material in each of the fourteen works to justify a whole study in its own right. Our purpose here will be to examine major landmarks in the respective reception-histories and to see the fourteen works in relationship to each other and to literature and art which is contiguous with their chosen material.

J.D. Levenson: *The Book of Job in its Time and in the Twentieth Century*[6]

Levenson's eighty-page essay summarises the state of biblical scholarship relating to the Book of Job thirty years ago and gives a chapter each to H.G. Wells's *The Undying Fire*, to Archibald MacLeish's *J B*, and finally to Robert Frost's *A Masque of Reason*. His order reverses the chronology of publication of the latter two works. Rather surprisingly, there is no mention at all of Carl Jung's *Answer to Job* or of Joseph Roth's novel, *Job, the Story of a Simple Man*.

---

6   J.D. Levenson: *The Book of Job in Its Time and in the Twentieth Century* (Cambridge Mass: Harvard University Press, 1972).

Wells offers the reader the story of Job retold as a modern novel. MacLeish creates a sort of modern mystery play about Job, though Job was never really a part of the medieval mystery play tradition. Frost creates a burlesque on the theme of a reunion between Job and God, a '43rd Chapter of Job,' set a thousand years after the events recounted in the Bible, with Job's wife recognizing God from Blake's picture. It is Frost's work which Levenson feels does most justice to the original.

Comment

Levenson never discusses the possible influence of the earlier of these works on the later and yet, reading MacLeish, it is hard to believe he had not read *The Undying Fire*. MacLeish's rejection of the historical process could well be a negative response to the dominant theme of the Wells novel, although it is also the foil for his existentialist quest.

For Levenson it is fidelity to the tone and even the theology of the original which is the litmus test of a successful twentieth-century retelling of Job. He believes that Frost achieves such fidelity by burlesque, preserving the biblical book's campaign against the sufficiency of reason and therefore arguing for mystery. Others have situated *A Masque of Reason* in the context of Frost's other writing, emphasising the capriciousness and darkness of the Frostian deity, forever experimenting and improvising and unable to plan ahead.[7]

MacLeish, for Levenson, stands condemned by his own commentary on his play, inferred by Levenson from a sermon preached by MacLeish in Connecticut three years before the play's premiere.[8] In the sermon MacLeish had told the congregation that love (following St Paul) was the supreme Christian virtue and concluded that love even creates God. This humanistic philosophy Levenson

---

7   See for example Dorothy Judd Hall: *An Old Testament Christian*, essay in J.A.C. Tharpe (ed.): *Frost Centennial Essays III* (Jackson, Mississippi: University of Mississippi Press, 1978), pp. 316–49.

8   Levenson, ibid., p. 47.

found wanting. Yet it is hard to see why the sermon (as Levenson reads it) should control the meaning of the play, where there is a concerted and anguished attempt to deal with the issues of God and suffering raised by the Book of Job. *J B* may be minimalist in its theology but this does not make it reductionist.

Similarly, *The Undying Fire*, whilst hailed by Levenson as a neglected masterpiece, is finally dismissed as defective in theology. Yet of the three works it is the only one which treats God unequivocally as a force for good operating upon human life. Whilst a progressive historical, social and political education is to be the instrument of salvation, the driving force is the 'Spirit of God in Man,' a force both external to human beings and personal.[9] Even if one agrees with the view of a biography of Wells that in this novel 'the Captain of mankind has been replaced by the Great Teacher,'[10] the theology is more hopeful than in Frost's work.

The main theological theme of the Frost work, according to Levenson, seems to be that Job liberated God from the Deuteronomist.[11] Levenson himself points out that the Bible, for example in Genesis 18 and in Habbakuk 1 and 2, already rejects the Deuteronomic doctrine of strictly administered rewards and punishments.[12] So one wonders why this liberation should be sufficiently novel to provide the thrust of Frost's Masque. Perhaps the key to this conundrum lies in Frost's designation of himself as 'an Old Testament Christian'. Dorothy Judd Hall has demonstrated that Frost's version of the God of the Old Testament is a highly volatile and capricious being who creates unpredictable trials for mankind, with Christ finally just another in the long line of victims.[13]

We could say, therefore, that the difference between Frost's *Masque of Reason* and the biblical book of Job is the difference between human reason defeated by

9   H.G. Wells: *The Undying Fire* (London: Macmillan, 1912), p. 215.
10 Norman and Jeanne Mackenzie: *The Time Traveller, The Life of H.G. Wells* (London: Weidenfeld and Nicolson, 1973), p. 320.
11 Levenson, ibid., p. 65.
12 Ibid., p. 15.
13 Dorothy Judd Hall, ibid., p.

28

the breathtaking absurdity of the universe, albeit a god-inhabited universe, and human reason defeated by the breathtaking mystery and wonder of the divine creation. It is the difference between learning submission to unreason[14] and 'I know that my Redeemer liveth' (Job 19:25.) It is the difference between 'Deliver us from committees'[15] and 'Who is this that darkens counsel by words without knowledge?' (Job 38:1.)

Three further critical views of Frost's Jobean work are worth noting. Thomas McClanahan reads[16] *A Masque of Reason* in the light of Frost's statement that 'religion is merely consolation for what we do not know'. He rates Frost as an important poet of the decline of faith. Others find Frost superficial as religious poet and frivolous, at least in this particular work. For Malcolm Cowley, 'The poet seems more conventional than convinced, more concerned with prudence than with virtue, and very little concerned with sin or suffering; you might say he is more Puritan, or prudish, than he is Christian'.[17] Yvor Winters sums up the weaknesses of *A Masque of Reason*: 'There is no understanding of good or evil in themselves, of the metaphysical questions involved. Good is submission to an anthropomorphic and undignified God and is made to seem preposterous. Evil is made equally preposterous and for similar reasons.'[18]

At least it can be argued that *The Undying Fire* and *J B* are passionate works, Wells reacting to the horrors of the First World War, in a work which he himself put

---

14 Robert Frost: *A Masque of Reason* in *Collected Poems*, pp. 229–48 (London: Penguin, 1973), p. 238.

15 Ibid., p. 243.

16 Thomas MacClanahan: 'Frost's Theodicy: *'Word I Had No One Left But God'* in J.A.C. Tharpe (ed.): *Frost Centennial Essays II* (Jackson, Mississippi: University of Mississippi Press, 1978), pp. 112–25.

17 Malcolm Cowley, essay in J.M. Cox (ed.): *Robert Frost, A Collection of Critical Essays* (Englewoods Cliffs NJ: Prentice-Hall/Spectrum, 1962), p. 41.

18 Yvor Winters, in Cowley, ibid., p. 72.

great store by,[19] and MacLeish reacting to the horrors of the Second World War. There is a moral and spiritual seriousness in them, whereas the Frost work is, not only burlesque in form, but also sardonic in its outlook, a thoroughgoing lampoon.

Wells comes close to a sort of Gnostic dualism, with his battle between the Spirit of God in Man and Satan as the Mocker of Mankind[20] and with the dream-sequence allowing Job/Huss to see as if around a metaphysical corner.[21] If MacLeish, as Levenson suggests,[22] anticipates the tenor of the death-of-God theologians, he seems closer to Bonhoeffer than Altizer. Interestingly, MacLeish's drama, through the logic of its two-tier staging, maintains the dialogue with Nickles/Satan throughout, until the closing scene of existentialist minimalism ('We'll blow on the coals of the heart ...') with J B and his wife. Wells has no difficulty in returning to a naturalistic narrative, since the operation and dream-sequence form an interruption within it.

If one asks what are the dominant images of the three works, they might be described as dualistic, or at least binary. In *The Undying Fire* the dominant image would be the contrast between the desperate life of the U-boat crew and the work of the progressive school at Woldingstanton. In *J B* it would be the contrast between blowing on the coals of the heart (or the flowering jasmine) and the unfeeling processes of the cosmos. In *A Masque of Reason* it could only be the contrast between the solemnity of the biblical Book of Job and the low farce of this '43rd Chapter'.

Levenson, in his own Epilogue, ends on a rather pessimistic note: 'The very calamities which have brought forth new interest in the Book of Job have also rendered its resolution credible to fewer people. For a successful re-creation of the

---

19   H.G. Wells: *Experiment in Autobiography* (London, Cape, 1934/69), Vol. II, p. 499: 'one of the best pieces of work I ever did.'
20   *Undying Fire*, p. 210.
21   Ibid., p. 248.
22   Levenson, ibid., p. 53.

Job story, we must endure until such time as the tension that informs the Book of Job is again real in the lives of most people'.[23]

Perhaps, however, it is possible to re-frame or re-tell without re-creating. The tension uppermost in the minds of most contemporary readers may be that between modern secularism and biblical theism and the three works do address that tension in their own ways. They also modify our reading of the Book of Job by our having read them, just as surely as *Paradise Lost* affects our reading of Genesis. It may be a mistake to look for 're-creation' when a strong re-telling delivers the (willing) reader into a dramatic relationship with the ancient text whilst keeping her/him aware of the cultural distance. If so, the process could be described as a dialogue rather than a usurpation.

James B. Pritchard (ed.): *Solomon and Sheba* (1974)[24]

Pritchard's work is divided into two main parts, the first containing essays by two contributors (Pritchard himself and Gus W. van Beek) on the archaeological evidence for The Age of Solomon and The Land of Sheba respectively. He leaves what he calls 'The Legend and its Diffusion' to the second part, where there are contributions on the story in the Judaic tradition, the Islamic tradition, the Ethiopian tradition and finally the Christian tradition, the latter encompassing what Paul F. Watson identifies as the post-Christian era of Romantic and Modern Art and Literature.

The archaeological evidence tends to diminish the achievements of Solomon and to underpin the opulence of the Sheban civilisation, lending credence to the view that the text in the first eleven chapters of 1 Kings has been fashioned as propaganda for a period in the history of Israel five hundred years later.

---

23 Levenson, ibid., pp. 69–70.
24 James Pritchard (ed.): *Solomon and Sheba* (London: Phaidon, 1974).

Lou H. Silberman[25] covers the Judaic tradition, beginning with the Targum Sheni, the second Targum to the Book of Esther, which contains the legend of the hoopoe as the emissary between Solomon and Sheba. However, it is the Targum to Job 1:15 which seems to be the origin of the treatment of the Queen of Sheba as Lilith, the beginning of a process of demonisation which continued into the late Middle Ages. Silberman also discusses the Babylonian Talmud's denial of the existence of the Queen of Sheba, probably the outcome of a political struggle over the legitimacy of Solomon's descendants in the time of R. Judah the Patriarch. It was the *Alphabetum Siracidis* which developed the notion of the hairiness of the Queen of Sheba (leading to Solomon's invention of a depilatory), but which also made the Queen of Sheba the mother, or at least the ancestress, of Nebuchadnezzar. Finally, it was left to Aviad's 'Tale of the Queen of Sheba' to state, tout court, 'She came into him and he lay with her and from her went forth Nebuchadnezzar'.[26]

For one late tradition,[27] Tamar, Malkath Sheba and Rahab became one transmigrating soul, indicated by the name Tamar being composed of the initial letter of each name. Amongst the Cabbalists the Queen of Sheba's demonic nature was developed, an example being the fourteenth-century *Tzefune Tzioni* where she became the Queen of Demons, though not apparently associated with Lilith, who usually carries that title. In German Jewish folklore her role as a demonic seductress of unwitting men, hairy and often goat-footed, was prominent. It is significant that Marina Warner, the author of the second work in our chronology, and probably the most influential one, was to make the theme of the animal-footed Sheba a major feature of her work twenty years later.[28]

---

25   Ibid., pp. 65–84.

26   Ibid., p. 77.

27   Ibid., p. 78.

28   See Marina Warner: *The Beast and the Blonde* (London: Vintage, 1995), pp. 111–28, and 'In and Out of the Fold', essay in C. Buchmann and C. Spiegl (eds): *Out of the Garden: Women Writers on the Bible* (London: Continuum, 1995).

W. Montgomery Watt[29] covers the Islamic tradition, which, following the Quranic Sura 27:15–44, stresses the Queen of Sheba as the model of conversion to Islam from sun-worship. Watt cites the Jewish presence in the Yemen as an important source of influence on Islamic traditions, though orthodoxy tends at an early stage to resist the notion of Sheba's hairy legs, treating it as a product of false rumours spread by the djinn.

One of the most interesting Islamic versions of the story of Solomon and Sheba, nevertheless, treats her as the offspring of a djinn mother. This legend (mentioned here,[30] and actually recounted at length in E.L. Ranelagh's *The Past We Share*[31]) includes the episode in which Belkis (her name in the tradition) murders a tyrant in a wedding-night plot, assimilating her to the figure of Judith in the Apocrypha. Later Solomon marries Bilqis, after depilation, and in one version builds three great palaces for her. The largely positive view of Sheba in Islamic tradition is only negated by the Sufi tendency to treat Solomon as the type of the perfect man and Bilqis as the emblem of the soul attached to material things.[32]

Edward Ullendorff[33] covers the Ethiopian tradition, which turns the story of Solomon and Sheba into a national saga, the *Kebra Nagast*, with the Queen's visit to Jerusalem resulting in the transference of the Divine Presence to Ethiopia. In this tradition the Queen of Sheba is identified both with Candace, Queen of the Ethiopians in Acts 8:27, and with the Queen of the South in Matthew 12:42/Luke 11:33. Sheba becomes the heroine when Solomon takes advantage of her, tricking her into his bed. The resulting offspring, King Menelik, is venerated as the kinsman of Christ. It is Menelik who presides over the removal of the Ark of the Covenant

---

29   Pritchard, ibid., pp. 85–103.

30   Ibid., p. 96.

31   E.L. Ranelagh: *The Past We Share* (London: Quartet, 1979), pp. 21–41.

32   Pritchard, ibid., p. 1.

33   Ibid., pp. 104–114.

to Ethiopia. There is evidence of the conflation of the story of Solomon and Sheba with that of Alexander and Candace.

Paul F. Watson[34] covers the Christian tradition, which was influenced by Prudentius's treatment of the Queen of Sheba as the type of the conversion of the Gentiles and also by the treatment by Isidore of Seville of her as the type of the Church, the bride of Christ. The Queen of Sheba was connected with the Magi in the medieval *Speculum Humanae Salvationis* and in subsequent art. In the Legend of the True Cross she encountered the future cross in the form of a wooden bridge (or floating plank) which she refused to desecrate, preferring instead to wade through a river. The Queen became the magnificent subject of medieval and renaissance art, appearing as the consort of Henry VIII when he was portrayed as Solomon by Holbein.

Medieval typology wanes in favour of the courtly treatment of the subject but returns briefly in the eighteenth-century.[35] Handel's oratorio *Solomon* is a counterpart to the lavishness of the theme in Baroque art, but 'the religious side plays a modest part'.[36] By the nineteenth-century the story has become a poetic motif. In Flaubert's *Tentation de Saint Antoine* Sheba appears again as a temptress and in the Shaba poems of W.B. Yeats she becomes the image of sexual love as the instrument of mystical wisdom. In the USA, Romare Bearden's collage *SHE-BA* connects the theme with the black civil rights movement.[37]

Pritchard, in conclusion, sees the story as the buttress of ideas and institutions which might otherwise have faltered[38] and wonders what the future holds for 'the memory of a brief moment within the tenth-century BC which has cast such a long shadow'. Though he finally does not specify which ideas and institutions most

---

34   Ibid., pp. 115–145.
35   Ibid., p. 132.
36   Ibid., p. 134.
37   Ibid., p. 144.
38   Ibid., p. 151.

needed buttressing, leaving the reader to find clues in the text of the preceding essays, we have to assume that for a historian like Pritchard the most likely candidates were the Kings of Israel and the Ethiopian monarchy, though others might include aspects of the interface between Judaism, Islam and Christianity both in the Near East from the rise of Islam and in medieval Europe.

Comment

Issues emerging from the Pritchard work include the persistent tendency in the Jewish tradition to vilify or demonise Sheba, the political use of the story in all traditions, the Sheba legends as a rare instance of commonality with Islamic tradition, and the fate of the story in post-Christian western imaginative literature and art. A more recent study would have to take account of the feminist perspective on 'Solomon and Sheba'. Whilst Paul F. Watson in this volume, for example, notes the neglect of religious content in Handel's *Solomon*, he does not point out that the oratorio revolves around a quartet of stereotypical biblical women (Solomon's Egyptian wife, the two harlots with the baby, and the Queen of Sheba herself.)

Marina Warner, approaching the material two decades later than Pritchard and with a feminist and indeed postcolonial critique, is repelled by the 'black but comely' Vulgate translation of the Songs of Songs passage associated with Sheba but also mesmerised by the mystery of the goose-footed Sheba – first identified by Emile Mâle in a (lost) example of French medieval sculpture – and then finally optimistic about the story's potential as a bridge between the three great monotheistic religions.[39] Neither she nor any of Pritchard's contributors discusses the extraordinary King Vidor film of 1959, *Solomon and Sheba*,[40] which conflates

---

39 Warner, in *The Beast and the Blonde*, p. 103, discusses the influence of the Vulgate translation of Song of Solomon 1:5: 'Nigra sed Formosa'. The French medieval sculpture is described in Emile Mâle: *Religious Art in France: the Twelfth Century* (Princeton NJ: Princeton University Press, 1978), pp. 394–7.

40 *Solomon and Sheba* (Metro-Goldwyn-Mayer Studios, 1959).

the story with that of Jezebel, though with a happy outcome, at least for proponents of patriarchy, when an Ethiopian-style ending is adopted. Also unmentioned by these writers are the poem by Robert Browning *Solomon and Balchis* and other significant versions in more recent English writing;[41] there is also no mention of the very lavish ballet entitled *Belkis, Queen of Sheba*,[42] for which Resphigi wrote the music and which was first mounted by La Scala, Milan, in 1931. The place of the Sheba traditions in western orientalism is discussed by Warner in her essays and another writer, A. Norman Jeffries, links the Yeats poems with the author's effort to distance himself from his Irish Roman Catholic background, a case of off-the-peg exoticism.[43]

In later chapters, the 'conflation history' of the story will be discussed more extensively, as well as its relationship with feminist and postcolonial critiques. One thing common to both the 'Pritchard' view of Sheba and the 'Warner' view is that a certain threshold is passed when radical rewritings are expressed in visual form.

Marina Warner: *Alone of All Her Sex* (1976)[44]

Alone of All Her Sex is a very comprehensive account of narrative material relating to the cult of the Virgin Mary from the time of the Gospels through to Pope Paul VI. It is the first substantial, unified work of the genre we are considering, given that Pritchard's volume was devoted in its first half to archaeology and in its second half to essays by five different authors, and also that it was a collection of essays by different authors.

---

41 Sol Liptzin's *Biblical Themes in World Literature* (Hoboken NJ: Ktav Publishing, 1985), pp. 198–202, discusses the Browning poem and works by Arthur Symons, John Freeman and even Bertrand Russell.

42 See Edward Johnson's notes on Resphigi's *Belkis* (London: Chandos Records, 1985).

43 A. Norman Jeffries and K.W.G. Cross: *In Excited Reverie* (New York: St Martin's Press, 1965).

44 Marina Warner: *Alone of All Her Sex* (London: Weidenfeld and Nicolson, 1976).

Warner's overarching theme is the flowering and decay of a dominant social myth . Respecting what she calls the polyvalence of the figure of the Virgin Mary,[45] she steers a course between feminist critique of the subjugation of women through the idealisation of the Virgin Mary and aesthetic appreciation of the exaltation of the feminine in such themes as Mary as the Queen of Heaven. Mary is one of the few female figures to attain the status of myth.[46]

Like many other examples within the genre which Warner herself seems to have inaugurated with this work, there is little interest in concrete historical detail. Warner is pre-eminently a cultural theorist and on this foundation she builds an impressive edifice. Like some commentators on the Genesis text in relation to Milton's *Paradise Lost*, she notes that it requires 'a Herculean effort' to read the Gospel of Luke without the influence of later accretions.[47] In that sense, *Alone of All Her Sex* is a catalogue raisonné of later accretions. Of the four central doctrines about the Virgin Mary, only one can be traced directly to Scripture.[48]

Warner uses major thematic chapters to relate traditions about the Virgin Mary to their human social consequences. Virgin birth is part of Christian civilisation's differentiation of human reproduction from animal reproduction and its contempt for the lower, 'animal' passions. The Second Eve reverses the effect of The Fall and offers a new start. The Assumption promises the Afterlife not just to saints but to all believers, diminishing the value of the material world. The Queen of Heaven legitimises first the Byzantine ruling house and then the rules of numerous European royal families, a process expressed in art and also in liturgy, exemplified by the *Salve Regina*, a hymn prescribed in the twelfth-century for the feast of the Assumption and later to become the most popular of all Roman Catholic hymns.

---

45 Ibid., p. xxiv.
46 Ibid., p. xxv.
47 Ibid., p. 13.
48 Ibid., p. 19.

In other manifestations, the Nursing Virgin enjoins female humility in the role of nurturing; the Mater Dolorosa consoles the bereaved because she also is a sufferer; the Mother of Mercy makes the Black Death tolerable by sparing some.

Balancing this social and political critique, Warner is alert to the interplay of the Virgin Mary traditions with classical and other mythology. The association of the Virgin with the moon is the outworking of a long process,[49] as is her role in the protection of cities.[50] She has a complex literary relationship with the Book of Revelation.[51]

Warner's final argument[52] is that, sublime though it may have been in the past, the myth dangerously polarises the masculine and the feminine into irreconcilably opposed camps and is part of a spent social code. Like some of the other Epilogues in the genre which was to follow, it is a sort of farewell to a once-vital tradition.

Comment

To get a sense of how the tradition could be represented in the middle of the nineteenth-century, Anna Jameson's *Legends of the Madonna* is indispensable. Not discussed in Warner's text, but listed in her extensive bibliography, this work by one of the leading proto-feminists of the Victorian period is a measure of the distance we have travelled. For Jameson, writing an elaborate account of the treatment of the Virgin Mary in art, stands firmly within the camp of Christian orthodoxy, impressed with the Virgin as 'this grand and mysterious idea of glorified womanhood ...'[53]

Reviewing the book in the year of its publication, Piers Paul Read characterised Marina Warner as someone who had moved from being a devout believer in

---

49   Ibid., p. 259.

50   Ibid., p. 304.

51   Ibid., pp. 56, 246, 261.

52   Ibid., pp. 336–9.

53   Anna Bronwell Jameson: *Legends of the Madonna* (London: Longman, Brown, Green and Longmans, 1852), p. 4.

Mary as the Mother of God (like himself) to 'a kind of secular feminism with Roland Barthes, Claude Levi-Strauss and Simone de Beauvoir as her apostles'. He contrasted the book unfavourably with John de Sator's *Mary and the Christian Gospel* which he reviewed at the same time and regretted that the author had allowed her sense of the beauty (and, as he said, to a Christian the truth) of the material she discusses be overtaken by a sort of post-adolescent rebellion against Christian values. Shaking off the values associated with traditional belief in the Virgin Mary might lead 'not to a feminist paradise but might instead return women to the status of cattle'.[54]

If nothing else, that review indicates something of the fierce reaction which Warner's book provoked amongst some believers. In opining that the author's 'English and Italian natures' were at war with each other in the book, Read, though presumably unsympathetic to any sort of synthesis, may perhaps have articulated an unresolved tension which survives to this day between feminist critiques and traditional readings of biblical texts.

Geoffrey Ashe's *The Virgin*[55] was published in the same year as *Alone of all Her Sex*. The two books were clearly written without any sort of interplay, but it is interesting that Ashe's attempt to relocate the Virgin Mary tradition within a mystical quest for the Mother Goddess met with much less publishing success than Warner's feminist tour de force. But Ashe, in any event, could not match the weight of cultural material which Warner deployed so richly. *Alone of All Her Sex* was not just a polemical argument, but a very enjoyable cultural tour.

Warner's study has had a considerable afterlife of its own. In direct response to *Alone of All Her Sex*, Julia Kristeva, in her 1977 essay *Stabat Mater* suggested a new and positive feminist direction for the development of the Virgin Mary tradition, drawing on the theme of the Mater Dolorosa as a 'post-virginal' basis for

---

54   Piers Paul Read, review in *Times Literary Supplement*, 5th November 1976, p. 1393.

55   Geoffrey Ashe: *The Virgin* (London: Routledge & Kegan Paul, 1976).

what she called *herethics*.[56] In turn, Sarah Jane Boss in *Empress and Handmaid*[57] has produced a counter-argument, placing the development of the Mater Dolorosa tradition in the context of Christian unease at the onset of modernity's instrumental rationality.[58] Her entire book is a plea to return to full-strength Marian devotion, in order to release a Marcusian liberationist energy which will free humanity from its destructive slavery to technology.

Ricardo Quinones: *The Changes of Cain* (1991)[59]

More perhaps than any other example in our survey, Quinones's study raises the question of multivalency or literary ambiguity in its sharpest form. *The Changes of Cain* is a magisterial survey of the treatment of the Genesis 4 story in Western literature.

By relegating, not only the midrashic background to Philo, but also the mystery play material to the notes at the back, Quinones is able to marshal his reception-history into three major themes, those of Citizen Cain, the Monstrous Cain, and Cain as the Sacred Executioner. He in addition places great emphasis on distinguishing between those examples which differentiate between the brothers and those which do not differentiate, the latter exemplifying the motif of 'frères ennemis'. He finds the fountainhead of this distinction in Augustine's treatment of the theme in Chapter 15 of *The City of God*, where Cain and Abel are citizens respectively of the earthly and heavenly cities, whereas Romulus and Remus are both in quest of the earthly.

The author explores the influence of Philo on Augustine and Ambrose. Augustine's passage (above) is located as the origin of the foundation sacrifice

56 Julia Kristeva: *Stabat Mater*, reprinted in Toril Moi (ed.): *The Kristeva Reader* (Oxford: Blackwell, 1986) pp. 160–85.

57 Sarah Jane Boss: *Empress and Handmaid* (London: Cassell, 2000).

58 Ibid., p. 204.

59 Ricardo Quinones: *The Changes of Cain* (Princeton NJ: Princeton University, 1991).

40

motif under the Citizen Cain heading, a motif later developed in one direction as the New Prince of Machiavellian political philosophy. Meanwhile, it is left to Ambrose to subvert the Augustinian earthly city/ heavenly city polarity into the identification of Cain with the Synagogue and Abel with the Church.

Quinones passes quickly over the medieval period, referring the reader to Emerson's article of 1906, 'Medieval Legends of Cain',[60] but in doing so neglects the legend of Lamech's slaying of Cain which has significance for the notion of Cain as the Eternal Wanderer. The Monstrous Cain, however, is charted feeding into the sources of the figure of Grendel in Beowulf. The crux comes with Byron. For Quinones, Byron's Cain is a heroic figure, the Sacred Executioner, at the start of a character-reversal and a career as a regenerate which continues on into the writings of Melville, Conrad, Steinbeck, Herman Hesse, Unamuno and others.

Comment

The chief area which Quinines neglects in this otherwise masterly survey is the medieval period. Apart from the omission of the legend of Lamech's slaying of Cain (which admittedly is not very relevant to the high-point which Quinones discovers in the modern period of the reception-history), he does not discuss either the Saxon Genesis or the Wakefield mystery-play Mactacio Abel, both of which contain material which we will find relevant elsewhere in our study. There are also alternative readings of all of his central material, beginning most tellingly with the case of the Byron work.

Probably there is scholarly consensus that Byron marks a revolution in the reception-history of the Cain story,[61] even if there is disagreement over the nature

---

60 O. Emerson: 'The Medieval Legend of Cain' in *PMLA*, Vol. 21, 1906.

61 This perception should not be allowed to overshadow the importance of the Wakefield mystery play as a literary milestone, see for example Hans-Jürgen Diller: *The Middle English Mystery Play* (Cambridge: Cambridge University Press, 1992), p. 231. Quinones downplays this material.

of that revolution. It is easy to demonstrate, for example, the huge influence of Byron's *Cain* over Unamuno. It is also clear that the revolution, once wrought, released the story to become the vehicle of Hesse's immensely successful *Damian* and Steinbeck's meandering epic, itself the subject of great cinematic success.

Yet, whilst Quinones sees Byron's Cain as the overturner of the values of the biblical story, Wolf Hirst[62] depicts Byron succumbing to the structural imperatives of the original, and Harold Fisch[63] evens hails Byron as the pioneer in recovering the *urtext* which lies behind the present biblical version. If this is a revolution, is it driven by the new findings of science (à la Baron Cuvier)[64] or by an antediluvian foundation sacrifice myth which refuses to lie down? Or is it, after all, a failed revolution? There are further questions over the relationship to Blake's reading of Byron in Blake's own work, *The Ghost of Abel*, where Quinones ignores the reference to Elijah in Blake's 'Lord Byron in the Wilderness'. Leslie Tannenbaum, in an article cited by Quinones but not given any weight, argues that Blake wanted to reinforce his own version of a Byronic revolution by coming to the aid of his fellow poet.[65] More recently, Morton Paley has presented *The Ghost of Abel* as Blake's effort to convert Byron to the forgiveness of sins[66] and has even seen the work as a recanting of the 'Manichaeanism' of Blake's own theology in *The Everlasting Gospel*.[67]

---

62   Wolf Z. Hirst: 'Byron's Revisionary Struggle with the Bible' in Wolf Z. Hirst (ed.): *Byron, the Bible and Religion* (Newark: University of Delaware Press, 1991), pp. 77–100.

63   Harold Fisch: 'Byron's Cain as Sacred Executioner' in Wolf Z. Hirst (ibid.), pp. 25–38.

64   Morton D. Paley in *Apocalypse and Millennium in English Poetry* (Oxford: Oxford University Press, 1999, pp. 209–16) discusses Byron's affinity with the scientific theories of Baron Cuvier, which posited a series of 'revolutions' in the Earth's geological history, a notion which Byron found congenial because it supported a cyclical view of history as opposed to one expecting a Millenium.

65   Leslie Tannenbaum: 'Lord Byron in the Wilderness,' article in *Modern Philology*, Vol. 72, 1975.

66   Morton D. Paley: *The Traveller in the Evening, the Last Works of William Blake* (Oxford: Oxford University Press, 2003), p. 207).

67   Ibid., pp. 217–219.

42

Consideration of rival interpretations of Melville's *Billy Budd* introduces further complexity into our response to the 'strong reading' offered by Quinones. Is Melville here the subverter of colonial values or the guardian of conservatism? Similarly, is Conrad's *The Secret Sharer*, about which much has been written, only understandable as a counterpoint to *Under Western Eyes* or is it a self-contained retelling of the Cain and Abel story? If the latter, is it morally outrageous (in for example its dependence on slim chance for the final saving of the ship) or is it an extended morality tale about the impossibility of hiding a murder? As a psychological drama, is it a triumph of narcissism or of individuation?[68]

There are further questions to be addressed, such as whether Conrad's Captain is a reliable narrator and the relationship of Melville to Christianity and to the military politics of his time. The fact that *Billy Budd* contradicts several conventional assumptions about time, being written in the 1890s, with the surface narrative concerned with a specific period in British naval history in the 1790s, but only known to the public in 1924, adds to the problems of placing it in a chronological scheme of development.[69] Benjamin Britten's opera, based on a libretto by E.M. Forster, seems to be an effort to validate the interpretation of the main character as a Christ-figure, the victim of the Master-at-Arms's repressed homosexuality, whilst using an operatic frame story to explore the guilt feelings of the so-upright Captain Vere as a Pilate figure in retirement.[70]

68　See A. Robert Lee (ed.): *Herman Melville, Reassessments* (London, Vista, 1984); William Hamilton: *Melville and the Gods* (California: Scholars Press, 1985); Daphne Erdnest-Vulcan: *The Strange Short Fiction of Joseph Conrad* (Oxford: Oxford University Press, 1999); and Daniel R. Schwarz (ed.): *Joseph Conrad, the Secret Sharer* (Boston: Bedford Books, 1997).

69　On the chronology, see H. Robert Bruce Franklin's essay, 'From Empire to Empire: *Billy Budd, Sailor*,' pp. 199–201, in A. Lee (ed.), ibid.

70　E.M. Forster co-operated with Eric Crozier and Benjamin Britten himself in writing the libretto, living in the same house for a month. Forster found himself 'on a kind of voyage' in adapting *Billy Budd*, in words quoted by John Colmer in *E.M. Forster, A Personal Voice* (London: Routledge & Kegan Paul, 1975), p. 181. Colmer also quotes from Forster's *Aspects of the Novel:* here was a writer, Melville, able to reach 'straight back into the universal, to a blackness and sadness so transcending our own that they are indistinguishable from glory'. (Ibid., p. 180).

Quinones rather unconvincingly enlists H.G. Wells's *The Time Machine* in his account of the reception-history of the Genesis 4 story, but otherwise it is hard to argue with his assertion that the theme has occupied some of the most representative and influential authors of our time. By the end, not only Unamuno, but also James Joyce and Michel Tournier have been added to the roll-call.

East of Eden, generally disparaged by literary critics as an example of Steinbeck's decline into sentimentality, is rehabilitated in Quinones as a major epic. It becomes a novel of divided consciousness set in the spacious context of the settlement of the Salinas Valley in California, though Quinones glosses over the structural weaknesses of the novel. There is also no analysis of the text as an incipient movie script, for which there is some evidence.[71]

After handling Wouk's *The Caine Mutiny* and some other works as regressive treatments of the theme, Quinones hails James Joyce's *Finnegan's Wake*, Unamuno's *Abel Sanchez* and *El Otro*, and two novels by Tournier as mature modern treatments of the acceptance of Cain and Abel as balancing forces in the ongoing cultural life of the West. The story of Cain and Abel is presented as the dominant myth and anti-myth of western culture, Quinones relying on the quality of the authors who engage with the theme as evidence for its significance. The author acknowledges Unamuno's fascination with Byron's *Cain*, though he shows no interest in tracing the lineage of influence through other authors, post-Byron.[72]

---

71 Steinbeck attended a script conference in Hollywood before writing the novel. His dreams at the time constituted 'a kind of autobiographical motion picture, going way back, and curiously, in sequence'. See Jay Parkin: *Steinbeck, A Biography* (London: Heinemann, 1994), p. 417. Earlier, in 1940, when the film rights to *The Grapes of Wrath* were sold for 75,000 dollars, it was one of the highest prices then paid for a novel. (Ibid., p. 276). We discuss the film version of *East of Eden* in a later chapter of this book.

72 For an account of the influence of Byron's *Cain* on Goethe, Baudelaire and others, see Sol Liptzin: *Biblical Themes in World Literature* (Hoboken NJ: Ktav Publishing, 1985), pp. 18–21.

44

Apart from the other, probably inevitable, areas of neglect (there is no mention of Von Rezzaori's *The Death of My Brother Abel*, published in 1976[73]), the coverage of the modern period is very comprehensive. But one misses any attempt to address the question of the conflation of biblical stories in this reception-history or to evaluate the relative impact of different biblical stories on the works selected for discussion. For example, Harold Fisch in *New Stories for Old*[74] finds the Akedah in *Billy Budd* and Job in *The Brothers Karamazov*, both works central to Quinones' study.

Quinones, an acknowledged Dante scholar, offers us the prospect of a menu of great writers enlisted in support of claims about the cultural importance of one particular biblical story. Constructing a highway through literature, however, perhaps inevitably, involves choosing one reading over another and therefore comes into direct confrontation with the basic reality of literature as an unending source of ambiguity. The idea of this kind of reception-history as an accumulation of meaning gives way to the sense that it may actually constitute an accumulation of ambiguities.

The issues raised here will be discussed in a later chapter, as will the question of whether Byron's demonstrable respect for Milton's *Paradise Lost* can be used to subvert his alleged radicalism and therefore whether reception-history can be seen as a two-way street in hermeneutical terms.

---

73   Gregor Von Rezzaori: *The Death of My Brother Abel*, trans. Joachim Neugroschel (London: Picador, 1986). This novel was first published in German as *Der Tod Meines Bruders Abel* in 1976. It is a rambling and ironic reflection on the cultural life of postwar Germany, where 'Kultur' itself became the means of repressing the memories of fratricide. The first-person narrator is obsessed with his own role as a Cain figure.

74   Harold Fisch: *New Stories for Old* (London: Macmillan, 1998), pp. 145 and 81, respectively.

Susan Haskins: *Mary Magdalene* (1993)[75]

Haskins's book, like its author, is deeply immersed in art history and provides a very full account of the treatment of the theme, particularly in medieval and renaissance art.

Haskins is concerned ultimately to distinguish the true Mary Magdalene from the myth of Mary Magdalene, the myth itself relying heavily on the tradition of conflating 'the three Marys', these being Mary Magdalene herself, Mary of Bethany, and Luke's sinner, with the occasional addition of the Johannine woman from Samaria and the woman taken in adultery. However, the vast bulk of her narrative is concerned with the myth, up to and beyond the point where Roman Catholic pontifical doctrine finally differentiates Mary Magdalene from the rest, identified by Haskins as the year 1969,[76] when calendrical changes were made.

A further emphasis of Haskins is on Mary Magdalene as the alternative feminine symbol to the Virgin Mary, though she never really resolves the question of her relationship to Eve in this role. A postscript records the decision of the General Synod of the Church of England to ordain women, as though this were somehow the outcome of the whole narrative.[77]

In terms of balance, there is a dichotomy between the enormous range of Haskins in exploring the reception-history of the Magdalene myth and the slender, almost laconic references at the beginning and end to the 'scientific' biblical critical study of Mary Magdalene as the first witness of the Resurrection and prototype of women's ministry. The 'correct' picture of Mary Magdalene renders obsolete, it seems, the whole complex excursion into cultural history which makes up most of the text. There are, of course, conflicting 'correct' modern pictures. The most

---

75 Susan Haskins: *Mary Magdalene* (London: HarperCollins, 1993).
76 Ibid., p. 388.
77 Ibid., p. 400.

radical feminist account is probably Jane Schaberg's *The Resurrection of Mary Magdalene*,[78] which amongst other things gives great emphasis to the Gnostic texts and has a useful discussion of the conflation of the three Marys.

The text itself faithfully surveys the importance of Mary Magdalene in Gnostic writings, the long tradition of the subject as the emblem of both desert mysticism and of the repentant sinner, the whole history of prostitution's association with the vocabulary provided by the Magdalene myth, the use of theme in erotic art, and finally the importance of Mary Magdalene as the insistent symbol of the Independent Woman.

Perhaps emulating Warner, Haskins seems to treat the subject as a fascinating journey into a discarded world of meaning. Near the end,[79] she reflects on Mary Magdalene's chimera-like existence which 'has reflected the exigencies of the periods in which she has flourished'. But the old myth seems to have given way to a new one, namely that the defeat of paternalism will lead to an era in which Christianity (and presumably its scriptures) will speak unambiguously to its audience.

Comment

There seems to be a contradiction between the lavish attention which Haskins devotes to the intricacies of the reception-history of the Mary Magdalene story and her readiness to dismiss the whole tradition in the light of what she takes to be the findings of modern biblical scholarship. Thinking of the reception-history which Haskins records, is there material here which is of enduring value? Why be so confident that biblical criticism has dispelled centuries of ignorance and obscurantism? Could a different account of the same material have come up with a

---

78   Jane Schaberg: *The Resurrection of Mary Magdalene, Legends, Apocrypha and Christian Testament* (London: Continuum, 2002).

79   Ibid., p. 391.

narrative in which the feisty figure of Mary Magdalene continually triumphs over attempts to assimilate her to cultural norms?

In a review in the *Times Literary Supplement* in October 1993,[80] Julia O'Faolain puts the question differently, asking why, 'having warned us against the propagandist misuse of the Magdalene myth and presented us with a "true Mary Magdalene"', Haskins should dismantle one myth in order to create another, the new myth being the feminist polemic.

Within Haskins's own analysis of her material, there is to be found a differentiation between paintings which treat the Magdalene theme in a deliberate way and those which merely attach the title to a painting which might equally well portray an anonymous subject (see the discussion of William Etty[81]). On a bigger scale, one might ask whether the growth of the mythical life from its origins in the Legend of the Seven Sleepers[82] was inevitable or whether something latent in the biblical figure drove it. Haskins, following Elaine Pagels, speculates on a lost gospel tradition which the Gnostics may have transmitted via the Coptic *Pistis Sophia*.

Mary Magdalene's career as a hermit[83] is another example of her ability to act as a motif for a powerful extraneous idea. Perhaps the fusion of mystic and reformed whore was an irresistible dramatic or thematic idea, as Debora Shuger seems to demonstrate in *The Renaissance Bible*.[84] But she is also the Wise Virgin[85] and a vehicle for the affective medieval spirituality of the Passion.[86]

---

80   Julia O'Faolain, review in *Times Literary Supplement*, 8th October 1993, p. 44.
81   Haskins, ibid., pp. 344–5.
82   Ibid., p. 107.
83   Ibid., pp. 110 ff and 226.
84   Debora Shuger: *The Renaissance Bible* (Berkeley and Los Angeles: University of California, 1998).
85   Haskins, ibid., p. 218.
86   Ibid., p. 202.

When Haskins argues that the medieval Magdalene fitted into a vital niche between Eve and the Queen of Heaven,[87] does the argument have to be reductionist? Even on a progressive, feminist reading, the admission of a less extreme feminine figure into the pantheon of Biblical Women could be seen as a creative development in the way that Jesus's treatment of the Syro-Phoenician woman in Mark 7:26 is often seen today as an improvement on the contemporary norm. Then we might challenge Haskins's relegation of Hawthorne's *The Scarlet Letter*, Flaubert's *Madame Bovary* and Tolstoy's *Anna Karenina* to the category of novels on 'the theme of the fallen woman'.[88] Also, whilst Haskins is probably right to regret the over-concentration of the novel *The Wild Girl* by Michèle Roberts[89] on the sexuality of Mary Magdalene, it seems inconsistent to dismiss the novelist's recreation of her subject as the author of a Gnostic gospel ('Mary Magdalene has endless dreams and mystical revelations ... '[90]), when Haskins's own Chapter 2 relies on the extant Gnostic material to underpin her claims about a suppressed feminist gospel tradition.

Haskins's catalogue of pornographic uses of the Magdalene theme in art does not of course hint at a progressive influence on the part of the theme, but it is, however, balanced by some extraordinarily original productions, ranging from the works of Giotto and Niccolo del'Arca to David Wynne's sculpture of 1963.[91]

A cumulative approach to reception-history might count the visual artistic masterpieces as landmarks in the total story and the medieval cult of the Mary

---

87 Ibid., p. 141.

88 Ibid., p. 341. In the case of *The Scarlet Letter*, for example, the novel can be read less as a 'fallen woman' story and more as a tale of how Hester Prynne uses her outward status as a defence against incursions against her inwardness. 'She affirms her autonomy by forcing the public to accept an exterior and superficial view of her which she is instrumental in forming.' – Edgar A. Dryden, *Nathaniel Hawthorne, The Poetics of Enchantment* (Ithaca and London: Cornell University Press, 1977), p. 71.

89 Michèle Roberts: *The Wild Girl* (London: Minerva, 1991).

90 Haskins, ibid., pp. 385–6.

91 Haskins, ibid., 210 and 378.

Magdalene as a necessary part of the journey. The question which will need further exploration later in this book is why so many authors of our genre of reception-histories assume that the journey or the story is now over, either on the basis that Christianity is played out (Warner) or that the critical era in biblical studies has emancipated us (Haskins, Norris, Wroe and Paffenroth). Trexler and Quinones, however, offer different schools of thought, as does John Sawyer in *The Fifth Gospel*, his study of the (Christian) reception-history of Isaiah

An alternative approach might be to treat the legendary material as fantastic literature. Eric Rabkin in *The Fantastic in Literature*[92] argued that the fantastic offers a magical world, often the polar opposite of reality, which can introduce new perspectives on what are regarded as social and political norms. Seen in this way, the reception-history of Mary Magdalene could be interpreted as a dialectic between emerging notions of womanhood and received notions, the meaning inhering in the process as much as in any arbitrarily decided outcome. Rosemary Jackson (see below in the section on Pamela Norris and Eve) has a much less romantic view of fantasy literature.

Norman Cohn: *Noah's Flood* (1996)[93]

The subject-matter of this book is narrower than its title suggests. Cohn concentrates almost exclusively on what one might call the 'technology' of the Noah story, to the exclusion of the human story. There is much about ancient and more recent calculations about the dimensions of the ark. There is nothing about the tradition of Noah's wife as a shrew or, more recently, her emergence as a proto-feminist, about which there is a not insignificant literature.

---

92   Eric Rabkin: *The Fantastic in Literature* (Princeton NJ: Princeton University Press, 1976).
93   Norman Cohn: *Noah's Flood, The Genesis Story in Western Thought* (New Haven and London: Yale University Press, 1996).

The plan of the book moves in stately chronological order from the Sumerian flood story to depth psychology in the twentieth-century, but a very large proportion of the text is devoted to the seventeenth and eighteenth-century speculations of early scientists including Burnet, Whiston, Steno, Woodward and Scheuchzer

Chapter 8 proves to be the turning point, 'Shifting Time-Scales'. Whereas scholarly debate could accommodate a localised Flood in place of a universal one, whilst still keeping to a biblical time-scale, the work of people like James Hutton and William Buckland effectively localised biblical history itself. The six-thousand year biblical history of the earth was dwarfed by the new findings.

Cohn provides useful accounts of the Harmonisers and the Fundamentalists, giving details of the quest to find the remains of Noah's Ark on Mount Ararat, a quest which really began in earnest with an Estonian expedition of 1829. A short Epilogue records the modern revival of interest in the Flood story as a feature of world mythology and the interest in the story as a motif in psychology.

Comment

Although Cohn explains the connection in theological thought between a prehistoric Flood and the future catastrophe of Judgement, in which, according to 2 Peter, floods of fire would engulf the earth, he makes little or no attempt to examine these twin myths as part of the imaginative life of western culture. This is surprising in a work which is at pains to discuss Noah as an antetype of Christ and which finishes by reciting the impact of Frazer's *The Golden Bough* in a chapter entitled, 'Hidden Meanings Again'.[94] It is as though hidden meanings had gone underground for about seventeen hundred years.

Norman Cohn's *Noah's Flood* can therefore be classified as a detailed guide to the part which the Genesis story of the Flood played in the opening phases of modern western science, incorporating background material on Mesopotamian

---

94   Cohn, ibid., pp. 130–3.

flood mythology and early Jewish and Christian methods of exegesis, with a postscript on the reaction of fundamentalists to the new scientific findings and the revival of interest in mythology. In the overall context of our study Cohn introduces a sense of debates which have raged, and for some people still rage, over the veracity of biblical stories in relation to alternative truth claims, especially those thrown up by the engine of modern material culture.

Further on in our study, we will attempt to redress the balance in terms of Cohn's neglect of the literary tradition, by looking at David Maine's recent novel, *The Flood*, at the beginning of our Chapter 5, 'Vox Dei,' and by referring to other aspects of the Noah tradition in Chapter 10.

Richard C. Trexler: *The Journey of the Magi: Meanings in History of a Christian Story* (1997)[95]

With Trexler we are in another world, in many ways at opposite poles from Cohn's book, except that the world of the magi turns out to be a very material world, or at least series of worlds.

The subtitle of this work, 'Meanings in History of a Christian story,' conveys the sense of the priority of the story-form over what can be inferred as meaning, signalling a perspective on reception-history which the whole of Trexler's text bears out and which may have wider implications.

Trexler has both a pre-history and a post-history of his main narrative, an account of the heyday of the magi in European and South American culture. Unlike the valedictory essayists in our study, Trexler offers the prospect of his subject returning to favour at some future historical juncture.[96] The pre-history

---

95   Richard C. Trexler: *The Journey of the Magi, Meanings in History of a Christian Story* (Princeton NJ: Princeton University Press, 1997).

96   Trexler, ibid., p. 209.

consists of a description of the Roman practice of depicting the giving of tributary gifts ('strenae') by client monarchs to the Emperor, itself rooted in the domestic gifting rituals associated with Saturnalia.[97] The post-history alludes to the modern political cliché of referring difficult decisions to groups of 'wise men' and the inversion suggested by the modern journeys of westerners to the East in search of gurus.[98] The association of the Magi with the Christmas commercial advertising industry also receives attention.

The bulk of the narrative describes the growth of the Magi tradition from the depiction of the three and sometimes four kings in early catacomb art through to the civic and state festivals of medieval Europe and South America, the latter developing in the wake of the consciously magian journeys of Columbus and his successors. Amidst a mass of assorted Magi material, ranging from the depiction in late medieval art of black third kings with earrings (a subversive theme) to the early modern fashion for Magi automata, Trexler fashions some powerful themes.

One of these themes is the plasticity of the Magi as Christian icons. Trexler shows the Magi successively as symbols of legitimising power, based on the Roman model of tribute-giving, and also of the salvific benefits of giving (in catacomb funerary art). They also become symbols of the conquering power Christianity as a state religion, at other times metaphors for religious border-crossing, and at other times symbols of the three ages of man. They act as models for diplomatic traditions. Trexler marks their transition from wise men to kings and even to becoming the titular saints of inns. He connects them with the Prester John myth and the Crusades. He discusses the central significance in European history of the movement of their bodies to Cologne in 1164; the fashion for European kings being depicted as Magi; the growth of civic Magi dramas and liturgical Magi plays.

---

97   Ibid., pp. 17–21.
98   Ibid., pp. 202–3.

The author explores the Dominican cult of the Magi; the Magi traditions of the Medici and others in Florence; the polarity between the first two and the third Magi in art; the appearance of the black third Magi; and eventually a feminine third Magus. He describes the return to the theme's roots during the Quattrocento and then the quest for the Magi in 'India' and finally the Americas. He discusses colonial gifting by Indians and then the poor kings of Hispano-American drama; the arrival of begging princes in Europe; and then the 'trick or treat' style of begging by the European poor which followed. At the end he comes to the universalisation and inversion of the Magi myth in the twentieth-century quest for Shangri-La. A 1948 photograph of the bodies of the Magi being ceremonially removed from the ruins of Cologne cathedral is used to suggest that the myth is sufficiently robust to enjoy future resurrection 'when the world needs to justify a new world order'.[99]

For Trexler the Magi story has myriad possibilities, but it is fundamentally a myth about legitimation and about exchange. It has a unique capacity amongst Christian stories to handle the fundamental polarities and realities of life in relation to these themes, including the polarities of poverty and riches, youth and old age, familiar and exotic, institutional and subversive. The story's own slender grip on historical reality lends it the capacity to be a subversive as well as a legitimising icon. 'The story speaks to any society's fundamental task of creating and maintaining legitimacy both within and without its borders.'[100]

Comment

Trexler differs from most of our other reception-history writers in that he is primarily a social historian, rather than an art historian or a literary scholar or theologian. But he also differs from several of them in his upbeat assessment of the future viability of the story he treats. In common with most of the others, his account deals at different

---

99   Trexler, ibid., p. 208.
100   Ibid., p. 37.

stages with the issues of paternalism in religion, colonialism, anti-semitism, gender, and modern secularism. Even Cuba makes a 'guest-appearance', as in Wroe and Stocker. But because he sees his subject as essentially pliable in ideological terms, rather than linked inextricably to one doomed ideology, he can be optimistic about its future. It may be that Trexler's particular academic discipline gives his account a greater detachment from the background narrative of modern secularism (or of religious decline) which propels some of our other texts.

The Journey of the Magi here is about a mythic theme which is capable of serving subversive forces as well as the status quo. The question arises as to whether the reception-history of Eve, the Virgin Mary, Mary Magdalene et alii or et aliae could be seen in the same light. Before turning to an account of the Eve story, which to an extent inhabits the middle ground between the valedictory essayists and the optimists, we examine a study of the Judith story which shares some of the combative qualities of its heroine.

Margarita Stocker: *Judith, Sexual Warrior –* *Women and Power in Western Culture* (1998)[101]

One of the most densely argued texts of the genre we have identified, Stocker presents Judith as a persistently subversive myth within western culture, the subversion being done to male dominance. This study therefore presents the mirror image of Warner's *Alone of All Her Sex*, which is about a publicly dominant myth.

Because of its subject-matter, Stocker is also a history of decapitation in western culture and the special conditions appertaining to the reception-history of a book from the Apocrypha which (as Stocker shows) carries its own particular religio-political complexities. Part of her argument, on the other hand, is that,

---

101 Margarita Stocker: *Judith, Sexual Warrior: Women and Power in Western Culture* (New Haven and London: Yale University Press, 1998).

when the chips are down, scruples over the distinction between apocryphal and canonical works dissolve. This is, after all, a book about power. More radically, Stocker seems to argue in places[102] that Judith represents a more authentic voice of the Otherness of God than equivalent voices within the canonical text.

Stocker is a poststructuralist, deploying the full vocabulary of binary opposition, text and subtext, multiple signifiers and so on. The story of Judith sets up a binary opposition between Israelite and Assyrian, monotheist and pagan idolater, true and false religion, but also (subversively) male and female, with the female revealed as godly. The story's innate tensions are played out then on the stage of Western European history, with art and literature providing an echoing commentary. In the end the story is counter-cultural because it is 'unreceptive to the pattern whereby society placates its rebels'.[103]

The coverage is sweeping. The misogyny of the Early Fathers causes them to allegorise Judith as an ante-type of the Virgin Mary.[104] Prudentius, however, establishes Judith as the emblem of human virtues.[105] Judith is the archetypal femme fatale.[106] Judith is a major focus for erotica during the Renaissance.[107] Judith is the focus for fascination with femmes fortes during the Reformation, in turn representing the Protestant revolt against priestly dominance[108] and the defence of the Old Religion against Holofernes.[109] Judith becomes the model for gynaecocracy, culminating in the rule of Elizabeth I, celebrated as a second Judith by the poet Richard Barnefield, in much the same way as Joan of Arc had been in France.[110]

---

102 Ibid., pp. 11–13, for example.
103 Ibid., p. 23.
104 Ibid., p. 88 et passim.
105 Ibid., pp. 29–45.
106 Ibid., p. 55.
107 Ibid., p. 60.
108 Ibid., pp. 74–6.
109 Ibid. p. 94.
110 Ibid., p. 100.

Du Bartas in his epic struggled with the tension between Judith as ideal woman and murderess, whilst the myth itself resonated with the male tyranny/ female opposition agenda of the Renaissance debate about politics.[111] Judith's acteme became the model for French public executions, where the private citizen could even kill a king.[112] But it could be reversed when, on the scaffold, the state reduced the criminal's body to the vulnerable state of a female body.[113] But then the guillotine came to be seen as the Revolution's Judith,[114] although there were other Judiths (like Corday) on the opposing side.

During the Romantic period Judith became one of the vehicles of Orientalism, representing the Other, but also, in contradiction, being the emblem of Englishness in England.[115] Judith became the name of Punch's wife in the popular puppet play, revealing the alienation within Victorian marriage,[116] and at the same time straddled the binary opposition between Ruth/wife and Magdalene/prostitute.[117] Turgid oratorios and inert verse-dramas keep Judith in the public domain,[118] whilst her canonical alter-ego, Jael, maintains her standing in formal religious circles. But by the 1890s Judith is demonised by both masculinists and feminists.[119] Feminism receives a boost, however, from George Meredith's much-read novel *One of Our Conquerors* in which Stocker detects Judith in Mrs Marsett.

Judith continues to occupy the stage in oratorios by Chorley and Parry, and, in displaced form, Puccini's *Tosca* and *Turandot*. Murderous women become more numerous in popular literature, in response partly to well-publicised criminal cases.

---

111 Ibid., p. 107.
112 Ibid., p. 112.
113 Ibid., p. 133.
114 Ibid., p. 139.
115 Ibid., p. 140.
116 Ibid., pp. 140–4.
117 Ibid., p. 146.
118 Ibid., p. 176.
119 Ibid., p. 179.

Lombroso's definitive work, *The Female Criminal*, asserts the wickedness latent in every woman. Trollope's *Last Chronicle of Barset* finds its murderess portrayed literally as Jael, emblem of the uncanny. Hawthorne's *The Marble Faun* presents a self-repressing Judith, typical of the dark secrets of Europe, which, like America, has failed to understand the bitter but noble truths about its own religion.

The Decadent movement sees Klimt's Judith I and Judith II present a sado-masochistic image of death as sex, reversing the Renaissance image of Judith's acteme imaging sex as death.[120] Freud in *Moses and Monotheism* celebrates the paradoxical virgin widowhood of Judith, unwittingly repeating the view of the Church Fathers that widows were the next best thing to virgins.[121]

Meanwhile, against the background of the rise of the Suffragette movement, various plays on the subject of Judith continue to appear in the opening decades of the twentieth-century, which Stocker documents. Reaction comes in the form of Bartok's opera *Bluebeard's Castle*, with its murderous hero dispatching four wives, including a final Judithic heroine. But Honegger's *Judith* restates Judith's political value.

Stocker notes the Nazi propaganda machine attempting to make Hebbel's *Judith* into a Nordic heroine, thereby highlighting the threat of Judith as a counter-cultural myth to Nazism.[122] After the war, pro-Zionist ballets and films demonstrate Judith's resistance to political hi-jacking. Amongst Holocaust novels Andre Schwarz-Bart's *The Last of the Just* has a male protagonist but its most memorable figure is Mother Judith, the conveyer of true Jewish values.[123]

Stocker reviews the motif of the 'Woman With A Gun' in popular film and fiction, but fails to locate the name Judith in any of the characters. The discussion

---

120   Ibid., p. 196.
121   Ibid., pp. 199ff.
122   Stocker, ibid., p. 195.
123   Ibid., p. 206.

therefore becomes a more generalised debate about gender roles and the gun as the phallic symbol. However, there are actual Judiths as the radicalised vicar's wife in David Edgar's play *Ecclesiastes* (1990) and in a comic role as a terrorist in Monty Python's *The Life of Brian* (1979.)

Stocker, like Wroe, finds herself in Cuba in Chapter 12, with the CIA mesmerised by the Judith myth into giving Castro's mistress Marita Lorenz the task of assassinating the leader, albeit unsuccessfully. The discussion emphasises the contradictory messages engendered by the motif of the 'Woman With A Gun'. Le Carré in his thriller *The Little Drummer Girl* (1983) has a Judith figure who approaches the disturbing frontiers of the moral ambiguity of the war on terrorism but retreats into the safe harbour of romantic love. In Michael Baldwin's thriller *Holofernes* (1990) gender roles are changed when both Holofernes and Judith are male. But Judith in herself continues to be a mixed symbol of fear and reassurance in the ambivalent attitude of Western society to patriarchal power.

Nicholas Moseley's postmodernist novel *Judith* (1992) contains a drama within a drama in which the main male and female rediscover authentic behaviour through playing inauthentic mythic roles in a Judith play. Helen Zahavi's novel *Dirty Weekend* (1991) presents a Judith character, Bella, whose reaction to years of subjugation is to become a serial killer in an updated version of *The Revenger's Tragedy*. Reassuringly for some readers, Stocker sees the prescription as irony.

Stocker's conclusion is that the Judith myth continually resists pro-cultural assimilation, inviting us to examine what our cultural mythology has made us. 'She is an image of the autonomy that is constantly being wrested from us all, and an icon of the way to recover it.'[124] Quite unlike Warner in her study of the myths of the Virgin Mary, Stocker sees her subject as counter-cultural and, more than that, dynamically relevant to the modern age. The book ends therefore not on a

---

124 Ibid., p. 252.

valedictory note but on a challenging one, suggestive of a new Reformation which will free Western society from thralldom to patriarchy and other disabling errors.

Comment

This is certainly a reception-history of encyclopaedic dimensions. In a mixed review published in the *Times Literary Supplement* in January 1999, Tom Shippey suggests that Stocker fails to balance her depiction of Judith's 'feminist judo' with a sense of her mournful widowhood and is less than convinced that Reformation politics was largely dominated by women. He also contends that by the modern period Judith had become a name without Apocryphal connotations largely and that to treat all plots involving inveigling women as Judith stories is indiscriminate. He notes that at one point Stocker denies writing a study of an image or a myth, instead using myth as 'the clue to an alternative study of western culture', earlier signalled as 'the radical feminist alternative to the Oedipal myth'. His terse conclusion is that 'Judith as a sexual warrior is most convincing to those in a sexual war: not Bethulians, anyway'.[125] Shippey's final comment here seems to suggest that meaning is captive to the (supposed) original context and it raises the question of whether the Bethulians, anchored safely in a conjectural (though of course fictional) past, have the power to chain Judith down forever.

Whilst we can agree with Shippey that Stocker probably spreads her net too widely, she reveals some very striking features of the reception-history of Judith, not least in the propagandist use of her theme by opposing sides during the Reformation. Later on in this book, we will have occasion to consider this aspect of Stocker's subject more fully and also to look further at Nicholas Moseley's novel *Judith*, which is one of the hypertexts she discusses. We will also compare and contrast her master-narrative of Judith as a 'counter-cultural myth' with the master-narratives of the other authors we are examining.

---

125 Tom Shippey, review in *Times Literary Supplement*, 15th January 1999, p. 30.

Pamela Norris: *The Story of Eve* (1998)[126]

This wide-ranging survey of the figure of Eve in western culture traverses the territory from speculation about the likely original meanings of the Garden of Eden story through to modern literary rehabilitations of Eve. It also looks at the related figures of Lilith and Pandora.

For Norris, Eve begins as part of a mythical explanation for the arduous conditions faced by the Israelites on arrival in Canaan. She is then more or less totally neglected until the mysogynist Ben Sira specifies her as the origin of sin and therefore of death. Thereafter the story is progressively exploited by the Church Fathers and their successors to demonstrate the negative qualities which patriarchy associated with womanhood, including woman as temptress and as incarnation or familiar of the Devil; or to emphasise woman's subordinate role to man as 'help mete'.

Norris is particularly effective at identifying the linkages between Eve and kindred figures in literature and art and at discussing the conflation of Eve with the goddesses of classical mythology. However, this approach does allow the author to wander away from the specific reception-history of the Eve of the Genesis story, making the account at times into a reception-history almost of Woman. In fact, the author's premise is that Eve is Everywoman, which makes the excursions into the stories of Joseph and Aseneth or Mesuline or the real-life Perpetua or Macrina entirely justifiable. There are some fascinating byways, such as Erasmus's mistranslation of Pandora's jar as a box (conflating the story with that of Psyche) or Elizabeth Barrett-Browning's difficulty in addressing the actual Garden of Eden story and turning instead to the story of the Exile from the Garden.

Closer, in its rabbinic origins, than some of the classical myths, to the early development of variants on the biblical story, the story of Lilith receives an

---

126 Pamela Norris: *The Story of Eve* (London: Picador, 1998).

appropriate amount of attention.[127] Norris draws out some of the worryingly misogynist themes in George Macdonald's *Lilith*. She devotes a proportionately large amount of space to Mary Shelley's *Frankenstein*, Willa Cather's *The Professor's House* and Angela Carter's *The Passion of the New Eve* as feminist revisions of the Genesis story.

Comment

Given Norris's large canvas, we could not expect her to make space for multiple critical views of the material she discusses. But this does mean that her material can be read quite differently from the feminist master-narrative which she offers. For example, an interesting aspect of Macdonald's fantasy which Norris does not address, but which is discussed in Ziolkowski's *Disenchanted Images*,[128] is the idea that the real world is an illusion and that the mirror in the story gives access to an eternal world of truth in which the mythic contest between Good and Evil, represented by Adam and Lilith, is forever in progress. For Ziolkowski this novel is close to the high-water mark in the tradition of mirror fantasies.

The author provides no explanation for the neglect of the Garden of Eden story within the biblical canon itself, where its fate is in sharp contrast to that of the Exodus story. However, she provides ample evidence of the story's resonance for the modern period, with telling readings of Mary Shelley's *Frankenstein* (the classic feminist text) and of Willa Cather's *The Professor's House*. Her examination of significant recent novels on the theme (Bagnold, Brookner, Le Guin, Attwood and Carter) suggests that the feminist dialogue with 'The Story of Eve' is a major

127 A more precise mapping of the development of the story of Lilith is to be found in Sol Liptzin: *Biblical Themes in World Literature* (Hoboken NJ: Ktav Publishing, 1985), pp. 1–12. In particular, Liptzin links the Talmudic legend with the problem of the two creation stories in Genesis and with the Vulgate rendering of her name in Isaiah 34:14 as Lamia. This author takes a more positive view of Macdonald's *Lilith* than Norris was to, emphasizing the redemption of Lilith from dependence on The Shadow at the end of the novel.

128 Theodore Ziolkowski: *Disenchanted Images* (Princeton NJ: Princeton University Press, 1977), pp. 219–21.

crux for our version of Biblical Studies. Margaret Atwood's *The Handmaid's Tale* epitomises the issues at stake, in so far as it projects a neo-Puritan strong reading onto the Genesis text, setting it up for rejection. In our chapter looking at feminist and other radical reading strategies, there will be a review of conflicting readings of Atwood's novel and of Angela Carter's *The Passion of the New Eve*, as well as a consideration of the significance of Mary Shelley's *Frankenstein* for the feminist Eve-hermeneutic.

Norris seems clear that *The Passion of the New Eve* is a dismissal of the biblical urtext. But the question of how to read Carter's novel, in particular, whether as a relentless attack on the Genesis myth or as an ironic parody of feminist extremism, whether as a dismissal of the Earth Mother movement or as a return to it, as well as the question of the influence of Blake on this novelist, is the subject of an extensive literature which we will discuss. Shelley's *Frankenstein* will be seen to be significant not just for the development of feminist approaches to the Genesis myth but also for ideas about narrative. Rosemary Jackson in *Fantasy, the Literature of Subversion*[129] sees *Frankenstein* as pivotal in the Gothic inversion of romance images which leads on to the work of the modern feminist writers of fantastic fiction.

The Afterword[130] talks about demystifying Eve in order to leave her behind. If the Genesis story is, in Norris's terms, the Story of Eve as written up by patriarchy, and large tracts of reception-history are the same thing reinforced, then the question being posed by Norris is whether modern rehabilitations or rewritings of Eve must inevitably lead to an abandonment of the story itself. Later we will examine this proposition more extensively and also explore the alternatives. It might also be worth noting that in modern culture the Garden of Eden story is not invariably associated with gender issues. A recent report of the discovery of a 'lost world'

---

129 Rosemary Jackson: *Fantasy, The Literature of Subversion* (London: Methuen, 1981).
130 Norris, ibid., p. 403.

in the jungle in the Papua province of Indonesia included the observation by the team-leader of a group of Australian scientists, 'It's as close to the Garden of Eden as you're going to find on earth'.[131]

Ann Wroe: *Pilate, the Biography of an Invented Man* (1999)[132]

Wroe, in her Introduction, describes how friends suggested that she would be better off writing a novel about Pilate. In many ways this work is a set of notes for a novel. Not only does it catalogue an enormous amount of material about the historical background to its subject (the story of the tribe from which Pilate probably originated; the Roman system of governorships), and give a very full account of the folkloric traditions about Pilate (together with a brief analysis of the gospel material), it also incorporates passages of purely novelistic invention by the author, including an excursus into Castro's Havana,[133] an episode involving a Black Rights protester in the USA in 1992,[134] and a slightly bizarre Epilogue with Pilate on an Arnoldian beach.[135]

It is no wonder that Leslie Houlden, inclined anyhow by his own background in conventional New Testament studies to be more interested in Helen Bond's *Pontius Pilate in History and Interpretation* (which was reviewed by him in tandem with Wroe's book in the *Times Literary Supplement* in 1999), remarked that 'the reader may find the precise genre hard to pinpoint'.[136] The Bond work[137] confines its attention to the material relating to Pilate which can be found in Philo, Josephus

---

131 Comment of Bruce Beehler, reported in *The Guardian*, 8th February 2006, p. 22.

132 Ann Wroe: *Pilate, the Biography of an Invented Man* (London: Jonathan Cape, 1999).

133 Ibid., p. 124.

134 Ibid., p. 181.

135 Ibid., p. 366.

136 Leslie Houlden, review in *Times Literary Supplement* 1999.

137 Helen Bond: *Pontius Pilate in History and Interpretation* (Cambridge: Cambridge University Press, 1998).

and the four canonical gospels. It also insists on a sharp distinction between 'the Pilate of interpretation' and 'the Pilate of history,' a distinction which Wroe tends to override by constantly interweaving legendary material with the more solidly historical and by her much wider canvas.

Comment

Wroe's book is certainly a curious hybrid and exists in a tantalising relationship to Bulgakov's novel, *The Master and Margarita*, to which it refers occasionally. There is a debate in literary circles about whether the inner novel in *The Master and Margarita* (which is about Pilate) can be equated with the whole of *The Master and Margarita* or whether it is only a figura for it.[138] The strange thing is that, if Bulgakov's novel is finally about the redemption of Pilate as a 'real' contemporary character, his Jesus is that of Renan, whereas Wroe resolutely contrasts Pilate as 'an invented man' with Jesus as the supernatural but fully historical figure assumed by Christian orthodoxy. The other curious relationship with the Bulgakov work is that the latter is one of literature's most unstable texts, known in considerably differing extant versions.

Despite this conundrum, one could not hope for a fuller account of the cultural history of the subject-matter. There is everything here, from the Coptic treatment of Pilate as a saint to Tolstoy's championship of Nicolai Gay's painting, *What is Truth?* and from the inscription recovered from the sea at Caesarea bearing Pilate's name to the folklore connected with Mount Pilatus in Switzerland. There is extensive use of the material from the *Acta Pilati* and also a detailed account of the treatment of Pilate in the Mystery Plays, where he became an important part of the development of the villain role in English drama.[139]

---

138 See J.A.E. Curtis: *Bulgakov's Last Decade, the Writer as Hero* (Cambridge: Cambridge University Press, 1997), p. 141.

139 Wroe, ibid., pp. 32, 121 and 170.

Wroe covers the development of Pilate's life as a character[140] and the Golden Legend's fabular connection of Seth with the Cross.[141] Closer to the interests of modern novelists are the accounts of Pilate's temperament inferred from Josephus, Philo and the Gospels.[142] The author's compendious digressions on a variety of historical subjects, ranging from aqueducts to suicide in the ancient world,[143] whilst relevant to the traditions about Pilate, are also characteristic of the modern, 'informative' popular novel (especially the thriller) where the reader is engaged not only by the narrative flow but also entertained by the imparting of esoteric snippets of information, as Bruce Merry has shown.[144]

The text touches on the topic of anti-semitism at various points, something which we will see coming to the fore in the reception-history of the Judas story with which Pilate is intertwined.

This book is an ingenious compendium of 'Pilate lore', rendered more readable possibly by being handled within a quasi-narratory framework. The opening Prologue on Blackpool Beach in 1870 and the closing Epilogue on a beach which sounds like Scarborough form the framework for a journey from the Romanticism of the Victorian world to the more prosaic contemporary world of the United Beach Mission and the disappointments of the modern Sunday. A journey from enchantment perhaps to disenchantment, or at least from a world in which legends

---

140 Ibid., p. 36.

141 Ibid., p. 155.

142 Ibid., p. 94.

143 Ibid., pp. 11 and 98.

144 See Bruce Merry: *Anatomy of the Spy Thriller* (Dublin: Gill and Macmillan, 1977), pp. 176–7: 'So between the lines of the text, the thriller is in the process of assuring the reader that he is bound to be an expert at something, as he soon as he decides to put down the book and re-emerge into daily life. The reader is also pleased and impressed that his time spent on the thriller may also be made worthwhile in terms of new information: technical data which are "well researched" (as the book jacket likes to claim) on dolphins or the use of marlinspikes, or the history of Algerian nationalism, or the technique of *chemin de fer*, or wiring up a missile for take-off, or programming a computer.'

66

about Pilate were exciting for the general public to one in which the bare bones of the Crucifixion story are hardly known.

If Warner's style is in the end valedictory from a feminist perspective, Wroe is also valedictory in terms of her perception of the usefulness of a narrative tradition. It is hard to imagine the novel suggested by her friends having much vitality, even though the book she has actually written is a fascinating cultural tour. The question which needs to be asked is why cultural tours such as this and those of Gaines, Warner and Haskins in our genre of reception-history have to end in nemesis, rather like those blockbuster films where the set has to be blown up to round off the proceedings.[145] It would seem that the coda is just a further expression of the author's alienation from the central subject-matter, which the reader is invited to share in narrative form.

Janet Howe Gaines: *Music in the Old Bones, Jezebel Through The Ages* (1999)[146]

Music in the Old Bones is an exhaustive trawl through theological and literary commentary on the Jezebel of I and II Kings. The book is divided into two halves. Part One explores facets of the biblical text and rabbinic and Christian commentary thereon. Part Two catalogues the treatment of the Jezebel theme in prose, fiction, poetry and drama (including films). The author regards the midrashic tradition as wholly negative about Jezebel, ignoring Ginzberg's slightly more nuanced reading of some of the material.[147] Gaines makes a distinction between 'biblical' and 'non-

---

145 Examples would be the James Bond films or *The Guns of Navarone*.

146 Janet Howe Gaines: *Music in the Old Bones, Jezebel through the Ages* (Carbondale and Edmundsville: Southern Illinois University Press, 1999).

147 Louis Ginzberg, *Legends of the Jews* (Philadelphia: Jewish Publication Society of America, 1938/1966), Vol. IV, p. 189, refers to Ahab's appearance in a dream to R. Levi, pleading with him to agree that Jezebel was the instigator of all his sins. Ginzberg also records a tradition that Jezebel had redeeming qualities (sympathy with those experiencing joy and grief) and

biblical' literary treatments, apparently differentiating between examples where the queen is directly involved and those where the reference is oblique or passing. There are anomalies, inevitably. The World War Two novel *Jezebel the Jeep*, centred on the adventures of a 'high-spirited' military vehicle, seems rather tangential to the theme (Gaines remarks that it 'sets a new low for foolishness'),[148] whilst the play *Jezebel's Husband* by Robert Nathan is as much about Jonah as Jezebel.[149]

The book's title and sometimes its text seem to promise a rehabilitation of Jezebel, of the Stalin Was Misunderstood genre. But in the end it is only Jezebel's fortitude in facing her death which provides the focus for this argument, culminating in Masefield's play,[150] though even Thomas Hardy is recorded as admiring her only in the way he admired Lady Macbeth.[151]

Gaines's book makes its mark as a contribution to reception-history by recording all the major (and many minor) treatments of the Jezebel story from the author of Deuteronomy onwards, by amplifying the background not only of the biblical text but also of most of the authors mentioned 'through the ages', and by highlighting the turns in the progress of the theme represented by such seminal works as John Knox's *The First Blast of the Trumpet Against The Monstrous Regiment of Women* and Margaret Atwood's *The Robber Bride*. Knox and Atwood are at opposite poles in terms of the Gaines thesis about the use of Jezebel in misogynist propaganda, though united in recognition of her as the epitome of evil.

In deconstructionist terms, the 'hidden voice' which Gaines uncovers is less that of the negative treatment of women (or of assertive women) within the biblical canon and its reception-history than that of Canaanite fertility religion. It is the

---

that the organs and limbs involved in expressing these qualities were left unmarked when the horses trampled her to death. Ginzberg's notes in Vol. VI admittedly assign a quite late date to the latter tradition (PRE 17, Amsterdam 1709 or Warsaw 1852).

148 Ibid., pp. 127–8.
149 Ibid., p. 181.
150 Ibid., p. 175.
151 Ibid., p. 159.

Tom Robbins novel *Skinny Legs and All* which in its flippant or ironic way sums up the case for a reassessment of the value of the sort of earth-goddess religion which Astarte is thought to have represented and therefore the case for the pluralism and religious tolerance which the Deuteronomic text fiercely resists.[152]

Comment

Given that *Music in the Old Bones* is fundamentally a rehabilitation-project, rather than an attempt at a more balanced or objective reception-history of the Jezebel story, it inevitably places great reliance on the few hypertexts which are sympathetic to its theme. Therefore, it is surprising that Gaines, in describing the Wilkie Collins novel *Jezebel's Daughter*, with its extremely convoluted plot, fails to discuss the evidence that the villainess, Madame Fontaine, is a partly redeemed character.[153] The treatment of the admittedly slender references to Jezebel in Faulkner's novel *Light in August* also ignores the potential to explore the full significance of the name as a term of abuse.[154] There is an extensive literature on Faulkner's relationship to Calvinism and to the Bible and also a recent essay by Irene Visser, which will be relevant to our discussion of the diffusion of biblical stories later in this study.[155]

As a reception-history, *Music in the Old Bones* demonstrates that resistance to the Deuteronomic view of Jezebel is an extremely rare phenomenon even in the modern period and that, in the case of this particular story, there is no stronger reading on offer. This is in spite of narrative experiments which make Jezebel the secret lover of Jehu or of Naboth[156] or films which allow her to be reformed.[157]

---

152 Gaines, ibid., p. 138.
153 Ibid., pp. 119–20.
154 Ibid., pp. 123–4.
155 Irene Visser: 'Faulkner's Mendicant Madonna' in *Literature & Theology*, Vol. 18, No 1, March 2004.
156 Gaines, ibid., pp. 133–6 and 173–8.
157 Gaines, ibid., pp. 82–3 and 221.

Recent feminist biblical studies likewise seem more concerned with valorizing the worship of Asherah or Astarte within Canaanite religion than with the rehabilitation of Jezebel herself.[158]

Tina Pippin: *Apocalyptic Bodies,*
The Biblical End of the World in Text and Image[159]

Apocalyptic Bodies, despite its neutral-sounding title and sub-title, is as much a rejection-history as a reception-history of the Book of Revelation. Pippin dips into a range of treatments of the Apocalypse in medieval art and in modern film, as well as making a passing reference to the Reformers' use of the text, but in all other respects her account of the impact of the text is driven by her own personal experience of the text's relationship with the Klu Klux Klan movement and Southern fundamentalism. The main argument consists of a feminist critique of the 'hypermasculine' deity of the Apocalypse and an examination of the biblical book as an extreme example of the genre of horror literature.

Chapter 1 relates the seven seals of the Apocalypse and other uses in the text of the notion of seals and sealing to its etymological connection with the word, 'sequel'. The Apocalypse then is the sequel to the rest of the Bible and partakes of the disturbing attributes of horror-film sequels, in which the body count steadily rises. Pippin is much concerned in this chapter and elsewhere with the violent and vengeful sentiments which she finds associated with Christian fundamentalist 'endism'. Despite the best intentions of some liberal Christian exegetes, the

---

158 An example would be Judith M. Hadley:'From Goddess to Literary Construct: the Transformation of Asherah into Hokmah' in Athalya Brenner and Carole Fontaine (eds): *A Feminist Companion to Reading the Bible: Approaches, Methods, Strategies* (Sheffield: Sheffield Academic Press, 1997). Here the linking of Asherah with Baal in I Kings 18 is regarded as Deuteronomic propaganda. 'It may be that the prophets of Asherah are not mentioned again because Elijah had no quarrel with them.' (Ibid., p. 306).

159 Tina Pippin: *Apocalyptic Bodies, the Biblical End of the World in Text and Image* (London: Routledge, 1999).

Apocalypse's destructiveness remains inscribed in the culture, not least in the author's own state of Georgia, where Trident submarines are manufactured and the 'White trains', the School for the Americas and Newt Gingrich are among the dominant public images. There is an extensive discussion of horror fantasy in setting up the Other as the horrible, obscene Thing which has to be obliterated, as in Nazi fantasies about the Jews.

Chapter 2 explores the world of the Klu Klux Klan in North Carolina and relates it to the 'little apocalypse' of Mark 13 and Flannery O'Connor's short story *A Good Man is Hard to Find.* Chapter 3 looks at the story of Jezebel in 2 Kings 9 and Revelation 2, re-reading the different texts about Jezebel both within these urtexts and in their retellings in American culture, in order to confront the complexities of this figure and the significance of the persistence of the 'cursed woman' theme for women claiming autonomy. Doré's illustrations are an important part of the material discussed, together with Tom Robbins's *Skinny Legs and All.* Chapter 4 explores the image of the Tower of Babel in Doré (again), in advertising and in art, as well as the 1916 silent film *Intolerance* and the 1993 Maguire opera *The Tower.*

Chapter 5 examines images of the Abyss, seeing them ultimately as related to negative images of women and the confronting of the hated Other. This is, for Pippin, a return to the formless void of Genesis, the Bible having come full-circle back to its beginnings. The chapter ends with the musing sentence, 'Maybe this time the story will be different'. But the next two chapters, on 'Apocalyptic Horror' and 'Apocalyptic Fear' seem to crush this hope. These chapters deal with horror films about the end of the world and with theoretical models about fantasy offered by Rosemary Jackson and Tzvetan Todorov, as well as Kant and the idea of the sublime, Kristeva and the emotive aspects of horror, and Noel Carroll's analysis of monsters. They also cover pornographic treatments of apocalyptic images, including the Whore of Babylon; Freud's notion of the monster as the externalisation of repressed fears and desires; Moretti's study of gothic monsters; and an outdoor enactment of the Four Horsemen of the Apocalypse, known as the 'Tribulation Trail', in which the spectators are terrified by the coming of the Rapture and Judgement.

Chapter 8 is the Conclusion, *The Joy of (Apocalyptic) Sex*, which asks why violence is condoned 'when it is in scripture and when God is the actor?' The author notices three major features of the Apocalypse read as a text from a postmodern perspective: it is full of fissures which can serve as entry-points for interpretation (gender, violence, beasts, hymns, eating, Jezebel, Babylon etc.); it has a strong hold on western culture; and thirdly, the Apocalypse makes the body the site for the inscription of a set of stories, not least that of the Bride (which Pippin sees as emblematic both of women's victimisation and of homoerotic impulses). Her conclusion is that the Apocalypse is a 'male misogynist fantasy about the future' and that the images of women are thoroughly vindictive. '... the Bride is made into polis, city, the Whore gang- raped and burned and eaten, the Woman clothed with the Sun is a reproductive vessel who is exiled subsequent to giving birth, and Jezebel is destroyed'.[160]

Comment

Although Pippin catalogues ways in which mainstream Christian exegesis sets out to marginalize this biblical book,[161] she herself reads it as a guide to the entire biblical canon. Not only does the Book of Revelation conclude the Bible, but its apocalyptic themes permeate the rest of the Bible. She reads Christ himself as the incarnation of the Fear[162] which is the correlate of the wrathful God of the whole master-narrative. She finds horror and the heavenly constantly interlaced in the

---

160 Pippin, bid., pp. 117 and 119.
161 Ibid., pp. 113–114.
162 Ibid., pp. 100–6 and 115.

72

text, with the New Jerusalem at the end of the narrative, but still no prospect of an end to horror.

Pippin partly echoes Auerbach's emphasis on the lacunae and silences of the biblical text but her deconstructionist strategy is to use them to challenge the text's authority. It is her use of the term 'The Other' which indicates the polar opposition of her exegesis to the approach of George Steiner, for whom The Other is the ineradicable trace of the Transcendent.

The short chapters on the reception-history of Jezebel and of the Tower of Babel are quite illuminating in places, if taken as one particular reading (amongst others) of the material selected for discussion.[163] The author also provides an extensive discussion of the notion of the Sublime and of Rudolf Otto's analysis of Holy Fear. But all of this is affected by the reductionism of her basic position, which is that the Apocalypse encodes submission to a terrorising and misogynist deity, intolerant of all pluralisms; and that, in doing so, this particular biblical book 'reveals' the true drift of the Bible as a whole.

The scholarly position that the text is historically rooted in the early Christian experience of persecution is judged irrelevant to the contemporary understanding of the text, partly on the basis of the poststructuralist rejection of the past setting as normative for later meaning, and partly because Pippin detects a sort of defeatist encouragement to acquiescence in a text which uses horror to catharise fear. Similarly, Pippin shows no interest in the details of the pre-modern reception-history of the Apocalypse.[164]

---

163   There could not be a greater contrast than that between Pippin's negative reading of the story of the Tower of Babel in art, film and literature and the optimistic view of André Parrot in an earlier generation, treating the story as an outworking of memories of the Mesopotamian ziggurat, itself for him 'the essential step' towards 'looking beyond this world.' See André Parrot: *The Tower of Babel* (London: The Camelot Press, 1955. Trans. Edwin Hudson. First published, Neuchâtel: 1954, as *Le Tour de Babel*).

164   In an earlier generation, M.R. James produced a scholarly study of the depiction of scenes from the Apocalypse in illuminated manuscripts. See M.R. James: *The Apocalypse in Art* (London: The British Academy, 1931). It seems worth noting that this author's stance is to

The author emphasises that she is not out to replace the aggressive God of the biblical text with a female-god warrior and rewrite the text in that way, and although she repeatedly talks of the necessity of rewriting or of resistant reading, the general thrust of *Apocalyptic Bodies* is that the text itself should be rejected.[165]

This book seems to throw up in an extreme form (appropriate to its immediate subject-matter) all the issues which are central to our study. Does a feminist or post-colonial reading of reception-history have to be either totalising or rejecting? What are the implications of treating one biblical book or one biblical story as the key to the whole Bible? Does a more respectful treatment of the text demand a degree of religious investment? Can the same material (in Pippin's case, the paintings of Dieric Bouts or Stanislau Lepri, the drawings of Gustav Doré or various horror films or *Skinny Legs and All*) be read in a different way? Given a degree of agreement over the morphology of fear and horror, can there not be a pluralism of ontologies? How can a text be received expectantly in the Steinerian sense and yet critiqued ideologically? What about the ambiguity of all literary texts? I hope to demonstrate that these are theological as well as literary or aesthetic questions.

If we take just one of Pippin's major intertexts for her reading of biblical apocalypse, Flannery O'Connor's *A Good Man is Hard to Find*,[166] we may ask whether her dismissal of the aesthetics of O'Connor's 'southern gothic' fiction is justified or whether she simply rides roughshod over a whole literary tradition when she concludes, 'For O'Connor as for Mark, salvation is through violence'.[167] This particular short story has given rise to a wealth of divergent interpretations, but

---

record the polemical use of images from the text at certain junctures (such as the insistent use of the Lamb as an image of Christ by Pope Sergius I or the depiction by Protestants of the Papacy as the Scarlet Woman), rather than to enlist the text in the service of an authorial polemic.

165 Ibid., pp. 82–3 and 121.

166 Flannery O'Connor: *A Good Man is Hard to Find*, edited by Frederick Asals (New Brunswick NJ: Rutgers University Press, 1993).

167 Pippin, ibid., p. 26.

mostly they take the violence at more than face value.[168] It is, in any case, hard to treat a text which embodies such improbabilities as the tragic meeting of the family with the Misfit (the very bogey they were intent on avoiding) as realistic narrative. Taking this further, William Scheick[169] has shown that G.K. Chesterton's fantastic story *Man Alive* is an important 'pretext' for the brutal shootings which dominate the narrative. Whether one considers O'Connor, after her own reckoning, as a 'Catholic' writer, or as the apologist for a typically Protestant view of salvation, it is hard to avoid the sense that this story is about the ridiculing of bourgeois norms and a dramatic confrontation with reality. It can also be read, de-constructionist fashion, as the exposure of human personality as the product of language.[170] The fact that this story, like other works of Flannery O'Connor[171] uses violence as part of its technique as a piece of 'grotesque' fiction, does not mean that its author is the mouthpiece for the doom-laden misogyny which Pippin associates with the reception-history of biblical apocalyptic in the Southern States.

Meanwhile, it is important to note that the Book of Revelation itself as a text has been received and interpreted in a multifarious way in the past. Taking Revelation 17 as an example, Ian Boxhall[172] has demonstrated the use of the image to describe the early Christian experience of persecution, to describe the excesses of the medieval papacy, to revile Protestant attacks on the Catholic Church, to describe the Byzantine Church, to defend the Church against oppression in Muslim Spain, to provide an image of apartheid to sustain its victims or to support campaigns for justice in Latin America. In their recent reception-history commentary on

---

168 See essays in Asals, ibid.

169 William J. Scheick: 'Flannery O'Connor's *A Good Man is Hard to Find* and G.K. Chesterton's *Manalive* in Asals, ibid., pp. 113–118.

170 See Mary Jane Schenck: *Deconstructed Meaning in A Good Man is Hard to Find* in Asals, ibid., pp. 165–74.

171 A good example would be *Wise Blood*, probably Flannery O'Connor's best-known work.

172 Ian Boxhall: 'The Many Faces of Babylon the Great: Wirkungsgeschichte and Revelation 17' in Steve Moyise (ed.): *Studies in the Book of Revelation* (Edinburgh: T. & T. Clark, 2001).

Revelation, Judith Kovacs and Christopher Rowland balance the negative portrayal of woman as harlot in Revelation 17 with the presence of negative male figures like Balaam in the text and also the fact that the text represents the Beast as the driving force behind the harlot. They also refer to the reliance of 'female prophets and mystics down the centuries' (including Perpetua and Felicity, Teresa of Avila, and Hildegard of Bingen, together with Anna Trapnel, the seventeenth-century visionary) on the Book of Revelation as a source of inspiration and as the scriptural warrant 'to transgress convention and to function in a male dominion'.[173]

Christopher Burdon[174] has described the great and multifarious influence the Apocalypse had on English life and letters during the early modern period, from Newton to the Muggletonians, from Wesley to Coleridge, and as rewritten by Shelley and Blake. Frederick van der Meer[175] has shown us the rich heritage of the treatment of the Apocalypse in western art, created despite the common recognition that this is a book which defies visualisation. As Alison Jack remarks, 'Its use of female symbols and characters are obvious starting points for any reading from a feminist perspective. However, whether a purely feminist reading gets to the heart of the text is another matter'.[176] An attempt to bridge theological and postmodernist literary-critical approaches to the text is made by Judith Lee ('A secular reading evokes horror, while a theological reading evokes awe. Neither ... is adequate by itself').[177] Her solution is to treat the Apocalypse as an exercise in

---

173 Judith Kovacs and Christopher Rowland: *Revelation* (Oxford: Blackwell, 2004), pp. 62, 188–9.

174 Christopher Burdon: *The Apocalypse in England, Revelation Unravelling, 1700–1834* (London: Macmillan, 1997).

175 Frederick van der Meer: *Apocalypse, Visions from the Book of Revelation* (London: Thames & Hudson, 1978).

176 Alison Jack: 'Out of the Wilderness: Feminist Perspectives on the Book of Revelation' in Steve Moyise, ibid., p. 162.

177 Judith Lee: 'Sacred Horror' in George Aichele and Tina Pippin (eds.): *The Monstrous and the Unspeakable: The Bible as Fantastic Literature* (Sheffield: Sheffield Academic Press, 1997), pp. 220–39. The quotation is from p. 233.

theological fantasy, borne out of intense pain, which ends by warning us off the short-cut to transcendence to which the text itself ostensibly points.

More positively, Steven Goldsmith[178] sees the Apocalypse as a foundational text in Romantic writing, culminating in Mary Shelley's *The Last Man*, seen not just as the site of a feminist argument but as the summons to perpetual ideological struggle. In our chapter entitled 'Variations on a Theme' we will look in more detail at *The Last Man* and at two other texts which retell the Apocalypse in ways which do not totally accommodate themselves to Pippin's argument.

Finally, as a further counterbalance to Pippin's seeming obsession with gender politics, we might cite the exhibition mounted at The British Museum during the period December 1999 to April 2000, entitled *The Apocalypse and The Shape of Things to Come*,[179] where the reception-history of the Apocalypse was traced through western art, literature and cinema. In the modern period, the Apocalypse was shown as a key theme in Russian literature and in Surrealism and also in the early cinema, as the latter responded to the experience of The Great War. The anxiety which found articulation here was more to do with seismic political upheavals, the degradation of civilized values and the sheer human cost of war than with the issues raised in *Apocalyptic Bodies*.

Yvonne Sherwood: *A Biblical Text and its Afterlives, The Survival of Jonah in Western Culture* (2000)[180]

This book is a fairly exhaustive survey of the treatment of the biblical Book of Jonah in Jewish and Christian exegesis and in Western literature and art. The author gives

---

178 Stephen Goldsmith: *Unbuilding Jerusalem, Apocalyptic and Romantic Representation* (Ithaca, New York: Cornell University Press, 1993).

179 See Frances Carey (ed.): *The Apocalypse and the Shape of Things to Come* (London: British Museum Press, 1999).

180 Yvonne Sherwood: *A Biblical Text and Its Afterlives: the Survival of Jonah in Western Culture* (Cambridge: Cambridge University Press, 2000).

particular weight to the Jewish midrashic tradition, which she sees as the precursor of the postmodern approach to the text and also as existing in a more fruitful relationship with the 'non-official' (here termed 'Backwater') tradition than the Christian version of 'Mainstream' exegesis. The book is remarkable for moving through reception-history *to* an analysis of the text rather than the other way round.

Sherwood clearly sees this unruly text with its reception-history as a paradigm for viewing the rest of the biblical corpus or at least as a microcosm of the wider history of the imaginative treatment of the Bible.[181] She uses the above-mentioned terminology of Bakhtin ('Mainstream' and 'Backwater') to set up a dichotomy between the doctrinal use of the text and a freer, imaginative response. The doctrinal use she sees as constraining the text by forcing universalist themes upon it or reinforcing the *heimlich*. The Backwater tradition, in contrast, concentrates on the particularity of the text and tends towards the fantastic and quirky.

Chapter 1, 'The Mainstream,' looks at Christian exegesis of Jonah from the Early Fathers through to Luther and Calvin and onwards through Pusey to the twentieth-century. Typological readings cast Jonah as Christ, the ship as the Church or the Synagogue, the sailors as the disciples or the Romans, the fish as the Devil or Hell. The untidiness of the text[182] and recalcitrant traits in Jonah[183] give way to Jonah as the exemplary prophet and proto-Christ figure. However, the next major development in Christian exegesis was to have far-reaching implications, with Jonah the Jew cast as the embodiment of the carnal character of the Jewish faith in contrast to spiritual Christianity, a theme which was inaugurated by Augustine but only fully developed by Luther, for whom Jonah signifies the weakness of the flesh. By the-mid nineteenth-century the text's iconic moment has shifted from Jonah's escape from the fish's mouth to Jonah glowering over God's

181 Sherwood, ibid., pp. 3–4, 206, for example.
182 Ibid., p. 19.
183 Ibid., p. 20.

78

forgiveness of Nineveh,[184] setting up the contrast between Christian universalism and Jewish particularism, making the Jew the Monstrous Other rather than the fish. The (unnamed) Author becomes the hero of the text,[185] the possessor of visionary qualities and protégé of the Christian usurpation of the text. Totalising discourses, Sherwood notes, always leave a residue, an antithesis, and here it is anti-Semitism.[186] Jonah becomes the site of Enlightenment supersessionism.[187]

Yet another trajectory, originating with Calvin, treats Jonah as the model of the chastised Self, brought into subjection by a disciplinarian God. 'The book becomes a tractate about the production of docile bodies ... '[188]

Anxieties generated by scientific discoveries lead the conversion of the fish into a more believable entity (such as an inn, 'The Great Fish ... ') and to Pusey's attempt to classify the fish, mystery defused.[189] There follows a lengthy digression on (Stanley) Fish and reader-response theory and then the Christian treatment of the Jew as 'the ultimate site of frenzied incoherence, loaded with the "awesome ambivalence of parricide and fratricide",[190] with all the positive values assigned to Jonah the text and all the negative values to Jonah the character, assimilated to the laziness and clownishness of the Others of colonial discourse'.[191]

Chapter 2 deals with 'Backwaters and underbellies' and treats Jewish midrashic exegesis as the gateway to a more free-floating and associational treatment of the Jonah story, and almost, most importantly, one which allows unrestricted questioning

---

184 Ibid., p. 26.
185 Ibid., p. 27.
186 Ibid., p. 30.
187 Ibid., p. 32.
188 Ibid., p. 42.
189 Ibid., pp. 42–8.
190 Ibid., p. 73.
191 Ibid., p. 81.

of the text.[192] The Zohar[193] reads Jonah allegorically as the story of Everyman. But the Palestinian version of the Talmud witnesses the effect of the need to counter Christian readings of the text, tending to defeat a positive picture of the Ninevites.[194] The ninth-century Midrash, the *Pirke de Rabbi Eliezer*, engages the reader in a fantastical underworld journey, converting Jonah from anti-prophet to super-prophet and anticipating by many centuries the magic realism of postmodern fiction.[195] But exotic though it is, this work is profoundly religious, celebrating the power of God over Chaos. In the Midrash Jonah the prophet's sufferings are elaborated, aligning him with the figure of Job.[196] A second-century midrash, the *Mekilta de Rabbi Ishmael*, revises the notion of prophet, making him a mediator, an uncomfortable riven figure, between God and nation.[197] Sherwood makes no reference to the haggadic tradition that Jonah was one of the select few allowed by God to go straight to Paradise without dying.[198] Though it counters Christian anti-Jonah polemic, this tradition might seem to negate the emphasis on Jonah as the rebel.

Sherwood discusses rabbinic discourse as resistant to the disembodied truths of metalanguage and supportive of the dialogical qualities found in the Jonah text.[199]

She discusses Assyria as an icon of the threat to Israel's existence[200] and the fundamental split between Jewish and Christian exegesis,[201] in the sense that Jews can oppose God as long as this is in defence of God's creation. Jewish exegesis,

192 Ibid., p. 103.
193 Ibid., p. 105.
194 Ibid., p. 105.
195 Ibid., p. 110.
196 Ibid., p. 119.
197 Ibid., p. 120.
198 'Jonah's suffering in the watery abyss had been so severe that by way of compensation God exempted him from death: living he was permitted to enter Paradise.' The quotation is from Louis Ginzberg: *The Legends of the Jews* (Philadelphia: The Jewish Publication Society of America, 1938/1966), Vol. IV, p. 253.
199 Ibid., p. 120.
200 Ibid., pp. 124–5.
201 Ibid., p. 127.

however, stops short of the nihilism of Melville.[202] The Shoa marks a decisive break in the relationship to the biblical text,[203] with Wolf Mankowitz's play, *It Should Happen to a Dog* (1956) and Eugene Abeshaus's painting, *Jonah in Haifa Port* definitely on the other side of the divide. A Jonah-based dream-sequence episode from the Canadian soap-opera, *Northern Exposure*, is explored[204] as an ironic collapsing of the modern into the ancient. There is an illuminating excursion into the literalistic imagery of sixteenth-century Dutch art,[205] which can be seen as providing a counter-blast to conventional notions of the disembodied sacred.

Melville's *Moby Dick*[206] is read in the light of the Calvinist preaching of the character Mapple and becomes a sort of desperate rejection of the punishing Calvinist God, with man railing against his creator 'with all the poignancy of Frankenstein's monster'.[207]

The medieval poem, *Patience*, is read as a meditation on the trials of being in a masterplot where resistance is useless.[208] Sherwood acknowledges that her 'whistle-stop' tour cannot due justice to this work.[209] More space might have allowed her to explore *Patience* as a work which oscillates between a Christological reading of the biblical urtext of Jonah and a reading which takes Jonah to be Everyman.[210]

Contemporary reductionist authors Julian Barnes (in *A History of the World*) and Terry Eagleton (in an essay on Jonah), although contributors to Backwater exegesis, are seen ultimately as purveyors of monologism.[211] But even modern

---

202 Ibid., p. 129.
203 Ibid., p. 134.
204 Ibid., pp. 146–50.
205 Ibid., p. 151.
206 Ibid., pp. 152–62.
207 Ibid., p. 162.
208 Ibid., p. 166.
209 Ibid., p. 144, note 161.
210 See Sandra Pierson Prior: *The Fayre Formez of the Pearl Poet* (East Lansing, Michigan: Michigan State University Press, 1996), pp. 87–96 and 145–57.
211 Ibid., p. 180.

secularism is no barrier to the octopus-like capacity of the Jonah to spread its *meme*. Sherwood considers that Christian biblical interpretation has yet to absorb the implications of the Holocaust.[212] She distrusts the teleological thrust of modern Christian commentaries on Jonah, with their happy ending in the assertion of God's love for the gentiles.[213]

Whilst the Mainstream is at pains to normalise the Jonah story,[214] the Backwater readings insist on and elaborate on its strangeness. It is almost Qoheleth in narrative form, 'a kind of theistic Camus'.[215] She even casts the Book of Jonah as a kind of 'biblical Judas, surviving precisely by betraying the Bible as a lofty cultural icon'.[216] Contemporary culture has a midrashic relation with the biblical,[217] in the sense that it treats the Bible as a repertoire of semiotic elements which are ready to be reconfigured in a new discourse. The mixture of violence and nostalgia in the relationship seems to confirm Harold Bloom's picture of creativity as an Oedipal struggle between sons and fathers. The privatisation of religious belief increases our sympathy for biblical dissenters and outcasts such as Jonah. In our era, the Bible, like over-familiar celebrities, has 'lost control over the dissemination of its own image',[218] part of the semiotic repertoire of modern culture, available and familiar to us, but on our own terms.

Near the end, in a section entitled, 'Salvific properties of the Bible and literature,' the author warns that both the Mainstream Christian and the Freudian religion-as-wish-fulfilment school treat the biblical text as metanarrative, designed to bring order and security to human life,[219] a 'drive to order' similarly evident in concepts

212 Ibid., p. 182.
213 Ibid., p. 185.
214 Ibid., p. 204.
215 Ibid., p. 217.
216 Ibid., p. 222.
217 Ibid., p. 226.
218 Ibid., p. 281.
219 Ibid., p. 217ff.

of secular literature which treat fiction as the provider of consoling structures. But postmodernism's critique of all metanarratives[220] has led to a rediscovery and revaluation of the disorderly in literature, the disruptive and anarchic tendencies of works like *Tristram Shandy*, presided over by a god called 'Muddle'. In Jonah interpretation there is a battle against the ideology of univocal meaning.[221]

Freeing the text of Jonah to allow exposure to dialogue with intertexts previously ruled out by the conventions of the Mainstream will uncover new resources of meaning. This is true also of intertextual dialogue with prophetic biblical books such as Jeremiah and Ezekiel, if read outside the framework of the Christian supersessionist metanarrative.

Jonah is a typical *traditional* story (like Oedipus or Ulyssses or Shylock) in that the plot is preclusive, the challenge is forced upon the hero (he does not choose it) and the hero is caught up in a double bind.[222] These traditional stories mediate the experience of powerlessness, just as the Hebrew prophets mediate the Otherness of God .[223] 'Jonah can be seen as an experiment in what it would feel like to occupy the strangely defamiliarising world of prophecy – albeit a world that in this case is taken to exaggerated, comedy-insulated extremes.'[224]

If Jonah gives the reader the interpretative strategies to read the entire Hebrew Bible as 'an extended meditation on questions of identity and survival, marked by an exposure to the raw vacillations of life (war, famine, plague), from which we in the West are deeply insulated,[225] it also is the antidote to hermeneutical closure and the catalyst for carnivalesque and restless questioning of that same Bible.[226]

---

220 Ibid., p. 287.
221 Ibid., p. 292.
222 Ibid., p. 281.
223 Ibid., p. 283.
224 Ibid., p. 287.
225 Ibid., p. 284.
226 Ibid., pp. 288–91.

Comment

A Biblical Text and its Afterlives has had a generally very warm critical reception. Avril Hannah-Jones[227] declares it 'an unqualified success' as Cultural Studies, 'challenging the common view of the Bible that sees it as occupying a transcendent zone and speaking an eternal message'. She thought that as Biblical Studies, the book 'prompts more questions than it answers', though clearly intended this as a positive comment, as she concludes: 'Sherwood certainly succeeds in countering popular and academic images of a bland and certain Bible'. For John Barton,[228] the book 'sets a new standard for the study of reception-history,' pointing out that Sherwood's own reading (beyond her survey of the reception-history, which focuses a great deal on the Christian 'othering of the Jew') goes beyond seeing the text as a protest against the alleged exclusivism of Ezrah and Nehemiah and becomes 'a much more profound exploration of the puzzling God of the Hebrew Bible, who defies our theological definitions and cannot be captured in the language of Christian (or Jewish) dogma'.

George Aichele[229] perceives Sherwood's book as a sign of the great changes underway in biblical studies and describes the author as tracing 'the ways in which this "mongrel text" has reproduced itself, both within and especially outside of the Bible ... ' He remarks that because the book's final chapter draws on 'the numerous interpretative "voices" that she has acknowledged, it is more of an anti-commentary than a commentary, an explosion of semiosis in which the book of Jonah becomes almost infinitely polymorphic'. Tod Linafelt[230] describes it as 'an almost impossibly rich book'.

---

227 Avril Hannah-Jones, review in *Melbourne Historical Journal*, Vol. 30 (2002).

228 John Barton, review in *Journal of Jewish Studies*, Vol. LV (Spring 2004).

229 Gorge Aichele, review in *The Princeton Seminary Bulletin*, 23rd March 2002.

230 Tod Linafelt, review in *RBL, Society of Biblical Literature*, October 2004.

84

Later on in this study, we will see *A Biblical Text and its Afterlives* more in relationship with other reception-histories. In correspondence with the author,[231] I found that she was not particularly conscious of being a contributor to a genre. Though aware of the work of Haskins and Stocker, two of our other authors, she was more conscious of relating to 'the emergent strain of Biblical and Cultural Studies' represented by people like Alice Bach, Cheryl Exum, David Clines, Stephen Moore, and the Biblical Studies/Cultural Studies Colloquium at Sheffield'.

One could challenge her reading of Melville's *Moby Dick* on the grounds that there are more optimistically 'theological' readings of the text.[232] But these could be seen as mere extensions of the Christian metanarrative which the author seeks to peel away. Sherwood's book inevitably has omissions. There is no mention of the Chester mystery play,[233] a very typical typological treatment of Jonah, or of James Bridie's satire, *Jonah and the Whale*, published in 1932,[234] where Jonah is portrayed as a petty tyrant who finally discovers that he has been deluding himself: 'My whole life has given way beneath me. I thought I was a great prophet. Everything I did or said was on that understanding. And now I find I am nobody. I am an ordinary man.' She omits discussion of Robert Frost's *A Masque of Mercy*, but justifies this in a footnote, noting (rightly according to most critical opinion) that the work is inferior to *A Masque of Reason* and merely regurgitates Christian mainstream readings.[235]

---

231 Private correspondence with Yvonne Sherwood, 24th June 2004.

232 Nicholas Boyle, in *Sacred and Secular Scriptures* (London: DLT, 2004), has a chapter in which he struggles to construct a Catholic interpretation of the novel, finally settling on a Melville short story of 1856, *Norfolk Isle and the Chola Widow*, to act as a sort of authorial intertext, in order to correct the moral and religious vacuum which he finds in *Moby Dick*. Boyle's book is discussed in our chapter, 'The Theorists'.

233 The entry under 'Jonah' in Lyle Jeffries (ed.): *A Dictionary of Biblical Tradition in English Literature* (Grand Rapids: Eerdmans, 1992), pp. 409–11, lists the Chester mystery play and a number of more substantial works, including the play by Thomas Lodge and Robert Greene, *A Looking Glasse for London and England*, dated circa 1590, and Gordon Bennett's more recent *So Why Does That Weirdo Prophet Keep Watching the Water?*

234 James Bridie: *Jonah and the Whale* (London: Constable, 1968), p. 61.

235 Sherwood, ibid., p. 96, note 20.

Since Sherwood's aim was not to construct an exhaustive chronological survey of her subject, but rather to identify 'some of the major historical trajectories' in interpretation, 'the stories that are told about the story,' her selective approach is both understandable and inevitable. Nevertheless, one wonders whether it might not be possible to examine the so-called 'Christian Mainstream', covering works like the Chester play, and find that they do not completely conform to the stereotype.

Two further issues arise from Sherwood's study, these being her treatment of Jonah as a sort of hermeneutical key to the whole Bible and the theology which emerges from her reading of Jonah and its reception-history.

In the correspondence, I asked whether, if you take Jonah as offering interpretative strategies to read the whole Bible, the same case could not be made for other biblical texts. Her reply[236] was that her aim was to show that Jonah was not a misfit, but could be read 'as a paradigm for prophetic and biblical literature in general,' and that even the centre of the canon was 'in some respects resistant to the dominant themes and ideas that we place on it'. Hence recovering books like Jonah, Ecclesiastes and Job from the margins to which we have consigned them could help to free up the rest. Jonah therefore becomes the model for using other peripheral biblical texts to disencumber biblical interpretation from the domesticating tendencies which are so strong, a model for resistance to hermeneutical closure.

On theology and, in particular, on the question of whether a sort of negative theology emerged from her study, Sherwood was more cautious. She admitted to 'trying to do something theological at the end,' but stated that her emphasis was less on the indefinability of God ('which can be a comfortable and easily domesticated notion') and more on the idea of 'God not on my side or God defined as the opposite of what I desire for myself'.[237]

---

236 Private correspondence, as above.
237 As above.

In many ways, *A Biblical Text and its Afterlives* seems itself to be a model for a kind of imaginative reception-history of a biblical story, one which eschews the claim to construct an objective survey of all the material (more or less impractical, anyhow, given the sheer volume of material) and which nevertheless offers a cogent argument on behalf of a reading which encompasses major variants. Her dichotomising of 'Mainstream' and 'Backwater' traditions seems to be a highly useful tool, but one which obviously has to be balanced by the recognition that some works straddle the boundary and also that other binary classifications could be introduced, such as Optimistic and Pessimistic or Conflating and Non-Conflating Narrative experiments play a very prominent part in our final example of the genre.

Kim Paffenroth: *Judas, Images of the Lost Disciple* (2001)[238]

Paffenroth's study begins and ends with what seem to be autobiographical thoughts on the part of the author. In the preface he describes his fascination since 1980 with the band named *Judas Priest*. The epilogue presents the vision of a happily married Judas who got on well with Jesus and circulated the rumour of his own suicide for reasons of social convenience.

The master narrative concerns the account of Judas's movement from being the product of narrative necessity in the gospels increasing vilification, and on to various sorts of rehabilitation in modern novels through and drama, the most famous example being the Judas of *Jesus Christ Superstar*. The chapter headings describe the progress from Object of Curiosity to Object of Hatred and Derision to Object of Admiration and Sympathy and finally to Object of Hope and Emulation.

---

238 Kim Paffenroth: *Judas, Images of the Lost Disciple* (Louisville: Westminster/John Knox Press, 2001).

Judas begins as a blank canvas, the perfect cypher for later story-tellers.[239] He is the vehicle for the venting of anti-semitic sentiments, as Paffenroth extensively discusses, and also the personification of the debate over fate and free will.[240]

Comment

Rehabilitation of the biblical villain seems to be a strong characteristic of the modern period; something which Paffenroth describes very fully through his examples, but scarcely analyses. If he were writing in or after 2006, he would find it impossible to avoid commenting on the publication of the Gnostic text known as *The Gospel of Judas*.[241] As it is, the two novels with similar titles which he does discuss[242]are not related to the hitherto lost Gnostic Text. It may be said, though, that the newspaper coverage[243] of the publication of the Gnostic *Gospel of Judas* has borrowed some of the religious frisson associated with the band named *Judas Priest*[244] which Paffenroth asserts has influenced him. Gnostic texts as a commodity may be a far cry from Gnosticism and perhaps closer to the world of pop-music promotion.

In common with a good number of our reception-histories, Paffenroth's study connects its subject at various points with the blaming of women in the Judaeo-

239 Ibid., pp. 2 and 15.
240 Ibid., pp. 70ff.
241 Rodolphe Kasser, Marvin Meyer and Gregor Wurst (eds): *The Gospel of Judas* (Washington DC: National Geographic Society, 2006).
242 These are R.S. Anderson: *The Gospel according to Jesus Christ* (Colorado Springs: Helmers & Howard, 1991) and E.S. Bates: *The Gospel According to Judas Iscariot* (London: Heinemann, 1929). Interestingly, Paffenroth does not mention or discuss the novel by Henryk Panas: *The Gospel According to Jesus Christ* trans. Marc E. Heine (London: Hutchinson, 1977) only listing it (in its Polish edition) in his bibliography.
243 For example, the banner heading of *The Daily Mail* of 7th April 2006 reads 'SAINT JUDAS? Inside the same paper, a fairly measured short article (on page 27) is eclipsed by a banner heading which reads, 'SAINT JUDAS? An ancient manuscript, discovered in Egypt and unveiled yesterday, not only 'proves' that Judas was the hero of the Crucifixion, but even casts doubt on the resurrection itself ...'
244 This particular example of religious frisson could be experienced on 19th June 2006 on the *Judas Priest* official web-site at http:/judaspriest.com where the opening page carries the subtitle, *Angel of Retribution*. The next page features a menacingly robotic angel, rotating.

Christian tradition (see the discussion of the role of Judas's wife[245]) and with the Holocaust.[246] There is detailed and disturbing discussion of the Nazification of the Oberammergau Passion play, relying heavily on a study by James Shapiro.[247] The emphasis on Nazism in the play tends somewhat to eclipse the evidence that violently anti-semitic portrayals of Judas were a specific feature of German (and French) medieval drama and of German medieval art.[248]

As a cultural tour, the Judas theme here takes in the New Testament, the Early Church Fathers, Dante, Shakespeare, the Mystery Plays, Mark Twain and the modern rock-operas, *Jesus Christ Superstar* and *Godspell*. In doing so, it successfully adds Judas to the map of western culture or demonstrates the usefulness of this figure as a means of navigating the terrain, rather like English history seen through the medium of the history of the City of Hull.

But as a reception-history of the Judas story, the treatment is incomplete. The movement of the narrative towards a progressive rehabilitation of Judas is effectively taken for granted. Of course, the fact of rehabilitation is incontestable. Indeed, further modern examples could have been given, including Henry Panas: *The Gospel of Judas*[249] and Peter Van Greenaway: *Judas*.[250] There is no discussion of how the modern 'rehabilitation' novels may have influenced each other or of how such strong 'misreadings', to use Harold Bloom's terminology, may represent a sort of backhanded tribute to biblical canonicity. Perhaps in Paffenroth there is an unstated and unexamined argument that the rehabilitation of Judas is the inevitable

245 Ibid., pp. 102 ff.
246 Ibid., pp. 41, 95, and 155–6.
247 James Shapiro: *Oberammergau* (London: Little Brown, 2000). This book documents the history of anti-semitism in the many recensions of the Oberammergau Passion Play and in the history of that Bavarian community.
248 See Shapiro, ibid., p. 162, on the effects of a return to medieval sources in the 1934 production and Hyam Maccoby: *Judas Iscariot and the Myth of Jewish Evil* (New York: Free Press, 1992), pp. 108 and 111.
249 Henryk Panas: *The Gospel According to Judas* (London: Hutchinson, 1977).
250 Peter Van Greenaway: *Judas!* (London: Panther, 1976).

outcome of the defeat of anti-semitism or of the triumph of pluralism. The Preface makes a passing reference to William Klassen's *Judas, Betrayer or Friend of Jesus?* (1996)[251] but does not explore the arguments of that book, which is a radical attempt to formulate a sympathetic portrait of Judas based on a rereading of the gospels.[252] Klassen's book emphasizes the neutral character of the Greek verb *paradidomi*, as found in the gospels, to 'hand over' rather than to 'betray', using this to support the conjecture that Judas was a sort of theological whistle-blower, either with a sort of misplaced loyalty to the religious authority of the High Priest or as an agent acting with the full complicity of Jesus. He also (unlike Paffenroth and Paffenroth's major source, Maccoby[253]) assumes the authenticity of the accounts of Judas's suicide and is at pains to state that suicide was free of stigma in the pre-Augustine Christian community.[254]

Paffenroth's narrative is very much a journey towards the rehabilitated Judas of novels such as William Rayner's *The Knifeman*.[255] In this it agrees with the tenor, at least, of Klassen's study, although that work confines itself largely to the New Testament material. He does not entertain the possibility of rejecting the Judas story altogether (as Maccoby's study does[256]) or of exploring the theme of guilt as a leitmotif in the overall reception-history. If he had, he might have considered, beyond the scope of the 'rehabilitation novels,' the novel by Günter Grass, *Cat and Mouse*, where the betraying figure is named Pilenz, reminding us of the close association of Pilate and Judas in the tradition.[257] Here there is no relief for the guilt of betrayal.

---

251 Paffenroth, ibid., p. xv.
252 William Klassen: *Judas, Betrayer or Friend of Jesus* (London: SCM Press, 1996).
253 Hyam Maccoby: ibid.
254 Klassen, ibid., pp. 165–7.
255 See Chapter 6.
256 See Maccoby, ibid., p. 166.
257 Günter Grass: *Cat and Mouse* (London: Penguin, 1966).

90

Although the medieval material is assumed by Paffenroth (and one of his main sources, Shapiro) to be uniformly bleak in its anti-semitism, the actual picture is more mixed. P.F. Baum, for example, in his extensive survey, notes the Swedish version of Oedipal legend of Judas where the reader is adjured to learn from the lesson of Judas, for there are worse people.[258] There is also the humanness of the figure of Judas in the English mystery play tradition to be considered.[259] Other areas omitted by Paffenroth are the Islamic legend that Judas was crucified instead of Jesus[260] and the possible origins of the St Brendan legend (which he *does* mention) in the apocryphon *The Acts of Andrew and Paul* (which he does not mention), where St Paul dives into the sea to meet Judas who had spurned the pardon of Jesus by accepting a second commission from Satan.[261] A more literary study, or a study more attuned to the description of the supernatural in literature, might have looked at the treatment of this legend in a Victorian poem, *Judas Iscariot's Paradise*, by Sebastian Evans.[262]

Finally, we may note the omission of references to visual art in this study, in contrast to Maccoby, who is able to deploy some major examples (including Giotto's famous wall painting, *The Kiss of Judas*) in the service of his thesis.[263] A recent study of the reception-history of Doubting Thomas has drawn attention

258 P.F. Baum: 'The Medieval Legend of Judas Iscariot', *PMLA,* Vol. 24 1916, p. 551.

259 'Judas is shown as a human being moving along the path to damnation and does once, writ large, what everyone else does often in miniature, and the treatment of him is for this reason deliberately designed not to distance him from the audience. People can relax with the comfortable feeling that they are not Cain or Herod, but they cannot be so certain that they are not Judas, and therefore he is portrayed in such a way that his fate, unlike for instance that of Herod, arouses a mixture of horror and compassion.' Rosemary Woolf: *The English Mystery Plays* (London: RKP, 1972), p. 240.

260 See Joseph Gaer: *The Lore of the New Testament* (Boston: Little Brown, 1952), p. 220.

261 See J.K. Elliott: *The Apocryphal New Testament* (Oxford: Oxford University Press, 1999), pp. 301–2.

262 Printed in Charles Williams (ed.): *Victorian Narrative Verse* (Oxford: Clarendon Press, 1927), pp. 268–75.

263 Maccoby., ibid., pp. 111–115.

to the close similarity between Caravaggio's portraits of Judas and of Thomas,[264] something which reinforces other connections between the two figures in the tradition.[265] A recent study of the treatment of Judas in films, another area not discussed by Paffenroth, sees the filmic Judas emerging as 'the alienated victim of a malign monotheism' or at least as 'the sacrifice that founds Christian discourse';[266] a less soothing outcome than that offered by Paffenroth.

Final Comments

Later in this book we will examine the relationship of the tendency to rehabilitate Judas, which Paffenroth so clearly identifies and underlines, to the larger context of such narrative upheavals. Hugh Pyper in an article[267] discusses 'modern Gnosticism' as a dominant feature of twentieth-century treatments of the Judas theme. For the moment we can observe the great journey which the figure of Judas has made in reception-history from its quasi-demonic status in medieval literature (a subject to which Paffenroth could have done more justice[268]) to the de-supernaturalising and rehabilitation it undergoes in modern popular literature.

---

264 Glenn W. Most: *Doubting Thomas* (Cambridge Mass: Harvard University Press, 2005), pp. 210–215. Most's book is discussed in the Appendix B.

265 Maccoby, ibid., pp. 87 and 188, speculates that Thomas may have been the twin brother of a Judas whom the New Testament seeks to differentiate from Judas Iscariot. Most observes that there is at least a thematic link between the two figures in the gospels: '… it is remarkable that of all the four brothers of Jesus reported by the Gospels, the only one that Thomas is ever identified with is Judas …' (Most, ibid., p. 98).

266 Richard Walsh: 'The Gospel According to Judas, Myth and Parable', article in *Biblical Interpetation*, Vol. XIV No 1 / 2 2006, pp. 37–53.

267 Hugh S. Pyper:'Modern Gospels of Judas, Canon and Betrayal' in *Literature & Theology*, Vol. 15, 2001, pp. 111–22.

268 The fullest coverage of this subject is still in P.F. Baum:'The Medieval Legend of Judas Iscariot' (*PMLA*, Vol. 24, 1916). But Maccoby goes much further in interpreting the demonic status of Judas as a sign of the working out of a myth of two Christs, a White and a Black Christ. For Maccoby the negative treatment of Judas in western culture is inextricably linked with the history of anti-semitism. In particular, he equates the extreme anti-semitism of the portrayal of Judas in medieval and later German art and Passion-story drama with the road to the death-camps. See Maccoby, ibid., pp. 108–111.

We may also contrast the final rejection of the 'Myth and Cult of the Virgin Mary' by one of our genre's pioneers, Marina Warner, at the outset of this survey, with the concluding acceptance of Judas as 'one of us' by one of the genre's most recent practitioners; even if the intervening years produced works which sought to look afresh at the Virgin Mary,[269] valorizing her story in both pro-feminist and pro-theological terms, or one which called for the final rejection of the Judas story.[270]

Though varying in the depth of their scholarship, our fourteen reception-history writers all attempt to account for the significance of their respective biblical stories in the inherited literary and iconographic culture and to provide an assessment of the current status of the reception-history. Weighted as many of them are towards the modern period, they deal with the challenges presented by modern gender and postcolonialist studies quite differently from scholars whose work is concentrated on the early stages in the development of biblical reception-history.[271] For, whether individually friendly or hostile towards the urtext, our fourteen authors deal with material which breathes the air of modern and postmodern skepticism towards traditional biblical authority. They each find themselves engaged in a revisionist campaign, either to rescue the biblical story and its reception-history or to consign it finally to oblivion.

Whether waged against an assumed consensus or on behalf of a lost consensus, all of these revisionist campaigns confirm the sense that there is much at stake, culturally, in the reputation of the protagonists of biblical stories. At the same

---

269 The examples we have cited are Kristeva's article *Stabat Mater* of 1987 and Boss's book *Empress and Handmaid* of 2000.

270 Hyman Maccoby: ibid.

271 Two very erudite collections of essays on the early period are Michael E. Stone and Theodore A. Bergren (eds): *Biblical Figures Outside the Bible* (Harrisburg PA: Trinity Press, 1998) and Athyla Brenner and Jan Willem van Henten (eds): *Recycling Biblical Figures* (Leiden: Deo, 1999). Both provide abundant evidence of the acculturation of biblical figures in the early centuries CE. The second work also contains two feminist rejections of 'later constructions,' with H.A. McKay comparing N.T. portraits of O.T. women figures unfavourably with the earlier texts and Caroline Vander Stichele making a foray into Fin de Siècle representations of Jezebel and Herodias which uncovers the artistic cliché of the Fatal Woman.

time, the reappraisal of 'reputation' can also be taken as a code for the approach of our reception-history writers to the evaluation of rewritings of biblical stories in relation to their own particular master-narratives.

Having given an outline-description and critique of each of the fourteen reception-histories in this chapter, we will go on later to explore much more fully the question of the handling of the transcendent in the material they discuss and in related literature; the concept of 'The Other' both in theology and in postmodernist thinking; the literary structures of the fourteen reception-histories themselves; what they reveal about the conflation of biblical stories with each other or with other narratives; the extent to which they cover the available ground; the extent to which they focus on a small number of texts as keys to the rest of the material; and the issues of closure in relation to the rewriting of biblical stories. We will also make a comparison between our fourteen biblical reception-histories and three reception-histories of non-biblical literature.

Before all this, it may be useful to take advantage of some theoretical perspectives on the subject and so, in our next chapter, we turn to the work of some major theorists of rewritten scripture, Northrop Frye, Piero Boitani, Robert Alter, David Brown, Nicholas Boyle, Harold Fisch, Larry Keitzer and George Steiner. It should be noted that none of our fourteen writers of reception-histories finds occasion to refer to these theorists and, even among those theorists who could have referred to any of our fourteen reception-histories, there is no mention, except for one footnote in David Brown's *Tradition and Imagination* referring to Trexler and two extremely brief references to Warner and a few brief references to Haskins in the same author's *Discipleship and Imagination*.

Chapter 3

REWRITING SCRIPTURE: EIGHT THEORISTS

The question of the theological status of rewritten biblical stories, of the kind which form the subject-matter of this book, cannot effectively be separated from the question of the theological status of secular literature in general. In many cases the authors are the same authors, whether it be H.G. Wells producing a deliberate retelling of Job in *The Undying Fire* and something less overtly biblical in reference in *The Time Machine,* or Shakespeare consistently preferring non-biblical stories in his frame-stories but somehow alluding to biblical stories and apocryphal biblical material in the most complex ways more or less throughout his oeuvre. It is equally true that finding a piece of imaginative literature or visual art with a biblical theme is no guarantee that it will support interpretations which imply transcendence. Apart from these issues, there is always the matter of ambiguity in literary texts, which extends to ambiguity in critical works. As Robert Carroll says of George Steiner, 'Does (he) think it makes any difference whether the sense of transcendence has a referent?'.[1]

Eight theorists will be discussed below: Northrop Frye, Piero Boitani, Robert Alter, David Brown, Nicholas Boyle, Harold Fisch, Larry Kreitzer, and George Steiner. They are the most prominent theorists of the rewritten biblical story and, as a body, include both conservative and radical positions on the status of the biblical urtext. They also represent both Christian and Jewish approaches. What the eight theorists have in common is a belief that the subject-matter of rewritten

---

1   Robert P. Carroll: 'Toward a Grammar of Creation: On Steiner the Theologian', in Nathan A. Scott and Ronald A. Sharp: *Reading George Steiner* (Baltimore: John Hopkins Press, 1994), pp. 262–74.

biblical stories is centrally important for an understanding of western culture and even for an understanding of the Bible itself. In the modern period in particular, they have to cope with the distinction between theology implied within a creative work (or denied) and a theology *of* such a work. Although not discussed by any of these theorists, Ben Elton's comic popular novel, *This Other Eden*,[2] with its distressing vision of a coming ecological dystopia driven by consumerism, could be considered a good example of a work which shows no interest in transcendence but yet invites theological comment.

Northrop Frye

Northrop Frye's *The Great Code* (1982),[3] although its focus is on the literary qualities of the biblical text itself, is remarkable for what it suggests about the relationship of the Bible to other writing. A literary critic of considerable standing, noted for his classic work on Blake, Frye maps the mythic patterns which he finds throughout the Bible, from Genesis to Revelation, and also argues for the dominance of typology across the whole text. He begins by discussing the word 'God',[4] which he thinks we would understand better in its biblical sense if we took it as a verb rather than as a noun, 'a verb implying a process accomplishing itself'. This view of theological language is set in the context of a threefold recurring pattern in which imaginative language as a whole oscillates from the poetic to the mythic to the metaphorical and back again throughout history.

The term 'mythical' as applied, not only to the Bible in Europe up until at least the eighteenth-century, but also to the significance of the Odysseus story for

---

2   Ben Elton: *This Other Eden* (London: Black Swan, 1993).
3   Northrop Frye: *The Great Code* (London: Routledge & Kegan Paul, 1982).
4   Ibid., p. 17.

the Greeks means the opposite of 'not true'.[5] Individual myths gain their charge from their interconnectedness with other, related myths in a canon. This is what differentiates them from folktales, which Frye argues are nomadic and form the basis of profane literature. 'In Western literature Dante and Milton chose their major subjects from within the mythical area; Chaucer and Shakespeare stay with folktale and legend. This process is possible because of the structural analogy, if not identity, of sacred and profane story.'[6]

Frye argues[7] that the Bible is a 'violently partisan book'. He notes that 'as with any other form of propaganda, what is true is what the thinker thinks ought to be true; and the sense of urgency in the writing comes out much more freely for not being hampered by the clutter of what may actually have happened'. When, later in this study, we look at the extremes of feminist response to the biblical text, it may be useful to recall this perception.

Frye robustly asserts[8] that we have no access to the 'real Jesus' and that 'mythical accretions' are what the Bible is. The importance of these observations for the validation of the imaginative reception-history of the Bible will be evident if we also note that Frye in the end treats the Bible itself not as literature but as being 'as literary as it can be without being literature'.[9]

Amidst a welter of other insights, Frye treats narrative as a 'movement in time', finally dismissing the notion of 'narrative structure' as too architectural and static.[10] The Bible as a historical myth frees conventional history to do its work and at the same time generates many secondary and discursive meanings, as evidenced by the

---

5   Ibid., p. 33.
6   Ibid., p. 38.
7   Ibid., p. 40.
8   Ibid., p. 42.
9   Ibid., p. 62.
10   Ibid., p. 63.

98

release of the text after the Reformation from the Catholic Church's restriction of meaning to 'a very narrow orbit'.[11]

Frye notes glimpses of the earth-goddess or image of *natura naturans,* set in contrast to the Sky Father, at many points in the Bible, all of which he sees as eclipsed by the text's escape from cyclical thinking.[12] He discusses biblical typology extensively, seeing it as central to the onward momentum of the Bible which finally defeats the cyclical pattern. Biblical typology, though it has classical analogues,[13] is finally unique, representing a specialised form of the repeatability of myth. Unlike allegory, typology is about real people and real events[14] and biblical typology also points to a transcendent world, in the shape of the Apocalypse, which subverts the overweening authority of the earthly Church. More radically, Frye sees cultural pluralism as the modern form of prophecy,[15] water metaphors as a constant reminder of the Deluge as the annulment of Creation,[16] the Oedipal story as the demonic mirror image of the Christ story,[17] the calendrical cycle as a form of reversion to mythical thinking,[18] albeit inevitable, and the Ark as a central biblical symbol reaching its apotheosis in the manger of the Nativity (Psalm 132:6 provides a connecting link) which completes a historical cycle which will finally recur (Rev 11:19) with the appearance of the ark of the Covenant in heaven. The Crucifixion is a demonic parody of the image in Zechariah 4 of the Messianic figure flanked by the figures of David and Joshua.[19] Kafka's *The Trial* is a midrash on Job.[20]

---

11 Ibid., p. 65.
12 Ibid., pp. 68–9.
13 Ibid., p. 80.
14 Ibid., p. 85.
15 Ibid., p. 128.
16 Ibid., p. 146.
17 Ibid., p. 156.
18 Ibid., p. 175.
19 Ibid., p. 179.
20 Ibid., p. 195.

The biblical kerygma as a form of rhetoric assumes a symbolically female body of readers addressed by a symbolically male God.[21] Finally, the Bible is a liberating text which human anxiety structures constantly seek to suppress or to distort, treating it often in the way the Philistines did Samson's hair.[22]

Frye's text is rich and suggestive, if not easy to assimilate. Taken as a whole, it stands as a plea to consider the Bible as an autonomous and unique mythopoetic entity which somehow delivers a kind of ontological and ethical seriousness which is unavailable in the rest of human literary production. It sees the Bible as standing in a complex relationship not only to history but also to the other mythic systems which exist alongside it.

The Great Code is ultimately a version of the Protestant perspective on revelation which comes close to a sort of immanence-within-the-text but still asserts the notion of God as a force or process outside the text. If Roland Barthes alerts us to the universal human propensity to live by myth, Frye's Bible offers the prospect of a way out, rather like a cigarette-substitute for smokers. The human condition is deeply immersed in mythical structures which are ready to defeat any incoming message but these structures equally are the main or only means by which anything worthwhile is communicated.

Piero Boitani

Piero Boitani in *The Bible & Its Rewritings* (1999)[23] has a similarly oblique approach to revelation, this time summed up by the notion that God cannot be known, only recognized. The work is a close literary study of recognition scenes, connecting the experience of Abraham at Mamre in Genesis 18 with that of Adam

---

21 Ibid., p. 231.
22 Ibid., p. 233.
23 Piero Boitani: *The Bible and Its Rewritings* (Oxford, Oxford University Press, 1999).

and Eve in Book XI of *Paradise Lost*; celebrating Thomas Mann's *Joseph and His Brethren* as a monumental recapitulation of the Genesis story and its whole tradition of imaginative interpretation; discovering in the Roman catacombs the link between the story of Susanna and the Elders and resurrection, leading to the development of two complimentary Susannas, the biblical figure and the saint,[24] then tracing the origins of Orwell's *Animal Farm* in Chaucer's treatment of an animal fable, itself a revisited Garden of Eden story. He goes on to examine the biblical and postbiblical traditions which lend resonance to Faulkner's *Go Down Moses*, before (in the concluding chapter) unpacking Shakespeare's *Pericles* as a reworking not only of Euripides but of the medieval legends of Mary Magdalene, themselves stemming from the ultimate 'recognition scene' of the Johannine empty tomb, a narrative identified as owing a huge debt to Alexandrine romance. The last work to be considered is Joseph Roth's *Job*, which manages to roll the story of Job up with a 1920s Jewish Exodus to America and a devastating restoration/ recognition scene.

Following in the steps of Auerbach, Boitani finds in the biblical text an inner space which in 'its silences and sudden, extreme flashes of emotion' opens the way for readerly speculation,[25] something which persists through 'centuries of elaboration'. If typology is the key to the Bible for Northrop Frye, rewriting itself is the key for Boitani, exemplified by the way the author of the Gospel of John rewrites both Genesis and the other gospels, as well as by all the other rewritings mentioned above. Rewriting is endless. Shakespeare's *Pericles* is in turn rewritten by T.S. Eliot in his poem, *Marina*. What all of Boitani's examples have in common is an underlying biblical recognition scene, leading to his final formulation, 'to recognize God is to rewrite the Scriptures'.[26]

---

24   For the sketch of an alternative reception-history of the Susanna story, see Chapter 11, 'Nodal Points,' pp. 281–3.
25   Ibid., p. 47.
26   Ibid., p. 203.

Although it could be argued that there is a great deal of assertion rather than persuasive argument in Boitani's account of the relationship of biblical rewritings to revelation, as a thematic *tour de force* it is rather impressive. In due course we will examine the usefulness of its insights to the material which underlies our fourteen reception-histories.

Robert Alter

Robert Alter, famed for his detailed literary analysis of the Bible in *The Art of Biblical Narrative* and *The Art of Biblical Poetry*, turns his attention to modern literary reworking of biblical material in *Canon and Creativity* (2000).[27] Like Boitani, he reiterates the Auerbachian contrast between the Bible and Homer: '... unlike the lucid, leisurely narrative of Homer's sunlit world, it is a kind of abrupt story that turns on dark places, that is riddled with unsettling enigmas'.[28] Alter finds the same qualities reflected in Faulkner's prose, in this case in the novel, *Absalom, Absalom!*

What is most interesting about Alter here is his assertion that writers like Kafka and Joyce are 'alert to the Bible in ways not available to the conventional reader'.[29] Also of importance is his argument that a canon is a 'transhistorical textual community'.[30] He even hails the modernists as those who save the canon from disappearing.[31] One of his chief examples is Kafka, whom he sees as at once traditional and iconoclastic, the author of a heretical midrash on the Tower of Babel story[32] and a similarly radical rewriting of the Genesis Eden story combined with

---

27 Robert Alter: *Canon and Creativity* (New Haven and London: Yale University Press, 2000).
28 Ibid., p. 15.
29 Ibid., p. 9.
30 Ibid., p. 5.
31 Ibid., p. 19.
32 Alter does not discuss the likelihood that Borges's *Three Versions of Judas* may owe something to the author's reading of Kafka. Instead, he describes the Kafka as 'like an anticipation of

102

Exodus in the novel, *Amerika*. He quotes Scholem to the effect that Kafka treads the boundary between religion and nihilism, thereby placing himself outside the canons of traditional exegesis but *inside* the modern canon.[33] Joyce similarly, in *Ulysses*, relies on the Hebrew Bible, in his case coupled with *The Odyssey* as intertexts.[34] Alter observes: 'The background of transcendence of the polytheistic Homer and of the monotheistic biblical narrative is largely absorbed into a secular foreground, though a potent residue of the sacred remains palpable in Joyce's novel ... '[35] He connects this sacred residue in the case of the Bible with 'its beckoning prospect of milk and honey, its urgent injunctions to be fruitful and multiply and to choose life over death'.[36]

Although at the minimalist end of the spectrum in theological terms, Alter, or the works he considers, are important as representative of the encounter between the process of biblical rewriting and the outlook of some major modern authors, not least in the light of the human suffering which is the backdrop in the twentieth-century to all writing and artistic production.

Our final five theorists belong to a much more sanguine and, in their own separate ways, orthodox world.

David Brown

David Brown's *Tradition & Imagination* (1999)[37] is an argument for the sense of an ongoing revelation which takes account of the stimulus ('triggers') which experience after the closure of the biblical canon has lent to the adaptation of

---

Borges ... ' (Ibid., p. 74). For a discussion of the Borges work, see Appendix A.

33   Ibid., p. 66.
34   Ibid., p. 167.
35   Ibid., p. 169.
36   Ibid., p. 171.
37   David Brown: *Tradition and Imagination* (Oxford: Oxford University Press, 1999).

biblical material. An important example for Brown is the development of traditions surrounding the Nativity, taking in works by Dürer, Caravaggio and Berlioz, amongst others, which fill out the significance of the birth of Christ for human life.[38] Brown affirms the (lost) Christian symbolism of the Christmas tree and mistletoe, challenging, as he puts it, 'the common assumption that the power of revelation is necessarily undermined if external material from the surrounding culture is used to illuminate it or even rewrite its story'.[39]

We are introduced to Jewish methods of scriptural exegesis, which again, contrary to common assumptions, are not backward-looking, but seen as the vehicle of progressively revealed truth. Brown discusses the sense of revelation as ongoing[40] and affirms that it is 'utterly implausible to think that God built into the biblical narrative the ability to anticipate all possible future scenarios ... '[41] He explores the notion of a flexible canon[42] and describes revelation as a moving stream rather than a fixed deposit.[43] After this Brown, who seems to be handicapped throughout by a very cautious and conservative readership, notes that the magi as kings are nonsense as history but 'more profoundly true than scripture itself'[44] and finds truth revealed through the Jewish mystical tradition and the Islamic *hadith*.

Part Two, entitled 'The Moving Text', is more adventurous, rehabilitating the Greek myths as sources of meaning and religious disclosure, and affirming the value of postbiblical writings about Abraham, including Kierkegaard's treatment of Genesis 22 in *Fear and Trembling*. Chapter 7 discusses 'art as revelation', being a survey of European religious art, particularly as it explored a developing sense of the humanity

---

38 Ibid., pp. 73–105.
39 Ibid., p. 105.
40 Ibid., p. 111.
41 Ibid., p. 116.
42 Ibid., p. 118.
43 Ibid., p. 127.
44 Ibid., p. 135.

of Christ, though the author admits that this sadly went with 'a diminution of respect for the humanity of others'.[45] A concluding chapter looks at tensions engendered by modernism and postmodernism (mostly in cinematic portrayals of Christ) and directs attention to some of the neglected treasures of pre-modern Christian art.

The most valuable contribution Brown offers to our study is his positive assessment of the notion of an ongoing revelation and his sense of a 'moving text', which has 'trajectories which can provide a critique of the biblical text itself'.[46] If, compared with Alter and Boitani, this all seems rather pedestrian, it at least marks progress away from the stronghold of conventional and conservative biblical studies, whilst holding firm to a Barthian understanding of the Otherness of God.[47]

Nicholas Boyle

Nicholas Boyle in *Sacred and Secular Scriptures*, subtitled *A Catholic Approach to Literature* and published in 2004,[48] approaches the subject from a very different angle. A noted Goethe scholar and a committed Roman Catholic, Boyle has no difficulty with the idea of the Bible as literature and instead seeks to pursue the idea of literature as Bible for Catholics, basically on the premise that the prayerful reader can find theology in secular literature, though the author grounds his approach in a thorough survey of the history of hermeneutics from Herder to Ricoeur. In Chapter 6 the Jewish philosopher, Levinas, is invoked as offering an alternative approach to bibliolatry, with his notion of the interdependence of the interpreting community and scripture, and his insistence on the priority of the kerygma as ethical demand and on transcendence as the enlivener of obligation to neighbour.

---

45   Ibid., p. 364.
46   Ibid., p. 273.
47   Ibid., pp. 67 and 74. For clarity's sake, the reference here is to the thought of Karl Barth.
48   Nicholas Boyle: *Sacred and Secular Scriptures* (London: Darton, Longman & Todd, 2004).

Later Boyle explores Pascal's *Pensées*, challenging received ideas about the wager of faith in the light of a close reading of the fragmentary text. For Boyle the work presents a limit situation in which the reader is confronted with the demand to live life as if it mattered infinitely, escaping from the prison of the Cartesian Self. 'Unlike sacred texts which are written by the Spirit, secular texts are written by authors. The failure to make this distinction was the principal error of the Herder and Schleiermacher School, which set out to read the Bible as poetry when it should have been trying to read the Bible as Law and poetry as prayer.'[49]

Boyle explores Goethe's *Faust* as a reversal of the *Pensées* and Faust himself as no wagerer of his eternal soul (like Marlowe's Faust) but as the freethinker who chooses not to believe, the protagonist of the venture-capitalist life lived at the highest possible intensity, where to stop is to die. Melville's *Moby Dick* is examined in another chapter, where the reduction of life to patterns of ruthless exploitation presents the shadow image of the world-as-it-ought-to-be. Boyle contrasts *Moby Dick* with a short story in Melville's *The Encatadas*, which he finds more compatible with the Christian story, using a minor work in the writer's output to form an intertext with and to critique his *magnum opus*.[50] Next, Jane Austen's *Mansfield Park* presents the unspectacular world of religious vocation set against the machinations and avarice of early nineteenth-century English society. Tolkien finally offers us an alternative idea of England from the post-imperial one we know so well and reclaims the myth of England for Catholicism, using that myth both to represent the more general twentieth-century experience of historical uprooting and to give new sense to the old tradition of the ascetic life lived in imitation of Christ and in the communion of the saints.[51] Tolkien is careful to ensure that his book is read as commentary rather than mistaken for Bible.

---

49   Ibid., p. 167.
50   Ibid., pp. 203–4.
51   Ibid., p. 266.

Boyle delivers us from a modern sort of bibliolatry, at the same time revaluing secular literature as the material for a religious response to human experience. The Bible is the medium through which the voice of command is conveyed to the believer. Secular literature provides the arena in which human aspirations, motives, hopes and fears are turned into prayer. The deficiency in Boyle's approach, which David Jasper notes in a review, is his very selective approach to the literary canon and his tendency to reduce his chosen authors to the terms of his theory.[52]

Perhaps Boyle's greatest strength is his pinpointing of the thought of Emmanuel Levinas as the source for an ethical and pro-theological critique of what he calls 'secular literature'. We will return to Levinas in Chapter 7, in our discussion of 'Otherness' in theology and in literary studies.

If Boyle offers us a 'Catholic' approach to hermeneutics, our next two theorists offer us approaches which distantly reflect their backgrounds respectively in Judaism and the preaching wing of Protestantism.

Harold Fisch

Harold Fisch's *New Stories For Old* (1998)[53] bears the subtitle, *Biblical Patterns in the Novel*, and is a detailed examination of the impact, in absorption and rejection, of biblical models by ten major authors, beginning with Defoe.

In Chapter 1, 'Dialogue and Repetition', Fisch finds the basis of the retelling of biblical stories within the text of the Bible itself, specifically in Exodus 10:2 and 13:8, where the retelling of the salvific narrative is enjoined. The story is to be told and retold down the generations, entailing, as Fisch argues, 'the potentiality for change inherent in the process of recapitulation ... In retelling the story, he or she

52 'Both Melville and Austen are simply larger and more complex novelists than Boyle allows them to be ... ' Review of *Sacred and Secular Scriptures* by David Jasper in *Theology*, January/February 2006, pp. 69–70.
53 Harold Fisch: *New Stories for Old* (London: Macmillan, 1998).

affirms its unexhausted meanings or possibilities'.[54] Because the reader continues to have an active role to perform, 'the tale is never completed'. Fisch finds that the stories of the Bible resist closure because of their very structure and context.[55] The threefold Aristotelian framework in Exodus of beginning, middle and end (Egypt, wilderness journey, and arrival in Promised Land) surrenders to the idea of a new beginning, just as the death of Joseph marks not a conclusion but the start of the tumultous history of the northern kingdom.

For Fisch, realistic narrative is the dominant mode of the Bible, with Apocalypse as a sort of marginal genre which makes occasional intrusions. When Robinson Crusoe experiments mentally with substituting a hope for metaphysical deliverance in place of one for physical rescue, he temporarily reflects this intrusion. Most of the time the reader is in a dialogic relationship with a biblical story which is as this-worldly as his or her own. Fisch regards the biblical presence as formative in English and American novel-writing from Bunyan to Hardy and Melville, but he distrusts Northrop Frye's 'monomyth' of an overarching, integrated biblical mythic structure, instead finding a diverse interplay of different voices and genres.[56] It is this same biblical polyphony which informs Dostoevsky and Rabelais.

Buber is enlisted to underline the this-worldly nature of the predominant biblical pattern ('God and man encounter one another not in heaven but on earth'[57]), as instanced in the story of Ruth and paralleled in the stories of Tamar and Judah and of Lot's daughters, where different perspectives are invited, just as they are in the Joseph narrative, whose own polyphony is echoed in Fielding's *Joseph Andrews*.

If the term 'dialogic' is borrowed from Bakhtin, Fisch feels impelled to resort to the language of *midrash* to describe the sort of radical hermeneutic which

---

54   Ibid., p. 4.
55   Ibid., p. 5.
56   Ibid., p. 10.
57   Ibid., p. 14.

108

permitted the 'reinvention' of biblical stories by authors like Fielding.[58] Eventually Thomas Mann in his trilogy, *Joseph and his Brethren*, was to make a monumental use of midrashic techniques, if in a typically sceptical modern style.

Fisch asserts that for the main novelists which whom he is concerned, however, the biblical story remains unsubverted. 'There are unlimited possibilities for new readings, but they are new readings of a textual constant which remains to be joyfully re-encountered or else, in some cases, to be fought against and resisted. Either way the Bible is a presence not easily put by; it asserts its authority with a certain importunacy.'[59]

In the rest of his book, Fisch, for whom 'the novel is rooted in exegesis',[60] conducts a detailed examination of Defoe's *Robinson Crusoe*, Fielding's *Joseph Andrews* and George Eliot's *Silas Mariner*, in all of which the biblical source is much more than a departure point. It is a text which compels interpretation and reinterpretation and has an insistent authority. 'The relation to it will be more genuinely dialogic than the relation of Bennett to Maupassant, because the source text will be urged to speak, will be argued with, listened to, or resisted.'[61]

It is only with Kafka that the character of the dialogue changes in Fisch's account. *The Trial* can be read as a midrash on the Book of Job. But here, at the outset of the modern era in fiction, the rupture between 'our secular world and the sacred texts which it has inherited' becomes a major challenge. Kafka reverses the story of Job, as had numbers of previous writers, but breaks new ground by 'foregrounding' the reversal.[62] In *The Trial* there is no 'answer to Job' and instead an unremitting exploration of alienation and despair. But the unrequited search for transcendence, according to Fisch, is so intense itself that it takes on a 'transcendent

58 Ibid., p. 17.
59 Ibid., p. 20.
60 Ibid., p. 25.
61 Ibid., p. 59.
62 Ibid., p. 97.

value'.[63] He goes on to look at Roth's novel, *Job*, and then at the work of Saul Bellow and of A.B. Yehoshua and S.Y. Agnon, with the latter demonstrating a return to a more vivid encounter with the biblical presence.

Perhaps the most valuable part of *New Stories for Old* from the point of view of this book is the author's definition of the boundary between texts which remain in a sort of active encounter with the biblical original and those which exist in a relationship of subversion. The fact that he does not treat this as necessarily a linear historical progression lends hope or at least open-endedness to our project.

Larry J. Kreitzer

Larry J. Kreitzer in *Gospel Images in Fiction and Film, On Reversing the Hermeneutical Flow*[64] examines the interpretative relationship between biblical text, literary text and film in the case of five images or themes, the Journey of the Magi, the Abomination of Desolation (Heart of Darkness), Darkness at Noon, the Handmaid's Tale and an episode in the TV series *Star Trek* which is entitled 'Bread and Circuses' and which is about Christian history.

Kreitzer is able to demonstrate common trends shared between T.S. Eliot's *The Journey of the Magi* and epic films such as *Ben Hur* and the films of Pasolini and Zeffirelli about Jesus (connecting the Nativity and the Passion) and also the dependence of the film *Apocalypse Now* on the film of *Heart of Darkness* and on Conrad's original short story, which itself draws on apocalyptic passages in Mark 13 and Revelation 17. Kreitzer's argument here is that not only do the images flow from past to present, but that imperialistic atrocities in the present shed light on the range of meanings supportable by the ancient text. *High Noon* as a film

---

63   Ibid., p. 99.
64   Larry Kreitzer: *Gospel Images in Fiction and Film* (London: Sheffield Academic Press, 2002).

releases a flood of meanings connected with Doomsday timetables, the isolation of saviour-figures, salvation itself and Judgement, which the biblical text both drives and chimes with. *The Handmaid's Tale* as a novel and film extends a short biblical phrase into a whole futuristic dystopia, which in turns points back (as does *High Noon*) to Old Testament prophecy.

However, whilst George Aichele in his Foreword robustly claims Kreitzer's book for a postmodernist perspective in which 'the meaning of a text must be negotiated and continually re-negotiated between that text and its reader',[65] a world in which the cinematic image of Conan the Barbarian can influence of our views of the Crucifixion, making Jesus into a sorcerer, the author himself seems to belong to a more pious world in which 'the films *High Noon* and *Outland* provide us with wonderful opportunities to consider afresh the significance of the Crucifixion of Jesus Christ which took place at the sixth hour, when the sun was darkened, and something wonderful, beyond the limits of human comprehension, happened within the life of the cosmos'.[66]

Summary of Frye, Boitani, Alter, Brown, Boyle, Fisch and Kreitzer

In this survey we have encountered a wide range of approaches to the significance of rewritten biblical stories. Before we move on to our eighth author, who is much less concerned with specific biblical rewritings than the first seven, it may be useful to list some of the key points so far.

a) We began with Northrop Frye's ambitious project to reconstruct a pan-biblical mythology, existing in a symbiotic relationship with classical mythology, but

---

65   Ibid., p. 8.
66   Ibid., p. 142.

driven ultimately by an overriding apocalyptic vision of transcendence. Frye's argument that the Bible is a 'violently partisan book', his concept of cultural pluralism as prophecy, and his sense of the Bible as the source of stories which human anxiety-structures seek to suppress are themes to which we will return.

b) Boitani interprets the rewriting of biblical stories as a 'recognition' experience.

c) Alter points to a 'transhistorical interpretative community' which somehow still breathes despite the nihilistic air of modernism. He also argues that the imaginative writer may be a better interpreter of scripture than the theologian.

d) David Brown argues the case for revelation as something ongoing.

e) Nicholas Boyle introduces the significance of Levinas for a critical theological approach to literature. He also, incidentally, provides the model for using an unexpected work as the intertext for a rewritten biblical story (in this case, *The Encatadas* for *Moby Dick*).

f) Harold Fisch insists that the urtext always remains the urtext and the rewritten story exists in a condition of dialogue with it. He finds biblical polyphony echoed in Dostoevsky and Rabelais. He distinguishes between rewritings which actively engage with the biblical urtext and rewritings which seek to subvert it.

g) Larry Kreitzer underlines the continuing use of the biblical vocabulary in modern literature and film, suggesting that we can read the biblical text in the light of the new material as well as vice-versa.[67]

In terms of conventional theology, we can choose between the Rudolf Otto-style numinous religion of literary critic Northrop Frye and the Buber-inspired this-worldly relational theology of literary critic Harold Fisch. But all of these authors discuss the boundaries between places where transcendence (in the religious sense)

---

67   Ibid., p. 4.

is upheld and places where it is subverted. This is where the argument of the rest of this book will focus, illuminated by the insights of our theorists, who have much to say about those boundaries and who will also serve to remind us, most of them, that there can be a theological response to subversion.

George Steiner

Our final theorist, George Steiner, is less concerned with the examination of specific texts or authors and more with the ontological status of aesthetics and of creative literature in general. In *Real Presences* (1989),[68] Steiner argues that a 'wager on transcendence' has been the key to almost all creative literature, visual art and music in the West. Only the post-Freudian and postmodern 'hermeneutics of suspicion' have reversed this assumption in favour of creative endeavour having its roots in the encounter with the transcendent Other.

Steiner challenges the Nietzschean assertion that God is a grammatical fossil[69] and makes a plea for the rediscovery of the 'immediacies' of aesthetic experience which are generated by great works of literature. Our world is dominated by the secondary and the parasitic, with literary reviews in newspapers and the whole industry of ephemeral academic output serving to insulate the reader from the full impact of great works. The most powerful act of interpretation is that offered by the performer of a piece of music or the re-writer of a novel, as when Dostoevsky 're-visions' *Madame Bovary* in his own novel, *Anna Karenina*.[70] Similarly, the translator and the parodist can shed new light on a past work.[71] 'The best readings of art are art.'[72]

---

68   George Steiner: *Real Presences* (Chicago: Chicago University Press, 1989/1991).
69   Ibid., p. 3.
70   Ibid., p. 14.
71   Ibid., p. 15.
72   Ibid., p. 17.

Behind all great literature, art and music can be detected the 'pulse of a distant source'[73] but this effect is muffled by the distancing of the consumer-reader in modern society and by the annexation of the living arts. One of the worst examples of this is the notion of the 'visiting artist or writer' on the university campus, where the voice of alterity is domesticated.[74]

There follows a potted history of hermeneutics, ranging from the rabbis through medieval scholasticism, through the Catholic attempt to close hermeneutics (with heresy understood as unending re-reading) and on to the methods of free association sponsored by analytic psychology and its offshoots. The idea of the canon is seen as the product of accumulated human experience,[75] though it is formulated by the few.[76]

Every work of art is a contingent singularity and works of literature re-write previous works.[77] Meaning is not susceptible to scientific measurement, for there is always an excess of the signified over the signifier.[78] Steiner, though he respects postmodernist critique when it is aware of its own reductiveness, is deeply opposed to the nihilism engendered by the deconstructionists, who threaten the act of trust which is basic to linguistic discourse[79] and lead to the 'autism of total scepticism'.[80]

The 'death of God' has been only a partial articulation of the havoc wrought by the destruction of reference,[81] with words denoting absence in the new dispensation; and the concept of the Self, as well as that of the author, dissolving. For the

---

73   Ibid., p. 28.
74   Ibid., p. 38.
75   Ibid., p. 63.
76   Ibid., p. 68.
77   Ibid., pp. 76–7.
78   Ibid., p. 84.
79   Ibid., p. 89.
80   Ibid., p. 91.
81   Ibid., pp. 93–5.

deconstructionists, texts cannot be stabilised and all readings are misreadings.[82] The reader creates the text, whilst the great writer conceals his meaning and the great exegete problematizes the text ad infinitum. Steiner believes this fashion is unsustainable and is akin to the Cretan saying all Cretans are liars.[83]

The second half of *Real Presences* is a counter-blast to postmodernism and relies on building up evidences of creative works as transformative entities which draw on and impart a sense of the Transcendent Other, the 'Real Presences' of the title. Kant established the autonomy of the artist[84] and Rilke's call, 'Change your life', expressed art as synonymous with moral (or immoral) persuasion. Buber and Levinas connected philosophy and art with the encounter with the Other.[85] The biblical scenes of Jacob's wrestling match and the encounter on the Emmaus road are emblematic of the process of recognition which is foundational for this view.

The experience of discovery which is associated with reading a great novel or hearing a great symphony or seeing a great painting arises from the meeting of two freedoms in the self's encounter with the Other.[86] Such an experience depends on the practise of courtesy, *courtesia*, towards the work of art, which allows Balzac or Dickens to change our perception of the world.[87]

Although the concept of authorial intention is under intense critical pressure in our time, the idea of authorial unreliability is nothing new.[88] Authorial obfuscation or confusion is properly the meat of critical research. But obliterating intentionality is a way of denying the otherness of the text. Here we might note that it is

---

82   Ibid., pp. 123–6.
83   Ibid., p. 129.
84   Ibid., p. 142.
85   Ibid., p. 146.
86   Ibid., p. 154.
87   Ibid., p. 164.
88   Ibid., p. 170.

interesting, that from a completely different perspective, Julie Sanders argues that intentionality is basic to the concept of rewriting.[89]

Steiner accepts that there is great modern embarassment over claims for the mystery of otherness in art.[90] but insists that the sense of otherness is fundamental to 'reception', even taking into account the 'idiolectic' aspects of personal reception, which he connects with our disposition to assemble personal canons from the public 'syllabus' of important works.[91]

When it comes to the battle with nihilism, we have to accept that nihilism is not in itself refutable.[92] The only way is to echo Leibniz's question, 'Why should there be being and substance? Why not nothing?'[93] Steiner goes on to assert that there is artistic creation because there is *creation,* whether this is understood in traditional theistic terms or in relation to the Big Bang theories of modern cosmology. He claims that 'deep inside every art-act lies the dream of a leap out of nothingness'[94] and that human artists and writers are driven by a feeling of rivalry with the given creation. The world is the 'unnameable rival' to the 'counter-worlds' which they create.[95]

Alterity tends to be rationalised as The Unconscious in modern critical thought, but this does not do justice to transcendence.[96] The word 'character' denotes more than the marker on the page, when we think of figures like Odysseus or Falstaff or Anna Karenina.

---

89   Julie Sanders: *Adaptation and Appropriation* (Abingdon: Routledge, 2006), pp. 2–14.
90   Ibid., p. 178.
91   Ibid., p. 183.
92   Ibid., p. 199.
93   Ibid., p. 200.
94   Ibid., p. 202.
95   Ibid., p. 204.
96   Ibid., p. 211.

Steiner resorts repeatedly to the idea of music as the medium of transcendence or 'unwritten theology'[97] and claims also that the great Christian myths have a 'double life' both as pillars of Christian doctrine and as symbols of a more diffuse sense of transcendence.[98] Artists continue to defy the deconstructionists and to make metaphysical assumptions about their work, but the twentieth-century as a whole is characterized by the forgetting of God.[99]

In conclusion, Steiner talks about the necessity of 'as if' in artistic wagers on transcendence. Kafka witnesses to a 'receding presence'.[100] He sees the Sabbath (Saturday) as emblematic of the human situatedness between the suffering of Good Friday and the resurrection-hopes of Sunday. But without the Sabbath's intimations of the Transcendent, asks Steiner, 'How could we be patient?'.

The relevance of *Real Presences* to our study must lie in Steiner's arguments about the centrality of a sense of the Transcendent Other in creative literature, art and music; in his insistence that the most powerful interpretation comes when art reads art; and in his belief that all literature is a re-writing of previous literature. Steiner's warnings about the domesticating and nullifying effects of the modern critical and journalistic mediation of the arts seems justified by the commoditification of literature in the Sunday press, where the 'top ten' are exhibited for admiration, rather like the Visitor Centres which welcome tourists to national parks and at the same time seem to cordon them off. But Steiner's point is a yet more serious one, about the taming of the transcendent reference.

If the author prompts Robert Carroll[101] to ask whether it would make any difference whether or not transcendence had a reference, this is a question for mainstream apologetics rather than specifically for George Steiner. He is in

---

97   Ibid., p. 218.
98   Ibid., p. 219.
99   Ibid., pp. 226–8.
100   Ibid., p. 230.
101   See above, note 1.

good company when he talks about the epic and the novel as the highest form of 'penetrative authority over our consciousness'.[102] Stephen Prickett argues similarly that spirituality and high literature are inextricably linked.[103] Whether any given reader takes the Transcendent in the Steinerian sense to refer to an objective theological presence or entity or to a form of ultimate seriousness is a matter for that reader, rather than for any final form of conclusive argument, whether pro-theological or anti-theistic. Steiner's achievement is to have lifted the argument about aesthetics beyond the terms of a stalemate between faith-orientation and reductionism.

Conclusion

All eight of our theorists provide us with valuable ingredients with which to formulate a conceptual framework for the discussion of rewritten biblical stories. They also provide a useful selection of vocabulary from which to draw. During the rest of this study, for example, we will have occasion to refer at various points to the Steinerian sense of transcendence; to Harold Fisch's view of the status of what we call the 'urtext' when it comes into dialogue with a rewriting; and to Nicholas Boyle's robust confidence in the viability of partisan pro-theological readings in the postmodern era. More generally we will bear in mind Robert Alter's claims about the special strengths of the creative writer as interpreter, Northrop Frye's picture of the constant battle between the revelatory text and human anxiety-structures, and Larry Kreitzer's campaign to 'reverse the hermeneutical flow'.

---

102 Steiner, ibid., p. 189.

103 Stephen Prickett: 'Orality, Literacy and the Idea of the Spiritual' in Liám Gearon (ed.): *English Literature, Theology and the Curriculum* (London: Cassell, 1999), pp. 35–43.

Chapter 4

FINDING THEOLOGY IN THE FOURTEEN RECEPTION-HISTORIES

Once again we will take the reception-histories in chronological order of publication. This has the advantage of decoupling our study from a too-ready adhesion to a Fall-to-Apocalypse schema and also of giving a sense of cultural change during the thirty years we are covering.

Levenson's title, *The Book of Job in its Time and in the Twentieth Century*, signals its author's belief that the biblical Book of Job has a peculiar resonance for the period following the First World War. He senses that the calamities of war and economic upheaval have, in destroying the shallow optimism of ideas of progress, engendered a new interest in theology. 'Creative writers, as well as theologians, joined in the new movement. It was natural that several of them should take the Book of Job as a model, for in no other book are characteristic themes of the twentieth-century – "disaster", "unimagined evil", "frustration", "bewilderment", "a sense of despair" – so central.'[1]

These themes are certainly central to the three literary treatments of the Job story which Levenson selects for attention: H.G. Wells's *The Undying Fire*; Archibald Macleish's *J B*; and Robert Frost's *A Masque of Reason*. But he gives no indication why he ignores Joseph Roth's *Job, the Story of a Simple Man*[2] or Carl Jung's *Answer to Job*,[3] both of them important twentieth-century retellings

---

1   Levenson, ibid., p. 3.
2   Joseph Roth: *Job, the Story of a Simple Man*, trans. Dorothy Thompson (London: Granta, 2000), first published as *Hiob, Roman eines einfachen Mannes*, 1930.
3   Carl Jung: *Answer to Job*, trans. R.F.C. Hull (London: Routledge & Kegan Paul, 1963).

and both highly significant ingredients in post-Holocaust reflection. He also fails to explain why the literature of the previous centuries can be safely ignored.[4] For example, it might be possible to show a renewed interest in *King Lear* in the twentieth-century, taking into account radical modern productions of the play, which would bring Shakespeare's play within the register of twentieth-century retellings of Job.

Even without taking into account direct twentieth-century revisiting of the literature and drama of previous centuries, it is hard to bracket out the origins of modern literature in traditions spanning many centuries. Lawrence Besserman[5] has demonstrated the vigorous medieval tradition of retelling of the Job story, culminating in the French mystery play, *La Pacience de Job*. This can be seen as a form of cultural accumulation which could have kept the Job story within the repertoire of mainstream European culture. Amongst the many traditions about Job which developed in the Middle Ages, the connection between Job and physicians at least suggests a specific literary background to the H.G. Wells novel which Levenson does discuss.

The question of seriousness is, however, the central theological issue of the material Levenson discusses and the material he does not discuss. Given that two of his selected retellings are post-Holocaust and that the Book of Job is first of all a Jewish text, what evidence do they show of reflection on this devastating horror? The issue is not one of form. In dealing with a subject of this enormity, it is impossible to specify what is and what is not an appropriate literary medium. So the comic theatre offered by MacLeish and Frost in their very different treatments

---

4   Harold Fisch in *The Biblical Presence in Shakespeare, Milton and Blake* (Oxford: Oxford University Press, 1999), pp. 117–149, argues that Job and Genesis 27 are major subtexts for *King Lear*.

5   Lawrence Besserman: *The Legend of Job in the Middle Ages* (Cambridge Mass: Harvard University Press, 1979).

of the Job story may possibly be as valid as anything else, if, in however convoluted a way, it addresses the issues.

To help state the issues we turn to the volume edited by Tod Linafelt, *Strange Fire, Reading the Bible after the Holocaust.*[6] In the discussion between Elie Wiesel and Timothy Beal, surviving is linked with remembering and it is surviving through and not surviving beyond. The silence of Job after the divine whirlwind is seen as a defiant silence and it is connected with the silence of Abraham in the Akedah. In this Akedah the father does not return, only the son.[7] The Midrash tradition often involves a dead figure from the past returning to address a new historical situation,[8] just as in Wiesel's own play, *The Trial of God*, the innkeeper becomes a latter-day Job,[9] challenging God. God in this case sides with Job against his comforters but offers no explanation of the truth of the situation. There is no voice from the whirlwind, only a silence. At the end of their discussion, Wiesel remarks 'sometimes when no words are possible, silence is an alternative language'.

Elsewhere in the volume Richard Rubinstein asserts that the German people firmly believed they were carrying out a just war against the Jews during World War II (raising severe questions about popular piety),[10] and that God has to be redefined as a suffering God,[11] and Stephen Kepnes argues that (according to Buber) Job continues to believe in justice in spite of an unjust God, a God who is willing to support Job paradoxically in his protest.[12] Job is the model of persistence, in the hope that justice, God and reality will come together in the future.[13]

6　Tod Linafelt (ed.): *Strange Fire, Reading the Bible after the Holocaust* (Sheffield: Sheffield Academic Press, 2000).
7　Ibid., p. 25.
8　Ibid., p. 26.
9　Ibid., p. 30.
10　Ibid., p. 248.
11　Ibid., p. 250.
12　Ibid., pp. 264–6.
13　We must note the position of Emmanuel Levinas, who calls for 'a faith without theodicy.' See, for example, Emmanuel Levinas: *Entre Nous* trans. Michael B. Smith and Barbara Harshav

Applying this amalgam of post-Holocaust theology to the works Levenson discusses, we can begin by acknowledging that the atrocities of the First World War which form the background to H.G. Wells's *The Undying Fire* were those of mechanized battleground warfare and therefore that Wellsian optimism in this novel has to do with a morally acceptable, if wildly idealistic, attempt to create a new world based on mass education as an antidote to militaristic propaganda. The God of *The Undying Fire* may be a rather cardboard figure, but somehow Woldingstanton School is a force for good, even a divine instrument, in a world where science and technology have run amok. A happy ending to the story of Job Huss is part of the campaign for a better world.

Historically, of course, the Wellsian Utopia did not materialise, and if the author today has regained some of his reputation as a novelist of the picaresque, he himself died disillusioned, 'a mind at the end of its tether'.[14] This was in 1946, when the full reality of Auschwitz and Buchenwald was dawning on a world recovering from war. Robert Frost published *A Masque of Reason*, which he dubbed 'Chapter Forty-three of Job', the year before.

Although there are some grounds for accepting Dorothy Judd Hall's picture of Frost as a sort of reluctant theist,[15] based on a survey of his poetry as a whole, *A Masque of Reason* presents the picture of a dilettante deity who is more concerned about experimenting with his own freedom than with the consequences in terms of human suffering.

(London: Continuum, 1998/2006), p. 86.

14 *Mind at the End of its Tether* (1945) was the last work which H.G. Wells published in his lifetime. It reflects his pessimism by that stage about the future, a deepening gloominess which was accentuated for him by the explosion of the first atom bomb. See Norman and Jeanne Mackenzie: *The Time Traveller, the life of H.G. Wells* (London: Weidenfeld & Nicholson, 1974), pp. 444–6.

15 Dorothy Judd Hall: 'An Old Testament Christian' in J.A.C. Tharpe (ed.): *Frost Centennial Essays III* (Jackson, Mississippi: University Press of Mississippi, 1978), pp. 316–49.

In lines 72–82 of the play Frost's God addresses Job, thanking him for release from being chained to his moral obligations to humanity. For this had meant that only man, rather than God, had free will. The deity had been trapped in a mundane scheme of rewards and punishments devised by 'the Deuteronomist'. Now at last, casting mystery aside, he could declare Job 'The Emancipator of your God'. Grateful for his new-found freedom, God promotes Job to the status of saint.[16]

Compared with the agonised reflections of a Buber on the unjustness of an inscrutable God, in the shadow of the Shoah, and the ultimate silence of Wiesel's theology, the Frostian deity appears as a sort of embarassing private joke in the post-Puritan Jamesian universe of Frost's America.[17]

MacLeish's *J B* may be pastiche, but it seems to spring from deeper concerns than the ridiculing of Puritan theodicy. MacLeish is concerned to rescue some sort of convincing theology from the ruins of the past and it seems to be a theology in which human love of God finally defeats the destructive power of Satan. Yet in his 1955 sermon[18] (which Levenson uses to overdetermine the meaning of the play by reducing it to an ethic of purely human love), MacLeish shows clearly his awareness of the impact of the Holocaust and the serious challenge it presents to all meaning, but then dilutes this by saying, 'These are the questions we in our generation ask ourselves. But they are not new questions'.[19] The whole tenor of what the contributors to the Linafelt volume are saying is that the Holocaust marks a decisive rupture in human history and that any reading of biblical texts, including Job, must reflect this.[20]

---

16 Robert Frost: *Selected Poems* (London: Penguin, 1973), p. 233.
17 Thomas McClanahan: *Frost's Theodicy* in J.A.C. Tharpe (ed.): *Frost Centennial Essays II* (Jackson, Mississippi: University Press of Mississippi, 1978), pp. 112–26, discusses the influence of the ideas of William James Sr. on Frost, building on Emerson's notion that evil is merely the privation of Good, rather than something absolute.
18 Reproduced in Nahum Glatzer: *The Dimensions of Job* (New York: Schocken Books, 1969), pp. 278–86.
19 Ibid., p. 279.
20 Linafelt, ibid., see especially pp. 36–51 and 221–32.

The most recent of our reception-history authors, Yvonne Sherwood, writing (as we have seen) about Jonah and not specifically about Job, argues that Christian culture still has not fully engaged with the impact of the Holocaust.[21] If she is right, then Frost's and MacLeish's retellings of the Job story could be seen as part of a rather frighteningly slow shift in the direction of greater awareness, with Levenson's study of 1972 itself a furtherance of the process, except that the author favours Frost over against H.G. Wells and MacLeish as a revitaliser of the original text. This is because Levenson sees the other two works as efforts to supplant the original and takes *The Masque of Reason* at face value as a 'meditation upon Job',[22] presumably on the basis of the closing self-reference of the play as the '43rd Chapter'.

We should note Harold Fisch's assertion that strong retellings of biblical stories are *all* in a dialogue with the original.[23] To this might be added the insight that every text from the past *becomes* a contemporary text in the reading of it. The recent republication of Joseph Roth's *Job, the Story of a Simple Man*,[24] is surely a case in point. First published in 1930, the novel concerns the exodus of a modern Job, Mendel Singer, and his family from the ghettos of Tsarist Russia to the disappointing Promised Land of New York in the Depression Era. Like other works of Roth, the fascination lies in the recreation of a lost European Jewish culture, but also here in the restoration of Job's fortunes through the unexpected emergence of his once mentally-debilitated son as a great musician.

Reading this novel in 2000 (the year of its republication in English) must be a different experience from reading it in 1930.[25] Harold Fisch thinks that, even

---

21 Sherwood, ibid., pp. 79–87.

22 Levenson, ibid., p. 68.

23 Harold Fisch: *New Stories for Old, Biblical Patterns in the Novel* (London: Macmillan, 1996), p. 7.

24 Joseph Roth: *Job, the Story of a Simple Man* (London: Granta, 2000).

25 For the impact of post-Holocaust thinking on a different rewritten biblical story, Mendelssohn's *Elijah*, see Appendix A.

though Roth was dead by 1939, 'this work should be considered among the great literary testimonies of the Holocaust'.[26] For him it is a 'prevision' of the crisis of faith which Judaism would experience through the Holocaust. In the novel, the main protagonist, Mendel Singer, who eventually boldly confronts God, is a model of dogged persistence in the outward observances of Judaism. This is the epic of the quotidian, 'an epic without distance',[27] in which the final miracle of Menuchim seems as ordinary as the suffering which envelopes the bulk of the narrative. For Boitani[28] the genius of the work is its ability to support both a naturalistic and a theological reading, with its hidden God lurking somewhere in the background, inviting but not compelling recognition. The sheer drabness and ordinariness of Mendel, set against the historical background of the mass Jewish emigrations to America, lends a matter-of-factness to the novel which is at the extreme opposite pole from the contrived theatrical pieces examined earlier.

When Carl Jung wrote his *Answer to Job* in 1952, he seems to have found a way of combining all the theological contradictions of the Job story and fusing them into a divine psychological drama which both alienated Christian orthodoxy and at the same time anticipated the feminist exegesis of a much later time. For Jung the central crisis in the story is Job's tenacious insistence that God can be met on the basis of justice and morality, a stance which brings to a head the contradiction whereby God is both a persecutor and a helper in one. Yahweh is not split, but is an antimony, a totality of inner opposites and this is 'the indispensable condition for his tremendous dynamism'.[29]

By forcing Yahweh to confront his own moral failure in flaunting might over right, Job is instrumental in propelling the deity to seek a reunion with Sophia,

26   Fisch, ibid., pp. 106–7.
27   Fisch, ibid., p. 109.
28   Boitani, op cit, pp. 204–5.
29   Carl Jung, ibid., p. 23.

126

his estranged consort (represented by the Virgin Mary) and the product is the Incarnation, 'God's birth to self-consciousness'.[30] Even in Christ, however, there is a manifest lack of self-reflection until the despairing cry from the Cross, 'My God, my God, why hast thou forsaken me?, which becomes the true answer to Job. God experiences what it is to be a mortal and 'drinks to the dregs what he made his faithful servant Job suffer'.[31] In the era of the Paraclete God has had to suffer from man, since this is the only means of reconciliation between the two.[32]

As an expression of the Promethean character of modern man and as a vehicle of the incipient reaction against patriarchy, Jung's *Answer to Job* clearly has a place in the reception-history of the biblical story, but it also seems superficial when placed alongside the contributions to the Linafelt volume. The Suffering God motif, however, has been a persistent theme in theology ever since,[33] and in that sense Jung displayed a degree of acumen which not all of the orthodox religious thinkers of his time shared.

The Pritchard compendium on Solomon and Sheba, our next text, could be taken as a metonym for the state of scholarship in 1974, in that archaeology, the Jewish tradition, the Christian tradition, the Muslim tradition and the Ethiopian are handled by separate specialists and thereby is implied a compartmentalisation of the topic, very different from recent pluralistic and inter-disciplinary studies. In the more recent book by Warner, *From the Beast to the Blonde*,[34] we find a more integrated treatment of aspects of the Sheba tradition, with the Queen herself seen as the Christian encrypting of hopes for the conversion of the Moor, but also as a

---

30   Ibid., p. 70.

31   Ibid., p. 114.

32   Ibid., p. 115.

33   See for example Jürgen Moltmann: *The Crucified God* (London, SCM, 1974) and Michael A. Chester: *Divine Pathos and Human Being: The Theology of Abraham Joshua Heschel* (London, Vallentine Mitchell, 2005). Apart from Heschel and Moltmann, two other theologians associated with the theme of the Suffering God are Dorothy Sölle and Kazoh Kitamori.

34   Marina Warner: *From the Beast to the Blonde* (London: Vintage, 1995).

folkloristic bridge between the three monotheistic faiths, especially in the tradition of her goose-foot. She is at the same time the embodiment of the exotic Other in Renaissance art and, in her role as the 'black, but comely' beloved of the Vulgate translation of the Song of Songs, she is the vehicle of the medieval Church's ambivalence about blackness,[35] otherwise the colour of the underworld. Sheba's part in the Legend of the True Cross locates her, nevertheless, within what Warner calls the 'tie-beam' of the Christian master-narrative.[36]

In theological terms, the Sheba nexus of legends can be seen as a reminder of the luxuriant character of scriptural elaboration in the era of oral folktale transmission, but also as evidence of the link-making proclivity of the central religious tradition. The *Golden Legend* is perhaps a literary counterpart of the typology of the Church's mainstream teaching in the pre-Reformation world.[37] More importantly for the future of hermeneutics, it is possible to see the apparently bizarre development surrounding Sheba's left foot as indicative of the tradition's capacity to anticipate subliminally new demands on its resources. In this case we have a development (first noticed by the art critic, Emile Mâle[38]) which surely qualifies for the category of 'strangeness' which we associate with transcendence in the context of the imaginative appropriation of biblical stories and motifs.

In terms of the inter-faith dialogue, the presence of Sheba as a common feature in the traditions of Judaism, Christianity and Islam has an obvious binding effect. The *Kebra Nagast* presents a variant narrative outside the limits of that particular conversation. Although it will no doubt maintain its hegemonic status within Ethiopia as a national epic, non-Ethiopians can take this text as a sort of alternative

---

35 Ibid., p. 103.

36 Ibid., p. 99.

37 Jacobus de Voragine: *The Golden Legend*, trans. William Granger Ryan (Princeton NJ: Princeton University Press, 1993).

38 Emile Mâle: *Religious Art in France, the Twelfth Century* (Princeton NJ: Princeton University Press, 1978), pp. 394–7.

128

history of salvation. The literary equivalent in English fiction would be the Kingsley Amis novel, *The Alteration*,[39] in which there has been no Reformation and electricity is banned. At a time when, as many of the reception-history texts examined in our study demonstrate, the biblical salvation-history metanarrative is under pressure from various kinds of ideological critique, a variant which can be seen to ironize that metanarrative from a pro-religious stance may be of specific theological value.

We now move on to the remaining twelve of our fourteen reception-histories, considered still in publication order. We begin with the first in our list to be both the work of a single author and to cover all or nearly all of the historical and cultural territory from the urtext's inception to the modern period.

Our next text, Warner's *Alone of all her Sex*, presents us with many of the issues about feminism and patriarchy which remain in the foreground of current hermeneutical debate. Warner cannot be said to belong to the ranks of feminist theologians. Whilst scrupulous in her scholarly attention to detail in the literary and iconographic treatment of the Virgin Mary theme in European culture, she appears to have no time for a 'goddess cult', even one associated with the advancement of the New Woman and she dismisses institutional Christianity as fundamentally androcentric. The theological options for understanding the material which underlies her study can therefore be outlined as:

1. To fall in with Warner's own valedictory approach to the history of the 'Myth and Cult of the Virgin Mary'. This effectively relegates religion to a benighted past from which the sophisticated reader is grateful to have been delivered.

2. To see the post-biblical tradition as the continuance of a suppressed goddess-cult, hidden or thinly disguised within the Bible itself.

---

39   Kingsley Amis: *The Alteration* (St Albans: Triad/Panther Books, 1978).

3. To seek to re-cast patriarchal theological images in terms which are either gender-neutral or positively feminist and to transpose these onto historical material.

4. To affirm the validity of unmodified patriarchy.

5. To accept that theology moves through the same process of change as culture (or a parallel process) and that we are currently at the point where a major shift is underway.[40]

Whichever of these options we favour will cause us to read the Coventry Annunciation play or Piero della Francesca's *Madonna della Misericordia* in a distinctive way. It is possible that any of them (except probably the first option) could be the basis of the sort of 'recognition' experience which Boitani describes, in which the artistic work reads us just as we read it.[41]

However, if we incorporate into our hermeneutic the moral impetus which Nicholas Boyle recommends from the writings of Levinas,[42] we must surely side with some version of Option 5. This might be an approach which respects the cultural situatedness of, for example, Dante's Beatrice, but also knows about Faust and Gretchen and about Primo Levi and about Margaret Atwood. Option 3, as pursued by Julia Kristeva, relies on being highly selective and extracting one element of the tradition, the Mater Dolorosa, whilst dismissing much of the rest.[43] As I shall argue later, the intertextual dialectic does not necessarily have to

---

40 For a treatment of the stories of the Virgin Mary and other women figures of the Bible which assumes seismic shifts in western culture, see Gloria Naylor's novel *Bailey's Café,* discussed in my article 'Latecomers: Four Novelists Rewrite the Bible' in J Cherlyl Exum (ed.): *Retellings: The Bible in Literature, Music, Art and Film* (Leiden: Brill, 2007).

41 On Boitani and recognition experiences in the rewriting of biblical stories, see Chapter 3, pp. 107–8.

42 On Boyle's reading of Levinas, see Chapter 3, pp. 112–114.

43 Julia Kristeva: *Stabat Mater* in Toril Moi (ed.): *The Kristeva Reader* (Oxford: Blackwell, 1986), pp. 160–85. One can respect the force of this highly influential feminist text without regarding it as a complete solution to the problem of how the Virgin Mary tradition as a whole might be read.

130

include works which are consciously or even unconsciously theological, as long as they are morally serious and at least open-ended ideologically.

We now move from an approach to reception-history which is highly resistant to theology (that of Warner), on account of what one might term the 'ideological closure' of the author's own metanarrative, to one which is much more open-ended and respectful of the urtext. Quinones in *The Changes of Cain* covers a denser concentration of major works of literature than any of our other reception-history writers, bearing out perhaps his claim that the Cain and Abel story is the fundamental myth of the western imagination.

If we take for a moment Nicholas Boyle's prescription of secular literature as the barometer of human spiritual need (described in Chapter 3), what are the needs which the main texts explored by Quinones express, given that we are dealing with rewritten Scripture? Obviously the relationship of violence to political necessity is an inescapable thread running throughout the reception-history, from Augustine to Melville. In the modern period, the Romantic revolt is associated with widening cosmological horizons, epitomized by the bewildering empty vastness of space in Byron's *Cain*.[44] The treatments of the Cain and Abel story by Melville, Conrad and Tournier all, by critical consent, explore the theme of homosexuality.[45] Unamuno raises in its starkest form the identification of Otherness in fellow human beings, which we can relate to Buber's I-and-Thou theology. All of these approaches represent partial readings of the respective texts, in that they can be interpreted in a multifaceted way, like all major works of literature. If we say 'like all canonical literature,' we will have come to the heart of the confrontation or interface between

44 Cain: 'How silent and how vast are these dim worlds!' In *Cain, A Mystery*, Lord Byron: *The Poetical Works* (Oxford: Oxford University Press, 1961), p. 531. The same vertiginous sense can be found in the two works of Mary Shelley discussed elsewhere in this book, *Frankenstein* and *The Last Man*.

45 See for example Harold Beaver's Introduction to the Penguin Classics edition of Hermann Melville: *Billy Budd, Sailor and Other Stories* (London: Penguin, 1985), p. 43, or Ross Murfin's essay on 'Gender Criticism' in Daniel R Schwarz (ed.): *The Secret Sharer – Joseph Conrad* (London: Bedford Books, 1997).

celebrated literary appropriations of the biblical text and the biblical text as sacred story.

The very fact that Byron and Conrad and the other authors have chosen the biblical story as the locus for their literary creations is a signal that the biblical text is being interrogated. For Alter such writers constitute a transhistorical textual community which may be more perceptive about the biblical story than conventional exegesis.

Given that, as Fisch reminds us, the biblical text always remains itself and therefore the new work exists in a condition of dialogue with it, we can assume that transcendence is taken care of, particularly in the case of those literary appropriations where we are not dealing with a severely secularist form of partisanship. In other words, where it is not transcendence as a topic which is at stake, at least ostensibly. One should add this final caveat, because there is a sense in which, for a writer like Melville, bleaker readings are always in the offing to derail such certainties.[46]

A *theological* reading of the main works discussed by Quinones would draw attention to the dignity of the Byronic Cain's stance before God, in which he accepts responsibility for succumbing to the determinism induced by Lucifer's conducted tour of the universe. It might find in *Billy Budd* the destruction of a Christ-figure[47] resulting from the unacknowledged and suppressed homosexual feelings of Captain Vere and others. In *The Secret Sharer* it might find the ship saved by the successful resolution of the Captain's homosexuality and in Tournier's *Gemini* it would observe the creative and the destructive potential of homosexuality across a panoramic sweep of French life from wartime occupation to postwar Algeria. It

---

46   See, for example, William Hamilton: *Melville and the Gods* (California: Scholars Press, 1985).

47   This was very much the reading offered by F.W. Dillistone: *The Novelist and the Passion Story* (London: Collins, 1960), pp. 45–68, though Dillistone describes the emotional forces faced by Billy Budd as 'the mystery of irrational hatred'. (Ibid., p. 49.). We have already referred to Benjamin Britten's opera in Chapter 2.

132

would find in the juxtaposition of Unamuno's two treatments of the Cain and Abel theme the final resurgence of Abel in a move which reverses the dominance of Cain in modern literature, prophetic perhaps of a return to other suppressed aspects of the biblical story (such as the deity).

Haskins, in writing the reception-history of Mary Magdalene, taps into another trope of theological revival. The huge readership attracted to Dan Brown's *The Da Vinci Code*,[48] blockbuster thriller with sales running into the millions, should be sufficient evidence that the idea of Mary Magdalene as the source of some esoteric 'revelation' about Christianity or about God is a powerful one at the beginning of the twenty-first-century. One may conjecture that this is the outworking in the popular imagination not only of feminist theology but of the sense that the Dead Sea Scrolls and other newly rediscovered ancient texts have upset the apple-cart of institutional Christianity, opening the way for an as-yet ill-defined alternative form of spirituality.[49]

Haskins herself, as we have seen, is far less sensational. If the General Synod of the Church of England's decision to ordain women is the culmination of the revolution, then orthodoxy perhaps has little to fear. But what may seem a slightly bathetic conclusion to Haskin's narrative should not divert attention from the central content of her book. This includes a magisterial survey of the treatment of Mary Magdalene in European visual art (predominantly) and literature.

If we seek to identify examples of 'strangeness' amongst the works Haskins discusses, the discussion should begin with the Gospel of Mary and the *Pistis Sophia*. This is as much on account of the modern and postmodern constructions which have been put on these texts as in response to their conjectured meaning in their equally conjectured Sitz-im-Leben. The speculative Sitz-im-Leben we take to be a 'lost

---

48   Dan Brown: *The Da Vinci Code* (London: Corgi Books, 2004).
49   See further discussion of this topic in Chapter 13.

tradition',[50] supplying a feminine deity of the kind familiar from what we know of the ancient religions of Egypt, Babylonia, Greece, Rome, Africa and North America. The reason for the tradition's suppression would have been the threat to the hierarchical system of patriarchy in the region of the three great monotheistic faiths.

The discovery of the Nag Hammadi library in 1945[51] released the Gnostic texts on the modern world and, in terms of their absent reception-history, we can describe them as new texts. The fragmentary nature of the Gospel of Mary is conducive to imaginative development and also meshes very well with the Romantic attachment to fragments which, Stephen Prickett[52] argues, lies at the very fountain-head of modern and postmodern attitudes to literature, from Lessing to Derrida.

Haskins's study is packed with striking treatments of Mary Magdalene in art. If we take as just one example, Botticelli's *Lamentation*, in which the head of Christ and that of Mary Magdalene are closely juxtaposed, almost fused,[53] we can see the progress of a line of development which culminated in Kazantzakis's novel, *The Last Temptation* or in the D.H. Lawrence short story, *The Man Who Died*.[54] The Lawrence short story came before its time in terms of public acceptability.[55] More prosaically, perhaps, it is worked out in Dr Barbara Thiering's *Jesus the Man* which, as Haskins notes, has Jesus married to Mary Magdalene, who 'left him after the crucifixion (which he survived for thirty years), having borne him a girl and two boys'.[56] This, and novels like *Wild Girl* by Michèle Roberts, we may

50   Haskins, op cit, p. 44.
51   See Kurt Rudolph: *Gnosis, The Nature and History of Gnosticism* (Edinburgh: T. & T. Clark, 1983/1998), pp. 34–44.
52   Stephen Prickett: *Origins of Narrative, the Romantic Appropriation of the Bible* (Cambridge: Cambridge University Press, 1996), pp. 187–9.
53   Haskins, ibid., pp. 208–9.
54   See Haskins, ibid., p. 372–3. Both the D.H. Lawrence short story and the Kazantzakis novel are discussed more extensively in Chapter 5, *Vox Dei*.
55   T.R. Wright in *D.H. Lawrence and the Bible* (Cambridge: Cambridge University Press, 2002), records Lawrence's disillusionment at the rejection of his vision of the relationship between Christ and Mary Magdalene.
56   Haskins, ibid., p. 374.

presume, are among the texts which form the basis of the popular speculations about the role of Mary Magdalene which are one element of *The Da Vinci Code*. In between Boticelli and the current era, we have the Victorian fascination with the Penitent Mary Magdalene, of which several novels by Wilkie Collins,[57] as well as Mrs Gaskell's *Ruth,*[58] are important expressions.

The Wild Girl,[59] though far from orthodox Christianity in its endorsement of a version of free love as part of the essence of the gospel, is nevertheless a bold attempt to imagine the situation of an impoverished young woman swept into prostitution and then transformed by her encounter with Jesus of Nazareth, who releases her mystical side. A decidedly Pauline shipwreck leads to an accidental arrival in Provence, where the first-person narrator and her companions establish a simple community and she herself is finally encouraged to write her own version of the gospel. It is her daughter's daughter, we learn on the novel's final page, who unearths the hidden text, which we understand to be identical with the novel itself. In terms of 'strangeness', though, it is Chapter 12 itself (immediately preceding the unearthing) which is most original. Here we find a series of dreams rewriting elements of the Apocalypse, in which the Great Mother redeems the harlot, Babylon the Great, and the male and female sides of God are reconciled. It seems that Mary Magdalene's final commission from God is to leave the tranquillity of her rural life in Provence, her earthly paradise, and 'to travel anew, through cities and deserts and the wilderness, to proclaim the Word'.

The effect of revisionist novels, such as *Wild Girl*, is to invite us to reconsider the past as something more than a closed book, suggesting that history is something other than a relentless linear progress to the world we have inherited.

57 Examples include *No Name* (1862) and *The New Magdalene* (1873), both discussed in Chapter 6.

58 Mrs Gaskell's *Ruth*, as a campaigning novel on behalf of women driven into prostitution, brought its author fierce social hostility at first. See Winifred Gerin: *Elizabeth Gaskell* (Oxford: Oxford University Press, 1980), pp. 127–41.

59 Michèle Roberts: *The Wild Girl* (London: Minerva, 1991).

135

The construction of a 'new past' may be one of the features of our current cultural upheaval. Again, Prickett has shown how important it was for figures like Chateaubrand, one of the theorists of the French Revolution and one of the originators of Romanticism, that the Revolution was seen to be continuous with a re-written past.[60]

Norman Cohn's *Noah's Flood*, as we have argued, is a valuable account of the hermeneutical crisis over the Genesis version of geology which occurred roughly between 1655 and 1840. The crisis had important implications for the perceived plausibility of Christianity in the Victorian period. However, the reception-history both before and after the crisis is much richer than Cohn allows, as several studies of the material demonstrate.[61] We could cite the Newcastle Flood play and the very recent novel by David Maine as further evidence.[62]

But, confining ourselves to Cohn's book, we find amongst the excellent illustrations, though hardly discussed in the text, some of the most powerful images of western art, including an illustration from the *Silos Apocalypse*; the twelfth-century mosaic in San Marco, Venice; Roelant Savary's *Noah's Ark*; and John Martin's *The Deluge*.[63] These are major examples of the imaginative appropriation of the biblical story in the visual language of their respective cultures. They show that the Flood story is about something much closer to human existential concerns than the fate of scientific theories and one could argue that in the contemporary world of acute ecological concern the story has the potential to be revitalised once again. We could classify Cohn's text itself therefore as characterised by an *absent*

60 Stephen Prickett, ibid., pp. 170ff.
61 See J.P. Lewis: *A Study of the Interpretation of Noah and the Flood in Jewish and Christian Literature* (Leiden: E.J. Brill, 1968) and Francis Landy: 'Flood and Fludd' in J. Cheryl Exum and Stephen D. Moore: *Biblical Studies/Cultural Studies, The Third Sheffield Colloquium* (Sheffield: Sheffield Academic Press, 1998), pp. 117–58.
62 David Maine: *The Flood, A Novel* (London: Canongate, 2004) is discussed at length in Chapter 5.
63 See Cohn, op cit, pp. 39, 10, 13, x, and 108 respectively for these illustrations.

presence of theology, which the illustrations serve to emphasise. The other *absent presence*, of course, is the impact of the new science on writers of imaginative fiction, such as Byron and Mary Shelley, whose output is central to the course of reception-history traced in other parts of this study.

We have already outlined the coverage in Richard Trexler's *The Journey of the Magi* of a great landscape of literary and iconographic appropriations of the Magi. Trexler's work was dismissed by David Brown (whom we considered as a theorist of rewritten scripture in Chapter 3) as an example of the study of the Magi as figures of social and political legitimation.[64] However, a close examination of the work reveals numerous examples of the Magi as subversive figures and there is also a persistent 'strangeness' about the third (sometimes fourth) magus which is the equivalent of the goose-footed Sheba. Here, again, we find an encounter with the Exotic Other. There is also the capacity of the story to attract acts of self-negation (which Brown himself celebrates[65]) and for it to march back into history like some ghost from the past, as demonstrated by the photograph of a military convoy returning the remains of the Three Kings to the bomb-blasted Cologne Cathedral at the end of the Second World War.[66] Despite the Magi's low credit-rating in New Testament Studies,[67] their story seems to have accumulated a transcendent charge which is independent of the rest of the Nativity story.

Stocker's *Judith* is, amongst other things, a study of the use of the Judith story in propaganda. She is able to demonstrate the story's remarkable capacity to be adapted to the purposes of quite opposite factions, as well as the feminist perspective of the story as a persistent challenge to patriarchy. Far from being

---

64 See David Brown: *Tradition and Imagination* (Oxford: Oxford University Press, 1999), p. 91.

65 Brown, ibid., pp. 90–1.

66 Trexler, op cit, pp. 208–9.

67 See, for example, J.C. Fenton: *The Gospel of Matthew* (London: Penguin, 1974), p. 44: 'There are no parallels to this chapter in the other Gospels: Matthew has probably composed it himself ... and we cannot discover what basis, if any, it had in history'.

137

reductionist in theological terms, the author asserts that the symbolic logic of the Book of Judith is that 'divinity is feminine when in epiphany on earth.[68] Judith reappears in the New Testament as Salome, as an inversion, according to Warner,[69] but Stocker sees the treatment of Judith as Salome (where it arises in reception-history) as an example of the death-drive.[70] Stocker's Judith displays considerable resilience against relegation to the ranks of biblical villainesses, emerging as the Victorian embodiment of the uncanny and as the spiritual heroine in Miriam in Hawthorne's *The Marble Faun*.[71] For Stocker, Judith is a resource in the construction of a counter-culture, a persistent challenge to patriarchy, stigmatised as The Woman With A Gun in some contemporary fiction.

Finally, Judith is 'an image of the autonomy that is constantly being wrested from us all, and an icon of the way to recover it'.[72] Nobody could claim that Stocker's study records the 'blunting of the text' and, in that sense, it is powerful evidence of the vitality of another avenue in the reception-history of biblical stories.[73] Perhaps Stocker's 'theology' is most fully expressed in her reading of Hawthorne's oeuvre as representative of his 'obsession in all his work, Anglo-American society has wholly failed to understand its own religion. Christianity is for Hawthorne a real of

---

68   Stocker, op cit, p. 11.
69   Marina Warner: *Monuments and Maidens* (Berkeley: University of California Press, 2000), p. 167.
70   Stocker, ibid., pp. 169–72.
71   Ibid., pp. 210–34.
72   Ibid., p. 252.
73   Lyle Jeffries in the Epilogue to his *People of the Book* (Grand Rapids: Eerdmans, 1996) echoes George Steiner's conclusion that there is little sign of writers being willing to surrender the authority which they have on loan from the 'spiritual capital' of the biblical tradition, despite the efforts of people like Matthew Arnold in our literary tradition to blunt the text by poeticising it. On this view, writers might be divided between those whose use of the 'trope of transcendence' is justified by their openness or allegiance to the biblical tradition and those who want a free ride.

138

dark, bitter, yet nobly romantic mystery, and its most profound secret is that 'only Lucifer – only a fallen angel – knows how to love good'.[74]

Norris's *The Story of Eve* tackles a topic which is central to feminism and to feminist theology. Milton's *Paradise Lost* is placed in the context of the misogynist theology[75] to which Charlotte Bronte's *Shirley* and later women's fiction are the antidote.[76] Mary Shelley's *Frankenstein* marks a turning point, not only in feminist appropriations of the Garden of Eden story, but also in the feminist response to the Creation story, with its dire warning of the consequences of the unbridled licensing of technology.[77] Later, Ernest Hemingway's *Garden of Eden* problematizes masculinity[78] and Angela Carter's *The Passion of the New Eve* dissolves gender boundaries in an ironic *tour de force*.[79]

There are, as we have already suggested, alternative readings of Norris's material.[80] It is possible to acclaim the theological genius of Milton whilst still recognizing that his attitude to women is time-bound and unprogressive.[81] It is

---

74 Stocker, ibid., p. 171. Clearly this reading of Hawthorne relies heavily on the sense of him as a literary descendent of Milton or as the preacher of a variant of the Fortunate Fall theme. Despite its religious unorthodoxy, it has the merit of giving due weight to transcendence as a theme within Hawthorne's romances. A recently-published essay by Emily Budick emphasises the intractability of human experience in *The Marble Faun* and sees this novel as a plea for respecting the unknowability of others.' See Emily Mary Rudick: 'Perplexity, sympathy and the question of the human: a reading of *The Marble Faun*' in Richard H Millington (ed.): *The Cambridge Companion to Nathaniel Hawthorne* (Cambridge: Cambridge University Press, 2004).

75 Norris, op cit, pp. 284–90.

76 Ibid., pp. 292–300.

77 Ibid., pp. 365–72.

78 Ibid., pp. 276–79.

79 Ibid., pp. 397–9.

80 See Chapter 2, p. 58.

81 For a rebuttal of claims that Milton was a misogynist, see Philip J. Gallagher: *Milton, the Bible and Misogyny* (Columbia: University of Missouri Press, 1990). For Milton as the theological critic of power, see Gale H. Carrithers, Jr & James D. Hardy, Jr: *Milton and the Hermeneutic Journey* (Louisiana: Louisiana State University Press, 1994). For an assessment of Milton's intellectual and literary stature, see William Kerrigan: 'Milton's Place in Intellectual History' in Dennis Danielson (ed.): *The Cambridge Companion to Milton* (Cambridge: Cambridge University Press, 1999).

possible to recognize the imaginative innovation in Macdonald's *Lilith* as a fantasy without being too preoccupied with the fact that the monstrous cat is linked with the negative cultural history of Lilith in general.[82] Carter's novel can be read as either the final triumph of feminism or as its ironization.[83] What perhaps Norris's study teaches us is that transcendence is a more complex topic than that of convergence with or departure from a particular ideological reading. Ideological readings, whether good or bad (Stocker has telling examples of the Nazification of Judith) have the tendency to flatten out their material.[84] But that does not mean that the texts of which feminism, for example, approves are themselves necessarily resistant to a transcendent frame of reference. Mary Shelley's *Frankenstein* can be read as a feminist tract or as a moral warning against the excesses of capitalism or as a story of the Uncanny.[85]

Wroe's *Pilate* refers to the different endings to Pilate's story available in the tradition. If the author had been theologically inclined, she might have discussed the radical difference between Pilate's suicide and caged submersion in the sea (on the way to Hell) in the *Mors Pilati* and his receiving of forgiveness in Bulgakov's *The Master and Margarita*. Bulgakov's novel is extraordinary in making Pilate the main subject of the narrative rather than Christ, but may be seen as the outworking of both the Eastern Orthodox stance towards Pilate (itself a 'trajectory' of Christ's words of forgiveness in the gospels) and the novelist's own experience as an artist.[86] We discuss *The Master and Margarita* more extensively in Chapter 5.

82 See Stephen Prickett: *Victorian Fantasy* (Cambridge: Cambridge University Press, 1979), pp. 189–93.

83 On *The Passion of New Eve* as a satire, see Linden Peach: *Angela Carter* (London: Macmillan, 1998), pp. 112–30.

84 Stocker, op cit, pp. 193–7.

85 See essays in Fred Botting (ed.): *New Casebooks, Frankenstein* (Basingstoke: Palgrave, 2002).

86 On Bulgakov and Pilate, see J.A.E. Curtis: *Bulgakov's Last Decade, the Writer as Hero* (Cambridge: Cambridge University Press, 1987). Curtis suggests that Bulgakov's own failure of nerve in relation to the censors is reflected in the Master's worries about his own cowardice in the Moscow sections of the novel. (Ibid., p. 155.)

140

If Norris's *The Story of Eve* is a work of feminist polemic, then Gaines's *Music in the Old Bones, Jezebel Through the Ages* is a sort of experiment in feminism. The attempt to rehabilitate Jezebel fits in, of course, with the wing of feminist hermeneutics which seeks to reclaim or annexe Canaanite religion, though, as one feminist writer has observed, one cannot assume that all goddess cults were favourable to women.[87] On the side of feminist hermeneutics, there is plenty of evidence of the malevolent use of the name 'Jezebel' in literature, particularly that of the American South, as evidenced for example in Faulkner's *Light in August*.[88] But Tom Robbins's *Skinny Legs and All* seems an unreliable ally in the rehabilitation of Jezebel when the novel reads like and surely *is* a pastiche; whilst Margaret Atwood's *The Robber Bride*, despite its strong feminist ethos, makes no attempt to valorize its villainess. In fact, *The Robber Bride* has been recognized as an example of magic realism, a genre which lends itself to the sense of the transcendent.[89] This novel and Atwood's other main entry into the field of biblical rewriting, *The Handmaid's Tale*, are examined in Chapter 7.

Pippin's *Apocalyptic Bodies* seems to represent the extreme of wrong-headedness, in that the feminist hermeneutic seems inappropriate to a text which, though possibly misogynist in some areas, is about something quite different from gender politics. Whatever the difficulties in pinpointing the exact historical setting of the biblical Book of Revelation, there seems to a scholarly consensus that the text is a response to the experience of intense suffering and living on the brink

---

87 'The most important cult of the Goddess practised in the world today is the cult of Maha Diva in India; its existence tells nothing about the position of women in Indian society; even though women have a strong position in that cult.' Luise Schotroff, Silvia Schroer, Marie-Theres Wacker: *Feminist Interpretation, The Bible in Women's Perspective* (Minneapolis: Fortess Press, 1998), p. 166.

88 See Irene Vasser: 'Faulkner's Mendicant Madonna' in *Literature and Theology*, Vol. 18, No 1, March 2004.

89 See, for example, Marina Warner's placing of *The Robber Bride* within this context in her *Signs and Wonders* (Vintage: London, 2004), p. 275. There is no need to accept her psychological reductionism.

of annihilation under Roman imperial persecution.[90] It seems perverse to dismiss this as a factor in a modern reading of the text and almost as perverse to ignore alternative readings offered by modern literary rewriters. In Chapter 6 we explore three literary works, by Mary Shelley, Kafka, and D.H. Lawrence respectively, which open up fresh perspectives on the potentiality of The Book of Revelation as a source of literary inspiration. In the Survey Chapter, we questioned whether one of Pippin's own chosen texts, Flannery O'Connor's *A Good Man Is Hard To Find*, really supports her rejection of biblical apocalypse (and its reception-history) as destructively misogynist. O'Connor is particularly interesting in this context as an avowedly pro-theological writer of fiction,[91] whatever status we accord to authorial intention.

Yvonne Sherwood's study of the afterlife of the Jonah story returns us to more fruitful territory, with Melville's *Moby Dick* inevitably at its heart.[92] Sherwood is concerned to emphasise the subversive aspects of Jonah as a theological text, drawing on her sharp distinction between 'Mainstream' and 'Backwater' in interpretation. Whereas mainstream exegesis (equating to Christian orthodoxy) finds in Jonah an allegory of the Passion Story or (as with Calvin) a cautionary tale, 'a testimony to the horror of dissidence and the pain of correction',[93] the midrashic and literary tradition celebrates the viscous nature of Jonah's experience in the belly of the whale and the growing perception of Jonah as a heroic clown confronting the caprices of a fickle deity.

---

90 For a survey of several alternative modern readings of the Apocalypse, see Steve Moyise (ed.): *Studies in the Book of Revelation* (Edinburgh: T. & T. Clark, 2001).

91 Flannery O'Connor in essays in *Mystery and Manners, Occasional Prose,* Sally and Robert Fitzgerald (eds.) (New York: Farrar, Straus & Giroux, 1970) repeatedly discusses her own situation as a 'Catholic novelist'.

92 For a study which situates Melville's *Moby Dick* within the novelist's interest in world religions or world mythologies, see H. Bruce Franklin (op cit).

93 Sherwood, op cit, p. 39.

142

Sherwood goes on[94] to propose that the Book of Jonah be seen not as a 'maverick misfit' in the canon, but as a sort of hidden key to the whole Bible. In this schema, God becomes 'a giant and unguessable force'[95] and Jonah the model of human reaction or adjustment to this reality. In correspondence with the author, I asked whether she thought that a sort of negative theology emerged from her study. She acknowledged that she was 'certainly trying to do something theological at the end' but cautioned that her emphasis was 'less on the indefinability of God (which can be quite a comfortable and easily domesticated notion)' and more on the idea of 'God not on my side, or God defined as the-opposite of what I desire for myself at this particular moment'. The author, at the same time, pointed out that the presumption that God and the Bible's role is to teach us lessons in precisely what the Backwater readings deliver us from.[96] Instead of seeing polemic (and authoritarian polemic) as the real stuff of the Old Testament, we can be helped by the Backwater readings of Jonah to discover another, less preachy and more playful approach to biblical literature.

This may be a suitable juncture to recall that the whole body of imaginatively-appropriated biblical material which underpins our fourteen works of 'reception-history' is evidence of a rich diversity of responses to the text and in many ways an antidote, taken in its entirety, to monolithic or partisan readings, whether anti-semitic, misogynist or illiberal in any other sense. But, of course, Sherwood's point goes further. Her study implies that, within the Bible itself (and its literary or exegetical appropriation), we can find a paradigm for destabilising settled notions about divinity or reality. Instead of relegating texts like Jonah, Ecclesiastes and Job to the margins of the canon, we can, by placing them more to the fore, encourage more dialogue between these texts and those which have previously been treated

---

94   Ibid., p. 284.
95   Ibid., p. 285.
96   Private correspondence, May 2005.

as central. 'In fact reading these texts and taking them seriously may change some of the ways in which we see the centre.'[97]

Paffenroth's *Judas, Images of the Lost Disciple*, though it shares something of the perverse sensibility of the Jezebel study by Gaines, does accurately reflect the tendency in modern fiction to rehabilitate Judas.[98] The theology of rehabilitation has its foundation, in any case, in the early doctrinal position that Judas was a necessary agent of the Passion. Modern novels like William Rayner's *The Knifeman* or the film *Jesus Christ Superstar* merely, one might say, take this further. Paffenroth devotes a considerable amount of space to the anti-semitic history of the Oberammergau play, but fails to connect this fully with the history of the reading of the gospel Passion story[99] or with the treatment of Judas in medieval drama. If Judas is a demonic figure in literature, then he is also the vehicle of the dark undertow of Christian theology in Europe[100] and it is questionable whether domesticating him (which is the drift of Paffenroth's book and some of his modern examples) does any service to the agenda outlined in the Linafelt volume, any more than Frost's treatment of Job does.

Summary

Taking Sherwood's argument about using peripheral biblical texts (and their afterlife) as a tool to reframe the total biblical picture of divinity and incorporating

---

97 As above. Sherwood makes a similar point in the closing section of *A Biblical Text and Its Afterlives*, where she argues (p. 289) 'the only fair presentation of biblical literature is a variegated one'.

98 For an overview of this tendency, see Hugh S. Pyper: 'Modern Gospels of Judas', in *Literature & Theology*, Vol. 15, 2001, pp. 111–22.

99 For a discussion of anti-semitic aspects (or readings) of the Passion story, see Gerd Lüdemann: *The Unholy in Scripture* Trans. John Bowden (London: SCM Press, 1996).

100 For a survey of Christian anti-semitism during and after the Middle Ages, see Heiko A. Oberman: *The Roots of Anti-Semitism in the Age of the Renaissance and Reformation* (Philadelphia: Fortess Press, 1984).

the problematizing of a 'central' biblical text which Warner or Norris, for example, offer us, in their particular versions of reception-history, may point towards a theology which is both more adventurous and more tentative than that which has traditionally propelled orthodoxy. But it would have the important strength of avoiding imposing pre-packaged or domesticating religious themes on the text and instead allowing, perhaps, more disturbing theologies to emerge, in line with the Fifth Option outlined above. Instead of reception-history being the history of the blunting of the text, it could be seen as the liberator of the text. Whilst within the whole field we may find plenty of individual cases of what we might consider 'blunting' (Quinones's study would suggest *The Caine Mutiny* as a prime example), the weight of the material would point towards 'revelation' rather than to blunting. The purpose of our next chapter will be to examine the extent of the strong material, termed for convenience the *Vox Dei.*

Chapter 5

VOX DEI

The purpose of this chapter will be to examine a dozen or more of the key literary and artistic works which underpin the fourteen reception-histories, in order to examine the concept of a *Vox Dei*, whether presented in a literal or an ironic mode, or in a voice which simply represents strangeness. Most of these works are discussed by the writers of our fourteen reception-histories. But some are examples which we have chosen because of the light they throw on one or more of the fourteen subjects, in spite of not being mentioned by our authors, whether because the example postdates publication of the respective reception-history or is excluded for some other reason.

In order of discussion, the works are: David Maine: *The Flood*; Milton: *Paradise Lost*; Willa Cather: *The Professor's House*; Ernest Hemingway: *The Garden of Eden*; Byron: *Cain, A Mystery*; Unamuno: *El Otro*; Kazantzakis. *The Last Temptation*; D.H. Lawrence: *The Man Who Died*; Michel Tournier: *Gemini*; Joseph Roth: *Job*; Michel Tournier: *The Four Wise Men*; and Bulgakov: *The Master and Margarita*.

David Maine: *The Flood*

David Maine's recent novel *The Flood*,[1] although obviously not discussed in Cohn,[2] will be a useful starting-point, since it is an example of a literary text which deals directly with the issue of the *Vox Dei* and also, incidentally, reminds us of

---

1   David Maine: *The Flood* (Edinburgh: Canongate, 2004).
2   Norman Cohn's *Noah's Flood, The Genesis Story in Western Thought* was published in 1996, eight years before Maine's novel.

the central area which Cohn's study ignores, namely the history of the imaginative treatment of a biblical text.

The Flood is a very entertaining and indeed convincing rendition of the Noah story, offering the picture of a primitive, post hunter-gatherer society, situated somewhere in the Nile Delta just a thousand years after the Creation. The six-hundred year-old Noe is a brutal patriarch, given to visions and to hearing the divine voice in the words of the biblical text. There are sympathetic portraits of his sons and particularly their long-suffering wives, and of Mrs Noe herself, the most long-suffering of all. Once Noe has received the command to build the Ark, the extensive preparations are met with a series of uncanny events, 'miracles', which confirm the divine purpose, such as the wind which suddenly facilitates Beria's voyage to collect rare animals and the long-lost daughter scene which forms her reception by dying head-man, Pra, and also the very diverting solar-eclipse episode. Much of the central part of the narrative is taken up with the arduous conditions aboard the Ark, once the Flood arrives, but this is only the prelude to the episode of the vindication of Noe's mission when the Flood finally recedes.

At the beginning, the location of the divine voice is established as 'not so much outside his (Noe's) head as inside'[3] but it is no less persuasive for that and, of course, it is backed up massively by events. The final instance of the voice is when it congratulates Noe after the safe arrival of the Ark's passengers on dry land and gives the final command for Noe's sons and wives to 'go forth into the world, each in a different direction, and multiply, and so refill the land'.[4] When the divine voice concludes with 'Hear then this My promise. Nevermore shall I send forth a flood to destroy the earth. Never shall I curse mankind and his works. He is prone to evil in his very nature, but I shall not destroy him again', we are told that Noe 'gropes for an appropriate response' and comes up with 'Thank you'. After this, Noe receives no

---

3   Maine, ibid., p. 6.
4   Ibid., pp. 185–6.

further auditions, 'the Lord's silence is universal',[5] and his wife, just before she dies, welcomes him back to the human race, 'Now you're just like the rest of us'.[6]

At the end, Mirn, wife of Jeptha, speculates on whether 'God reigns' or 'God rains' is the best way to tell the story of the Flood,[7] but the overall drift of the narrative is to emphasise the utter rareness and oddity of encounter with the divine voice, which becomes the *absent* voice of God perhaps in western culture. Maine refuses to demystify the Genesis story (as one reviewer notes[8]) but, at the same time, produces a sort of matter-of-factness which again is the equivalent of the plain prose of the original, though with the difference that huge amounts of novelistic detail are included both in terms of circumstantial detail (the problems over the supply of bitumen; the realities of keeping wild animals in a wooden ship) and in terms of the emotions of the different characters, including the mix of stoicism and hope which we find amongst them. The extraordinary *Vox Dei* is set in counterpoint to the lives of the human protagonists who, except for Noe, never hear it. They simply experience the physical events of the Flood which, we are reminded, has the capacity to become the story to end all stories. The novelist makes no effort to moralise the story in relation to current ecological warnings. We are presented instead with the Flood story speaking for itself and, at the heart of it all, the divine voice speaking for *Itself*, albeit in a very private way.

Milton: *Paradise Lost*

Returning now to Milton's *Paradise Lost*, the work so central to Pamela Norris's account of *The Story of Eve* and obviously to the whole history of the literary

---

5   Ibid., p. 250.
6   Ibid., p. 252. These words might equally apply to the Cain of David Maine's most recent novel *Fallen*.
7   Ibid., pp. 258–9.
8   Josh Lacey, review in *The Guardian*, 9th October 2004.

148

appropriation of biblical texts, we find a *Vox Dei* which dominates the discourse as much as it dominates the action. In fact, direct speech constitutes a very large part of the whole epic, even though much of it is language *about* Heaven and Hell rather than the actual voice of God.[9] Significantly, the dominant non-human speaker in Books I and II is actually Satan, whose reality is as convincing as that of God. God's own debut as a direct speaker is in Book III, where he is the author of a theodicy whose main characteristic is the rebuttal of Predestination. Later, Satan notoriously gives the Serpent a voice, setting up the drama of the Temptation in the Garden and much of the rest of the poem consists of pro-divine speeches made not directly by God but by Raphael and Michael and other angelic figures. God himself becomes, as a result of the Fall, less available as a voice heard on earth, but he continues to manifest himself in dreams (Book XII, 610–612). Meanwhile, Adam and Eve journey out of Eden, guided by Providence rather than a direct divine communication. In *Paradise Lost* divine speech is the basis of reality even if, for reasons of divine sovereignty, it tends to be remote from the human scene. Meanwhile, the Muses which guide Milton himself are the same Muses which inspired the Hebrew Scriptures:

> Sing, heavenly Muse, that on the secret top
> Of Oreb, or of Sinai, did inspire
> That shepherd, who first taught the chosen seed,
> In the beginning how the heavens and earth
> Rose out of chaos.[10]

---

9   We should note Harold Bloom's assertion, 'The true God of *Paradise Lost* is the narrator, rather than the Urizenic schoolmaster of souls scolding away on the throne or the Holy Spirit invoked by the Arian Milton ... ' See Harold Bloom: *Ruin the Sacred Truths* (Cambridge Mass: Harvard University Press, 1989), p. 92.

10 *Paradise Lost* I, 6–10, quoted in Regina Schwarz: 'Milton on the Bible' in Thomas N.Corns (ed.): *A Companion to Milton* (Oxford: Blackwell, 2001/2003), p. 46. It is clear that Dante held a similarly strong view of his own work as the outpouring of the Holy Spirit. See Peter S. Hawkins: 'Dante and the Bible' in Rachel Jacoff (ed.): *The Cambridge Companion to Dante* (Cambridge: Cambridge University Press, 1993), pp. 120–35. 'Standing in the line of biblical authorities, and receiving from them the Spirit's inspiration, he proposes himself as a vessel of election. It is as if a third testament will flow from his pen.' (Ibid., p. 132.) The Gawain

If Milton seems narrowly 'religious' to some modern readers, we need to observe his (in musical terms) Mahlerian approach to reality in the shape of the pagan gods and the way in which he daringly borrows from the Prologue to Job to reconstruct the story of the Fall, at the same time giving Satan all the best speeches, as is often remarked. Milton's God is ultimately a rational Being, coping with human irrationality as well as human waywardness, and his speeches reflect this.

Willa Cather: *The Professor's House* and Ernest Hemingway: *The Garden of Eden*

Two of the examples Pamela Norris in *The Story of Eve* gives of modern retellings of the Eden story are Willa Cather's *The Professor's House*[11] and Ernest Hemingway's *The Garden of Eden*.[12] Both novels, in their different ways, involve the interruption of the narrative by a primitive voice from the past. In *The Professor's House*, it is the flashback to the journey of the Professor's friend, Tom Outland, into a remote part of New Mexico where he and his companions discover an ancient Mesan hill-top civilisation. The mummified remains of the Mother Eve whom they disinter becomes the voice of a repressed matriarchal religion with which the Professor himself has been struggling, both professionally and domestically, all his working life.

In narratological terms, the flashback constitutes an 'embedded narrative'. It is a device which can be used to provide a perspective on the total narrative into which it is inserted and, in the hands of Cather, it fits into a pattern of quarried mythological stories which seem to offer meaning and resonance to 'present events'.

---

poet reveals similar tendencies in *Patience*, as discussed by Sandra Pierson Prior: *The Fayre Formez of the Pearl Poet* (East Lansing, Michigan: Michigan State University Press, 1996), pp. 155–7.

11   Willa Cather: *The Professor's House* (New York: Vintage, 1990).

12   Ernest Hemingway:*The Garden of Eden* (New York: Scribner, 2003).

In *The Garden of Eden*, Hemingway's final novel, there is also a flashback. Here it takes the form of the account which the writer-protagonist, David Bourne, has written of a childhood experience in Africa in which his father had brutally and ruthlessly hunted two elephants to destruction, for the sake of their tusks. He writes the story at intervals in the latter half of the novel, where it is interspersed with the love triangle of the surface narrative and also the contents of David's dreams. David's guilt for his own part in betraying the wounded bull elephant and his horror at the pulp to which his father reduces the animal's face and eyes means that the elephant replaces his father as his hero. The inner story is counterpoised against the decadence of the sophisticated, leisurely life in the South of France which forms the content of the rest of the novel and is like a trumpet call from the Paradisal Eden, whilst at the same time pinpointing the moment of the writer's own childhood Fall.

Although the two novels share the technique of the flashback to a primeval past, it is that by Cather which offers the bleakest diagnosis of the human condition, with the remains of the murdered Mother Eve an insistent reminder of the brutal realities of the human sexual drive.[13] The wound in her side can be read, as Norris notes,[14] as a sort of parody of the wound in Adam's side resulting from God's removal of the rib to create the first woman. Norris does not make the point, since she does not treat the two novels in tandem; but, considered as intertexts, Hemingway's *The Garden of Eden* and Cather's *The Professor's House* respectively offer escape to a paradisal past and the refusal of such an escape, two very different voices. In terms of our definition of the Vox Dei as the inruption of the voice of strangeness, both of these examples seem to qualify, in that in both cases a naturalistic contemporary narrative is interrupted by a flashback to a past sequence of events which evokes a

---

13 In her biography of Willa Cather – *Willa Cather, A Life Saved Up* (London: Virago, 1997) – Hermione Lee treats the flashback as symptomatic of a major fissure in the life of the main character and remarks of the fall of the mummified Mother Eve into the canyon: 'Cather leaves us to make what we like of this, but strongly suggests the inescapable nature of 'cruel biological necessities'. (Ibid., p. 249.)

14 Norris, ibid., pp. 378–9.

vision of the primordial. In the case of the Hemingway novel, the vision posits an original state of blessedness before its corruption by human action. In the case of the Cather novel, the vision is a sort of horror from which the present must recoil. Either way, the vision is a normative one.

Byron: *Cain*

In Byron's *Cain*, in many ways the key text in the Quinones survey, there is no direct divine voice, but the Angel mouths the exact biblical words of the Genesis *Vox Dei*: 'Where is thy brother, Abel ...?'[15] The chief dialectical value of Byron's drama, in terms of this chapter's concerns, is the meeting between the biblical text and the Romantic revolt. In a sense it is mainly through appropriations of Byron's work, particularly by Unamuno, that this dialectic comes to fruition.

Unamuno: *El Otro*

Unamuno, in *El Otro*,[16] provides a gloss on Byron, making the voice of The Other the voice both of God and of the murder-victim, Abel, who recognizes the close identity of murderer and murdered. The ambiguous character, The Other, declares, 'God is also the Other ... the Other in Heaven who has brought on this confusion!' The play revolves around uncertainty over whether the character, The Other, is Cain or Abel (Cosmo or Damian) and which of the two is the corpse in the basement, until the surviving twin commits suicide. It is the character, The Other, who is also the mouthpiece of the biblical God's question, 'Where is Abel thy brother. What have you done with him?' Finally, the mystery remains in place (Unamuno was himself fascinated by the details of Byron's drama, including the

---

15   Byron: *Cain, a Mystery*, Act III, Scene I, Line 466.
16   Miguel de Unamuno: *El Otro* in *Ficciones* (Princeton: Princeton University Press, 1976).

title, *Cain, A Mystery*) and we are assured in the Epilogue that this is connected with the mystery of fatality:

> The mystery? Mystery is fatality ... Destiny. And why clarify it? Could we live at all if we knew our destiny, our future, the exact day of our death? Can a man with a summons from death really live? Close your eyes to the mystery! It's the uncertainty of our supreme hour which allows us to live at all, and it is the secret of our destiny, of our true personality, which allows us to dream ...Let us dream, then, and not seek a solution to the dream. Let us dream *la forza del destino, la fuerzo de sino* ...[17]

Kazantzakis: *The Last Temptation*

Kazantzakis, in *The Last Temptation*,[18] uses dream sequences to handle supernatural events, including the quasi-supernatural visit of the Magi to the manger and, most central to the plot of this novel, the devil-temptation episode in which Christ dreams on the Cross of a alternative erotic life with Mary Magdalene and then with Martha and Mary. Theodore Ziolkowski links Kazantzakis's vision of the amatory temptation of Christ with an episode in the writer's own history, which was resolved through the intervention of a Viennese psychiatrist.[19]

D.H. Lawrence: *The Man Who Died*

D.H. Lawrence, in *The Man Who Died*,[20] went further than Kazantzakis in making Christ abandon the ascetic life for one of sexual fulfilment, though only after

---

17 Unamuno, ibid., pp. 295–6.

18 Nikos Kazantzakis: *The Last Temptation* (London: Faber & Faber, 1975). Both this work and the D.H. Lawrence short story mentioned below feature in Haskins's *Mary Magdalene*.

19 Theodore Ziolkowski: *Fictional Transfigurations of Jesus* (Princeton: Princeton University Press, 1971), p. 127.

20 D.H. Lawrence: 'The Man Who Died' in *Love Among the Haystacks and Other Stories* (London: Penguin, 1960).

crucifixion. In Lawrence's short story, the Christ-figure narrowly escapes death before being taken down from the Cross ('They took me down too soon. So I have risen up.'[21]). The appearances to Mary Magdalene and the other disciples, including the meeting on the Road to Emmaus, are in fact encounters with a man recovering from just avoiding death, a man disillusioned with trying to shape the lives of others and now bent on finding another way. The words to Mary Magdalene become a *leitmotif*, 'Noli me tangere',[22] as he modulates from being a messiah to a discovery of pure aloneness, 'which is one sort of immortality'.[23] Eventually, he becomes the lost Osiris for the female guardian of the Temple of Isis, before sailing off into the sunset to avoid recapture by the Romans and final crucifixion. 'For here on the bay the little life of jealousy and property was resuming sway again, as the suns of passionate fecundity relaxed their sway.'[24]

The Man Who Died represents a deviant version of the Passion story, which attracted considerable hostility in Christian circles at the time of its first publication. Surprisingly, despite the main character's approval of Judas ('I know I wronged Judas ... '[25]), the story goes unmentioned in Paffenroth, though it does feature in Haskins as a stage in the modern development of the character of Mary Magdalene. We may agree with Haskins[26] that, in christological terms, Lawrence's work is part of a wider discussion about the full humanity of Christ. As a piece of rewritten scripture, it is remarkable for its erotic use of gospel images (for example, the tethered cock which is central to the first half of the story) and for the way in which it goes beyond Kazantzakis's *The Last Temptation*, though it preceded that novel by a quarter of a century. Treating the two works as intertexts, *The Last Temptation*

---

21 Ibid., p. 130.
22 Ibid., pp. 135, 155, 157.
23 Ibid., p. 142.
24 Ibid., p. 171.
25 Ibid., p. 136.
26 Haskins, op cit, pp. 372–3.

154

could be read as the orthodox rejoinder to *The Man Who Died*, whether or not the author had read Lawrence. This would make conservative Christian rejection of the Kazantzakis work (largely as filtered through Scorsese's film) more illiberal than it has seemed.[27]

Scorsese's film[28] emphasises the contest between the competing voices experienced by Jesus, those of God and Satan. The Temptation in the Wilderness in a sense becomes the matrix for the whole film, though it is only there and in the angel-scene during the Crucifixion that the voices are directly represented. William Telford has observed that in the contemporary period, Scorsese is the only film director to tackle head-on the problem of depicting Christ's divinity, 'offering us a Jesus genuinely struggling between the two sides of his nature, the human and the divine, the flesh and the spirit. It is no wonder then this brave endeavor has excited such controversy'.[29]

Michel Tournier: *Gemini*

Michel Tournier has no *Vox Dei*, but the authorial viewpoint, a stage on from the Victorian omniscient narrator, is capable of spanning a panoramic segment of recent history and, at the same time, offering the persistent authorial theme of twinship. In *Gemini*,[30] the struggles of the identical twins, Paul and Jean, with the tension between the quest for individuation and the satisfying completeness of twinned communion, takes place against the background of the internecine strife of the Second World

---

27 '*The Last Temptation of Christ* ... condemned for blasphemy by evangelical Christians for its sensual portrayal of Jesus.' Jon Lewis: *The New American Cinema* (Durham and London: Duke University Press, 1998), p. 27.

28 *The Last Temptation of Christ* (Universal Pictures, 1988).

29 William R. Telford: *The Depiction of Jesus in the Cinema* in Clive Marsh and Gaye Ortiz (eds): *Explorations in Theology and Film* (Oxford: Blackwell, 1997), p. 130.

30 Michel Tournier: *Gemini* trans.Anne Carter (London: Minerva, 1989). Discussed by Quinones in *The Changes of Cain*, pp. 232–7.

War, the tragic quest of their homosexual uncle, Alexandre, for brotherhood, and the dysfunctional marriage of their parents, Edouard and Maria-Barbara, leading to the latter's arrest as a leader of the Resistance. The tragic plight of the children from St Brigitte's, near the beginning of the novel, signals the disorder which is to come as the innocents are swept to sea in a small boat. The detailed meteorology of that passage is echoed by the novel's closing section, where we part from north-eastern France in a weather-system sweeping over the region.

However, the heroic effort of Paul in helping escapees through a tunnel under the Berlin Wall, costing him his left arm and leg, finally overcomes the Cain and Abel myth which has propelled the rest of the novel.

If the omniscient narrator has no trouble in spanning wartime Brittany and Paris, and then post-war Casablanca, Venice, Iceland, Japan, Canada, Tunisia and Berlin, and arriving and departing with the weather-system,[31] it is the inner forces of the Cain and Abel story which count for most in determining the course of the characters' lives. Paul's act of heroism finally vindicates the Genesis banishment of Cain, in that altruism triumphs finally over violence. Having said this, it has to be observed that the novel as a whole is overloaded, by a complex marriage of the millennial ideas of Joachim of Fiore, postmodernist philosophy, the Christology of Eastern Orthodoxy, and the author's characteristic predilection for scatology as a foil for his interest in the dualities of the settled and the nomadic life.[32] It was in recognition of this overloading[33] that Tournier reverted to a much simpler narrative form in his next novel, *The Four Wise Men,* which we will examine a little further on.

---

31 In his autobiography, Tournier discusses Jules Verne's *Around the World in Eighty Days* as one of the intertexts for *Gemini,* centred around 'the triumph of chronology over meteorology'. See Michel Tournier: *The Wind Spirit, an Autobiography* trans. Arthur Goldhammer (London: Collins, 1989), pp. 225–8.

32 See Susan Petit: *Michel Tournier's Metaphysical Fictions* (Amsterdam, Philadelphia: John Benjamins Publishing Co, 1991), pp. 47–73. Also Colin Davis: *Michel Tournier, Philosophy and Fiction* (Oxford: Clarendon Press, 1988), pp. 64–115.

33 See Petit, Ibid., p. 123.

James Joyce: *Ulysses*

James Joyce in *Ulysses* treats assorted biblical material as though it were secular literature denying, apparently, the transcendental referent of the text in its setting. Yet, if Alter's reading is accepted,[34] the effect of the inclusion of biblical material is to offer a 'horizon of redemption'[35] through the life of Leopold Bloom, a latter-day 'light to the Gentiles'.[36] In terms of this chapter, we could say that the *Vox Dei* is almost lost in a welter of other voices, including the Homeric voice of the frame-narrative. It is certainly subjected to Joyce's ironising and mocking decontextualisation of all source material. But at the same time, since parody is a form of respect-paying, the divine voice remains in place, off-stage, as it were. In his final major work, *Finnegan's Wake*,[37] Joyce took the unscrambling of the familiar landmarks of western discourse still further.

Joseph Roth: *Job*

Joseph Roth's *Job*[38] has, as its *Vox Dei*, the long-delayed miracle of the healing of the son of Mendel and Deborah Singer. The Russian Jew's life of doggedly persistent prayer and poverty is finally lifted by the family's opportunity to emigrate to America, when their son Shemeriah (now 'Sam') makes good in New York as a businessman. But the journey involves leaving the invalid child, Menuchim, behind. Menuchim is the catatonic son whom nothing seemingly can cure. But Deborah's earlier visit to the renowned miracle-working Rabbi of Kluczysk has secured the promise that one day Menuchim will be miraculously cured and that she is on no

---

34 Robert Alter: *Canon and Creativity* (New Haven: Yale University Press, 2000), pp. 151–83.
35 Ibid., p. 182.
36 Quoted in Ibid., p. 174.
37 Discussed in Quinones, pp. 217–26.
38 Joseph Roth: *Job, the Story of a Simple Man* (London: Granta, 2000).

account to abandon the child. Despite Deborah's angst at leaving Menuchim behind, the family go ahead with their plans to emigrate, which are reinforced by the need to separate their daughter Miriam from her liaisons with local Cossack soldiers.

Settling in New York, the fortunes of the Singer family keep rising until, just at the point where it seems it will be possible to send for Menuchim, war breaks out in Europe. The family assume that their other son, Jonas, has died, serving in the Russian army. Sam enlists as an officer in the US army and then the news comes of his death, which is followed by Deborah's own death. Mendel's psalm-singing seems increasingly futile and he comes to wish, in a phrase which anticipates the Holocaust so dreadfully, that he could 'burn God'.[39] Finally, the arrival of a brilliant Jewish musician in New York attracts the attention of Mendel Singer and there is a denouement in which 'Alexis Kossak' turns out to be none other than Menuchim. There is then news that Jonas may, in fact, still be alive, serving in the White Guard, and Miriam, who by now is in a mental hospital, may be cured.

The narrative is punctuated by thoughts about Menuchim and about whether God still performs miracles on earth, all of which is in a sort of counterpoint to the traditional Jewish prayers and observances of Mendel Singer. The allusions to the story of Job are most overt in the episode of his 'comforting' which comes shortly before the arrival of Menuchim in New York. God himself remains doggedly unresponsive until the final turning-point when he 'speaks' through the unveiled miracle and the other improved news for this modern Job.[40]

Joseph Roth is often regarded as the elegist for the lost world of Eastern European Jewry, but he can also be seen as the prophet of the theology of endurance which Martin Buber came to represent in his post-Holocaust writings. This *Vox Dei* is deeply buried in the processes of history and in the shifting conditions faced by

39   Ibid., p. 166.
40   For a rewritten version of Job which challenges the happy ending of the urtext, one should turn to Muriel Spark's *The Only Problem*, discussed in my article, 'Latecomers: Four Novelists Rewrite the Bible' in *Biblical Interpretation*, Vol. XV, No. 4–5, 2007.

his Chosen People. If America at first seems to the Singer family to be the Promised Land, its values are quite alien to the spirituality on which they have been reared, and the miracle itself has to occur back in Russia, the country which represents suffering rather than plenty. Significantly, when the novel was made into a Hollywood film, the religion of the main protagonist became a Roman Catholic.[41]

It is surely no coincidence that Martin Buber's thoughts about *Bewährung*, in his essay on Biblical Humanism and elsewhere, were being forged in Germany at much the same time as Roth was writing his novel. Just as Buber taught about *Bewährung* ('a proving true through life of God's living presence. Not works or faith, then – but justification through a faithful realization of the divine truth of the hour. This is Martin Buber's third alternative.'[42]), so Roth wrote about Mendel, a Job-figure, whose life as a Jew was stronger than either his works or his faith.

Michel Tournier: *The Four Wise Men*
and Mikael Bulgakov's: *The Master and Margarita*

Our final two novels are rewritings, one slightly oblique and the other very oblique, of New Testament stories relevant to our fourteen reception-histories. These are Michel Tournier's *The Four Wise Men* and Mikael Bulgakov's *The Master and Margarita*.

The Four Wise Men[43] is not mentioned in Trexler but is mentioned, though only very briefly discussed, in David Brown's *Tradition and Imagination*.[44] It must,

---

41 See Michael Hofmann's Introduction to Joseph Roth: *The Radetsky March* (London: Granta, 2003), p. vi.

42 See Michael Fishbane: 'Justification through Living – Martin Buber's third alternative' in William G. Dever and J. Edward Wright: *The Echoes of Many Texts, Reflections on Jewish and Christian Traditions* (Atlanta: Scholars Press, 1997), p. 226.

43 Michel Tournier: *The Four Wise Men* trans. Ralph Manheim (Baltimore: John Hopkins University Press, 1997).

44 David Brown: *Tradition and Imagination* (Oxford: Oxford University Press, 2004), p. 92, where the author commends Tournier's novel as a 'particularly powerful version of this tale,'

nevertheless, be considered a major example of a literary appropriation of the story of the Magi. Tournier develops the background to the convergence of the Three Kings on Jerusalem and then Bethelehem. A Fourth King, a latecomer, is too late to visit the infant Jesus but does witness the Massacre of the Innocents and, after a long spell of imprisonment in a salt mine (thirty-three years), becomes the first recipient of the Eucharist by arriving too late for the Last Supper.

Tournier gives convincing portraits of the Four. There is Gaspar ('I am black but a king',[45] echoing the Vulgate text used of Sheba), who is liberated from his obsession with a white slave-girl through the discovery that the Infant Jesus is in fact a black baby with white parents. There is the aesthete, Balthasar, who discovers in the Child the reunification of 'image and likeness' which were sundered at the Fall.[46] There is Melchior, the poor and dispossessed king, who is on a journey of discovery about power.

After an elaborate account of the life and times of Herod the Great,[47] whose guests the Three Kings become, we are given a glimpse of the stable at Bethlehem, mainly from the point of view of the ass,[48] before the narrative shifts to the story of Taor, Prince of Mangalore,[49] the spoilt would-be regent whose life is driven by a futile quest for the source of Turkish Delight and whose expedition of men and elephants ends in spectacular disaster beside the Dead Sea.

The genius of the novel is to dramatise the individual spiritual journeys of *The Four Wise Men*, who only actually become *wise* through their encounter with Christ. At the same time, the wealth of 'occidental' detail, from the court life of Gaspar to the necrophore trees encountered by Taor, provides an exotic background to what

---

referring to the tradition of the four kings.

45 Tournier, ibid., p. 3.
46 Ibid., pp. 70–71.
47 Ibid., pp. 79–96 and 111–38.
48 Ibid., pp. 143–58.
49 Ibid., pp. 161–249.

160

in the Gospel of Matthew is an exotic intrusion in the narrative. The episode in which Taor feeds the children of Bethlehem with exotic sweetmeats whilst their brothers are being massacred is an example of the acerbic edge to what might otherwise at times seem a sentimental tale.[50] When the angel Gabriel explains to the Ass that animal sacrifice is being replaced by the sacrifice of God's son, the background is a discussion which puts Yahweh in the wrong from the time of Cain and Abel until the birth at Bethlehem. The lengthy account of life in and around the salt-mines of Sodom, where an unreconstructed population still revere Lot's wife provides the foil for the self-sacrifice of Taor, whose imprisonment results from an impulse to rescue a man about to receive a lengthy prison sentence as a debtor. Similarly, the vivid depiction of the malignity of Herod and the corruption inherent in power politics acts as foil for the spiritual journey of the Magi.

First published in French in 1980, with the English translation appearing in 1982, Tournier's *The Four Wise Men*, along with *Gemini*, demonstrates the possibility of the production of a robust novelistic and, at least ostensibly, pro-orthodox retelling of a biblical story within the consciously postmodern period of the literary reception-histories with which we are concerned in this book. When the author, no doubt for publicity reasons, asked that his new novel be given the *imprimatur* by the Roman Catholic Church, the refusal was explained in terms of the cessation of that practice.[51] If it had been awarded, there would surely have been a considerable stir, since *The Four Wise Men* is a resolutely postcolonial text, placing the Black King at the forefront of the narrative and presenting a black Christ-child. Significantly, the 'Postscript' consists mainly of a direct reprinting of the AV text of Matthew 2, verses 1–16. Parody and magical realism are clearly not the only alternatives to literalistic retelling.

---

50 The Massacre of the Innocents is foregrounded even more sharply in José Saramago's *The Gospel According to Jesus Christ*. See my article: 'Against the Grain and with the Grain' in *Theology*, November/December 2008.

51 See Petit, ibid., p. 124, for Tournier's application to the Bishop of Versailles.

Finally, we return to Bulgakov's *The Master and Margarita*,[52] this time examined in its own right rather than as a rather shadowy presence in Wroe. (We will recall that Wroe treated Bulgakov's novel as just one ingredient in an assortment of literary and folkloric responses to the gospel 'story of an invented man', a kind of ragbag from which she might have assembled her own putative novel if she had not decided, instead, to trace her account of the reception-history of *Pilate*.)

If we consider *The Master and Margarita* in the context of Russian writing of the period, it is clearly part of a rare and undervalued literary strand set against the monotonous conformity of so much of the 'officially approved' fiction of the early Soviet era. In the words of Martin Amis, 'Bely's *Petersburg*, Bulgakov's *The Master and Margarita* and Zamyatin's *We* – exalted, fizzing with humour and licence – are the flagships of a vanished literature'.[53]

From our point of view in this study, Bulgakov's novel hinges on the cultural weightiness of the story of Pontius Pilate. Without the project contained within the novel of writing a novel about Pilate, the whole fantastic and satirical edifice of demonic and supernatural interventions in 1930's Moscow would be pointless.But the relationship of these events to the writing of a novel about Pilate is anything but straightforward, leading to the question posed by at least one critic as to whether the novel about Pilate and *The Master and Margarita* are coterminous.

Certainly, both the 'internal novel' and the 'external novel' are concerned with the question posed by Pilate in John 18:38, 'What is truth?', even though these words are not quoted in the text itself. The Pilate of the internal novel seems, in an after-life setting, to be in an obsessive state of denial about the Crucixion: 'The execution, of course, had been a pure misunderstanding: after all, this same man,

---

52 Mikhail Bulgakov: *The Master and Margarita* trans. Michael Glenny (London: Vintage, 2004).

53 Martin Amis: *The War on Cliché, Essays and Reviews 1971–2000* (London: Jonathan Cape, 2001), p. 395.

with his ridiculous philosophy that all men were good, was walking beside him – consequently he was alive. There had been no execution! It had never taken place! This thought comforted him as he strode along the moonlight pathway'.[54]

As part of a satire on Stalin's Russia, the possibility of rewriting history to conform with ideology is obviously highly suggestive. The fragile but resilient state of the internal novel, which is burned to ashes and yet somehow survives, is set against the iron certainty of life in a régime where rent books can be falsified to obliterate the identity of people: 'Koroviev threw the case-history into the fire. "Remove the document and you remove the man", said Koroviev with satisfaction'.[55]

Right from the start of the novel, human identities are subject to degrees of uncertainty. The Master himself, the author of the novel about Pilate, is presented as the poet Ivan Nikolayich Poniryov, but writing under the pseudonym of Bezdomny. The novel's commissioning editor, Berlioz, soon to be decapitated under a tram wheel, is concerned 'to prove to the poet that the main object was not who Jesus was, whether he was good or bad, but that as a person Jesus had never existed at all and that all stories about him were mere invention, pure myth'.[56] Jesus himself is referred to within the quoted section of the internal novel variously as Ha Nostri and Yashua, as though to point to some documentary reality beneath the commonplace name.

Both the Master and Berlioz are part of a writers' syndicate which, with the exception of the internal novel about Pilate, seems to be sterile in its effects and largely preoccupied with the provision of fringe-benefits for its members. The novel's heroine, Margarita, escapes a lifeless marriage to become the Master's lover and the champion of the novel-writing project, but she only achieves this at

---

54   Bulgakov, ibid., p. 361.
55   Ibid., p. 329.
56   Ibid., p. 15.

the expense of a Faustian pact with Woland, the Satan-figure, whose techniques are those of the régime which the external novel satirises, with his ability to make persons and objects magically appear and disappear.

Woland, in a pivotal scene in the external novel,[57] makes his début as a performing magician with his extraordinary assistants in a Moscow theatre. He literally mesmerises the audience, granting them wish-fulfilment in the form of bank-notes and *haute-couture* fashion, only for them to be cruelly disappointed when the money turns to blank pieces of paper and the Muscovite women find themselves in a state of public *déshabillé*.

The transcendental reference of *The Master and Margarita* emerges both from the ironic and satirical light which it casts upon early Soviet society and from the mysterious indestructibility of the internal novel. The ironising of what was, after all, the most hideously successful totalitarian regime of history, revealing it as a conjuring trick of mass hypnosis, was an act of authorial courage and a testimony to the strength of an alternative world-view. This other world-view can be identified not only as everything which the oppressive world of Moscow in the 1930s was not (freedom of expression, unrestricted travel, the availability of desirable clothing and a solid currency; the recognition of the reality of the supernatural), but as the other world of the events which made Pontius Pilate famous.

Finally, as the Master and Margarita themselves set out towards eternity, the work of the novelist at last complete and the author at peace, we are told that Pilate has been redeemed. 'He had been freed, just as he had set free the character he had created. His hero had now vanished irretrievably into the abyss; on the night of Sunday, the day of the Resurrection, pardon had been granted to the astrologer's son, fifth Procurator of Judaea, the cruel Pontius Pilate.'[58] Pilate ultimately is defined not by his own cruelty but by the forgiveness ('Father, forgive

---

57   Ibid., pp. 139–53.
58   Ibid., pp. 431–2.

them, for they know not what they do.') of the character, Yeshua, in the internal novel. The external novel, in its Epilogue, restores us to real-time Moscow. As in Shakespeare's *The Tempest* or *A Midsummer's Night's Dream*, everyday reality reasserts itself, but the springtime full moon is a persistent, though infrequent, reminder of a different reality for Professor Nikolayich Poniryov of the Institute of History and Philosophy.

Strangeness has won a victory over the sameness imposed upon human experience by a political system of unprecedented barbarity and bureaucratic efficiency and the victory has found its locus in the writing of a novel, a piece of rewritten scripture, about the contest between two sorts of power, represented respectively by Pontius Pilate and Yeshua.

If, at times, the field of literary appropriation or rewriting of biblical narratives can seem to verge on a form of aestheticism, *The Master and Margarita* is a powerful example of the reverse. Here we have an experimental novel which is, at the same time, an exploration of literary issues about the relationship between fiction and reality and a theological protest against totalitarianism. In a cultural climate which insisted upon treating the gospel story as fiction ('mere invention'), it took the production of a radically fictional work, a piece of fantastic writing, to relativise the mental world of materialist-realism.

Summary

Milton believed in the continuance of the scriptural Muse through his own work. Taking the main works discussed in this chapter in order of mention, and following Milton's prescription, we could interpret the *Vox Dei* in Maine as silhouetting the biblical voice itself against the imaginative reconstruction of the primitive Noachic world. In Milton it would be the fundamental challenge to hegemonic power-structures which the author's work represents. In Unamuno's *El Otro*, the voice would be the existential and life-enhancing challenge of uncertainty. In Kantzakis's *The Last Temptation*, considered partly as an intertext for Lawrence's *The Man Who Died*, it would be an alternative to the hegemony of the Freudian world-view. In Tournier's two novels, *Gemini* and *The Four Wise Men*, it would be respectively the overcoming of the Cain and Abel myth as a manifesto for bloodshed and the overcoming of colonialism. In Roth's *Job* it would be the call for endurance in the face of the seemingly relentless forces of atrophy. In Bulgakov's *The Master and Margarita* it would be the affirmation of radicalising fiction itself as a possible means of salvation in the face of totalitarianism.

All of the examples we have considered are works of great originality and 'strangeness', in the sense that they re-work the biblical urtext drastically to confront new cultural realities. They have also achieved, in each case, a degree of critical acclaim and recognition which places them somewhere in the canon of major, as opposed to ephemeral, literature. They are evidence that beneath our fourteen reception-histories there lies a literary substratum of significant dimensions. In Chapter 13 we will examine further the relationship of major rewritings of biblical stories to sacred and secular notions of a canon.

Chapter 6

VARIATIONS ON A THEME

The purpose of this chapter will be to examine a selection of the more minor works discussed by our reception-history writers, works which are, mostly, confined to the edges of the literary canon, in order to see whether they shed a distinct light on the by-roads of the imaginative appropriation of biblical stories or what Sherwood in her Jonah study calls the 'Backwater tradition'.[1] As in the Vox Dei Chapter, we will occasionally venture into the area of works not discussed by our fourteen authors, but which are highly relevant to their subject-matter.

Here we will take the works to be considered in biblical thematic order. They are: George Macdonald: *Lilith*; Daphne du Maurier: *Rebecca*; the Wakefield mystery-play, the *Mactacio Abel*; John Steinbeck: *East of Eden*; Wilkie Collins: *Jezebel's Daughter*; Nicholas Moseley: *Judith*; Robert Southwell: *The Death of Our Ladie*; Gloria Naylor: *Bailey's Café*; Wilkie Collins: *The New Magdalene* and also *No Name*; William Rayner: *The Knifeman*; the film: *Jesus Christ Superstar*; Mary Shelley: *The Last* Man; Kafka: *The City Coat of Arms*; and D.H. Lawrence: *Apocalypse*.

George Macdonald: *Lilith* and Daphne du Maurier: *Rebecca*

We begin with two pieces of fiction centred on the Lilith/Eden story, George Macdonald's *Lilith*[2] and Daphne du Maurier's *Rebecca*.[3] Whilst both works sit on the fringes of literary respectability, the Macdonald novel is now little read

---

1   Yvonne Sherwood, op cit, pp. 1–8 and 88–209.
2   George Macdonald: *Lilith* (Grand Rapids: Eerdmans, 2000).
3   Daphne du Maurier: *Rebecca* (London: Virago, 2003).

but famous for its influence on C.S. Lewis,[4] whereas the du Maurier novel has run into many reprintings but is more known for the film adaptation by Alfred Hitchcock[5] than for its literary influence. The English country house seems to be the fundamental reality, apart from Lilith herself, common to these otherwise completely dissimilar books.[6]

Macdonald's *Lilith* was first published in 1890 but went through a series of revisions by its author, with the final 1925 version three times the length of the original. The work is a highly elaborate fantasy, consisting of a series of journeys to the Other World, mostly beginning with the passage (in Lewis Carroll fashion) through the ancient mirror in the attic of the country house belonging to the narrator, Mr Vane.[7] The Other World turns out to be the scene of epic mythological struggles between Good and Evil. It is also both a more real world than the everyday world and, at the same time, a version of the biblical world. In the Other World, we encounter Mr Raven, the deceased librarian of the country house and sexton of the after-life, who is also Adam, with Mrs Raven as Eve.

Lilith herself is the evil leopardess who wreaks havoc in the Other World, terrorising its inhabitants by devouring their children. She is finally defeated by another wild animal, the Cat-Woman, Mara (the other name for Naomi in Ruth 1:20), who is also Mary Magdalene. Mr Vane's contribution is to take the severed hand of Lilith from the mortuary which is also a sort of Purgatory, enabling Lilith herself to

---

4   See C.S. Lewis in Macdonald, ibid., Introduction, pp. v-xii.

5   ABC Motion Pictures Inc, 1940.

6   The place of the English country house in English literature is explored in Richard Gill: *Happy Rural Seat* (New Haven and London: Yale University Press, 1972). Although he does not refer to either George Macdonald or Daphne du Maurier, Gill's general observations on the symbolism of the country house seem relevant: '… In a significant number of works – in, for instance, Ben Jonson's 'To Penshurst' or in *Mansfield Park* – it is obviously much more than a literal setting: it is the chosen emblem of what the author considers humane order and enduring values. This is particularly so in the fiction of the late nineteenth century and twentieth centuries … ' (ibid., p. 7).

7   See Macdonald, ibid., pp. 11, 41, and 251.

be redeemed, and (through the burial of the hand in the Wasteland) to release the curse which has previously held The Little Ones in a permanent state of childhood. Whereas Norris, in *The Story of Eve*, condemns the Macdonald work, along with Rider Haggard's *She*, as an example of the sadistic exploitation of the potential of feminine evil,[8] others have emphasised the sheer power of Macdonald's invention in creating a religious fantasy which boldly insists on making the Other World more real than the earthly one.[9] By turns an adventure story and a mystical meditation on human identity with animals and nature, *Lilith*, even if unfashionable today, is definitely a very serious work and highly original even if in places sentimental, in its thoroughgoing depiction of a self-contained supernatural world. A postmodernist analysis would certainly focus on the prominence of the library[10] and, at one stage, a sort of supernatural book[11] in the narrative, showing us an anti-materialist text which cannot escape its identity as a literary artefact

The feminist critique may be justifiable within its limits, but it cannot be used to invalidate a work which is so optimistic theologically[12] and which, even though its subject-matter is an ancient rabbinic myth generally taken to be misogynist,

---

8   Norris, op cit, pp. 335–6.

9   Prickett points out that central to Macdonald's argument in *Lilith* is the complete inversion of 'life' and 'death.' He quotes the words of Mr Raven in the cemetery scene: 'None of those you see,' he answered, 'are in truth quite dead yet, and some have but just begun to come alive and die. Others had begun to die, that is, come alive, long before they came to us; and when such are indeed dead, that instant they will awake and leave us. Almost every night some arise and go ... This is the couch that has been waiting for you'. See Stephen Prickett: *Victorian Fantasy* (Hassocks, Sussex: Harvester Press, 1979), p. 190.

10   The library is the departure point and terminus for the adventure, see Macdonald, ibid., pp. 5–10, 237 and 251. Mr Raven, the bird, sexton and Adam-figure, is also the librarian, see Macdonald Ibid., pp. 8, 15, 29 and 147.

11   Macdonald, ibid., pp. 37–42 and 147.

12   It should be noted that an alternative reading can be found in Robert Lee Wolff: *The Golden Key, A Study of The Fiction of George Macdonald* (New Haven: Yale University Press, 1961), pp. 326–71. Wolff charts the expansion of the text threefold from the first version of 1890 to the third and final version of 1895, concluding that 'the consolations it professes to offer seem to have lost their meaning for the author himself.' (Ibid., p. 332.) Wolff's views are based on what he calls his 'close reading' of the text, but also on the negative reaction of Macdonald's wife to the work and his contextualisation of the work in Macdonald's years of personal decline.

seems to be driven by something quite different from antipathy to feminism. *Lilith* ultimately is a forceful, if eccentric, assertion of the reality of the transcendent. For one brief moment even Astarte, the pagan goddess of fertility, makes an appearance in a definitely positive role as the panther-messenger of Mara,[13] again fogging the feminist attack on Macdonald's stance.

Rebecca appeared in 1938 and was an instant publishing success. In outline, the plot concerns the romance between the anonymous female narrator and Max De Winter, the wealthy owner of a country house in the West Country called Manderley. The couple meet in Monte Carlo, where the narrator is enduring the role of paid companion to a widow named Mrs Van Hopper. Meeting the glamorous but mysteriously reserved De Winter leads to a whirlwind marriage and the sudden installation of the narrator in the plush setting of Manderley, where there is a gradual unfolding of the fate of the previous Mrs De Winter, the Rebecca of the title, who turns out to have had a promiscuous life-style, ending in a boating tragedy. The drama of the main part of the novel pivots around the obsessive loyalty of the housekeeper, Mrs Danvers, to the dead lady of the house and the secret that Max De Winter himself engineered the drowning of Rebecca. In the novel's dénouement, Max narrowly escapes being discovered as the murderer he is, but only at the cost of a conflagration which consumes Manderley, resulting in the consigning of the newly-married couple to an itinerant life spent in continental hotels.

The novel has numerous biblical references. In general terms, Manderley and its grounds feature as an Eden, from which the couple consisting of the narrator and Max De Winter are eventually exiled.[14] The sense of Rebecca as the quasi-demonic

---

13   Macdonald, ibid., p. 79.
14   See du Maurier, ibid., pp. 1–4 for Manderley as Eden.

former wife of Max[15] evokes the legend of Lilith and there are numerous passages in which Mrs Danvers takes on the characteristics of Satan.[16]

It is possible to read the novel as a downbeat commentary on patriarchal values, with the narrator doomed to follow Rebecca into enslavement (fatally resisted by Rebecca herself finally) to the values of a property-centred male society, ruthless in its determination to secure clear lines of male inheritance.[17] But it is equally possible to read it as the defeat of such values, with Manderley itself destroyed, and the newly-empowered narrator now the dominant partner in a marriage exiled to foreign hotels.[18]

Either way, the author's enigmatic insistence on an anonymous narrator and the novel's repeated indulgence in novelistic speculation by the narrator, who is forever devising melodramatic scenarios,[19] are evidence for the case that *Rebecca* is more than a page-turner.

Norris sees *Rebecca* as a rite of passage for the female narrator,[20] whereby she trades her Edenic innocence for complicity in the plot to cover up Max's guilt, and Max himself forfeits his purchase on Paradise through his efforts to cling to the outworn social pieties of the land-owning classes. This is a reasonable interpretation of the novel but perhaps it underplays the central part which the house Manderley plays in the proceedings. Hitchcock observed that, despite the presence of four major human protagonists in the novel, the dominant figure

15   For example, see ibid., p. 305.
16   Ibid., pp. 223, 224, 240 and 276.
17   See Sally Beauman's Introduction in ibid., p. xiii.
18   The novel really has two openings, the description of Manderley (pp. 1–4) and the episode in the modest hotel restaurant (pp. 5–10) in some unspecified European resort. The latter provides the sense that the anonymous narrator, Maxim's second wife, has prevailed in the reduced circumstances of the post-Manderley era.
19   For examples of the narrator's indulgence in melodrama, see ibid. pp. 98, 100, 168 and 224.
20   Norris, ibid., pp. 384–6.

was really that of the house itself.[21] At one stage, Max complains that Christian preaching underestimates the pull of property ('They don't preach about it in churches. Christ himself said nothing about stones, and bricks, and walls, the love that a man can bear for his plot of earth, his soil, his little kingdom. It does not come into the Christian creed.'[22]).

Certainly, a large proportion of the novel is taken up with a painstaking description of life in the archetypal country house which Manderley is. Max may have forfeited his right to live there and the anonymous narrator, through her complicity after the fact, may share in the condemnation. But we, as readers (male or female) are left with the strong sense that Manderley is where we would like to be and, in that sense, any moralistic lesson about rites of passage or the defeat of petty male tyrants seems to be eclipsed by the vision of the lost mansion. We could therefore argue that the novel *Rebecca* is at least as much a celebration of a (lost) Paradise as a drama of the Fall.

The Wakefield Mystery Play: the *Mactacio Abel*

In our examination of Quinones's *The Changes of Cain*, we remarked on the neglect of the medieval period, relegated by the author to end-notes. Here, we take the opportunity to draw attention to the Saxon poem *Genesis* and to the Wakefield mystery play, the *Mactacio Abel*, generally regarded as a masterpiece of the medieval theatre. Both this play and the other Yorkshire play, that in the York cycle, have been taken to stand out from their counterparts in English and European drama.[23] But it

---

21 Beauman (in du Maurier, Ibid., p. vii) quotes Hitchcock to the effect that *Rebecca* is the story of two women, a man and a house; and of the four the house, Manderley, is the dominant presence.

22 See du Maurier, ibid., p. 306. For Christ himself escaping 'the little world of property and jealousy', see D.H. Lawrence's *The Man Who Died*, as discussed in Chapter 5, p. 160.

23 See Hans-Jürgen Diller: *The Middle English Mystery Play* (Cambridge: Cambridge University Press, 1992), p. 228, or Lynette R. Muir: *The Biblical Drama of Medieval Europe* (Cambridge:

is the Wakefield play which develops the character of Cain as a villain, described by Rosemary Woolf as a 'study in damnation'[24] and by Hans-Jürgen Diller as 'the Wakefield master's great achievement'.[25] It is beyond the scope of this book to speculate on the subterranean influences on the Wakefield play deriving from the work now described as *The Saxon Genesis* (composed some five hundred years earlier [26]), but we are bound to note A.N. Doane's claim that the Cain-Abel story within that text stands out as a 'systematic rewriting of the original',[27] presenting the sense of Cain as a man experiencing damnation from within, and that its genius lies in postponing the divine judgement on the first murderer until the end.[28]

In the play, Cain is portrayed as a bad tither. Evidently an affluent farmer (he has a servant-boy), he resents Abel's suggestion that he should offer as a sacrifice his best produce when his toil has been rewarded only with poor harvests and blighted crops. He responds to Abel's argument that all good things are only on loan from God in his grace with the words:

Lenys he me? As com thrift apon the so!
For he has euer yet beyn my fo;
For had he my freynd beyn,
Othergatys it had been seyn.
When all mens corn was fayre in feld,
Then was myn not worth a neld.

Cambridge University Press, 1995), p. 71.

24 Rosemary Woolf: *The English Mystery Plays* (London: Routledge & Kegan Paul, 1972), p. 128.

25 Diller, ibid., p. 231.

26 The *Saxon Genesis* is thought to have been composed around 900 and the Wakefield *Mactacio Abel* in the 15th century. See A.N. Doane: *The Saxon Genesis* (Madison and London: University of Wisconsin Press, 1991), p. 54 and A.C. Cawley (ed.): *The Wakefield Pageants in the Towneley Cycle* (Manchester: Manchester University Press, 1958), p. 130.

27 Doane, ibid., p. 154.

28 Doane, ibid., p. 158: 'By postponing The judicial sentencing until last, the scene is closed not with Cain's domestic disgruntlement and fate but with the cosmic image of God as Lord and Judge. The impending punishment of Hell that appears to the anxious and guilty Adam is here completely internalized in the psyche of the sinner, while God's words echo in the external proclamation of an already established state of things'.

When I shuld saw, and wanted seyde,
And of corn had full grete neyde,
Then gaf he me none of his;
No more will I gif him of this.
Hardly hold me to blame
Bot if I serue him of the same.[29]

Cain's words in the early stages seem designed to attract the sympathy of the medieval audience but, as his language becomes coarser and more blasphemous, he becomes a more diabolical figure. Finally, he makes his offering, but selects only the worst sheaves, offering them with a prayer that his tithe may go as a figure of his soul. He curses when his offering fails to burn and grows angry at God, 'that hob ouer the wall'.[30] He murders Abel out of resentment of his brother's righteousness. After this, Cain is terrified by the divine curse, but reads God's refusal to allow the murderer himself to be murdered as a royal proclamation of pardon, though he is mocked by his servant. Cain's parting words to the audience underline his state of damnation:

Now fayre well, fellows all, for I must neyds wend,
And to the dwill be thrall, warld withouten end:
Ordand there is my stall, with Sathanas the feynd.[31]

Although in part a comic figure, this Cain must also have struck terror into the hearts of his medieval audience. He was, no doubt, on the mind of Shakespeare's Bolingbroke when he told Exton, the murderer of Richard II, 'With Cain go wander through shades of night, And never show thy head by day or night'.[32] It seems likely that Byron, though he is assumed not to have been acquainted with

---

29 A.C. Cawley (ed.): *The Wakefield Pageants in the Towneley Cycle* (Manchester: Manchester University Press, 1958), p. 4. These are lines 117–129.

30 Ibid., p. 8: line 297.

31 Ibid., p. 13: lines 463–5.

32 William Shakespeare: *Richard II*, Act 5: Scene 6, Line 43.

manuscripts of the mystery plays, was aware of the force of this play, as evidenced by his drama's title, *Cain, A Mystery*.[33]

We move on to a work which Quinones *does* discuss in its original form as a novel, though not in its form as a film.

John Steinbeck: *East of Eden*

Some films expand an originally very thin idea in a piece of literary fiction. Others compress or simplify something much more complex. *East of Eden*[34] seems to be one of those films which enhances the original through compression of what is a very sprawling novel. By reducing the story-line essentially to that of Caleb's journey through rebellion to maturity and that of Aron's doomed idealistic journey into oblivion in the trenches of the First World War, Elia Kazan's 1955 film of the Steinbeck novel faithfully conveys the rejection of biblicist idealism in favour of a hard-bitten realism which is the novel's basic theme. Instead of an expansive saga, we have a fairly straightforward account of sibling rivalry for the affection of Adam, Adam's failed experiment with lettuce-refrigeration, Caleb's twin discovery of his estranged mother and the business opportunities opened up by the war in Europe, the transfer of Abra's affections from Aron to Caleb and, finally, the death-bed scene in which the dying Adam is reconciled to Caleb. Vast sweeps of narrative discourse are dismissed in favour of this simple story, which is punctuated by a small number of vivid and dramatic cinematic images: Caleb and the ice-blocks, the train with the melting vegetables, the fairground episode, and Aron smashing his forehead through a train-window.

---

33 Morton D. Paley: *Apocalypse and Millennium in English Poetry* (Oxford: Oxford University Press, 1999), p. 217: 'Although Byron could have read some of the mystery plays, there is no indication that he did'. He notes the view of Philip W. Martin that Byron read about the Mysteries in two secondary works, Thomas Warton's *History of English Poetry* and Robert Dodsley's *A Select Collection of Old Plays*.

34 Warner Brothers, 1954.

176

In *East of Eden* the biblical Paradise is irrecoverable and the only viable way forward is that of a compromise with the realities of human nature (the brothel-business in Salinas) and the realities of modern commerce, where the future lies literally in Futures rather than in old-fashioned codes of honour or in naïve attempts to avoid the profit-motive. Adam's failed attempt to be a dominant patriarch matches his failure as an altruistic innovator in agriculture. The divided but driven personality of the New Cain figure (Caleb) holds the key to progress in the world which is emerging. Adam's only consolation is to die in his arms.

Wilkie Collins: *Jezebel's Daughter*

The latter-day Jezebel who takes the shape of Madame Fontaine in Wilkie Collins's *Jezebel's Daughter*,[35] published in 1880, is another driven character, borrowed from the pages of the Old Testament. The novel, like *East of Eden*, is a confrontation with modern realities. But, in this case, they are the realities of the success of reformist ideas in improving the care of lunatics and the fact that lunacy nevertheless persists beyond the confines of the asylum. Mrs Wagner, the widow of an asylum-reformer, successfully applies non-restraint techniques to the case of Jack Straw, who becomes her personal servant, but falls victim to the machinations of the cornily-named, poison-dispensing, Madame Fontaine, the scheming mother of the innocent Minna, who plots to install her daughter as the wife of a successful Frankfurt businessman. The obstacle to Madame Fontaine's plans is presented by the business interests of Mrs Wagner, who has a controlling interest in the firm. The means adopted by the villainess is the untraceable poison which her late husband devised, known as Alexander's Wine, which turns out to have an antidote which is not always available when needed. Minna, as the daughter of the title, is herself the antidote to her wicked

---

35   Wilkie Collins: *Jezebel's Daughter* (Doylestown, Pennsylvania: Wildside Press, no date. Original publication, London, 1880).

mother ('It was always in Minna's power to lift her above her own wickedness.'[36]) and we see this worked out through the purity of Minna's behaviour and through her mother's avoidance of the possibility of making Minna the vehicle for the communication of a lie at a critical moment. The novel, in its closing pages (through the medium of the closing pages of the diary of Madame Fontaine, which she meant to destroy), also points out the redeeming feature of Madame Fontaine's avoidance of the convenient opportunity to poison Jack Straw.[37]

Jezebel, in the terms of this novel, is a predominantly unredeemed character but is survived by a daughter who is her opposite. The novel's contribution to the accumulated reception-history of the biblical story of Jezebel is to make the villainess the unwitting executioner of herself and also to convey, through its highly contrived and convoluted plot, the sense that wickedness of this kind is very difficult to bring off. Along the way it throws a sympathetic light on asylum-reform[38] but also makes a gratuitous contribution to anti-semitism or, at the very least, racial stereotyping, in the episode in the ghetto in Frankfurt connected with the jewellery district.[39]

Nicholas Moseley: *Judith*

Nicholas Moseley's novel, *Judith*,[40] appeared a century after *Jezebel's Daughter* and takes us from the Victorian world of the early thriller to the near-contemporary world of magic realism. This postmodernist work, as Stocker points out, sets the

---

36   Ibid., p. 67.
37   Ibid., p. 260.
38   Ibid., p. 22.
39   Ibid., p. 189: 'By twos and threes at a time, the Jews in this quaint quarter of the town clamorously offered to the lady who had come among them. When the individual Israelite to whom she applied saw the pearls, he appeared to take leave of his senses. He screamed; he clapped his hands; he called upon his wife, his children, his sisters, his lodgers, to come and feast their eyes on such a necklace as had never been since Solomon received the Queen of Sheba'.
40   Nicholas Moseley: *Judith* (London: Minerva, 1992, revised from the 1986 edition).

farcical outworking of a Victorian melodrama about Judith and Holofernes into opposition with the pervasive presence in modern society of scripted behaviour driven by inherited stereotypes and myths.[41] It is precisely when the estranged husband-and-wife partnership of actor and actress attempting the roles on stage of Judith and Holofernes allow their true relationship to break through that the play comes alive, albeit as a theatrical disaster.

The rest of the novel comprises a series of dream-like tableaux which take the female narrator (named Judith) through the London drugs scene, then an Ashram in India, and finally a demonstration against the presence of nuclear weapons at an American base in East Anglia. Biblical motifs abound, above all those of Judith and Holofernes, the Tower of Babel and Lilith. 'God' is the name given to the guru in the Ashram, whose gnomic utterances point towards either self-realisation or a typical form of Western escapism, and whose final contribution is to dissolve the Ashram before disembarking for California. If the Ashram is a temporary Eden, then the military camp and war games area becomes another one, with its 'Keep Out' signs and the presence of the façade of the country house once inhabited by Bert's family and the life-size toy village, sinister in its clichéd neatness. In this world in which human beings observe themselves and each other in the performance of stereotyped roles, the police and demonstrators alternate between being actors and audience.

One of the hopes which the novel holds out is that human beings will learn to eat from the Tree of Life (as opposed to the Tree of Knowledge), that neglected aspect of the Garden of Eden story.

> Supposing the American airbase was a place where were stored the fruits of the Tree of Knowledge of good and evil (those missiles like snakes with death in their heads) ... Well, it has often been said often enough, has it not, that there was a prohibition only against eating from the Tree of Knowledge of good and evil; there was no prohibition against eating from the Tree of Life. So human beings, having language, ate the fruit of the Tree of

---

41   Stocker, op cit, p. 241.

knowledge of good and evil. Language is counter-productive; they did not eat of the Tree of Life. But a mutation (like a god) would know this.[42]

Thus a gap in the Genesis story becomes the resource for an escape from scripted behaviour.

The novel's comic sense of God as a sort of wild card surfaces repeatedly. It is there in the destruction of the romantic earnestness of the Judith and Holofernes play at the outset. We are told that the playwright told the story 'without bringing in much about God; sexual passion had taken God's place'. In the new performance we find that 'romantic passion was as much out of favour as ideas about God's will'[43] and it is the spontaneous but, unfortunately, unrepeatable prat-falls of the two thespians which enliven the production, suggesting that the Judith story itself is resistant to commodification. Later, the Professor, who appears to be involved in the narrator's drug-addiction therapy, sets up an experiment with students which is supposed to demonstrate randomness but somehow another element interferes, just as the apparently sham spirituality of the guru in India seems to release an authentic form of awareness almost by accident.

The narrator persistently experiences life through the medium of remembered stories and paintings based on biblical or classical themes. But one of the central stories is a completely reworked version of the story of Achilles and Penthesilia, Queen of the Amazons, derived from a play by Kleist, in which Penthesilia hacks Achilles to pieces.[44] So, in terms of the novel, we are invited to see the biblical Judith story, along with the Eden story, as a sort of liberating myth in a human culture which is otherwise a maze of debilitating myths. Like Sheherazade, we depend on stories but they also imprison us, with this possible exception.[45]

42   Moseley, ibid., p. 280.
43   Ibid., p. 5.
44   Ibid., p. 57.
45   Moseley, ibid., p. 76, mentions 'Queen Sheherazade.' Later in the text, the narratorial voice remarks, 'But then how dependent human beings are on making up stories! Did they

Robert Southwell: *The Death of our Ladie*

Turning to New Testament themes, we now consider, as a counterbalance to Warner's *Alone of all Her* Sex and the author's deprecating conclusions about Mariolatry, her warm appreciation of Petrarch's poetic invocation of the Virgin as the guiding star, the Stella Maris, of his life:

Vergine chiara stabile in eterno,
Di questo tempestoso mare stella,
D'ogni fedel nocchier fidata guida,
Pon'mente in che terribile procella
I'mi ritrovo sol, senza governo ... [46]

Two centuries later, Robert Southwell composed his poem, *The Death of our Ladie*, highlighted in Louis Martz's *The Poetry of Meditation*,[47] another literary pinnacle, this time lamenting the loss of the Queen of the Earth:

Weepe, living, of life the mother dyes;
The worlde doth loose the sum of all her blisse,
The queen of the thinges Earth, the empresse of the skyes;
By Mary's death mankind an orphan is:
Lett Nature weepe, yea lett all graces mone,
Their glory, grace, and gyftes dye all in one.
Her face a heaven, two planettes her eyes,
Whose gracious light did make our clearest day;
But one such heaven there was and loe! It dyes,
Deathe's darke eclipse hath dymmed every ray:

---

remember this: I mean remember not only what they wanted to remember, but how much they were limited by their dependence on stories? The huge facades of churches are always, I suppose, to do with the preservation of stories.' (Ibid., p. 150.)

46   Warner, op cit, p. 263. The translation given is:
O shining Virgin, steadfast in eternity!
Radiant star of this tempestuous sea,
And every faithful mariner's trusty guide!
Incline your thoughts to the terrible squall
In which I am beset, alone and rudderless!

47   Louis L .Martz: *The Poetry of Meditation* (New Haven: Yale University Press, 1962), p. 105.

Sunne, hyde thy light, thy beames untimely shine!
Trew light sith wee have lost, we crave not thine.

The point of quoting both texts is to emphasise that, in terms of the imaginative appropriation of biblical themes, there is a whole world of literary achievement and human experience which is different from that of the modern period. Martz argues that Southwell's poem is closely related to a neglected form of the rosary, known as the '*corona* of our Lady'. The very archaism of Southwell's diction and spelling, like the Italian of Petrarch, projects us into a different arena of sensibility from that of battles on behalf of feminism or other modern viewpoints.

We might equally well have discussed the influence of the Cherry Tree Carol[48] within medieval English culture or the descent of the Virgin into Hell in *The Apocalypse of the Virgin* or the 'profound and gentle humanity' which Warner herself finds in the painting, *The Madonna and Child*, by a follower of Giotto.[49] All of this is of major importance in the reception-history of the story of the Virgin Mary, as evidence of the imaginative appropriation of the urtext, and it cannot simply be written off as 'history', any more than Shakespeare can be abandoned because of the view of kingship propounded in his plays. By the same token, the Stabat Mater, in the words of Julia Kristeva, 'enthrals us today through the music of Palestrina, Pergolesi, Haydn and Rossini'.[50]

Warner omits all reference to the theme of the Virgin Mary in modern literature. If she had covered the topic and had been writing twenty years later, she might have had found space to consider the novel by the African-American feminist novelist Gloria Naylor, *Bailey's Café*. This work is, amongst other things, a magic-

48 Rosemary Woolf in *The English Mystery Play* (London: Routledge & Kegan Paul, 1972), pp. 177–8, discusses the influence of the Cherry Tree Carol on the *Ludus Coventriae* and the carol's own roots in Pseudo-Matthew.

49 Warner, ibid., p. 293, illustration 52.

50 Julia Kristeva: 'Stabat Mater' in Toril Moi (ed.): *The Kristeva Reader* (Oxford: Blackwell, 1986), p. 176.

182

realist reworking of some biblical themes in a parody of Chaucer's *Canterbury Tales*. The 'Virgin Birth' which occurs here is to a rape victim, but the whole tenor of the narrative, rather than being deconstructive of the biblical urtext, tends towards a sort of wistful homage to it. It is as though the biblical story points up the sordidness of the conditions in which Naylor's characters are forced to live.[51]

Wilkie Collins: *The New Magdalene* and *No Name*

Turning now to Haskins and reworkings of the Mary Magdalene story, Wilkie Collins in *The New Magdalene*[52] produced a novel in which the main protagonist finds redemption finally in migration to America. Although Haskins emphasises Mercy Merrick's dependence on marriage to the Christ-figure, Julian Grey, for her salvation, the heroine in facts initiates the process herself through her daring attempt to pose as the (apparently) dead Grace Roseberry, even though the intermediate effect is failure. She also shares in, with Julian Grey, rejection by London society (in the shape of Horace Holmcroft) before the couple escape to start a new life across the Atlantic. To regret the part played by Julian Grey (as Haskins seems to) is to reject the story as a rewritten biblical story or to want to rewrite it without Christ.

Haskins similarly links the plot of *No Name*[53] with female reliance on salvation through the agency of a male Christ-figure (Captain Kirke)[54], but, as Deirdre David has shown, this novel is ultimately the most deconstructive of Wilkie Collins's novels. [55] In their very different ways both the heroine, Magdalene, and the truculent Mrs Wragg are thoroughgoing challenges to patriarchy and their anarchic

51 Gloria Naylor: *Bailey's Café* (New York: Vintage Books, 1993). See p. 117, note 40.
52 Wilkie Collins: *The New Magdalene* (Doylestown, Pennsylvania: no date. Original publication: London, 1873).
53 Wilkie Collins: *No Name* (London: Penguin, 1994).
54 Haskins, op cit, pp. 338–9.
55 Deirdre David: *Rewriting the Male Plot in No Name*, essay in Lyn Pykett (ed.): *Wilkie Collins, Contemporary Critical Essays* (London: Macmillan, 1998), pp. 136–48.

stratagems are what drive the whole narrative, even if Collins is compelled to wrap them in a conventional 'happy ending' envelope. In fact Magdalene's capacity for assuming a variety of female identities as part of her subterfuge in reclaiming her lost inheritance is central to the subversive mood of this text, which at a crucial point becomes almost postmodern in its self-reflexivity. 'Very strange....It's like a scene in a novel – it's like nothing in real life' remarks the loathsome Mr Noel when he becomes aware of Magdalene's scheming.

On this reckoning, *No Name* is less of a plank in the reformist agenda of the Dickens circle and much more of a step towards a vertiginous experiment in the destabilisation of the moral and cultural certainties which are held to underpin (or to be underpinned by) the comforting effects of the omniscient narrator of Victorian fiction. With established religious beliefs dethroned (on this view), the omniscient narrator provides a sort of refuge in the slippery downward path from belief to scepticism. In undermining this convention, Collins points towards Thackeray and the interrogation of all forms of authoritative pronouncement. 'Collins insists that we see the subjective, arbitrary nature of fictional representation, the hubristic nature of novelistic omnipotence.'[56] From a theological perspective, we could say that the Magdalene of Wilkie Collins is the agent of a relativising argument which is just as capable of supporting a transcendental reference as a sort of incipient nihilism. Either way, this alarmingly driven figure has moved a long way from the reformed sinner of conventional piety.

For the purposes of balance, it could be argued that Magdalene's sister, Norah, provides the foil to this maverick proto-feminism, in that her quiet passivity is eventually rewarded by marriage to George Bartram and thereby the family estate. She achieves what Magdalene set out to achieve by doing virtually nothing. But, in terms of the novel as a whole, she remains a decidedly minor figure. If she

---

56   Ibid., p. 141.

represents in some way the triumph of conventionality, her victory is no more compelling than that of the rest of the 'happy ending' wrapper.

Mary Magdalene, as Haskins shows, was a dominant trope for the rehabilitated female in western literature and piety. Judas as a rehabilitated figure features in our two next examples, William Rayner's *The Knifeman* and the Norman Jewison film of *Jesus Christ Superstar*, both of which are discussed by Paffenroth.

William Rayner: *The Knifeman*

The Knifeman [57] can be seen as one of the earliest of a wave of Judas novels which appeared in the late 1960s and during the 1970s, often purporting to be or to contain the lost manuscript either of the memoirs or of the gospel of Judas. Rayner's novel is exceptional for the sheer convolutedness of its plot. It is the ultimate expression of the Conspiracy Theory. Judas betrays Jesus in order to hasten the coming of the Kingdom but then escapes into an incognito life sponsored by the authorities, who again pay him to infiltrate the nascent Christian community. He learns that Jesus did not die on the Cross but was drugged and survived. Hired to kill him, Judas in fact saves his life and instead kills a fellow-agent before himself being killed by the forces of the Church.

The motivating factor for Judas is his disillusionment with God's treatment of Jesus, who in the novel has ended up as a feeble, sedated victim of a religious movement which needs to keep him out of the way.[58] *The Knifeman* is important as part of the literary background to the disillusionment of Judas which drives the much better-known *Jesus Christ Superstar* (as rock-opera and film) and also as an

---

57   William Rayner: *The Knifeman* (New York: William Morrow & Co, 1969).

58   'This was a cynical abasement of goodness and sacrifice. Jesus…was like a splendid butterfly who'd been outraged and despoiled by boys, his wings torn off and his being brought down to struggling impotence. If this was God's work, then what kind of God ruled the affairs of men?' (Rayner: *Knifeman*), ibid., p. 151.

example of the fascination with lost gospels which was and remains a feature of our culture and of thriller-writing in particular.

Norman Jewison: *Jesus Christ Superstar*

The rock-opera *Jesus Christ Superstar* was composed jointly by Tim Rice, who wrote the lyrics and Andrew Lloyd-Webber, who wrote the music. It was launched initially as an album and remains best known in that form in the United States. Turned into a 'rock-opera,' it in fact shared that description only ever with *Tommy*, and so the indefinite article is only just sustainable.

The film of *Jesus Christ Superstar* was produced by Norman Jewison,[59] with a screenplay by Melvyn Bragg. It was Bragg who introduced the idea of the theatre group arriving in the desert by coach in what came to resemble a student revue for at least one critic. Sir Tim Rice, the original lyric-writer, has made it clear that this work, one of only two examples of the genre of rock-opera, was not meant either to support or refute the idea of Christ's divinity. It is Jesus Christ seen from the point of view of Judas, who did not accept Christ's divinity.[60]

Judas plays a prominent role in *Jesus Christ Superstar*, appearing at the beginning on a desert hill-top, lamenting the fact that things had got out of hand with Christ's mission. He appears again to criticise Mary Magdalene's anointing of Christ and thereafter repeatedly as the disaffected disciple on the fringes. Driven forward by tanks in the film, Judas goes to the high priests, singing, 'I didn't come here of my own accord...Don't say I'm damned for all time,' a theme developed soon into the lyrics, 'I only did what you wanted me to do' and 'I don't know how to love him'. Before he hangs himself, Judas sings, 'God, I've been used,' and 'You

---

59   *Jesus Christ Superstar* (Universal Studios, 1973).
60   Sir Tim Rice, interview in DVD edition of *Jesus Christ Superstar* (Universal, 2005).

have murdered me'. The chorus, which sang, 'Good old Judas' at the meeting with the high priests now sings, 'So long, Judas'. Jets fly overhead.

In Gethsemane, Judas sings, 'I don't know why you let the things you did get so out of hand'. He makes his final appearance in the opera descending on a harness, singing the lyric, 'Don't get me wrong,' which leads directly to the main chorus number, 'Jesus Christ, Superstar, are you who they say you are? What have you sacrificed?' Finally, after the Crucifixion, the whole cast, apart from Jesus but including Judas, clamber back into the bus (Judas is last, hopping on at the final moment) to leave the desert.

Paffenroth claims that Jewison, in casting a black man, Carl Anderson, in the role of Judas provocatively 'used racial stereotypes to undermine racism,' whereas in the interview mentioned above, Sir Tim Rice denied that there was any significance in casting a black man in the role. What cannot be denied is that the work itself is provocative in the way it pushes the role of Judas into such prominence as a vehicle for its pressing (though not answering) of the question of the identity of Jesus Christ Superstar. Leaving Christ on the Cross at Golgotha at the end rather than having him rejoin the rest of the cast in the bus leaves the impression that, whatever else, the Crucifixion was real and beyond the realms of rock opera itself.

Finally, we consider three works which rework the Apocalypse, in order to see whether they offer alternatives to Pippin's determined rejection of the biblical text as a 'misogynist male fantasy of the end of time'. Taking them in chronological order of production, they are Mary Shelley's *The Last Man*, Kafka's short story, *The City Coat of Arms*, and D.H. Lawrence's *Apocalypse*. The treatment of these three works in analytic detail is obviously beyond the scope of this study, but our purpose here will be to consider them in summary form as independent readings of the text.

Mary Shelley: *The Last Man*

Mary Shelley's *The Last Man* [61]appeared in 1826 and is important as a corrective to the common picture of Mary Shelley as a one-work author, as the outworking of a nexus of literary interest in the theme of the Last Man, and as the novel which seems to close the door on Romanticism. *The Last Man* is a large-scale futuristic drama which begins in England in the year 2073, with the abdication of the King to allow the formation of an English Republic and the withdrawal of the royal family to Windsor. An elaborate family drama involves the narrator, Verney, who marries Idris, daughter of the former king; Raymond who becomes Lord Protector of England; the Greek Princess Evadne; the narrator's sister Perdita; and Adria, son of the former king. England is portrayed as a paradisal state, whilst out in Europe great upheavals are afoot as the Greeks prepare to overwhelm the Turks at Constantinople. However, the Plague intervenes, putting a stop to imperialism, and finally engulfing both the Continent and England.

In the end the human race is reduced to three people, Raymond, Adrian and the daughter of Raymond and Perdita, with Verney the narrator mysteriously surviving the Plague as a sort of ghost. The three survivors decide to sail for Greece but are shipwrecked, leaving only Verney to carry on, together with his dog. He climbs to the top of St Peter's in Rome to carve the inscription, '2100, the era of the end of the world'.

A great deal of scholarly interest surrounds the frame-story, in which the events described are vouchsafed by the Oracle at Sibyl, and the ironies which are attached to a text written for a manifestly non-existent readership. There are also stark reflections throughout the narrative of the tragic personal experiences of the author.

Nevertheless, this does seem to be a feminist text which does not reject the Book of Revelation but rewrites it to act as a cultural prophecy. In this speeded-up

---

61   Mary Shelley: *The Last Man* (Oxford: Oxford University Press, 1994/1998).

188

historical vision, the Other seems at first to be represented by the world beyond Europe, the non-western cultures which have yet to impinge. But there is a yet more powerful Other, which is the Plague or Death, [62]and it is this which finally overrides the English utopia, Romantic universalism, the novel as a literary artefact, and presumably all male-centred fantasies. Stephen Goldsmith concludes: 'In rewriting the Book of Revelation, *The Last Man* makes it impossible to remain free from contamination, free from the plagues of Babylon. The novel's distinctly feminine protagonist – the the plague itself- thus marks the persistence of all that the Book of Revelation seeks to end apocalyptically: historical, sexual and linguistic differences. But beyond its reversal of the patriarchal content, *The Last Man* assures that the literary *form* of apocalypse must remain a matter of ideological conflict, not a vehicle for the claim to transcend such conflict...it exposes the pretence of a privileged mode of apocalyptic representation, of a literary form that might transcend history, for all modes of representation have rivals; they are all inscribed by cultural circumstances that are never free of conflict.'[63]

The novel has been read by Audrey Fisch as a parable of western political inability to handle AIDS.[64] It might also be possible to read *The Last Man* today as an ecological warning about the irrelevance of inherited forms of humanism to the matter of coping with environmental catastrophe.

---

62   Barbara Johnson, in her essay on *The Last Man* in Audrey A. Fisch, Anne K. Mellor and Esther H. Schor (eds.): *The Other Mary Shelley, Beyond Frankenstein* (Oxford: Oxford University Press, 1993), p. 264, argues: 'Where western man expects to encounter and master his other, he finds himself faced with his absolute Other ... The Plague, which extends out over the entire world from the point of encounter between East and West, is thus in a sense that which replaces the victory of the West over the East. Its lethal universality is a nightmarish version of the desire to establish a universal discourse, to spread equality and fraternity throughout the world. Thus the universal empire of the Plague would not only be, as Camus suggests, what is *excluded* from western humanism, it would be its *inverted image*'.

63   Stephen Goldsmith: *Unbuilding Jerusalem, Apocalypse and Romantic Representation* (Ithaca, New York: Cornell University Press, 1993), pp. 312–3.

64   Audrey Fisch: 'Plaguing Politics: AIDS, Deconstruction and *The Last Man*' in Fisch, Mellor and Schor, ibid., pp. 267–6.

But the above discussion should serve to demonstrate that *The Last Man* is an early feminist text which does not reject the Apocalypse out of hand on account of its 'horror' content, but instead seeks to mobilise the text in a way supportive of a variety of types of cultural subversion.

Kafka: *The City Coat of Arms*

Kafka's *The City Coat of Arms*[65] was commended by Alter, as we saw earlier, along with several others of his minor works, as expressive of a whimsical, quasi-midrashic form of dialogue with the biblical text.[66] In this short 'parable,' the builders of the Tower of Babel become involved in a sort of technological procrastination, never actually commencing work because they anticipate the advent of superior methods of construction in the future. They fall out. Then a sort of anti-urban sentiment sets it, which questions the point of building the tower altogether. Alter points out that all of this reverses the order of the Genesis story, where the destruction of the tower by God is the explanation for human division.

Only at the end does Kafka reveal that the City emblem depicts the apocalyptic destruction of the city:

> All the legends and songs that came to birth in that city are filled with longing for a prophesied day when the city would be destroyed by five successive blows from a gigantic fist. It is for that reason that the city has a closed fist on its coat of arms.[67]

In this miniature literary treatment of the Apocalypse, the end-time is the cause not particularly of female subjection, but of general human inertia and of a ruralistic impulse to shun city life. An alternative view, equally distant from Pippin's feminist

---

65   Franz Kafka: *The Complete Short Stories* (London: Minerva, 1992), p. 433.
66   See Alter, op cit, pp. 70–3.
67   Kafka, ibid., p. 434.

reading, is proposed by Clayton Koelb,[68] who notes that the story begins with the chaos of the building preparations and the hopelessness of the task, making divine intervention a form of deliverance *from* chaos.

D.H. Lawrence: *Apocalypse*

D.H. Lawrence's *Apocalypse*,[69] like Kafka's short story, was published posthumously. It was written in about 1929, roughly five years after Kafka wrote *The City Shield*. It could hardly be more different. The book is a wholesale attack on the role of the Book of Revelation in propping up a priggish, self-glorifying Christian religion in place of the 'religion of tenderness' associated with Jesus in the rest of the New Testament. Drawing obliquely on the scholarship of R.H. Charles[70] in attempting to unearth different stages in the text's production, Lawrence finds a suppressed sun-religion at the heart of the Apocalypse's visions of sun and moon and stars, dragon and Andromeda. Successively hi-jacked by a scribal Jewish redactor and a perverted Christian writer, the biblical book was turned by a later editor into the textual equivalent of Judas. It is time to recover the organic wholeness between man and cosmos which the neglected and editorially-disguised visions of the Book of Revelation promise.

Lawrence's extraordinary work seeks to salvage the wholesome archetypes which the biblical book embodies but distorts. In many ways Lawrence is as suspicious of Christianity as Pippin, although from a rather different perspective. Both of them are in revolt against the power-worship which they find in the biblical Book of

68 Clayton Koelb: *Kafka's Rhetoric* (Ithaca, New York: Cornell University Press, 1989), pp. 149–53.
69 D.H. Lawrence: *Apocalypse* (London: Penguin, 1974).
70 Christopher Burdon in *The Apocalypse in England, Revelation Unravelling, 1700–1834* (London: Macmillan, 1997), pp. 211–212, discusses Lawrence's awareness of the scholarly work of R.H. Charles and Lawrence's own intuitive grasp of the cruces of Christian exegesis of the Apocalypse.

Revelation, but Pippin sees the driving force as patriarchy, whereas Lawrence sees it as driven by a narrow-minded Puritanism and also by a sort of inner dividedness which leads to insanity. Whereas Pippin wants to ditch the biblical book, Lawrence wants to rescue it from itself, by uncovering the pagan visions embedded within it. He sets up a dichotomy between the 'Christianity of the Apocalypse' (the 'dark side of Christianity') and 'the things the human heart secretly yearns after.'[71]

Like Pippin's reading, D.H. Lawrence's *Apocalypse* is an oppositional reading, but it is so in the service not of a rejection of the text but of an effort to restore the text's suppressed pagan vitality and also to release the biblical book's multivocality, as T.R. Wright argues, whilst documenting Lawrence's indebtedness to the ideas of Nietzsche and of Frederick Carter, as well as the commentaries not only of R.H. Charles, but of John Oman and Alfred Loisy.[72] There is a great gulf fixed between Pippin's campaign to expose the misogyny of the Apocalypse and D.H. Lawrence's exultation over the 'Magna Mater', the oriental goddess who is set to bring new life to the biblical text, in spite of the efforts of its redactors.

In conclusion, our three last works do indeed offer variant readings of the Apocalypse which are an alternative to Pippin's dismissal of the urtext and its reception-history as 'a misogynist male fantasy of the end of time'. They range between a post-Romantic feminist fantasy which can be taken to be subversive of western culture or of literary pretensions, through an ironic, modernist questioning of urban life, to a male fantasy of recovering the vitality of pagan imagery through condemning the biblical Apocalypse and valorising its sources. All three exist in a sort of creative dialogue with the biblical original, however extreme, and in this they differ from Pippin.[73]

---

71   D.H. Lawrence, ibid., pp. 124–5.

72   T.R. Wright: *D.H. Lawrence and the Bible* (Cambridge: Cambridge University Press), pp. 228–44.

73   For a look at Ingrid Bergman's film *The Seventh Seal*, considered as another alternative to Pippin's view of the Apocalypse, see Appendix A.

Conclusion

This chapter has explored a wide swathe of literary retellings of the biblical stories covered by our book. Apart from the final section on the Apocalypse, all of the examples are discussed within the pages of our fourteen reception-history writers. They can be distinguished very broadly from the works examined in the *Vox Dei* chapter in that they are slightly further removed from the biblical text, though Macdonald's *Lilith* is resolute in its supernaturalism, in fact probably more so than parts of the Bible. The Book of Ruth in the canonical Bible and the Book of Esther in the Apocrypha are examples of 'biblical' narratives more or less devoid of reference to the supernatural or to the deity, in contrast to *Lilith*.

What the works which we have discussed demonstrate is a rich seam of rewritten biblical material, responsive to changes and upheavals in culture, and often more complex than the readings offered by the fourteen theorists suggest. It may be useful to list our findings:

a) Macdonald's *Lilith* cannot be reduced to the terms of a misogynist tract, as Norris implies. It represents a bold, if rather eccentric, experiment in supernaturalism.

b) Daphne du Maurier's *Rebecca*, beneath the veneer of a popular romance, hides an ironic and subversive look at patriarchy, albeit wrapped in the seductive package of a Lost Paradise.

c) Steinbeck's *East of Eden*, particularly viewed through the prism of its more focused and condensed film adaptation, presents itself as a worrying blockade for 'biblical values' in the context of early American capitalism.

d) Wilkie Collins's *Jezebel's Daughter* is clearly rather more than the continuation of the Jezebel stereotype in its, admittedly melodramatic, attempt to inscribe insanity within a nineteenth-century European setting.

e) Nicholas Moseley's *Judith* can be read as a more exploratory novel than the summary offered by Stocker in her reception-history.

f) Rescuing some meditative poetry from the clutches of Warner's overreachingly reductionist account of the treatment of the Virgin Mary in literature, we have found the theme itself the subject of a powerful reworking in a modern novel, *Bailey's Café,* which is representative of a field ignored by Warner, even if this particular work was published some sixteen years after *Alone of All Her Sex.*

g) We have found in Wilkie Collins's *No Name* a much more self-reflexive, and even deconstructionist novel, than the male-hero-to-the-rescue saga described by Haskins in her reception-history, *Mary Magdalene.*

h) When the rehabilitation of Judas, inaugurated perhaps by William Rayner in *The Knifeman*, gets reworked in *Jesus Christ Superstar*, the results are not as unambiguous as Paffenroth in his reception-history implies.

i) Similarly, our excursion into the field of alternative modern retellings of the Apocalypse has revealed a much more diverse scene than that depicted by Tina Pippin in *Apocalyptic Bodies.*

Overall, the thirteen works we have examined lend themselves to readings which are far less constrained than those offered by our reception-history writers. Their chief protagonists, such as the unnamed narrator of *Rebecca* and Madame Fontaine in *Jezebel's Daughter* or Judas in *The Knifeman*, do not conform to the literary stereotypes propounded by some of our fourteen authors. Some of the works are more multi-faceted than our authors allow, as we find when reading Moseley's *Judith* or Macdonald's *Lilith.* In the case of Robert Southwell's poem *The Death of Our Ladie*, Naylor's *Bailey's Café* and the three works which we found to be hypertexts to the Apocalypse, we are dealing with material which is not discussed by Warner and Pippin in their respective reception-histories and confounds their dismissive approach to their main topic

We must conclude that the writing of a reception-history, particularly one with a pronounced ideological slant, involves a selective approach to the range of texts discussed and a selective approach to the available readings of those texts.

Chapter 7

THE OTHER IN THEOLOGY
AND POSTMODERN THOUGHT

Central to many of the critiques of rewritten biblical stories which we are considering is the concept of 'The Other'.[1] In the writings of the postmodernists[2] we may distinguish between the negative use of the term to signify everything which is culturally excluded by the dominant metanarrative and the positive use of the term to denote something elusive but appealing.[3] An example of the first type of use would be the exclusion of the Canaanite voice in the narratives of the Israelite settlement in Palestine or the suppression of the feminine voice in patriarchy. An example of the second would be the valorisation of Jewish fiction in post-1945 America.[4] Despite such variety within postmodernism, it has to be stated that a

---

1   Literary-critical uses of the term, 'the Other,' are not exhausted by our discussion here. For example, Edgar A. Dryden, in *Nathaniel Hawthorne, The Poetics of Enchantment* (Ithaca and London: Cornell University Press, 1977), posits a duality in Hawthorne's novels between untamed nature ('the Other') and European-rooted civilisation. See ibid., Chapter 2, 'The Enchantment of the Other'.

2   We refer to the school associated with the work of Lacan, Foucault, Derrida and Lyotard.

3   We do not discuss the literary concept of the Sublime here, largely because 'the Sublime' is not a term used by any of our fourteen reception-history writers; but also because the concept does not add anything to the contest between pro-theological and secularist senses of The Other. For a good example of the neutrality of the concept in contemporary literary criticism, see Philip Shaw: *The Sublime* (Abingdon: Routledge, 2006). Tod Linafelt, in an article mentioned in our 'Conflation' chapter (Chapter 9, p. 207, note 2), skilfully uses the term to distinguish between the quest for Beauty and the quest for the Transcendence in *The Wizard of Oz* and the Book of Job respectively.

4   See essay by Kevin McCarren: 'Inhabiting what remains of Jewishness and Alterity in the Fiction of Saul Bellow, Philip Roth and Bernard Malamud' in Stanley E Porter and Brook W R Pearson (eds).: *Christian-Jewish Relations Through the Centuries* (Sheffield: Sheffield Academic Press, 2000), pp. 284–97.

major factor in postmodernist usage has been Lacan's insistence that Otherness in Western literature is a signifier for the phallus; in other words, for patriarchy.[5]

In mainstream theology, 'The Other' has tended to denote the divine. From Rudolf Otto's account of the numinous in *The Idea of the Holy*[6] to Martin Buber's description of the uncanny encounter with the 'Youness' of other people in *I and Thou*,[7] the phrase has conveyed the sense of God as that which is supra-human and transcendent. Levinas seems to mediate between the inherited theological sense of Otherness and Otherness as the source of ideological criticism, with his quest to find the ethical voice in literature, addressing the reader and 'forcing us out of the bed of preformed and customary ideas that protect and reassure'. [8] A recent article on post-Holocaust theology by a Jewish theologian sums up Levinas's contribution to a theology of The Other: 'For Levinas one must recognize the difference between one's own finiteness and infinity. We glimpse the infinite when we acknowledge the unknown in the other, because that unknown has the capacity to be infinite. To presume to know any one completely is to eliminate otherness, and therefore to eliminate the Infinite.'[9]

Outside the writings of Levinas, the postmodernist usages and the theological usage seem at times to be on a collision course. As an example of collision, we may cite Regina Schwarz's polemical attack on biblical monotheism, *The Curse of Cain,*[10] Schwarz equates the defining of outsiders as the Other with violence: 'Violence is not only what we do to the Other. It is prior to that. Violence is the

---

5   See article on Otherness in Jeremy A. Hawthorn: *A Glossary of Contemporary Literary Theory* (London, Arnold, 2000/2003), pp. 249–50.

6   Rudolf Otto: *The Idea of the Holy* trans. John W. Harvey (London: Oxford University Press/ Milford, 1936).

7   Martin Buber: *I and Thou* trans. Walter Kaufmann (Edinburgh: T. & T. Clark, 1970).

8   Emmanuel Levinas: *On the Jewish Reading of Scriptures*, reprinted in David Jobling, Tina Pippin and Ronald Schleifer (eds.): *The Postmodern Bible Reader* (Oxford: Blackwell, 2001), p. 330.

9   Mark L. Winter: 'Dialogue on Holocaust Theology' in *Theology*, September/October 2006, p. 339.

10   Regina Schwarz: *The Curse of Cain* (Chicago: University of Chicago Press, 1997).

very construction of the Other'. She sees the Old Testament as the incubator of the colonialist treatment of foreign nations, with transcendence ascribed to a deity who is able to sustain a minority nation in the face of material scarcity.[11]

Another example of a collision between the religious sense of Otherness and Otherness seen as denoting cultural exclusion is found in Edward Said's highly influential *Orientalism*,[12] where the author describes the contours of the colonialist landscape, a place where the needs of the imperial power were projected onto the citizens of the conquered nation. Relevant to at least four of our biblical stories (those of Eve, Sheba, Judith, the Magi) is his listing of some of the *dramatis personae* of this world: 'In the depths of this Oriental stage stands a prodigious cultural repertoire whose individual items evoke a fabulously rich world: the Sphinx, Cleopatra, Eden, Troy, Sodom and Gomorrah, Astarte, Isis and Osiris, Sheba, Babylon, the Genii, the Magi, Nineveh, Prester John, Mahomet and dozens more ... '[13]

The colonialist exoticizing of foreign nations has been taken by feminists to extend to the general treatment of women in a patriarchal culture, with women and native Americans seen as parallel cases.[14] This may be both the expression of power relations and the outworking of anxieties, a way of enforcing boundaries, hence the binaries, 'Self/Other, Civilised/Savage, Male/Female, Home/Abroad' which Yvonne Sherwood[15] sees as characteristic of western thinking. At its most sinister, the phenomenon is manifested in the Holocaust as the marker of Jewish alterity.[16] The point being made is that this relationship to 'The Other' is both

---

11 Ibid., pp. 2, 4, 33, 80–3, 89–90, 114–17.

12 Edward Said: *Orientalism* (London: Penguin, 2003).

13 Ibid., p. 63.

14 See Mary Ann Tolbert, essay, 'Reading the Bible with Authority' in Harold C. Washington, Susan Lochrie Graham and Pamela Thimmes: *Escaping Eden, New Feminist Perspectives on the Bible* (Sheffield: Sheffield Academic Press, 1998), p. 160.

15 See Yvonne Sherwood, 'Colonising the Old Testament' in S.E. Porter and B.W.R. Pearson (eds.).: *Christian-Jewish Relations Through the Centuries* (Sheffield: Sheffield Academic Press, 2000), pp. 256–7.

16 See Ibid., p. 290.

198

instrumental and coercive. It is the very opposite of the upholding of 'difference', which is an attitude of receptivity to that which is not-us.

One of our fourteen reception-history writers occupies a position interestingly mid-way between the positive and negative uses of the term, the Other. In parts of her Judith study, Margarita Stocker seems to bridge the divide between the theological and postmodernist *sense* of the Other. Treating the apocryphal work as a subversive text in which 'even the divinity is feminine when in epiphany on earth,' she sees the Book of Judith as 'a counter-cultural view of how God acts'.[17] Judith embodies the culture's uncanny and this is the *source* of the text's power.

The Otherness of God in conventional theology was in opposition to the humdrum, limited focus of humankind or to human efforts to treat the not-self in instrumental ways. In postmodernist thinking, at least those parts of it where the term 'God' is not synonymous with the coercive treatment of subject peoples, this Otherness relies on being culturally subversive. It is like the contrast between George Steiner's 'Real Presence' and George Derrida's 'absence'. The question remains as to whether it is possible to be affirmative about some aspects of the inherited culture, whilst being critical about other parts. In other words, to find God in medical progress but not in the destruction of the rain forests. In literary or hermeneutical terms, this would mean recognizing the genius of Milton's *Paradise Lost* whilst resisting those aspects which appear to some to be misogynist. The corollary would be to affirm the eroticism of Flaubert's Sheba, whilst resisting the author's atheism. Similarly, the ironizing of Sheba which we find in works of modern art can signify for us the affirmation of the genuine difference or otherness of the Other. That is, the Other as a source of critique of ourselves rather than the object of our projections.

Access to another form of transcendence is described in Herbert Schneidau's analysis of the Modernists in his book, *Waking Giants: The Presence of the Past in*

17   Stocker,op cit, p. 11.

Modernism.[18] Schneidau finds that authors like Kafka, Joyce, Conrad and Pound bring us into contact with the primal realities of life, as they expose the fact that human pretensions are 'as baseless and as transitory as our joys'.[19] In that sense, the achievement of the modernists is to restore human awareness of the deep corridors of the past to which the Bible and Homer testify. We will look at the applicability of Schneidau's insights to some of the novels covered in this study.

Dealing first with Milton, the case for his intellectual stature is eloquently put in two separate essays by Stephen Fallon[20] and William Kerrigan.[21] Fallon charts Milton's impassioned battle in *Paradise Lost* against the Calvinist theodicy, his determined insistence on human freedom and on the reasonableness of divine justice. He demonstrates the innovative daringness of Milton's doctrine of the continuum of matter: 'Our souls are not different in kind from our bodies, but only in degree'.[22] Most importantly, the narrowing of the gap between divine and human reason in the early books is the driving force in his argument about human moral responsibility.[23] The Spirit which fuels Milton is the source of his magisterial authority and at the same time, ambivalently, his self-doubt, making *Paradise Lost* the epic of mental struggle which Wordsworth in *The Prelude* could only imitate.[24]

Kerrigan, on a still larger canvas, sets Milton's achievement against what he sees as the theologically-derivative secular philosophies of the period from Heidegger to Derrida. If Milton's Adam and Eve were temporarily exiled in an interim mental

---

18 Herbert Schneidau: *Waking Giants, The Presence of the Past in Modernism* (Oxford: Oxford University Press, 1991), p. 21.

19 Ibid., p. 135.

20 Stephen M Fallon: '*Paradise Lost* in Intellectual History' in Thomas N Corns (ed.): *A Companion to Milton* (Oxford: Blackwell, 2003).

21 William Kerrigan: 'Milton's Place in Intellectual History' in Dennis Danielson (ed.): *The Cambridge Companion to Milton* (Cambridge: Cambridge University Press, 1999).

22 Fallon in Corns, ibid., p. 337.

23 Ibid., p. 339.

24 Ibid., p. 347.

200

paradise between the First Paradise of Eden and the future Paradise, Heidegger in *Being and Time* offers a 'restlessness and homesickness' which is devoid of the authenticating context created by Milton's epic, but in a great way dependent upon it. Derrida similarly depends upon the trope of Exile for his 'deferral,' 'difference,' and *'difference'*. Freudian ideas such as 'displacement' and the 'uncanny' or *'unheimlich'* (= 'unhomely') and Marxist notions of 'alienation' are all examples of modern signs which gain their resonance from Milton's epic. Milton is the master of a literary 'argument' which ultimately transcends philosophical discourse.[25]

In an article in the same collection, Diane McColley[26] argues that in his historical context Milton is a progressive rather than a misogynist: 'Thanks to three centuries of progress which Milton helped to promote, the idea that woman was made for man, or that any segment of the human family is necessarily subordinate to any other, has been discredited'. She shows that the responsibility for the Fall in *Paradise Lost* is shared between Adam and Eve, with the weight finally in Book 10: 198–200 shifting towards Adam's culpability. To McColley's argument we could add that Milton's erudition extended to a quite remarkable knowledge of rabbinic midrash and it seems very likely that he was familiar with the strand in rabbinic commentary on Genesis 2 which tended towards lessening Eve's blame.[27]

If it is true that later feminist writers, beginning with Mary Shelley, were to treat Milton as the misogynist bogey-man against which they fought, we have seen evidence that this reading was misplaced, even if the broad target of an oppressive patriarchy in English culture found a convenient symbol in its most prominent religious artist. In the light of Harold Bloom's notion that artists need,

---

25 Kerrigan: 'Milton's Place in Intellectual History' in Danielson, ibid., p. 257.
26 Diane K. McColley: 'Milton and the Sexes' in Danielson, ibid., p. 179.
27 For this strand, see James L. Kugel: *The Bible As It Was* (Cambridge Mass: Belknap/Harvard, 1997), pp. 76–8.

in an Oedipal way, to supplant predecessors, or to 'misread' them,[28] we can see the *Paradise Lost* of Mary Shelley and others as a projection of their own literary anxieties. To say this is not to bolster a form of literary-critical or cultural reaction, but to recognize that there has been what military strategists euphemistically call 'collateral damage' in the feminist campaign.

Milton himself as a writer may be regarded as an embodiment of the Other in the theological sense, in that his resolutely oppositional moves against the cultural assumptions of his time (both Hobbesian philosophy and religious Calvinism), his poetic genius, his creative and summing-up approach to what we now call biblical reception-history, and his political radicalism, together with his immense and incomplete influence on the future, mark him out as totally extraordinary. Convinced, as Regina Schwarz shows,[29] that the same Muse which lay behind the Hebrew Scriptures drove him, Milton is the literary manifestation of transcendence. As ever, we may choose to bracket out ontological questions, but even if contemporary relevance were the only criterion (and there are critics who argue that all literature can only have validity for *now*[30]), then Milton's powerful sense of human rapaciousness in response to the divine gift of Creation would be enough to constitute a major counter-cultural challenge to the consumerism and carbon-fuel profligacy of the early twenty-first-century.

Before we go on to consider the modern and postmodern Sheba, it may be useful to examine the significance of Mary Shelley's *Frankenstein* and also that of Tennyson's *Maud*, both of which feature in Norris's *The Story of Eve*. Mary

28   See Harold Bloom: *The Anxiety of Influence* (Oxford: Oxford University Press, 1997), 2nd edn.

29   Regina M. Schartz: 'Milton on the Bible'in Corns, ibid., pp. 37–54.

30   This is really the nub of Stanley Fish's argument against E.D. Hirsch's definition, in *Validity in Interpretation*, of the text as 'an entity which always remains the same from one moment to the next.' For Fish in his later phase, texts, readers and authors are *all* the products of contemporary interpretation. See Stanley Fish: *Is There a Text in the Class? The Authority of Interpretive Communities.* (Cambridge Mass: Harvard University Press, 1980/1994), pp. 1–17.

Shelley's most famous novel has been the subject of hundreds of books and essays (Louis James in 1994 knew of three hundred[31]) and has been considered one of the basic 'pretexts' of the twentieth-century, in the technical (postmodernist) sense of texts which give rise to other texts.

A dizzying variety of levels of interpretation is available,[32] from the historical contextualisation of the text in connection with the bizarre assemblies of animal parts in human guise created by Charles Waterton at Walton Hall near Wakefield, as part of a Catholic protest against irreligion to studies of *Frankenstein* as the engine of modern cinematic horror.[33] The novel has been seen as the precursor of modern magic realism and as a regression to medieval primitivism.[34]

However, two strands of response are particularly relevant to the theme of this chapter of the book. The first is represented by an essay by Jerrold Hogle on 'Otherness' in *Frankenstein*.[35] The second we find in an essay, discussing a feminist critique of Science by Anne Mellor.[36]

Hogle's essay is a thoroughgoing poststructuralist reading of *Frankenstein*, in which the text is seen as having no external referent, except to other texts, which include most obviously Milton's *Paradise Lost* and Coleridge's *The Ancient Mariner*, both of which feature in the text as the reading matter of two of the characters. Hogle defines the Other as 'the intersubjective-intertextual ground of articulation',[37] which I take to mean the disguised projection of the author. Victor Frankenstein himself, the Monster and Robert Walton are all trapped in a play of

---

31   Louis James: 'Frankenstein's Monster in Two Traditions' in Stephen Bann (ed.): *Frankenstein, Creation and Monstrosity* (London: Reaktion Books, 1994), p. 77.

32   Stephen Bann, ibid., pp. 7–13.

33   See Michael Grant: 'James Whale's Frankenstein, 'The Horror Film and the Symbolic Biology of the Cinematic Monster' in Stephen Bann, ibid.

34   See John Louis Schefer: 'The Bread and the Blood' in Stephen Bann, ibid.

35   Jerrold E. Hogle: 'Otherness in Frankenstein, The Confinement /Autonomy of Fabrication' in Fred Botting (ed.): *Frankenstein -New Casebooks* (Basingstoke: Palgrave, 2002).

36   Anne Mellor: 'A Feminist Critique of Science' in Fred Botting, ibid., pp. 107–39.

37   Hogle in Fred Botting, Ibid., p. 208.

signs which stretches from the Lost Paradise of the moment of the Creation to an elusive Paradise Regained which never occurs. Instead of Presence, there is only absence, or the eternal deferral of desire which Clerval, a character in the novel, finds in the works of the orientalists.[38] In fact, the whole novel turns out to be a rehearsal of nothingness, as two different meaning-systems (the scientific method of classification and the religious idea of revelation) clash in a sea of floating symbols.

There is no doubt that *Frankenstein*, like many other literary productions, lends itself to poststructuralist discourse, which plays on the artificiality of narrative and the aporia and lacunae in the finished text. The very deliberate and ostentatious reference of Mary Shelley's work to previous texts, and indeed its own strong presence in subsequent literature, help make it a *locus classicus* for this approach. Adopting the stance of Nicholas Boyle, the pro-theological rejoinder would be that the nihilism of Hogle's reading describes the existential anguish which the gospel is there to address. On this reading, the Other would be more than a symbolic order of self-referring fragments but the real presence of something primal.

Mellor's essay takes us into different territory, as she contrasts Mary Shelley's approval of the 'good' science of Erasmus Darwin with her anxious response to the galvanic experiments of Giovanni Aldini on animal parts.[39] She places *Frankenstein* at the head of a tradition of mad scientists such as Dr Strangelove and which inspired Aldous Huxley's dystopian *Brave New World*. The novel, which for some lampoons *Paradise Lost*, becomes a serious prophetic tract, warning against the dangers of nuclear proliferation and the perils of the Enlightenment project.

Before we look at Tennyson's *Maud* and then return to Schneidau's view of the Modernists in relation to alterity, we can take up the question of the escapism which Mary Shelley's character, Clerval, found in the orientalists. In fact, one of

---

38   Ibid., p. 218.
39   Mellor in Fred Botting, Ibid., p. 113.

204

the many narratives-within-narrative that make up *Frankenstein* is the story of
Safie, an Arabian beauty who has been brought up by an Arab-Christian mother
who wants to help her 'aspire to higher powers of intellect and an independence
of mind forbidden to the female followers of Muhammad.[40] The girl's father is an
unreliable Turkish merchant, a manifestation of the imperialism which is a feature
of this text. This Sheba-figure fits into a pattern of European literature and art
which Edward Said documents in his study, *Orientalism*, in which the sterotypes
were set up by such works as Edward William Lane's *The Manners and Customs
of the Modern Egyptians*.[41] Therefore, as a progressive feminist text, *Frankenstein*
is deficient in so far as its inscription of imperialism locates it within a western
patriarchal framework. The lesson for ideologues is that historical cultural change
is often gradual and patchy. Mary Shelley's social attitudes outside the area of
her departure from convention are as historically situated as Milton's alleged
misogyny[42] or the historical Jesus' attitude to cosmology or (sadly) the anti-
semitism of John Buchan.[43]

Another Victorian text discussed in Norris's *The Story of Eve* is Tennyson's
poem or monodrama of 1854, *Maud*. The plot of this work is difficult to extricate
from the very diffuse text, but W.W. Robson has provided a very useful summary,
drawing attention to the similarity with the plot of popular novels and dramas of
the era:

---

40   Mary Shelley: *Frankenstein* (London: Penguin Books, 1994), p. 119.

41   Said, ibid., pp. 176–7.

42   For an attempt to clear Milton completely of misogyny, see Philip J. Gallagher: *Milton, the
     Bible and Misogyny* (Columbia:University of Missouri Press, 1990).

43   For anti-semitism in John Buchan's *The Thirty-Nine Steps*, see essay by Irene Wise, *Images
     of Anti-Semitism* in Porter and Pearson, ibid., pp. 328–50. Her quotation from page 8 of *The
     Thirty-Nine Steps* ('The Jew is everywhere, but you have to go down the backstairs to find
     him … ') is quite damning. David Daniell in *The Interpreter's House, A Critical Assessment
     of the Work of John Buchan* (London: Nelson, 1975), pp. xii and 137, flatly denies the charge
     of anti-semitism in Buchan's novels (already current when he wrote his survey), claiming that
     sympathetic portraits of Jews elsewhere in the novels invalidate what he designates as the
     anti-semitism of the character John Hannay, rather than the novelist.

First of all, it can be read for the story, which is not very clearly told and rather melodramatic, about a young man who has been ruined by the old 'Lord of the hall', falls in love with the lord's beautiful daughter, kills her brother in a duel and escapes to France, has a mental breakdown and is finally cured by responding to the call of his country at war and (as I interpret the poem) is killed in battle.[44]

(Robson goes on to suggest that the value of the poem lies outside its 'stagey plot', in its fineness as love poetry.)

Norris celebrates the work as a variant on the Song of Songs, with the enclosed garden of *Maud* echoing both that biblical text and also the theme of Mary Magdalene in the garden.[45] It can certainly be said that Tennyson's figure Maud bears, in the mind of the narrator, the ambiguous traits associated with the reception-history of Mary Magdalene ('the Female Other'),[46] but this chaotic and unruly poem also signals other sorts of Otherness. Critics have found the rising mercantile class to be the poem's Other (in the shape of the *nouveau riche* Lord of the Manor and his son)[47] and indeed Peace is a sort of Other to the poem's

44 W.W. Robson: *The Definition of Literature and other Essays* (Cambridge: Cambridge University Press, 1982), p. 60.

45 Norris, op cit, pp. 242–5.

46 The poem speculates on the ambiguities of Maud's behaviour:
'What if with her sunny hair,
And smile as sunny as cold
She meant to weave me a snare
Of some coquettish deceit,
Cleopatra-like as of old....' VI, iv.

The following lines actually occur twice (at VI,v, and VI,x):
'Yet if she were not a cheat,
If Maud were all she seem'd
And her small were all I dream'd,
Then the world were not so bitter
But a smile could make it sweet.'

These references and those below are all to the text of *Maud* in *The Poems of Tennyson* (London: Henry Frowde, 1904).

47 See David Goslee: *Tennyson's Characters, 'Strange Faces, Other Minds.'* (Iowa City, University of Iowa, 1989), pp. 135–56.

exultation in war as the purgative for human social ills. *Maud* also shares with a number of Tennyson's works a recoiling from the disturbing Otherness of a hostile universe. There is also the Other of madness which stalks the poem and its narrator, as it stalked Tennyson's own family. But it is Death which provides the defining Other, in the sense that Maud herself is only perfected in death and seems most present in the poem in the shape of the wraith which Maud becomes. It is likewise from the grave that we finally understand the narratorial voice to emanate.[48] *Maud* can be read as a 'Crimean war poem,' but this does not fully express the sense that Tennyson's monodrama represents a unique fusion of death-obsession and erotic longing. Also, the historical contextualisation may deflect from the sense in which the poem eulogises war in general.

The poem's own reception-history has been greatly influenced by the use of a few of its verses in M.W. Balfe's celebrated parlour-song, *Come into the Garden, Maud*.[49] The song can become a sort of distillation of the poem, recalling the subliminal horror which the poem both hides (in its deeply-veiled plot) and displays (in the ravings which threaten to engulf its narrator). The Christian God is present in the poem as its addressee (when the addressee is not Maud herself) and as conflated with Mars, the God of War. The pagan gods in general seem to be a chthonic presence, 'you tyrants in your iron skies,' associated with the 'sad astrology' which affected Tennyson even more than Byron. But the Transcendental Other of *Maud* is finally an authorial voice which has found a form of emotional and spiritual resolution in a projection of morbidity. In reductionist fashion, this can be explained as the last gasp of a nostalgia for squirarchy or the sublimation of Tennyson's grief at the loss of Hallam, as a requiem for chivalric love, or indeed as

---

48 On the voice from the grave, see *Maud*, I, ii and XXVII, 1–4. For Maud as wraith, see XXVII, vii.

49 M.W. Balfe: *Come Into The Garden, Maud* (London: W. Paxton, no date).

the sublimation of the horrors of the warfare which the poem otherwise commends.[50] But, taken on its own terms, *Maud* offers a rather disturbing experience centred on the elevation of love as death-obsession to centre-stage, long before the advent of Freud. The poem's alterity, we may conclude, consists in the way its chaotic formal structure, and its intermittent passages of great lyricism, are together the vehicle for a vision (albeit a morbid vision) which is unique in literature. The voice from the grave summons the 'spectral bride'[51] to witness to the superiority of martial values over the values of whose 'sole God be the millionaire'[52] and whose paltry Peace is the product of all-consuming commerce: 'Maud in the light of her youth and her grace, Singing of Death, and of Honour that cannot die ... '[53]

Maud may be supposed to articulate what many in the twenty-first-century would regard as a quaintly Victorian notion of death and glory. However, reading the poem in the light of recent history, it would be hard to argue that Britain as a nation has found any other sort of transcendence over 'turbo-capitalism' than the vision offered by Tennyson in this work. In that sense, *Maud* encapsulates the Otherness of the national psyche:

It is better to fight for the good, than to rail at the ill;
I have felt with my native land, I am one with my kind,
I embrace the purpose of God and the doom assign'd.[54]

---

50 See Joseph Bristow: 'Nation, Class and Gender in Tennyson's *Maud*', essay in Rebecca Stott (ed.): *Tennyson* (London: Longman, 1996), pp. 127–47. Bristow sees *Maud* as a Crimean war poem in which Victorian models of masculinity are shown in conflict. The eponymous female subject, he notes, has no voice of her own in the poem and can only be 'heard' through the male voices, for whom she is 'a female power that, if it is to be obeyed, must also be mastered by men, and thereby subsumed into the stuff of myth.' (Bristow, p. 142). Susan Shatto argues that 'the indistinctness of her narration suggests her function in the poem is not as a character at all, but as the obscure object of the narrator's desire.' (Susan Shatto: *Tennyson's Maud, a Definitive Edition* (London: Athlone Press, 1986), p. 37).
51 For the reference to Maud as 'a spectral bride,' see *Maud*, XXVII, viii.
52 'Nor Britain's one sole God be the millionaire ... ' (*Maud*, XXVIII, ii).
53 *Maud*, V, ii.
54 *Maud*, XXVIII, iii.

208

The Crimean War was fought on the fringes of a Europe which defined the Orient as its Other. Indeed, leaving aside the propensity of western Europeans in the nineteenth-century to treat Eastern Orthodoxy as exotic, the Crimea contained then, as it still does today, pockets of Islamic culture. We move on now to consider aspects of the reception-history of the Magi in terms of their encoding of Oriental Otherness.

Edward Said identifies Flaubert as one of the nineteenth-century authors who did most to reinforce the association between the Orient and sex[55] and in *The Temptations of St Antony* we find a vision of Sheba which is both a remarkable fusion of traditions about the Arabian Queen and highly erotic.[56] This is Otherness as colonialist projection. But with Yeats the erotic is coupled with a modern occultism, which is probably much more a post-Christian reflex than a colonialist one. It is only with Romare Bearden's *She-ba,* taken as symbolic of Sheba as the cultural heroine of the black community in the United States, that we enter the arena of what might be called a progressive Otherness, in which the image of the black queen gesturing with an imperial wave reverses imperialism.[57]

The Magi are in a way the New Testament counterpart of the exoticism of Sheba. We should note those parts of Trexler's study where legitimation gives way to something subversive. Four important examples are the uprisings at Epiphany which he records as occurring repeatedly in Mexico City and Lima between 1537 and 1667; the development of the black magus; the development of the feminine magus; and the arrival of poor, begging kings in Europe.[58]

We now move on to the work of four specific modern novelists, whose retellings of biblical stories form a significant part of the material handled in our fourteen reception-histories, and whose work also engages with the issues

---

55 Said, ibid., p. 188.
56 Gustav Flaubert: *The Temptation of St Anthony* (New York: the Modern Library, 2001).
57 See Pritchard, op cit, p. 144 and illustration 62.
58 See Trexler, op cit, pp. 155–6, 102–7, 107–118, 170–85.

of Otherness we are exploring. The works are: Herman Melville's *Moby Dick*; Miguel de Unamuno's *El Otro*; Michel Tournier's novels *The Ogre* and *Gemini*; and Margaret Atwood's *The Handmaid's Tale* and *The Robber Bride*.

As a preface, it may be worth remembering that the use of material quarried from ancient authors or authorities had gone out of fashion in the late Victorian period. But with the Modernists (Joyce, Harding, Forster, Pound) came a change. Herbert Schneidau's description of the return to the distant past as a source of meaning and transcendence (in the literary sense) may help us locate the new approach to biblical stories which emerges at about the same time: 'While most Westerners were still living as if they had to accept Tennyson's admonition to 'move upwards, working out the beast, And let the ape and tiger die,' the Modernists were able to look on the primordial past as the source of long-stored energy.'

Herman Melville: *Moby Dick*

We begin with Otherness in that proto-Modernist, Herman Melville. Yvonne Sherwood's reading of Melville's *Moby Dick*. incorporates a number of other contemporary readings by literary critics and creative writers. The sum of these readings is that the text of *Moby Dick* encapsulates or articulates two sorts of Otherness. The first is the Otherness of the totalising ideologies of the modern period, from 'rubber truncheons, Hitler, Stalin and Mussolini' to post-Imperial manifestations of totalising power; this is the Otherness of a power structure from which the reader feels alienated. The second sort of Otherness is the intractability of the natural order or of reality, manifested in the triumph of Moby Dick itself or 'Vietnam' or 'Afghanistan'.[59]

Whilst pietistic readings of *Moby Dick* were once seduced by the honeyed rhetoric of Father Mapple's sermon about Jonah, Sherwood demonstrates that

59   See Sherwood, op cit, pp. 152–75.

the sermon and the hymns sung at the service are self-deconstructive. This is Calvinism imploding on itself. Not only that, but the whole tenor of the sermon is rapidly dismissed by Ishmael-the-narrator's preference for 'a sober pagan rather than a drunken Christian'. Modern authors like Julian Barnes, meanwhile, are more pre-occupied by what they see as the collapse of the whole theistic master-narrative rather than the specifically Calvinist elements in it. Set against the exploitative discourse of a discredited master-narrative, the untameable force of the sea and the visceral strength of the great whale represent Otherness of a different order. For atheists like Barnes, presumably, this is the impenetrable rawness of Nature. Sherwood's alternative version of theology would find an elusive, maverick, unclubbable deity within this Otherness. Seen in these terms, the novel *Moby Dick*, taken as a whole, is an antidote to false projections of Otherness rather than a prescription in favour of one reformist programme or another.

This understanding of *Moby Dick* would fit very well with the scholarly consensus that Melville's great project was concerned with transcending the social matrices of the religion of his day as well as the cultural matrices of America's emergence from the colonial era. The first form of transcendence was interlocked with the author's interest in 'primitive' world religion (the 'South Sea Melville') and with the relativising of biblical truth-claims inherent in the new biblical scholarship. The second form manifests itself in the text's parodying of Shakespearean forms (the soliloquies; the low-life scenes on board the *Pequod*.)[60] The great white whale finally destroys not only Captain Ahab but the meliorism of liberal Protestantism and, emerging from its 'absent presence' in the first two-thirds of the novel, becomes the focus of a narrative action which leaves behind the rambling discourses of the previous text. Lawrence Buell equates this narrative takeover with the triumph of a

---

60   See John Bryant: '*Moby Dick* as Revolution' and Jenny Franchot: 'Melville's Traveling God' (sic) in Robert S. Levine (ed.): *The Cambridge Companion to Herman Melville* (Cambridge: Cambridge University Press, 1998/1999).

revelatory sacred vision, mimicking the preference of the biblical text for narrative action.[61] A more cautious approach would follow Rowland Sherrill in reading *Moby Dick*, like other imaginative literature, as a 'hypothetical version of reality'.[62] The place of *Moby Dick* within the canon of American literature, as a pivotal cultural icon and the subject of a huge proliferation of commentaries, nevertheless gives it an importance which makes it a quasi sacred text.

In *Religion and its Monsters*,[63] Timothy Beal traces the theme of the Freudian *unheimlich* as a site for encounter with religious Otherness. Although he does not discuss *Moby Dick*, Beal's reading of the horror novels of Howard Phillips Lovecraft (1890–1937) as a quest to locate religious experience in the context of cosmic fear, a search for the chthonic in contrast to the reassuringly beneficent deity of modern western religion, seems like an extension of the intractable religious presence which Sherwood finds in Melville's whale. It is only the evidence of a final lack of seriousness on the part of Lovecraft (in contrast to the earnestness of some of his devotees) which disqualifies him from the role of theologian of the Monstrous Other. For our purposes, the significance of this corner of America literature perhaps lies less in the intentionality of one writer of popular fiction than in the fact that he had identified the vulnerability of 'anthropocentric cosmological veneers' and had attempted to stitch together an alternative, albeit a hotch-potch of 'mutually incompatible religious discourses and ritual practices'.[64] We have the sense of unfinished business in the imaginative response to the horror literature of the nineteenth-century, including Mary Shelley's *Frankenstein*, Bram Stoker's *Dracula*, and (as we would argue) Melville's masterpiece itself.

---

61 See Lawrence Buell: '*Moby Dick* as Sacred Text' in Richard H. Brodhead (ed.): *New Essays on Moby Dick* (Cambridge: Cambridge University Press, 1986).

62 See Rowland A. Sherrill: 'Melville and Religion' in John Brant (ed.): *A Companion to Melville Studies* (New York: Greenwood Press, 1986), p. 485.

63 Timothy K. Beal: *Religion and its Monsters* (London: Routledge, 2002).

64 Ibid., p. 184.

Miguel de Unamuno: *El Otro*

Miguel de Unamuno, famous for his enigmatic and quasi-mystical work of theology, *The Tragic Sense of Life*, was also the author of a collection of equally enigmatic short stories and plays, which include *Abel Sanchez*[65] and *El Otro*.[66] In *Abel Sanchez*[67] he deals with the tragic recent history of Spain where the Cain and Abel story is validated, sadly, by the national experience. But Otherness is most explicitly handled in *El Otro* where, as Quinones puts it, 'Every Cain is an Abel because every murder is suicide'.[68] In this play, Cosme and Damian are twin brothers. They are in love with the same woman. Whilst one of them is away, the other marries the woman. When the absent brother returns, there is a struggle and one is killed. But nobody can tell who is the killer and who is the victim. The survivor is then called 'El Otro'. Finally, the plot is further complicated by the arrival of a second woman who claims she is also the wife of one of the brothers. This second woman turns out to be pregnant with twins. The play dramatises the sense that human identity is perpetually torn between the singleness of individual consciousness and the Other as a defining boundary. This is the human predicament. We are all Cain and Abel.

---

65 Miguel de Unamuno: *Novela/Nívola*, trans. Anthony Kerrigan (Princeton NJ: Princeton University Press, 1976), pp. 249–380.

66 Miguel de Unamuno: *Ficciones*, trans. Anthony Kerrigan (Princeton NJ: Princeton University Press, 1976), pp. 251–300.

67 Miguel de Unamuno: *Novela/Nívola*, trans. Anthony Kerrigan (Princeton NJ: Princeton University Press, 1976), pp. 249–380.

68 Quinones, op cit, p. 228.

Michel Tournier: *The Ogre* and *Gemini*

In Tournier's two novels *The Ogre*[69] and *Gemini*[70] Otherness becomes first the cause of human social disintegration and then, in the second novel, the path to reconciliation. In *The Ogre*, the outcast Abel Tiffauges represents the most unappealing and unassimilable aspects of human personality and only narrowly escapes annihilation at the hands of the Cainites, in the shape of the Nazis. This 'Rabelesian giant,' however longs for the day when he and his fellow nomadic types can finally purge the world of the citizens of Cain's city. However, in *Gemini*, after numerous destructive encounters between Cainites and Abelites, the character Paul in *Gemini* finally becomes the vehicle of the defeat of the determinism of the Cain and Abel story (according to Quinones's reading[71]), and the quest for individuation finally gives way to universalism.

Margaret Atwood: *The Handmaid's Tale* and *The Robber Bride*

Finally, Otherness in Atwood's *The Handmaid's Tale* [72]and *The Robber Bride*[73] takes at least three different forms. In *The Handmaid's Tale* it is the suppression of biblical transcendence and the narrow, fundamentalist exploitation of two or three biblical texts (chiefly Genesis 30 vv 1–3, and Genesis 3 v 16) to support a programme of legalised rape which signifies theological Otherness by its absence.[74] In *The Robber Bride*, the idea of Zenia as the latest incarnation of a

---

69 Michel Tournier: *The Ogre,* trans. Barbara Bray (New York: Doubleday, 1972).

70 Michel Tournier: *Gemini,* trans. Anne Carter (London: Minerva, 1989).

71 Quinones, op cit, p. 237.

72 Margaret Atwood: *The Handmaid's Tale* (London: Vintage, 1985/1996).

73 Margaret Atwood: *The Robber Bride* (London: Virago, 1994/2003).

74 Larry Kreitzer in *Gospel Images in Fiction and Film* (Sheffield: Sheffield Academic Press 2002), pp. 143–71, explores the sense in which *The Handmaid's Tale* is a parody of biblical themes. He also looks at two adaptations of the novel, one for film and one for radio.

form of evil which is unrelieved by any redeeming characteristics points towards a supernatural explanation, as does the importance of the main characters' dreams as source of guidance.

In her study of the novels of Margaret Atwood, Coral Ann Howells[75] reads *The Handmaid's Tale* as a dystopia depicting the effort by a future totalitarian version of American patriarchal society to eliminate the Otherness of women by reducing them entirely to the reproductive function. In this novel women are either the passive right-wing consorts of the dominating males or (in most cases) enslaved child-breeders, all living in a society which has turned the language of seventeenth-century New England Puritanism into a sort of fascist discourse. 'Offred,' the narrator, is the 'handmaid' of the Commander and has been procured in order to provide him and his wife with a child. The novel describes the furtive attempts of Offred to resist her own erasure as a woman, something evident in her clandestine love-affair with the Commander's driver and in her delight in time spent in the garden of the Commander's wife, seen by Howells as a 'Tennysonian garden'. It could be said that, in the terms of the novel, these are the two moments of transcendence in a narrative which otherwise is uncompromisingly bleak in its account of the successful erasure of Otherness. Howells points out that even Offred's own account of her terrible ordeal is threatened with a form of erasure by the fact that, in the frame narrative, it becomes the object of editing by a male professor, who sifts through her recorded words in a quest for 'objective history'. This is the story of the Virgin Mary translated into the form of a nightmare.

Comparing *The Handmaid's Tale* with H.G. Wells's *The Time Machine* (seen, we recall, by Quinones as a rewritten Cain and Abel story), we can say that Atwood's novel takes the Wellsian dystopia much further. In *The Time Machine* the unhappy co-existence of the spiritual Eloi and carnivorous Morlocks at least means that Otherness survives, pending, of course, the final glimpse of the end of

---

75   Coral Ann Howells: *Margaret Atwood* (Basingstoke: Palgrave, 1996, new ed. 2005).

life on earth, millions of years ahead. In *The Handmaid's Tale*, the 'present time' of the main narrative is an era of largely unrelieved gloom, even given the ironic standpoint offered by the fact that the reader turns out to hearing Offred's story through the medium of a post-dystopic society.

In our final example, Atwood's later novel *The Robber Bride*, Otherness returns as a more complex topic. Although in this study we have so far followed Gaines in focusing on the figure of Zenia as an unredeemed Jezebel figure, the chief concern of the novel, as Howells points out, is with Zenia as-seen-through-the eyes of the three foregrounded female characters, Tony, Roz and Charis. For all three, Zenia is the Other Woman, both in the immediate sense that she seeks to seduce their husbands, and in the more psychological sense that she represents the shadow side or reverse pole of their personalities. Even after her final demise (as opposed to the mock funeral which occurs near the beginning), Zenia continues to dominate the thoughts of the three women. She is the ruthless, overwhelmingly sexually attractive, enigmatic character that they are not; but she also embodies all the Othernesses of postwar Canada, including her status as a foreign immigrant, an émigré Russian princess, or alternatively the child of a Holocaust-survivor, the child of a mixed Roman Catholic and Jewish marriage, and as a drug addict and AIDS victim. She brings to the surface all the personal insecurities of the other three women.

Howells finds in Zenia the combining of a feminised version of the Robber Bridegroom of the Brothers Grimm tale, the biblical Jezebel (incorporating the Great Whore of Revelation 17) and the French Cathar woman warrior, Dame Giraude, the latter the subject of historical research by Roz in her professional life as an academic. She argues: 'Zenia represents the phobic underside of consciousness for the three friends, but she also represents the social neuroses and traumatic memories that are buried in the foundations of late twentieth-century Western culture. She remains un-dead, a vampiric figure … she derives her life from the insecurities and desires of the living'.

For Gaines, 'Atwood uses Jezebel as a symbol of eternal evil, reborn in every generation',[76] whereas for Howells Zenia reflects back on society its projections of Otherness, whether in the inexhaustible desirability of the *femme fatale* or the exoticism of the foreign immigrant. We may be inclined initially to interpret 'eternal evil' as a more promising channel of transcendence in the theological sense than the 'mirrors' which Howells understands as the novel's key *leitmotif*. However, the repeated references to mirrors in *The Robber Bride* do carry the connotations not only of Snow White's mirror (a clear magic-realist device), but also the whole theological and literary sense of mirrors as windows on the soul, from the medieval idea of unstained mirrors as tokens of the Virgin's purity, through the iconographic motif of emblems as *Veritas* and the Puritan's biblical emphasis on the mirror as a metaphor for God's Word, epitomised in the looking glass given to Mercy by the Shepherds of the Delectable Mountains in the second part of Bunyan's *The Pilgrim's Progress*.[77]

If we allow the tradition which culminates in Bunyan's mirror to act as an intertext for this aspect of *The Robber Bride*, then we have a transcendent reference independent of the sense of Jezebel as a demonic figure. This may finally offer a more meaningful route into theological Otherness than the resort to treating Atwood's Zenia as the incarnation of a diabolical force in some dualistic system.

In this chapter, we have explored the territory which stretches from Otherness as a fundamental theological category and 'cheer word' to Otherness as the problematic rock, blocking the paths of feminism and racial tolerance and integration. Given their influence on several of the authors of our fourteen reception-histories, we cannot ignore the claims of the school of Lacan that theological transcendence is a

---

76   Gaines, op cit, p. 131.

77   See entry, 'Mirror Without Stain', by James F. Forrest, in David Lyle Jeffrey (ed.): *A Dictionary of Biblical Tradition in English Literature* (Grand Rapids, Michigan: William B Eerdrmans, 1992), p. 515.

conceit for the phallic dominance of an androcentric, patriarchal culture, even if we reject those claims as themselves redolent of an ideological monoculture.

But moving beyond the stand-off between theism and non-theism, our argument must be that the examples of rewritten biblical stories considered above all support a dialogue between the traditional theme of Otherness in religious thought and Otherness as the problematic in contemporary discourse concerned with sexuality and ethnicity. Milton's *Paradise Lost*, both as read by modern critics and as read or misread by his rewriters, is an important site for this dialogue. But so is the unexpectedly varied cultural history of the Magi. Beardon's *SHE-BA* brings us female and colonialist Otherness fighting back. Mary Shelley's *Frankenstein* satirises patriarchy, and probably Milton, but also challenges the whole Enlightenment project. Tennyson's *Maud* is a discordant voice, eulogising morbidity. Melville's *Moby Dick* invites the reader to escape the clutches of all pre-packaged versions of reality. Unamuno rewrites Byron's Cain to interrogate the boundaries which denote individual consciousness. Tournier promises us the overriding of the negative aspects of Otherness. Margaret Atwood alerts us to the dangerous tendencies threatening the tolerance of Otherness in contemporary American culture (*The Handmaid's Tale*) and to the complex ways in which human personality is constructed in modern (Canadian) society, on the basis of projections of Otherness (*The Robber Bride*).

The fact that this list includes some of the major landmarks of Western literature, as well as some of its most unsettling texts, suggests that rewritten biblical stories will continue to constitute an important site for the confluence of the two senses of Otherness we have examined. In terms of the theology associated with the name of Levinas, we could say that those rewritten biblical stories (or hypertexts[78]) which

---

78 See Appendix C for a discussion of the definition of the urtext as 'hypotext' and the rewritten text as 'hypertext'.

218

force the reader to confront the inalienable Otherness of that which is culturally excluded bring about the disclosure of the divine.

Levinas's great plea is for human beings to respect the Otherness of other people, as well as the Otherness of the natural order, and in so doing encounter the divine. The antithesis of such respect is the violence, both physical and moral, which seeks to create of 'The Other' an object which can be manipulated, labelled, exploited, excluded or annihilated in the furtherance of the self-image or the interests of the perpetrator.[79]

Clearly for feminists, patriarchy, as it is encountered in many of the biblical urtexts and in a large proportion of their reception-history, is the site of exactly the violence which Levinas describes. The same could be said of those texts which have been used in the service of anti-semitism, racialism in general, and homophobia. But the reception-history also contains remarkable examples of works which challenge the abusive stance towards Otherness. In earlier chapters we have noted the subversive tendencies of the Magi hypertexts, as well as those of Sheba, Judith and the Apocalypse. In this chapter we have explored the subtle probing of Otherness in works by Milton, Tennyson, Mary Shelley, Melville, Unamuno, Tournier and Atwood, which form part of the afterlife of the biblical stories of Adam and Eve, Jonah, Cain and Abel, Jezebel, Mary Magdalene and the Virgin Mary.

Just as it is reputedly almost impossible to read Genesis 3 without the colouration provided by *Paradise Lost*, it could be argued that *all* hypertexts have an indelible impact on the sourcetext or urtext. In that sense, the works discussed in this chapter all contribute to a revisionary reading of their respective urtexts. They could be said to rescue those texts from what some see as their negative history. But another way to view the evidence is to see the hypertext as part of the outworking of the urtext. In other words, as the reception-history proceeds, it releases something

---

79   See Emmanuel Levinas: *Entre Nous* trans. Michael B. Smith and Barbara Harshav (London: Continuum, 2006).

latent in the urtext. After all, Unamuno found something compelling about Genesis 4 (refracted through Byron) as a vehicle for his own exploration of human identity in relation to Otherness and Melville's great novel was launched on the site of Jonah and not some other urtext. Mary Shelley chose the Miltonic Genesis 3 as the locus for *Frankenstein* and not a Shakespearean play.

However, as we know from such examples as Tennyson's *Maud*, not everything in the outworking of Otherness in the reception-history of a biblical story is healthy. It may indeed be pathological. The value of applying the insights of Levinas is having an ethical measure of the handling of Otherness as a theme. In the case of the morbidity of *Maud*, we could find that the corrective is the call to 'die the other's death', because of 'the priority of the other over the I'.[80]

More positively, the rich and varied manifestations of humanity celebrated in the novels of Michel Tournier and Margaret Atwood in the context of rewriting biblical stories may be taken as the literary counterpart to Levinas's call for the hallowing of Otherness.

We can therefore argue that the rewriting of biblical stories always has the potential to protect or to revivify the evocation of the Other in the urtext and that, far from leading to the blunting of the text, it may lead to the text's re-sharpening.

Clearly there *are* hypertexts which diminish the hypotext and clearly there *are* rewritten biblical stories which tend to extinguish the richness or the Otherness of the original, but there is enough evidence in the work of Milton, Blake, Unamuno, Mary Shelley, Margaret Atwood and others to suggest that what Julie Sanders calls 're-visioning' may indeed be precisely that.[81]

Conventionally it has been the task of biblical scholars and preachers to connect the biblical text with the demands and insights of later cultures. But the

80   Levinas, ibid., p. 188.
81   Julie Sanders: *Adaptation and Appropriation* (Abingdon: Routledge, 2006), where the author uses 're-visioning' to describe more generally both the playful and political dimensions of rewriting. See Appendix C.

220

literary reception-history of biblical stories offers an entrée into a world in which this process has been underway independently and, of course, dangerously. It may be that it is the dangerousness of Milton rewriting Genesis or of Blake rewriting Job which is required to reignite our sense of the Otherness contained within the biblical material, especially when that material has had such a long history of what we might call commodification for institutional religious purposes.

David Jasper refers to Blake as one of the very few poets who 'have dared utterly to follow scripture'.[82] Just as orthodox theology always seeks to insist on the priority of scripture as revelation, so perhaps we should learn to respect those creative writers who have surrendered to the influence of the biblical text, even to the point of obsession. For most of them it is pre-occupation with one particular biblical story (amongst our examples, Melville with Jonah or Unamuno with Cain and Abel), a fact which may indicate that the taming of the text is at least in part associated with the self-cancelling effect of an overabundance of words or of the sort of detachment which glosses over the great diversity found within the component texts to create a homogenized entity, 'the Bible'.

Even writers whose approach to rewriting biblical stories is more whimsical than obsessive may nevertheless may have the capacity to release a renewed sense of the Other, as we see in Chapter 6.

---

82 David Jasper: *The Sacred Desert: Religion, Literature, Art and Culture* (Oxford: Blackwell, 2004), p. 153.

Chapter 8

ANALYSING THE FOURTEEN STUDIES AS LITERARY STRUCTURES

The purpose of this chapter is to analyse the fourteen reception-histories as structures. Since we examine many of their chief arguments and much of their underlying material elsewhere, our purpose here is largely to bracket out content and to focus, firstly, on shared formats and, secondly, on the stance from which each reception-history is written. We will also have regard to the possible interplay between framework and argument.

It will be seen immediately that there are similarities of form shared by several of the reception-histories and also that there is a broad division between those clusters of reception-histories which attempt to maintain an objective stance in relation to their subject-matter and those which seem to wish to join in the fray. Our argument will be that the Prefaces and Epilogues are highly significant with regard to the second type of grouping. We will consider these two phenomena in turn.

Common Formats

The Pritchard volume of 1974, although unique amongst our fourteen studies in being a collection of essays by different scholars, sets the pattern of the dual background history/reception-history format which we find also in Norris and Gaines. In all three cases, roughly half the text is devoted to the historical background and/or explication of the biblical urtext and half to the reception-

222

history in imaginative literature. Each of the three has a distinctive terminology,[1] suggesting that the authors arrived at their dual pattern independently, something which is confirmed by the general sense in all these studies that the writers were not conscious of operating within a tradition or school of thought. Levenson's much more modest study shares in the same duality, here named 'Hebraic Vision' and 'the Book of Job in the Twentieth Century'.[2]

Warner in *Alone Of All Her Sex* is the master of the major themes/minor themes pattern in a text which is effectively one-hundred percent reception-history. The use of the major themes, Virgin, Queen, Bride, Mother, Intercessor, to control what the author makes the sub-themes (Maria Regina, Mater Dolorosa[3]) seems inevitable until one compares it with the quite different schema offered by Anna Jameson's *Legends of the Madonna* (1852),[4] which divides the field into two major parts (Devotional Subjects and Historical Subjects) and has even more sub-themes. Warner's study is extraordinary in being both the earliest full-scale reception-history in our survey and the only one which has an antecedent.

Quinones also has a two-layer approach to themes, but in his case the two layers interpenetrate each other, so that what he calls 'The Three Traditions' (Citizen Cain, Monstrous Cain, Sacred Executioner) crop up in and around the more-or-less sequential literary history of 'Regenerate Cain', 'Dramas of Envy', and 'Tomorrow's Cain'. This sophisticated pattern is slightly confused by the division of the text into four 'Parts', in which The Three Traditions constitute Part One and the Regenerate Cain, Dramas of Envy and Tomorrow's Cain constitute Parts Two, Three, and Four,

---

1   In Pritchard the reception-history is called 'The Legend and its Diffusion'; in Norris, 'Fantasies of Eve'; in Gaines, 'The Eternal Jezebel'.

2   The two subtitles relating to the two halves of Levenson's Job study, see Levenson, op. cit., pp. 1 and 5.

3   Warner, op. cit., p. vii.

4   Anna Bronwell Jameson: *Legends of the Madonna* (London: Longman, Brown, Green and Longmans, 1852), pp. iii–viii.

respectively.[5] The inclusion of H.G. Wells's *The Time Machine* (a work with little demonstrable connection to the theme) in Part Four[6] does suggest that the structure is slightly creaky in this otherwise very persuasive reception-history.

Paffenroth[7] offers a different version of the two-layer schema, in that the five chapters bearing the titles of the major themes ('Judas the Obscure', 'Judas the Arch-Sinner: Object of Horror', etc.) begin with a theme related purely to the early period and then discuss themes which cover the bulk of the reception-history (from the gospels to Oberammergau, for example), before shading off into a theme ('Judas the Penitent: Object of Hope') which, though rooted in the gospel tradition, represents a characteristically modern reversal. In fact, the title rather disguises the actual content of this final theme/chapter, which is chiefly concerned with the modern rehabilitation of Judas. Within the five thematic chapters, there are minor themes ('Judas as Avaricious', 'Judas the Lover', etc.), though these are mixed in with such topics as 'Judas's Name in Charms' and 'Judas's Red Hair', which we might call non-narrative themes. In this case, we have a thematic structure which tends to belie the author's underlying argument that the story of Judas is a movement from invented origins through demonisation and on to modern projections of Judas as a misunderstood fall-guy. The reason this happens is that treating each separate theme as a gospel-to-present-day progression disrupts the argument and, inevitably, the themes themselves are slightly arbitrary, unlike those in the Virgin Mary tradition, where the nomenclature is firmly established.

Haskins and Stocker both present us with a succession of themes which carry the burden of their arguments. Whilst Haskins's themes have a sort of historical glow ('Apostola Apostolorum', 'Beata Peccatrix') those of Stocker are more racy ('The Gorgeous Gorgon', 'The Monstrous Regiment of Judiths'). In both cases

---

5   Quinones, op. cit., pp. v–vi.
6   Ibid., pp. 201–5.
7   Paffenroth, op. cit., pp. ix–x.

224

there is a clear chronological progress. In Haskins, it is from biblical origins to nemesis. In Stocker, it is from biblical origins to untamed hermeneutical force and significance. Haskins is more concerned in the body of her text with art-history, acknowledging her book's origins in research into the iconography of Mary Magdalene in seventeenth-century art.[8] Nevertheless, she pays close attention to literature, at least from the Victorian period onwards. Stocker casts her net widely in art, literature, and popular fiction and drama, in order to explore her subject. The effect here is that of an exhaustive survey which, at times, stretches credibility, as when the puppet-theatre of Punch and Judy is enlisted.[9]

Haskins seems, in her argument, to be somewhat at variance with the range and richness of her material. If the whole legend was a false trail, why expend such a lavish amount of space on it? Stocker, by contrast, is so convinced that the Judith story is 'the' key counter-cultural myth of western culture[10] that she seems prepared to ransack every corner of cultural history to find it. These are structural matters in that they appertain to the relationship of the content-volume of the respective studies to their arguments. In one case, extensive erudition is deployed almost for its own sake, only to be swept aside by a feminist argument. In the other case, the feminist argument drives the whole survey and is repeatedly re-expressed in the different contexts, though Stocker is careful to locate degenerate uses of the theme[11] as well as those which accord with the recognition of the Judith story as dynamically counter-cultural.

Both Cohn and Trexler offer surveys which are controlled by chronologically-determined themes. In Cohn's case, there is an inner-core chronology which

8   Haskins, op. cit., p. ix.
9   Stocker, op. cit., pp. 135–7.
10   See Stocker, Ibid., pp. 2, 23, 251–2.
11   Examples include Judith's image in portraits in bordello-galleries (ibid., p. 38); Thomas Arne's Oratorio of 1761 (ibid., pp. 140–1); and John Le Carré's *Little Drummer Girl* (ibid., pp. 225–6).

225

records the rise of modern scientific approaches to geological history and changes in attitudes to biblical cosmology in the eighteenth- and nineteenth-centuries. Seven chapters out of eleven are concerned with this topic.[12] For this author, the biblical story of the Flood, its Mesopotamian pre-history, and the history of its early interpretation, form the prelude to the main story, with the return of 'hidden meanings' in the closing chapter, as a sort of brief sequel.

Trexler's chronological survey is much more evenly spread, giving extensive coverage to all the significant periods in the reception-history of The Journey of the Magi, though the author emphasises that his study is related to the 'political sociology of the magi in Christianity from their appearance in Matthew to the present',[13] rather than to a wider history of 'the magi cult'.[14] It could be argued that it is this approach which sharpens what might otherwise be a rather meandering reception-history. Three central chapters, Chapter 3: The Pageant of the 'Two Kings', Chapter 4: El Dorado, and Chapter 5: The Ancien Régime of the Magi, present an array of extraordinary material which, by its sheer volume, supports the author's thesis that the story of the Magi has great plasticity and inner reserves.

We have already noted that Wroe's Pilate is a hybrid between a novel and the history of a legend. Rather as with Haskins, we are invited by the authorial dismissal of the whole legend to ask why so much space should be devoted to a blind-alley in western culture, though the dismissal here is a secularist one rather than a feminist one. The author's unease about the status of legendary material is evident structurally in the constant interweaving of concrete historical 'fact' (like the Pilate inscription found at Caesarea[15]) with fantastic stories about Pilate (such as Pilate's crucifixion or damnation).[16] Because there is no critical attempt to evaluate the material, let alone

12   Cohn, op. cit., pp. 32–130. These chapters comprise nearly 70% of the book.
13   Trexler, op. cit., p. 4.
14   Ibid., p. 6.
15   Wroe, op. cit., pp. 82–3.
16   Wroe, ibid., pp. 248 and 353–7.

to explore the possible cultural or religious significance of apocryphal works, it all becomes part of a mélange of undifferentiated 'Pilate lore'.

The canonical gospels form a sort of monitoring element amidst all the accretions. 'Matthew ignored the actual setting of the guard, but medieval writers made the most of it', we read,[17] after which we are treated to a rendering of episodes from the mystery plays, unattributed and included as part of the ongoing narrative, as though unrelated to the gaps in Matthew. Elsewhere, the narrative moves from the summary of apocryphal material ('The Copts may have made a saint out of Pilate but they did not exculpate him ... so in another Coptic fragment, Pilate interrogated the soldiers, dismissed their feeble excuses, threw them into prison and went back to the garden himself') straight to realistic narrative: 'It was still early. The bushes of the garden were soaked with dew as he brushed against them ... '[18] The result is a variant on the stream-of-consciousness novel, with dream-like episodes of realistic narrative, often based on the legendary material, interwoven with historical comment, the canonical gospels being part of the historical comment. The overall movement of the frame story of Pilate moves from early beginnings at Rome to the fairly conclusive exorcising of his ghost on Mount Pilatus in Switzerland by 1585.[19]

Pippin's *Apocalyptic Bodies* is a very selective reception-history, in that its eight chapters are devoted to discussing the outworking of the 'horror' elements of themes from biblical apocalyptic in literature, film and art. This results in a highly episodic structure, passing quickly from billboards of the Klu Klux Klan to Mark

---

17 Ibid., p. 302.

18 Ibid., p. 310.

19 The Coptic tradition of Pilate as a saint and the association of Pilate with Mount Pilatus are given more specific documentation in J.K. Elliott: *The Apocryphal New Testament* (Oxford: Oxford University Press, 1993/1999), pp. 159–63 and 208–217. It is clear from this work that there is no evidence for a 'Coptic Gospel of Pilate', even as a lost work, and therefore that Wroe's shipwreck in her Prologue is more than just embroidery; it is pure invention. This certainly confuses the character of the authorial voice, making it veer from that of a diligent researcher in the London Library to that of a fabulist.

13 and then to the fiction of Flannery O'Connor (Chapter 2); the images of Jezebel in Dore's Bible illustrations and in Tom Robbins's *Skinny Legs and All* occupy Chapter 3; the Tower of Babel in art fills Chapter 4; the Abyss of Revelation as read by Nietzsche and by the postmodernists comprise Chapter 5; apocalyptic monsters and the Whore of Babylon lead to a discussion of modern horror fiction in Chapter 6; and examples of apocalyptic fear in Chapter 7 lead to a discussion of the horror-film genre. The Conclusion explores the destabilising of gender difference in Revelation, seeing it as ultimately misogynist.

Compared with most of our other examples, the absence of a chronological sequence in Pippin's thematic chapters highlights the arbitrary choice of examples from the arts. Why select Doré's engravings of Jezebel and not Dürer's The Marriage of the Lamb or Satan Cast Into The Pit? Why ignore D.H. Lawrence? Why should misogyny and perversity (literally) have the last word?[20]

Finally, Sherwood's book on Jonah demonstrates that it is, after all, possible to avoid a chronological sequence without riding roughshod over chronology. Despite the density of her argument, the actual basic structure of A Biblical Text and its Afterlife is very simple. As our outline above indicates, it is a three-part account of the orthodox Christian reading of the Jonah story ('the Mainstream'); the much more playful, disturbing and anti-domesticating readings of both Jewish midrash and the literary tradition; and the implications of all this for biblical hermeneutics and for theology. There is a sense that somewhere behind this book there lies a more 'catalogue raisonee' style of reception-history, just as the author herself indicates that a whole book could have been written about the relationship of Melville's Moby Dick to the Jonah text.

---

20   Pippin, op. cit., p. 125. The last two lines of the book read: 'What remains is the misogyny and exclusion by a powerful, wrathful deity. In the Apocalypse, the Kingdom of God is the kingdom of perversity'.

Objective Stances and Committed Stances

Objective stances we take to be those where the author declares no autobiographical link with the theme and displays a degree of objectivity about the reception-history and about its future prospects. Committed stances is the term we will use to act as (one hopes) an objective description of non-objective or paradigm-driven approaches.

Our earliest example, Levenson (1971) is, from this point of view, a fairly straightforward academic monograph and, despite its rather blinkered approach to the topic of Job-and-suffering in the twentieth-century, must be placed in the 'objective' camp. Pritchard, similarly, is an academic collection of essays, with an open-ended view of the future.

Quinones offers another academic monograph, with an open position about the future direction of the perpetually resonant story of Cain and Abel. If there is a lack of objectivity, it is in claiming this story to be supreme in western culture. Something similar could be said about Trexler and Stocker, both of whom claim to have found something like the key to reality in the western world. But we can take these hyperbolic positions to be the stock-in trade of the dedicated advocate. Only in the case of Stocker do we find this assuming a sort of transcendental, determinative function, where the myth or story itself becomes not merely a supreme myth amongst competing myths, but a tool for dissecting all mythological forms.

Sherwood has a similar optimism to that of Stocker, with the difference that her claims about the story of Jonah and its afterlife are more specifically related to their relevance for reading the Bible as a defamiliarised text and for unleashing a rawer sense of God/Reality on the reader. Whilst Stocker envisages release from oppressive myths (including patriarchy, but not just patriarchy),[21] Sherwood seems to be on the

---

21   Stocker, op. cit., p. 252.

229

trail of something still more elusive and exciting, the vision of a suppressed textual tradition which has the capacity to refresh our perception of reality.[22]

Meanwhile, back in the world we actually inhabit, we can also number Norris as a member of the objective group, in the sense that her version of the story of Eve (which she claims is really the story of Woman) is both feminist and moderate, being prepared to entertain the texts of Eden-and-its-afterlife but just read them differently.

The Committed Stance in reception-history really begins with Warner. A very thoroughly researched and documented account of the 'Cult of the Virgin Mary' is negated by an Epilogue which sees no future for a myth which has run its course. Haskins's study effectively mirrors this approach, like Warner recounting a Catholic upbringing in the Preface and closing with a marking of the demise of the myth. Wroe seems committed not so much to feminism as to secularism, recounting in novelistic fashion the remarkable twists and turns of the Pilate legend, before a downhill descent from Mount Pilatus towards the banalities of the United Beach Mission. She implies a contrast between Pilate as 'an invented man' and Jesus as a historical figure, without considering that Jesus may equally be, in terms of the gospel portraits, an invented figure, but yet both historical and of central significance for theology. Wroe's is a sort of literalist secularism.

Gaines's committed stance seems a little assumed, in the sense that the rehabilitation of Jezebel runs against the grain of most of her material. We have seen that there is a noticeable absence of a Conclusion or Epilogue in her book. Our only clue about the outcome of this study lies in the closing words of the final chapter, where we find more of a recognition of the destructive side of Jezebel.[23] Seen as a rather whimsical feminist tract, this reception-history has the merit of

---

22   Sherwood, op. cit., pp. 291–2.
23   Gaines, op. cit., p. 189.

drawing attention to the problematic situation of non-Yahwist religion in the First Testament and of questioning the stereotyping of women.

Both Pippin and Paffenroth seem committed to expunging radical evil from the biblical text and its reception. Pippin's agenda is related to the identification of misogyny in the Apocalypse. Paffenroth's agenda seems to be connected with making Judas conform to the stereotypical 'regular guy' of contemporary American culture. In Chapter 2 we suggested that Pippin had missed signals that the Apocalypse was about something other than gender relations. We also question whether erasing the demonic does full justice to the Judas tradition, once anti-semitism has been put aside. What is most significant here, however, is the strong autobiographical link to their subjects implied by both authors. We must ask whether the misappropriation of the Apocalypse in the American South and the hi-jacking of the Judas theme by a rock-band are sufficient grounds to abandon all objectivity in the handling of the reception-history of these two biblical stories. In the case of Pippin, the inclusion of photographs of Klu Klux Klan signs and of the selected iconographic images reinforces the partisan message.

Finally, we might note that with Cohn, objectivity is taken perhaps too far, in that the author seems detached from the whole importance of the Flood narrative as a literary text and iconographic subject. By making science-history the focus, he effectively demotes the biblical text and its reception-history (despite his subtitle[24]) to a secondary status. This relegation is transmitted structurally by the preponderance of science-history over the rest of the material.

In conclusion, we have seen the importance of prefaces and epilogues both in explaining the autobiographical interest of authors (notably Warner, Gaines and Paffenroth) in the subject-matter of their studies and in describing the 'tilt' of each study. The most extreme example of the latter is Warner's Epilogue, effectively dismissing the whole Marian tradition on feminist grounds, whilst Paffenroth's

---

24   *The Genesis Story in Western Thought.*

Epilogue achieves the same result by a different means, submitting the whole Judas tradition to the norms of modern Middle America.

The duality of biblical origins/reception-history seems to be a logical starting-point for those who are particularly conscious of the need to reiterate the findings of biblical criticism or near-eastern archaeology. The formats of the Levenson and Pritchard, our earliest examples, starkly reflect this approach, with a strict division of the text into two parts, 'before' and 'after'. Norris mixes biblical studies with classical-mythological studies in her Part One ('The Making of a Bad Reputation'), before leading on to her account of reception-history in Part Two ('Fantasies of Eve'). Haskins, Wroe and Paffenroth exhibit a sort of internalised duality, by emphasising the contrast between what they regard as 'objective biblical studies' and later tradition, largely to the detriment of the reception-history.

Chronological progress is a feature of most of the studies, with only Sherwood departing radically from this pattern. Warner, Haskins and Wroe progress from biblical origins to nemesis, whilst Stocker, in her Judith study, progresses from biblical origins to untamed hermeneutical force. Norris steers a middle course by suggesting that her material can be read in ways more hospitable to feminist concerns. Gaines moves directly from biblical origins to modern reception-history in her quest to find a liberated Jezebel, the outcome of which is not entirely clear. The studies of both Trexler and Cohn are driven by overarching chronological themes. With Cohn, it is the March of Science. With Trexler, it is changes in political sociology, a theme which proves more friendly to the biblical story of the Journey of the Magi than Cohn's theme does to the biblical story of Noah.

Both Stocker and Sherwood treat their respective biblical stories as hermeneutical keys. For Stocker 'Judith's acteme' (as she terms it) represents a counter-cultural myth and the reception-history demonstrates this. For Sherwood, the biblical story of Jonah is the catalyst for exposing a bifurcation between two divergent ways of reading, 'Mainstream' and 'Backwater'. In the case of Jonah, the Backwater reception-history reveals a text which is capable of defamiliarising the God of the narratives of the rest of the Bible. Whilst Stocker's argument is harnessed to a chronological history, Sherwood's approach is much more literary-critical.

We can say that Quinones, Stocker, Trexler and Sherwood are committed to the importance of their chosen biblical stories, whereas Warner, Haskins, and Gaines start from versions of the feminist master-narrative and Wroe from the secularist master-narrative. Pippin and Paffenroth for separate reasons are driven by the effort to expunge radical evil from the biblical text and its reception-history, Pippin by erasing the text altogether (on radical feminist grounds) and Paffenroth by domesticating the text in favour of contemporary American norms. Both Pippin and Cohn seem to have agendas (or master-narratives) which seriously misread their respective biblical stories by ignoring important dimensions in the history of their signification. The avoidance of material from the pre-modern period, which is a feature of several of the fourteen studies, is achieved in the case of Gaines and Paffenroth by simply ignoring it; in the case of Quinones by relegating the subject to the small-print notes; and in the case of Norris by an overtly selective approach to 'Fantasies of Eve'.

Conclusion

The most satisfying literary structures amongst our fourteen studies are those where the outcome seems to justify the scholarly expenditure (Quinones, Trexler, Stocker, Sherwood, especially) and the most confusing are those where the material is summarily dismissed in the Epilogue, with Warner and Haskins as outstanding examples. Pippin's study, despite what we argue is its wilful misreading of biblical apocalypse, has the merit of consistency in its rejection of the biblical text and its afterlife.

The most conventional structure is that based on the duality of biblical origins/ reception-history, which we find most evident in Levenson, Pritchard, and Gaines, but also, in a modified form, in Norris and Paffenroth. The most unconventional structure, as well as form, is Wroe's hybrid of reception-history and notes for a novel.

In terms of the chronology of the publication of the fourteen studies we are considering, there is an overall movement from structures based on a biblical origins/afterlife duality to more complex structures based on the discernment of recurrent themes in the reception-history. The breakdown of structures, where it occurs (for example in the strained complexity of the Quinones study, in the end of the book by Gaines and in the uncomfortable relationship of some of the prefaces and epilogues to their texts), is a testament to the richness of the material and a signal that no structure is final.

Chapter 9

CONFLATIONS, CONVERGENCES, CONTAMINATIONS AND INTERTEXTS

In this chapter we will look at evidence offered by our fourteen authors which is relevant to the relationship between rewritten biblical stories and other biblical stories; between rewritten biblical stories and stories from classical mythology and general folklore; and between rewritten biblical stories and other literature. The order of treatment this time will be roughly the biblical order of stories.

Conflations will be taken to mean examples where two biblical stories are merged (as with Judith and Jael in Stocker's study) or where a biblical story is merged with a non-biblical one, such as Judas and Oedipus. Convergences will be taken to be examples where the biblical story is rewritten to conform either with a strong literary non-biblical text (such as Job with Lear) or with a formulaic story (such as Judith in Daphne du Maurier's *Rebecca.*) Contaminations will be taken to mean examples where there appears to have been an accidental spilling-over between stories, as in the transfer of the jaw-bone used by Samson to kill the Philistines to become the instrument of Cain's murder of Abel.[1]

Intertextuality, as a concept, ranges from ideas about authorship and authorial intention through to the random juxtaposing of otherwise unrelated texts, as when the film, *The Piano*, is used to interpret St Mark's Gospel or when the *The Wizard of Oz* is used as an intertext for the Book of Job.[2] Here we will use the

---

1 Discussed extensively in M. Schapiro: 'Cain's Jaw-Bone That Did The First Murder', article in *Art Bulletin*, Vol. 24 (1942), pp. 205–12.

2 See David Rhoads and Sandra Roberts: 'From Domination to Mutuality in *The Piano* and in the Gospel of Mark' in Clive Marsh and Gaye Ortiz: *Explorations in Theology and Film* (Oxford: Blackwell, 1997), pp. 47–58 and Tod Linafelt: 'The Wizard of Uz: Job, Dorothy,and

236

term to signify allusions in a text which cause the reader to become conscious of resonances with other works of literature or art and which, therefore, help modify or amplify the text's range of meaning. An example would be the many references to Ovid in *Paradise Lost*.[3]

Eve and Gaia

Beginning then with the Eden story, Norris is surely right to draw attention to what she calls the 'prehistory of Eve as Gaia'. The Genesis narrative is widely agreed to have part of its origins in submerged mythologies of an ancient Earth Mother and it is, in any case, important, as Von Rad argued,[4] to *decontaminate* the story at this level from the familiar Christian doctrinal story of the Fall even if, for the purposes of reception-history, the Fall will be seen to have had a dominant influence on European and American readings of the Eden story. So, as with Jezebel and Astarte, we have the possibility of resonances for the earliest readers of Genesis which connect the text with the fertility cults of the surrounding Near Eastern religions.

Norris notes the fascination of the Early Fathers with the story of Pandora, as an alternative creation myth, recounting the loss of the Golden Age through Pandora's defiance of the gods in her opening of the jar of pestilences. There are direct comparisons between Eve and Pandora in Tertullian, and other Fathers of the Early Church. Erasmus reworked the story, introducing Pandora's famous box

---

the Limits of the Sublime' in *Biblical Interpretation*, Vol. XIV, Nos 1 & 2, 2006., pp. 94–109. The joint authors of the first article avoid the suggestion of any evidence of literary influence between the text of Mark and the film-script for *The Piano*, whereas Tod Linafelt implies that The Book of Job may have had an unconscious influence on Frank Baum.

3   See Sarah Anne Brown: *The Metamorphosis of Ovid, from Chaucer to Ted Hughes* (London: Duckworth, 1999), pp. 101–22. This book itself is discussed in Chapter 12 of this book as an example of a non-biblical reception-history.

4   Gerhard von Rad: *Genesis, a Commentary* (London: SCM Press, second ed., 1963), p. 85. Von Rad's contrast between 'the reticence, indeed soberness and calm, of the Biblical story' and 'the arrogant and harsh colors in the myths of other peoples' (ibid., p. 97) would surely attract a strong postcolonialist critique, if written today.

(instead of jar) and Milton inherited the comparison of Eve to Pandora through his assimilation of Ovid.[5]

Although Hesiod (the earliest source for the Pandora story) comes about 200 years after the Yahwist, we must assume that Christian appropriations of the Eden story are often tinted by that of Pandora. In any case, Pandora in Hesiod is also identifiable in places with the Earth Mother, Gaia, whose ancestry includes Araru, the mother goddess of the *Epic of Gilgamesh* and Mami in the Babylonian *Epic of Atrahasis*. By comparison with Pandora, as Norris acknowledges, the Genesis Eve is a much less misogynist production and, although early midrashic treatment of the Eden story often emphasises Eve's culpability, there are opposite strands, as James Kugel has shown.[6] In these cases, the emphasis falls on the subtlety of the serpent in tricking Eve into eating the forbidden fruit.

Cain and Analogues

With Genesis 4, we move into a different field of comparison with classical mythology. Quinones argues for the sharp contrast between Cain and Odysseus,[7] with the latter as the hero notably without a brother. It was Augustine who made the comparison between Cain and Abel and Romulus and Remus, but did so for the purpose of distinguishing 'between theme and motif, between the Cain-Abel theme, and the larger motif of brother-strife into which it may generally fit'. Thus the Cain and Abel story, drawn as the contrast between the earthly and heavenly cities, gains its force from being differentiated from the more universal motif of *frères ennemis*, which the story of Romulus and Remus is made to represent. Quinones later credits Machiavelli with reversing Augustine's (and Dante's) scheme of the two cities and

---

5   Norris, op. cit., pp. 111–34.
6   James Kugel: *The Bible As It Was* (Cambridge Mass & London: Belknap/Harvard University Press, 1997), pp. 76–8.
7   Quinones, op. cit., p. 20.

238

restoring the pagan concept of Romulus (Cain) as the Sacred Executioner, laying the ground for later rehabilitations of Cain.[8]

In our chapter on 'The Other,' we looked at Tennyson's *Maud*. One striking feature of that poem is the convergence between the theme of Mary Magdalene and that of Cain and Abel. In the work's rather shadowy plot, the narrator murders Maud's brother, an act which seems to result in Maud's own death and the narrator's own banishment to serve in the Crimean war, where he dies. However, nothing is straightforward in this dreamy poem and at one stage we read:

Who knows if he be dead?
Whether I need have fled?
Am I guilty of blood? (XXIV, ix.)

The poem's early reference to Cain connects him with avarice rather than with murder, confirming the bias in *Maud* in favour of warfare as an alternative to murky commerce:

Why do they prate of the blessings of Peace? We have made them a curse,
Pickpockets, each hand lusting for all that is not its own;
And lust of gain, in the spirit of Cain, is it better or worse
Than the heart of the citizen hissing in war on his own hearthstone? (I, vi.)

Tennyson's poem is evidence, on the one hand, of the loose use of biblical imagery and also, on the other, of a perversity in decoupling Cain from the killing that takes place in warfare, whilst the narratorial voice from the battlefield harks back to a private murder, using language borrowed from Genesis 4:

And there rang on a sudden a passionate cry,
A cry for brother's blood:
It will ring in my heart and my eyes, till I die, till I die. (XXIII, i.)[9]

---

8   Ibid., pp. 76–8.
9   Alfred Lord Tennyson: *Poems* (London: Henry Froude, 1904), pp. 445, 477, 479.

From Early to Joycean Typology

The stories of Cain and Abel and Noah's Flood were joined together in the Jewish tradition by the idea that the world was flooded *because of* Cain's deed. This idea, found by Kugel in Wisdom and the Testament of Adam,[10] naturally finds no place in Cohn's account of *Noah's Flood, the Genesis Story in Western Thought.* However, Cohn, despite his concentration on early modern science, finds the space to note the conflation of the End-Time of Noah's Flood with the apocalyptic End-time of 1 Enoch and Matthew 24 and Luke 17. He also mentions the typological treatment of Noah as John-the-Baptist and as Christ, with the Ark as the City of God, in early Christian exegesis.[11] Typology licences a large number of biblical cross-references and, of course, is pervasive in medieval drama and art. If modern scholarship shuns typology as the effacer of difference between texts, particularly in its supersessionist implications for the reading of the Hebrew scriptures, its historical impact should not be underestimated.

Quinones draws attention to the presence of the Cain and Abel story in the writings of James Joyce, particularly *Finnegan's Wake*, where Shem-Shaun are representatives of a duality which also includes Brutus and Cassius, the Roman Church and the Irish Church and Mensheviks and Bolsheviks.[12] Meanwhile, *Ulysses* is the great cultural signal that the biblical stories for this major writer are not privileged over against other great tales from the past, even if this great novel also marks a return to the past as the great treasure-house of meaning-giving stories.[13]

---

10   Kugel, ibid., pp. 99–100.

11   Cohn, op. cit., pp. 23–31.

12   Quinones, op. cit., pp. 217–26.

13   See Herbert Schneidau: *Waking Giants* (New York: Oxford University Press, 1991), pp. 3–24.

240

Sheba and Lilith

The Queen of Sheba was interpreted typologically, as shown in the Pritchard volume,[14] variously as the Virgin Mary and as the precursor of the Magi. Allegorised as Luxury, she also appeared in Flaubert's *The Temptations of St Anthony*. But the dominant conflation, evident indeed in Flaubert's work, was with the figure of Lilith, a conflation rooted in rabbinic and cabbalistic exegesis.[15] In this context the Ethiopian *Kebra Nagast* offers a meeting of Christian and rabbinic interpretations of Sheba, with Sheba combining the features of Lilith the Seductress and the virtuous Queen of the South and Queen Candace of Acts. Sheba, as we have seen, became a pivotal figure in *The Golden Legend*, linking the Tree of the Garden of Eden with both the time of Solomon and the Tree of the Cross. In many ways *The Golden Legend* is the great medieval hub for the convergence of biblical stories.[16]

Archetypes and Stereotypes

Taking the remaining reception-histories covered by our study, we find that there is a thin dividing line between conflation as an almost accidental process and conflation as a hermeneutical tool, allowing one biblical story to illuminate another.

Gaines argues that biblical women are stereotyped into three main groups: evildoers (like Jezebel), nondescript silent ladies and heroines like Esther. Pippin develops Mieke Bal's theory about ideo-stories to argue that Lilith, Jezebel, Delilah and Sappho are effectively conflated in the tradition to create a composite

---

14 Pritchard, op. cit., pp. 115–31.
15 See Sol Liptzin: *Biblical Themes in World Literature* (Hoboken NJ: Ktav Publishing, 1985), pp. 187–203.
16 It was Emile Mâle, the French art historian, who championed the rediscovery of *The Golden Legend* as the key to the stories and story-linkages which underpinned medieval art. In *The Gothic Image* (London: Dent, 1913, reprinted Fontana, 1961), he celebrates the fact that the work's 'absence of originality' makes it a faithful guide to tradition. (Ibid., p. 273).

figure. Resisting such patriarchal determinism, Alice Bach notes that, whilst Esther, Delilah, Salome and Jezebel share a group identity as women who 'threaten biblical heroes', by changing the reader's identity, a negative is changed into a positive and Delilah, Esther and Judith share a group identity as heroes in the mind of their own people.[17] This perception is related to Bach's further argument that such biblical characters have an afterlife in reader's imaginations independent of their immediate biblical context, to which, of course, reception-history of the kind we are considering bears witness.[18]

In fact, there is no need to limit this concept to female figures. As Sherwood demonstrates, there is a strand in the Jewish and Christian traditions which conflates Job and Jonah[19] and the treatment of Herod in Josephus probably owes a great deal to the portrait of Antiochus Epiphanes in 1 Maccabbees, to name but one further example.[20]

Stocker shows how the conflation of Judith with Jael allowed for the apocryphal heroine to gain a sort of canonical respectability,[21] whilst Warner shows how the existence of the Three Marys ('A Muddle of Marys') in the canonical gospels

---

17 Alice Bach: *Women, seduction and betrayal in biblical narrative* (Cambridge: Cambridge University Press, 1997), p. 190.

18 For example, she states, in the context of her own juxtaposing of the story of Susanna and the Elders and the story of Joseph and Mut-em-enet in the Testament of Joseph: 'Both stories stand as reminders of chastity as a code for female value. The deliberate strategy of bringing these two female characters together in the reader's mind has resulted in destabilizing the reader's perception of female characters as flat or unresisting commodities within the text. Insistence upon the inconsistency of character also allows the reader to subvert narrative closure. The characters, if not their stories, live on in the reader's imagination'. (Bach, ibid., p. 72). Bach's argument is that her style of intervention rescues the (female) biblical character from stereotyping. Later she incorporates parts of the imaginative reception-histories of both Bathsheba and Salome into the argument, though consigning their treatment in film and drama largely to errant male fantasies. (Ibid., pp. 158–65 and 210–62). The desired destabilisation occurs almost by default.

19 Sherwood, op. cit., p. 109.

20 See Helen K. Bond: *Pontius Pilate in History and Interpretation* (Cambridge: Cambridge University Press, 1998/2004), pp. 74–5 for a discussion of the characterisations of Herod, Pilate and Antiochus Epiphanes in Josephus. This author also highlights parallels in Matthew's Gospel between Herod in the birth narrative and Pilate at the trial of Christ.

21 Stocker, op. cit., pp. 145–6.

242

leads to a number of ambiguities and confusions, with only the Virgin Mary of the spurious Coptic work, the *Twentieth Discourse*, claiming to incorporate all three.[22]

Trexler finds the Magi conflated with the classical notion of the Three Ages of Man, as well as with more generalised Roman ideas about tribute-giving.[23] The connection with Prester John had more far-reaching economic and political consequences, in that it led to the quest for magian gold, frankincense and myrrh along the west coast of Africa from the late fourteenth-century onwards.[24] This ideologically-driven conflation makes the 'Muddle of Marys' seem quite innocent by comparison.

Haskins describes the association between Mary Magdalene and Venus in Renaissance art, a typical form of iconographical convergence, which flowered in the sixteenth- and seventeenth-centuries into a whole literature about Mary Magdalene as the Venus of Divine Love.[25] She sees the examples painted by Titian as expressive of the Christian humanism of the period, a true convergence of biblical and classical. Earlier on, she also notes the origins of the mythological life of Mary Magdalene in the location of her sepulchre near the entrance to the Cave of the Seven Sleepers at Ephesus, an interesting example of the almost random convergence of legendary material to create new forms of signification. Mary Magdalene meets the martyrs.

Wroe connects Pontius Pilate with the legend of the Wandering Jew; and Pilate and his wife, Procula, with Adam and Eve.[26] These are further examples of the luxuriant growth of folkloristic convergence. The effect of making Pilate the passenger of the unfortunate Wandering Jew was no doubt to provide a link

22 Warner, op. cit., pp. 344–6.
23 Trexler, op. cit., pp. 39, 18–20, 59, 101ff.
24 Ibid., pp. 73–4 and 103.
25 Haskins, op. cit., pp. 236–48.
26 Wroe, op. cit., pp. 346 and 355–6.

between the 'now' of medieval legend and the biblical story, but it also no doubt reinforced the anti-semitism inherent in the Wandering Jew legend. The effect of making Pilate and Procula into Adam and Eve, which finds its roots in *The Golden Legend* and its full flowering in medieval drama, was, on the other hand, perhaps to humanise them.

Paffenroth identifies *The Golden Legend* as the source of another important conflation, that between Judas and Oedipus.[27] The assimilation of the Judas story to that of Oedipus, including the generation of an elaborate childhood story, was anything but casual and found its way beyond Jacob de Voragine's work into medieval English and French drama. The drift of Paffenroth's argument is that, by assimilating Judas to Oedipus, the medieval authors began the process of exonerating Judas, seen increasingly as the victim of an ineluctable Fate. We might note that Paffenroth's source for the medieval period, P.F. Baum, emphasises the conflation of the Judas fratricide legend in Greek Version B with the Cain and Abel story (particularly in the use of a stone) and also the rather later tendency to associate Judas and Pilate as co-villains.[28] A further medieval link is that between Judas and the brothers of Joseph as betrayers, something highlighted by Shapiro in his study of the origins of the Oberammergau play.[29]

Finally, with Pippin, we find that the Apocalypse has been hi-jacked by a particularly extremist form of white racism and that the Tower of Babel has been appropriated as a symbol of the doomed aspirations and desires of western culture.[30] If we find Pippin's account of the reception-history of these two biblical themes rather one-sided, her study nevertheless serves to document the cultural

---

27   Paffenroth, op. cit., pp. 70 and 78–9.
28   P.F. Baum: 'The Medieval Legend of Judas Iscariot' in *PMLA*, Vol. 24, 1916, p. 525.
29   James Shapiro: *Oberammergau* (London: Little Brown, 2000), p. 159.
30   Pippin, op. cit., pp. 13–31 and 43–63.

conditions under which biblical stories can seem to be conflated with (in this case) destructive social myths.

Summary

Our survey of conflations, convergences, contaminations and intertexts has shown how stories transmit meaning, not only through being rewritten, but also through being aligned with other stories. The early period witnesses the playful midrashic inclination to mix stories and the patristic search for analogues between biblical stories and those of classical mythology. In the medieval period, *The Golden Legend* becomes the vehicle for summarising links across the Testaments which have already become established, often, but not exclusively, for doctrinal reasons. The Renaissance revives interest in the parallels between biblical stories and classical mythology. Thereafter, a total entity called 'The Bible' gains force, which, particularly after the Protestant Reformation, becomes a collection of sacred stories set apart from other stories,[31] though this does not prevent a high degree of mixing of biblical stories with political and social myths, as Stocker and Haskins demonstrate. The Romantic period releases biblical stories for more adventurous experiments in conflation (as we see with Tennyson), whilst the modern period finds one of the most important figures in twentieth-century literature, James Joyce, treating biblical stories as relics of a ragbag of stories from the past which are freely available for conflation and for intermixing with each other in the course of the production of a novel. We may wonder how much of the resonance of the original biblical story, let alone its reception-history, survives under these conditions, but, as a representation of the postmodern propensity to raid the culture for its own ends, Joyce's use of biblical material could be said to be emblematic.

---

31   See David S. Katz: *God's Last Words* (New Haven and London: Yale University Press, 2004).

Our review of conflations, convergences, contaminations and intertexts has revealed that reception-history as a field of discourse cannot ignore the strong cultural and affective impulses to mix biblical stories both with other biblical stories and with other myths and narratives which circulate in the west. These can vary, in the pre-modern period, from the apparent vagueness of the tradition of muddling The Three Marys to the imaginative athletics of the attempt to create a joined-up panoptic narrative of biblical stories and sacred legend which we find in *The Golden Legend.*

It can be argued that the Reformation raised biblical stories onto a new plateau of cultural prominence, only to let them succumb to the new political necessities of propaganda and stereotyping, before a more sceptical age exchanged faith in sacred stories for faith in the human capacity to write life-enhancing fictions. The irony is that the biblical stories continued to exert a powerful influence over the modern novel when it emerged, either as the direct source of narrative material for rewriting or as the model for realistic fiction. We can perhaps view the contest between biblical story and modern stereotype which Stocker, for example, finds in Le Carré's *The Little Drummer Girl*,[32] as indicative of a cultural battle in progress. At the same time, the ostensibly unlikely convergence of two very different biblical stories, those of Cain-and-Abel and Mary Magdalene, in Tennyson's *Maud,* may serve as the barometer of a sort of ontological crisis, just as surely as a film about Operation Desert Storm during the Gulf War being called *Three Kings.*[33]

---

32 Stocker, op. cit., pp. 225–8.

33 Directed by David O. Russell, US/Australia, 1999. The film is mentioned in John Pym (ed.): *Time Out Film Guide, Eleventh Edition* (London: Penguin, 2003), p. 1218.

Chapter 10

RANGE: HOW THE FOURTEEN
STUDIES COVER THE GROUND

In order to gain a perspective on the range of material covered by our fourteen authors, I have analysed the amount of space devoted to six very broad historical periods in each study, quantifying it by pages used in relation to the total page number of each work. Although a fairly crude form of measurement, it does reveal sharp disparities between the different studies, which may be related either to authorial choice or to the wealth or sparsity of source material in the relevant periods.

Author	Period					
	1	**2**	**3**	**4**	**5**	**6**
Levenson	41%	0%	0%	0%	0%	59%
Pritchard	40	18	20	8	11	3
Warner	6	20	63	8	1	2
Quinones	0	7	17	17	18	41
Haskins	8	6	43	20	15	8
Cohn	16	12	0	6	60	5
Trexler	1	8	43	32	4	7
Norris	6	33	14	11	23	8
Stocker	8	0	24	16	22	30
Gaines	49	0.5	0.5	5	15	27
Wroe	65	10	15	2	8	0
Paffenroth	24	6	12	1	8	25
Pippin	0	0	4	0	2	94
Sherwood	7	4	17	7	9	45

248

The six periods designated are:

1. The period of the biblical text's production.
2. The early period of rabbinic or patristic commentary or apocryphal writing.
3. The medieval period.
4. The Renaissance and Reformation.
5. The Enlightenment and Romantic Period.
6. Everything post-1900.

Taking the fourteen authors in turn:

1. Levenson, by virtue of his chosen theme and title *The Book of Job in its Time and in the Twentieth Century*, arrives at a predictable balance between Column One and Column Six, though his study still begs the question of why the intervening period can be ignored.
2. Pritchard's work, given that it is a collection of essays by different authors, achieves a remarkably good balance, except that the modern period seems underweight. This seems to be more to do with the richness of the medieval material than a paucity of modern material.
3. Warner is much more weighted towards the medieval period still, reflecting both the heyday of her subject-matter, but also her own preoccupation with that period at the expense certainly of both the biblical period and the modern period.
4. Quinones had a deliberate strategy to marshal the medieval material into footnotes, tipping the balance heavily in favour of the Romantic and Modern periods.
5. Haskins achieves a spread which appears to do justice very closely to the availability and distribution of material across the six periods.
6. Cohn's score reflects his book's heavy concentration on one historical period.

7. Trexler's low score for Column One reflects the thinness of gospel-material and high scores in Columns Three and Four reflects the importance of the Magi during those centuries.

8. The score for Norris is a little surprising, give her attention to the Genesis material and to the modern period, but faithfully records the space she gives to early commentaries.

9. Stocker's scores reflect the gradual increase in acceptance of Judith as a component book of the Apocrypha, leading to a high degree of interest in the modern period.

10. Gaines's approach seems to be less balanced than many of the others, despite the promise of her subtitle, *Jezebel through the Ages*. The main ages discussed turn out to be the biblical origins and the period from Victorian times onwards.

11. Wroe's coverage seems to be heavily tilted towards the conjectured historical background of Pilate's life and governorship, with everything else more thinly represented. Excluding the oblique references to Bulgakov, the modern period is neglected, despite the numerous treatments of Pilate in film which might have provided valuable material for an account of the dialogue between the biblical story of Pilate and twentieth-century romanticisation of history or that between the biblical Pilate and modern American notions of military governorship.

12. Paffenroth's coverage is reasonably balanced though, in reality, he largely neglects the treatment of Judas in the mystery plays. The quite high score for the modern period reflects the novelistic interest in rehabilitating Judas.

13. Pippin's score is biased almost exclusively towards the modern period (at 94% by far the highest), though her study makes no claims for historical balance, unlike that of Gaines, for example, with its sweeping subtitle, *Jezebel Through the Ages.*

250

14. Finally, Sherwood's scores, to a degree like those of Stocker, reflect the growth in interest in Jonah, reaching a sort of apotheosis in modern times. We are, as we note elsewhere, in the age of the deviant biblical text.

As we have said, this is a rather imprecise way of measuring the balance of space which each author devotes to the six rather broad chronological bands and it would clearly be impossible to devise a 'control' score to display the *actual* availability of material relevant to the fourteen studies across history. But it does have the merit of highlighting the large variations in coverage of the six historical periods between the fourteen authors. With the exceptions of Levenson and Pippin, these variations do seem to be related, if not to the quantative availability of biblical-appropriation material relevant to each of the fourteen underlying stories, then to the *qualitative availability* of such material, in the sense of significant variations on the various themes.

It would be possible to conclude that in the modern period the main focus of rewritten biblical stories has been on the Old Testament, except for the case of Judas. We might also conclude that, as the informal tradition of writing 'reception-histories' has developed, there is a rough divide between period-specialists (like Warner and Haskins) who are not necessarily committed to the continuing relevance of their material and semiotic enthusiasts who regard the modern or postmodern period as the time of the culmination or flowering of their chosen biblical story.

Finally, we will now sketch alternative ways in which the ground might have been covered by those of our reception-history writers whose coverage is very selective.

Beginning with Levenson, it is clear that there is a wealth of material relating to Jewish midrash on Job,[1] to interpretations of Job in the patristic period,[2] and to

---

1   See Nahum Glatzer (ed.): *The Dimensions of Job* (New York: Schocken Books, 1969).
2   Ibid., pp. 1–86.

the treatment of Job in medieval literature.[3] Even given that Levenson's chosen subject is 'The Book of Job in its Time and in the Twentieth-Century,' we have noted elsewhere the strange blindness of this study to works by Jung and Roth.[4]

Warner's coverage is very comprehensive until the early modern period, where she shows no interest in refractions of the Virgin Mary story in either Victorian or twentieth-century literature, or indeed visual art after the Renaissance. David Lyle Jeffrey in *A Dictionary of Biblical Tradition in English Literature* mentions the Marian themes in pre-Raphaelite poetry, the sublimation of Mary in nineteenth-century fiction (for example Dickens's Ada in *Bleak House* or Amy in *Little Dorrit*; the figure of Miss Virginia Hector in John Barth's *Giles Goat-Boy* and (in a more orthodox mode) Hopkins's *Rosa Mystica* and R.S. Thomas's *Pieta*.[5] Within the visual arts, we might add Epstein's *The Visitation*.[6] Within the field of feminist hermeneutics, Kristeva's highly influential essay *Stabat Mater* would form an unavoidable part of the picture if Warner's book were being rewritten today. We might even include Mary Wollstonecraft's novel *Maria* in an alternative feminist account of the reception-history, in which the desperate plight of the heroine as the victim of eighteenth-century marriage law could be seen as a trope in dialogue with the 'handmaid of the Lord' theme of Luke 1:38.[7] Therefore, abandoning

---

3   See Lawrence S. Besserman: *The Legend of Job in the Middle Ages* (Cambridge Mass: Harvard University Press, 1979).

4   See Chapter 2. We might also mention the significance of Blake for modern perceptions of Job. See Andrew Wright: *Blake's Job, A Commentary* (Oxford: Oxford University Press, 1972). There is also a link to be explored between the rediscovery of Job at the close of the nineteenth-century and a renewed interest in the theologically-unconventional. This is apparent in Hubert Parry's selection of *Job* as the subject for a condensed form of oratorio in 1891, a successor to *Judith* and *The Lotus Eaters*. See Jeremy Dibble's notes to the Hyperion recording of the work. (London: Hyperion records 1997), pp. 1–9.

5   David Lyle Jeffrey: *A Dictionary of Biblical Tradition in English Literature* (Grand Rapids, Michigan: Eerdmans, 1992), pp. 494–5.

6   See illustration and discussion in Frank and Dorothy Getlein: *Christianity in Modern Art* (Milwaukee: Bruce Publishing, 1961), pp. 138–9.

7   Mary Wollstonecraft: *Maria, or The Wrongs of Woman* (New York: W.W. Norton & Co., 1975, originally published London: 1798). Elisabeth Bronfen argues that the Monster in Mary Shelley's *Frankenstein* is modelled on Jemima in *Maria*. See Elisabeth Bronfen: 'Rewriting

252

Warner's heyday-and-decline schema, we could construct a more optimistic, or at least multi-layered, reception-history, with the sort of open-endedness we find in Pritchard, Trexler, Stocker, and Sherwood.

Quinones is not one of our valedictory authors, but he relegates the medieval period, except for *Beowulf* and Dante, to the end-notes. An alternative reception-history might build on the development of Cain as a figure undergoing damnation in the mystery-play tradition[8] and might also examine the iconographic material which is relevant to this area.[9] It might also explore the relationship of this Cain to the growth of the British theatrical villain.

Haskins's coverage is more comprehensive than that of Warner, but she nevertheless belongs decidedly to the valedictory camp. In this case, an alternative history would build on the same material as that discussed by Haskins, but might give more space to the Digby play[10] (which Haskins dismisses in two lines[11]); it might discuss the elaborate Protestant morality play of Lewis Wager, *The Life and Repentance of Marie Magdalene*[12] (not mentioned by Haskins); and it might give more weight to the handling of the figure of Mary Magdalene in modern fiction. It is clear that this story, far from petering out in the modern period, has gained more

the Family, Mary Shelley's *Frankenstein*, essay in Stephen Bann (ed.): *Frankenstein, Creation and Monstrosity* (London: Reaktion Books), 1994.

8   See Rosemary Woolf: *The English Mystery Play* (London: Routledge, Kegan & Paul, 1972), p. 128. Also Hans-Jürgen Diller: *The Middle English Mystery Play* (Cambridge: Cambridge University Press, 1992), pp. 228–31. For legends of Cain in the *Cursor Mundi*, see David C. Fowler: *The Bible in Early English Literature* (London, Sheldon Press, 1977), pp. 168–9 and 171–2.

9   See M.D. Anderson: *Drama and Imagery in British Churches* (Cambridge: Cambridge University Press, 1963), pp. 144–5 and 212.

10 For a discussion of the Digby play as a major dramatic elaboration of the life of Mary Magdalene, incorporating the assault on Castle Magdalene, a Passion narrative concentrating on Mary Magdalene's part in it, the raising of Lazarus, the Resurrection-garden scene incorporating imagery from the Song of Solomon, and finally Mary Magdalene's mission to Marseilles, see David C Fowler: *The Bible in Middle English* (Seattle and London, University of Washington Press: 1984), pp. 106–12.

11 Haskins, ibid., p. 167.

12 See Ruth H. Blackburn: *Biblical Drama under the Tudors* (The Hague and Paris: Mouton, 1971), pp. 131–6.

and more impetus. Jeffrey remarks: 'The 20th cent. has seen a dramatic resurgence of interest in Mary Magdalene'.[13] It might be useful to explore the reasons for this. Edward Coleman's *The Bible in English Drama* lists eighteen 'modern plays' about Mary Magdalene, none of which are mentioned in Haskins.[14]

Cohn's coverage is, as we have noted, driven by his focus on science-history. There is ample evidence of a wealth of material to support an alternative history of Noah and the Flood,[15] this time examining the story as a locus for human existential concerns or for variant depictions of the relationship of God to creation. The figure of Noah's wife is another theme worth exploring, right through from her prominent role in the English mystery plays[16] to the modern feminist novel by Michèle Roberts.[17]

It is hard to fault the coverage of Trexler, so we move on to Norris's Eve. Given that this is an enormous subject, the alternative reception-history might prove to be a mighty tome. It might give more coverage to Eve in rabbinic literature, to Eve in Early and Middle English literature (for example in *Genesis B*), to Eve in Spenser's *Faerie Queene*, and to a more balanced and in-depth study of Eve in Milton's *Paradise Lost*. Jeffrey lists Archibald MacLeish's *Songs for Eve* and Constance Beresford's *The Book of Eve* amongst twentieth-century rehabilitations of Eve.[18]

Stocker is the only example amongst our fourteen reception-histories where the coverage seems *too* comprehensive. The inclusion of Punch and Judy, as well as the excursion into the genre of thrillers subsumed under the title of 'Woman with a Gun',

---

13 Jeffrey, ibid., p. 488.
14 Edward D. Coleman: *The Bible in English Drama*, with Isaiah Sheffer: *A Survey of Recent Major Plays* (New York: New York Public Library & Ktav Publishing House, 1968), pp. 142–3.
15 For example, J.P. Lewis: *A Study of the Interpretation of Noah and the Flood in Jewish and Christian Literature* (Leiden: Brill, 1968).
16 Lynette Muir in *The Biblical Drama of Medieval Europe* (Cambridge: Cambridge University Press, 1995), p. 73, singles out an English tradition which uses an Eastern legend 'to justify an anti-feminist portrayal of Mrs Noah as disobedient and bad-tempered'.
17 Michèle Roberts: *The Book of Mrs Noah* (London: Vintage, 1999).
18 Jeffrey, ibid., p. 254.

seems to indicate a readiness to embrace material with a rather tangential connection to the central theme and it is possible that this otherwise very suggestive study might have gained from the excision of such elements. Gaines also has moments of rather wild inclusiveness, including the attention given to *Jezebel the Jeep*. But, as we have noted elsewhere,[19] the weakness in coverage lies more in a failure to explore more fully the negative use of the Jezebel theme in American literature (especially Faulkner) and in the absence of a conclusion to the whole study.

With Wroe, we have already mentioned the omission of any discussion of Pilate in twentieth-century film. Jeffrey lists an unfinished poem by Hopkins in which Pilate crucifies himself, the figure of Shaw in Conrad's *The Rescue*, and a number of modern novels, including Carlo Maria Franzero's *The Memoirs of Pontius Pilate: From the Autobiography of G. Pontius Pilate*, Paul Luther's *Pontius Pilate: an Autobiographical Novel*, Warren Kiefer's *The Pontius Pilate Papers* and Vincent O'Sullivan's *The Pilate Tapes*.[20] None of this material is mentioned in Wroe's study. The effect of including a discussion of these works, as well as the portrait of Pilate in Robert Graves's *King Jesus*, would be to counter the sense, very strong in Wroe, that the Pilate story is somehow defunct in the modern period.

In the case of Paffenroth, an alternative reception-history would examine the treatment of Judas in visual art (to which there is no reference in Paffenroth) and would attend more fully to the treatment of Judas in English literature. For example, Cynewulf's late eighth- or ninth-century poem *Elene* features a second, good Judas who assists Saint Helena in her discovery of the true cross, causing the devil to exclaim 'Once I was heartened by Judas, and now once again by Judas I am humiliated'.[21] This second, converted Judas might fit rather well into Paffenroth's account of the history of the rehabilitation of Judas.

---

19   Chapter 2, pp. 66–9.
20   Jeffrey, ibid., p. 623.
21   David C. Fowler: *The Bible in Early English literature*, p. 113.

Our alternative to Paffenroth would explore in much greater detail the treatment of Judas in the mystery-plays, including anti-semitic strands in that material. Relevant literary treatments listed by Jeffrey, but not discussed in Paffenroth, include those found in D.F. Strauss's *Das Leben Jesu*, George Moore's *The Brook Kerith*, and Norman Mailer's *The Executioner's Song*.[22] Edward Coleman's *The Bible in English Drama* lists a number of plays not mentioned or discussed in Paffenroth, ranging from a play of 1601, *Judas*, by Samuel Rowley and William Borne, to William Ford Manley's dramatic poem of 1930, *Judas Iscariot; a dramatic poem in six scenes.* [23] Elsewhere in this study we look at Borges's *Three Versions of Judas*, which again Paffenroth does not mention.

Pippin's *Apocalyptic Bodies* is so selective that we can only point to much more comprehensive studies of aspects of the treatment of the Book of Revelation, including Frederick van der Meer's *Apocalypse* (covering the visual arts extensively),[24] Christopher Burdon's *The Apocalypse in England* (covering mainly eighteenth-century English literature)[25] and a French compendium on the Angers Apocalypse.[26] Even confining one's purview to North American fiction, there is John R. May: *Toward a New Earth*, which examines the theme of apocalypse from Hawthorne to Vonnegut against the background of residual shades of Puritan influence and growing secularisation.[27]

---

22   Jeffrey, ibid., p. 420.
23   Coleman, ibid., pp. 135–7.
24   Frederick van der Meer: *Apocalypse, Visions from the Book of Revelation in Western Art* (London: Thames and Hudson, 1978).
25   Christopher Burdon: *The Apocalypse in England: Revelation Unravelling, 1700–1834* (London: Macmillan, 1997).
26   Jacques Cailleteau (ed.): *La Tenture de l'Apocalypse d'Angers* (Nantes: Inventaire Générale, 1987).
27   John R. May: *Toward a New Earth, apocalypse in the American novel* (Notre Dame, Indiana: University of Indiana Press, 1972). '... the literary phase of American apocalypse that develops with the maturation of our national literature, from the middle of the nineteenth century until the present, reflects a strong reaction against the easy optimism of the nineteenth and early twentieth centuries and later a poignant response to the succession of global hot and

256

The remaining reception-histories do not seem to be deficient in coverage or to provoke alternative emphases, allowing for the fact that there are always unmentioned examples in such works. For instance, Sherwood does not discuss Zachary Boyd's *The history of Jonah, a dramatic poem* (Glasgow, 1855) and the Pritchard volume does not mention C.J. Hanssen's *The Queen of Sheba; a Biblical drama for young ladies* (Chicago & New York, 1899), both listed in Edward Coleman's *The Bible in English Drama*.[28] More seriously, Trexler omits any reference to Michel Tournier's novel *The Four Wise Men*, discussed in our chapter on 'Variations,' which a more literary study could not ignore.

Conclusion

The value of examining coverage as a topic in the context of this book is that it provides evidence for a critique of the limitations of any particular study and also offers outlines for alternative reception-histories. It may also indicate areas which are neglected generally by the producers of reception-histories. In particular, it is evident that there is scope for re-evaluating a whole swathe of rewritten biblical stories in English literature from the Anglo-Saxon *Genesis*, through the mystery-plays, to Milton and Blake, as material to be enjoyed and to be quarried for semiotic significance and relevance today. Our distribution grid has highlighted the uneven coverage of reception-history in several of our authors, but has also suggested the value of distinguishing between fallow periods for particular biblical stories and their reception and the deliberate neglect occasioned by authorial wilfulness on the part of reception-history writers.

---

cold wars. It reflects as well the process of secularisation that began in the nineteenth century and blossomed into the anomie of the century of unrestrained technology'. (Ibid., pp. 32–3).

28   Coleman, ibid., pp. 77 and 72, respectively.

Clearly the mere fact that a rewritten biblical story or hypertext is mentioned in a reception-history, or even extensively discussed, is no guarantee that it is given appropriate weight. However, the absence of mention or discussion is a clear signal that the range of a reception-history is partial. This perhaps is a more significant issue when there exists only one treatment of a particular topic, as is largely the case at the present stage of reception-history writing, rather than where there are multiple accounts.

Chapter 11

NODAL POINTS

This section will consider the extent to which our fourteen studies contain, or rely on, nodal points in their treatment of their respective reception-histories. The term 'nodal point' is one I have borrowed from geography, where it refers to the place where several valleys meet to form a route-centre.[1] The node is also an important concept in cognitive psychology, where it signifies a neural crossing-point.[2] In terms of the texts we have been examining, Mary Shelley's *Frankenstein*, viewed as a proto-feminist response to Milton's *Paradise Lost*, could be considered as 'a' or 'the' nodal point in Norris's study of Eve. Our preliminary survey of the fourteen texts already indicated the tendency for certain literary or artistic works to dominate the reception-histories, sometimes at the expense of others. Looking at the specific question of nodal points will allow us to ask whether certain rewritten biblical stories or texts inescapably prevail or whether there is a degree of selectivity, high or low, on the part of the reception-history writer. In some cases, we may have to consider whether the reception-history writer has had to work hard to counteract the dominating effect of a particular work, such as Melville's *Moby Dick* in the case of Sherwood's study of Jonah.

---

1   See, for example, David Waugh: *Geography, an Integrated Approach* (Edinburgh: Nelson, 1990), p. 332.

2   See Michael W. Eysenck and Mark T. Keane: *Cognitive Psychology* (Hove and New York: Psychology Press, 2005), p. 13: 'The (connectionist) network consists of elementary or neuron-like *units* or *nodes* connected together so that a single unit has many links to other units. Units affect other units by exciting or inhibiting them'. See also Arthur S. Reber and Emily S. Reber: *Penguin Dictionary of Psychology* (London: Penguin, 2001), p. 468, where a node is defined as 'a point upon which a number of operations impinge'.

J.D. Levenson: *The Book of Job in its Time and in the Twentieth Century*

Taking the works in order of publication, we begin with Levenson's *The Book of Job in its Time and in the Twentieth Century*. The authorial premise is that the Book of Job, and the characteristic themes of twentieth-century literature, are uniquely suited to each other, justifying a purview which confines itself first of all to the twentieth-century and then to the three works which the author regards as 'the three prominent works in English' to have 'ostensibly recreated the Job Story'.[3]

The objection to this stance would be that it rules out an important work written in German but translated into English (Joseph Roth's *Job*)[4] and also excludes works produced in earlier centuries, in a variety of languages, including English (such as Shakespeare's *King Lear*), which may have been important to twentieth-century readers and audiences, or (in the case of Blake, as an artist in many ways a 'twentieth-century discovery') to those aware of visual art. The latter group would include the composer Vaughan Williams, whose *Job, A Masque for Dancing* was definitely a twentieth-century response to Blake's Job illustrations.[5]

However, within its limited remit, Levenson's study does make the claim that the three works it explores, H.G. Wells' *The Undying Fire*, Archibald MacLeish's *J B* and Robert Frost's *The Masque of Reason* are, in some sense, pivotal. We have already challenged Levenson's preferral of the Frost work over the others on theological grounds. But leaving that area aside for the moment, are the three works nodal points other than inside Levenson's study? The problem for us in 2006 is that none of these three works are very important in the literary canon. If anything, they have slipped progressively further into obscurity, whereas, of

---

3   Levenson, op. cit., p. 4.

4   Joseph Roth's *Job* is discussed in Chapter 5, pp. 164ff.

5   Vaughan Williams wrote the work in 1930. See Michael Trend: *The Music Makers, The English Musical Renaissance from Elgar to Britten* (London: Weidenfeld & Nicolson, 1985), p. 101. Hubert Parry had earlier written a choral work, *Job*, which was fuelled by the modern sense that the biblical book was a challenge to religious orthodoxy.

course, Joseph Roth's *Job* (reportedly Marlene Dietrich's favourite novel[6]) has grown in critical acclaim. In this case, therefore, we are left with what can only be described as discarded nodal points.

It may still be true that the H.G. Wells work is a neglected piece of valuable literature (along with many other examples of that writer's output), but in cultural terms Levenson's nodal points have been eclipsed. We may speculate that this is on account of a deepening sense of the implications of the Holocaust or because existential anguish no longer represents the mood of the reading public.

James B. Pritchard (ed.): *Solomon and Sheba* (1974)

Pritchard and his five co-contributors in *Solomon and Sheba* cover a vastly larger canvas than Levenson, taking in Jewish, Christian and Muslim imaginative responses to the story of Solomon and Sheba over three thousand years. Nevertheless, several nodal points do emerge. These include the *Targum Sheni* – the second Targum to the Book of Esther; the mystical treatment of the story in Jahal-ad-Din ar-Rumi's *Mathnawi*; the Ethiopic *Kabra Nagast*; the typological treatment of the theme in the *Speculum Humanae Salvationis*; and Romare Bearden's collage, *She-ba*. These can be said to be nodal points firstly because, in most cases, they have spawned new literary and artistic developments and, secondly, because they stand at significant cultural cross-roads in each case.

The *Targum Sheni* was the source for the legends about the throne of King Ahaseurus being actually King Solomon's throne, for the visit of the cock-of-the-woods to sooth Solomon, and for the idea of the Queen of Sheba as a deviser of riddles. The *Mathnawi* was an important development in the mystical reading of

---

6   See p. vi of Michael Hofman's Introduction to Joseph Roth: *The Radetsky March* (London: Granta, 2002). We cite this literary anecdote to illustrate the prominence of a work which Levenson ignores.

262

the Quran. The *Kabra Nagast* became, of course, the national epic of Ethiopia, as well as an extraordinary meeting-point of the three religious traditions. The *Speculum* was a very successful ecclesiastical attempt to suppress exotic variations on the story and to impose typology. Bearden's *She-ba* of 1970 put a Black African Queen into prominence in American culture,[7] the very antithesis of the decorative regal visitor of (for example) Handel's opera *Solomon and Sheba*.[8]

The importance of these nodal points in Pritchard's book is that they not only explain later developments in the tradition but that they clearly signal the existence of major break-points in the imaginative appropriation of the urtext. The fact that these break-points operate far beyond the bounds of and historically mostly very long before the rise of the modern novel indicates that the phenomenon of imaginative reception-history is driven by cultural forces much more universal than that of the modern writer in his or her garret.

Marina Warner: *Alone of All Her Sex* (1976)

Warner's *Alone of all her Sex* is, out of all of the fourteen reception-histories, the least concerned with the modern novel. Warner's study consists of a detailed exploration of the treatment of themes connected with the Virgin Mary in the Early Fathers, in medieval and Renaissance art and poetry and in its aftermath. Nodal points are difficult to identify in that the sheer wealth of material almost drowns out

---

7   In her Introduction to the feminist collection of new hermeneutical approaches to the Bible, *Searching the Scriptures* (New York: The Crossroad Publishing Company, 1993. UK edition: London: SCM, 1994), Elisabeth Schüssler-Fiorenza, chooses Sheba, rather than other female biblical figures, as the key to a new app.roach: 'In order to shift the paradigm of feminist biblical interpretation, I would like to introduce here Sheba, the black queen, who travels far from home to test the wisdom and knowledge of Solomon (I Kings 10:1–13; 2 Chron 9:1–12). Like Sheba the authors of *Searching the Scriptures* put 'hard questions' not only to the reigning epistemology of biblical studies but also to the scriptures themselves. Like the Queen of the South (Luke 11:31 [Q]), they search the 'rich dark depth' of submerged religious wisdom and knowledge that can inspire sacred visions for a *different* future'.

8   Described in Pritchard (ibid)., pp. 133–4.

individual works. However, in terms of Warner's thesis about the rise and decline of 'The Myth and the Cult of the Virgin Mary', we may take her to associate the *Book of James* with the rise in the doctrine of the Virgin Birth; St Augustine's *The City of God* with the sense of Mary as the Second Eve; the *Obsequies of the Holy Virgin*, a third-century work written in Syriac, with the rise of the doctrine of the Assumption; the sixth-century fresco in S. Maria Antiqua in Rome with the flowering of the idea of Mary as Queen of Heaven; the Songs of Songs in medieval exegesis with the sense of Mary as the Bride of God; Dante's Beatrice in the *Divine Comedy* with Mary as the inspiration for human love; the *Kontakion* of Romanos with the theme of the Mater Dolorosa; and Piero della Francesca's *Madonna della Misercordia* with the theme of the Mother of Mercy.

The importance of these nodal points is that they are the expression of deep religious currents flowing beneath the surface of Western culture, rather than turning points. So the experience of the Black Death in Europe in the fourteenth-century increased the urgency of treating the Virgin Mary as both Intercessor and Mother of Sorrows.[9] Warner herself, though, insists on a final nodal point outside the progress of the 'myth and cult' itself, namely the rejection of the whole tradition by a particular strand of modern feminism, supported by the work done by Roland Barthes to expose the inner workings of public myths.[10]

Ricardo Quinones: *The Changes of Cain* (1991)

With Quinones's *The Changes of Cain* the nodal points are quite distinct. They are Augustine's *City of God*; Dante's *Divine Comedy*; Byron's *Cain, a Mystery*; Conrad's *The Secret Sharer*; Melville's *Billy Budd*, Unamuno's *Abel Sanchez*, and Tournier's *Gemini*. On this framework, Quinones builds his argument about the themes of

---

9   See Warner, op. cit., p. 215.
10   Warner, ibid., p. 335. Barthes is further discussed in our chapter on 'Closure'.

264

Citizen Cain, the rise of the Monstrous Cain, and Cain as Sacred Executioner, and so on. The point about these nodal points is that they serve the rise of the modern novel, or at least the rise of modern literary consciousness, with Byron's drama (not in itself a great work of literature) acting as a sort of watershed. Whereas Warner seemingly deals with the rise and fall of a great cultural edifice, comprising works of ultimately mass appeal, at least historically, Quinones deals with a story which is continually gaining momentum through the literary activity of a few exceptional artists, whose work stretches into the future. The fact that multiple readings are available of the works cited by Quinones, not all of which agree with his own master-narrative, does not affect the sense that these works belong together as landmarks in the progress of the imaginative response to the Genesis 4 story.[11]

Susan Haskins: *Mary Magdalene* (1993)

Haskins's work, *Mary Magdalene*, is closer in concept to that of Warner; in fact the two works stand apart from the rest of our fourteen in their detailed study of medieval and Renaissance art and literature and in their valedictory approach to their respective themes. Nodal points in Haskins are the Gnostic material, particularly the *Pistis Sophia*; Gregory's sermons on Mary Magdalene; the *Grandes Heures* of Vezelay; Mary Magdalene as Luxuria in medieval preaching anthologies; the voluptuous Mary Magdalene of Titian; as Vanitas in art from the seventeenth to nineteenth centuries; and as the stigmatised Fallen Woman in Wilkie Collins's novels, *No Name* and *The New Magdalene*. Despite the high quality, particularly of the visual art discussed, these literary texts are nodal points for Haskins in the cultural exploitation of a negative view of women and, echoing

---

11   For alternative readings of this material, see Chapter 2.

Warner, her ultimate reference point lies in the escape from the whole tradition of the representation of her subject in western literature and art.[12]

Norman Cohn: *Noah's Flood* (1996)

Cohn's nodal points are the *Epic of Gilgamesh* as part of the prehistory of the Flood story; the typological treatment of the Flood in 2 Peter; the embroidering of the story in the Midrash *Genesis Rabbah*; Burnet's *The Sacred Theory of the Earth*, a high-point in the harmonisation of early modern science with the Genesis account; John Woodward's *Essay* and its problematic fossils; William Buckland's *Reliquiae Diliuvianae* with its elongated biblical time-scales; and James Frazer's *Golden Bough*, signifying the rise in interest in nature-mythology *per se*.

If Cohn's version of 'Western Thought' – as in his title, *Noah's Flood, the Genesis Story in Western Thought* – had extended to the literary appropriation of the Noah story, nodal points might have included the Newcastle mystery-play and more recent fiction such as Michele Roberts's *The Book of Mrs Noah*[13]and the short story about the Flood in Gesualdo Bulfalino's *The Keeper of the Ruins*,[14] even though David Maine's novel (discussed in our Chapter 5) came later. Cohn, or his publisher, does include illustrations of several significant paintings including John Martin's *The Deluge* of 1834, but these bizarrely are not discussed in the text.

Richard C. Trexler: *The Journey of the Magi* (1997)

Trexler's narrative in *The Journey of the Magi* is that of a legitimising story interrupted at intervals by subversive episodes. Therefore, his nodal points seem

---

12   See Haskins, op. cit., pp. 398–400.

13   Michèle Roberts: *The Book of Mrs Noah* (London: Vintage, 1999).

14   Gesualdo Bufalino: *The Keeper of the Ruins* trans. Patrick Creagh (London: HarperCollins, 1994).

to be breaks in what might otherwise be a smoothly continuous tradition. We think of the exotic black and then ambiguously gendered third kings; the Magi as three women; the riotous cabildo plays in New Spain; and, finally, the begging kings of early modern Europe. We are dealing here not with artistic masterpieces but with inruptions within the social fabric inspired by the story of the Magi and expressive of tensions, injustices and inequalities within society.

Margarita Stocker: *Judith, Sexual Warrior –*
Women and Power in Western Culture **(1998)**

Stocker's study, *Judith, Sexual Warrior*, is as densely textured as that of Trexler and similarly not reducible to a series of masterpiece-landmarks. The nodal points in this case are probably a number of nexuses which formed around the theme, or 'acteme', as the author terms it, of Judith. These would include the erotic use of Judith's image which Stocker describes as hugely evident in Renaissance portraiture of the biblical heroine-cum-*femme fatale*; the political use of the Judith image in Reformation and post-Reformation Europe; the Romantic and exotic criminal in Victorian fiction; the shrewish wife in Punch and Judy; and, finally, the woman-with-a-gun of recent fiction. In nearly all of these cases, the theme is much more significant than the individual work of art or literature though, especially within visual art, there are some notable masterpieces (paintings by Cranach, Botticelli, Goya, Caravaggio and Klimt). There are really no major literary works, though Du Bartas's epic, *La Judit*, and Nicholas Moseley's novel, *Judith*, play the role of symptomatic examples of the theme's development.

Pamela Norris: *The Story of Eve* (1998)

Norris's *The Story of Eve* is much more of a literary-landmark study. We can identify the nodal points here as the treatment of Eve in the *Midrash Rabbah*; in the *Vitae Adae et Evae*; of Pandora in Hesiod's *Theogony*; of Penelope in Homer's *Odyssey*; of Eve again in Augustine's *The City of God*; and in Milton's *Paradise Lost*; and in Mary Shelley's *Frankenstein*; and in Margaret Atwood's *The Handmaid's Tale*; and, finally, in Angela Carter's *The Passion of the New Eve*. The inclusion of Pandora and Penelope is justified by the strong comparisons made or implied between these characters and Eve from Tertullian onwards. Looking at the above list, we could say that the ultimate nodal point is Milton, since it is Milton who sums up the whole of the reception-history up till his time and it is clearly Milton to whom later feminist authors are reacting.

Ann Wroe: *Pilate, the Biography of an Invented Man* (1999)

With Wroe's *Pilate* the situation is more complicated, since the work itself seems to exist in the shadow of Bulgakov's *The Master and Margarita*, as the author herself seems to acknowledge,[15] but the Bulgakov work is never properly discussed, only alluded to. At the same time, of course, the *Acta Pilati* plays an important role as part of the evidence for the growth of Pilate-lore, as do a mass of classical sources, together with *The Golden Legend* and the texts of the York and Towneley plays. We therefore have a nodal point which functions rather like the Ghost in Hamlet, if we are discussing literary landmarks. In terms of Wroe's own, rather unusual, hybrid of a literary structure (part reception-history, part historical documentary, part folklore history, part fiction), we could say that the nodal points are the invented beach scenes at the beginning

---

15   Wroe, op. cit., p. xi.

and end, the invented Cuba episode in the middle, and the largely uninvented account of the rise and fall of the Pilate myth around Lucerne in Switzerland.

Tina Pippin: *Apocalyptic Bodies,*
The Biblical End of the World in Text and Image

Pippin's *Apocalyptic Bodies* begins with the contemporary experience of horror-films, citing *Scream, Scream 2*, the *Nightmare on Elm Street* series, and *The Rapture*. Although much of the discussion which follows is rigorously academic, these films provide the context for the discussion. The autobiographical section on life in North Carolina has a similar function, joined to the references to the stories of Flannery O'Connor, dealing with the same Southern culture. After this, the chapter on Jezebel leans heavily on the documented colloquial use of the name in southern culture, on Gustav Doré's illustrations, and (like Gaines) on Tom Robbins's *Skinny Legs and All*. The chapter on Babel begins with Coca-Cola as an emblem and again draws on the Doré Bible illustrations, together with the work of Pieter Bruegel the Elder, and more recent art. There is discussion around the silent film, *Intolerance* (1916), and Matthew Maguire's opera, *The Tower* (1993). Chapter 6, 'Apocalyptic Horror', refers to the horror fiction of Hal Lindsey and Stephen King, the films *Psycho* and the *Texas Chain Saw Massacre* and Kant's *Critique of Judgement*. There is a section on pornographic treatments of the Whore of Babylon. Chapter 7, 'Apocalyptic Fear', draws on the film, *The Last Temptation of Christ*, Frankenstein and Dracula as horror figures, and apocalyptic films, including *Dr Strangelove* and *Terminator 2: Judgement Day*.

These nodal points are really flash-points in an academic argument about the transmission of biblical images about the end of the world through culture. The culture explored is chiefly visual art from Bruegel to the present day, modern popular fiction, and film from its inception.[16]

Janet Howe Gaines: *Music in the Old Bones,*
Jezebel Through The Ages **(1999)**

Gaines's *Music in the Old Bones, Jezebel through the Ages*, seems much more stately by comparison, despite its slightly wild project to rehabilitate Jezebel. Here, the nodal points (after the extended discussion of the biblical background-setting) are literary landmarks of varying stature, including John Knox's *The First Blast of the Trumpet against the Monstrous Regiment of Women*, some minor novels of the twentieth-century, stereotyping Jezebel as a villainess, Margaret Atwood's *The Robber Bride*, and Tom Robbins's *Skinny Legs and All*. The main work in the section on drama is Racine's *Athaliah*. The remainder of the material discussed, whether prose, poetry or drama, is either of little literary or cultural importance or consists merely of a passing reference to Jezebel, as in Shakespeare's *Twelfth Night*, where in Act 2, Scene 5, Sir Andrew Aguecheek refers to Malvolio as a Jezebel.

The nodal points here, from the point of view of the author's project, are the works which revise the reputation of Jezebel, notably the Robbins novel and the 1929 one-act play of Edith Lombard Squires, *Queen Jezebel*.

---

16 For the discovery of a historical nodal point in the reception-history of the Apocalypse, see M.R. James: *The Apocalypse in Art* (London: 1931, The British Academy). This author points out the huge influence of Dürer's woodcuts on subsequent treatments of the Apocalypse in art. It is significant that Dürer began his work in 1498, on the brink of the approach to the millennial year of 1500.

Kim Paffenroth: *Judas, Images of the Lost Disciple* (2001)

In Paffenroth's *Judas, Images of the Lost Disciple*, which is also a rehabilitation project, the nodal points are more extensive, perhaps because Judas is a more central cultural figure than Jezebel. In terms of literary works which play an important part in the book (Paffenroth does not discuss examples in visual art), the list would include *The Golden Legend*, the Oberammergau play, William Rayner's *The Knifeman*, Kazantzakis's *The Last Temptation* (as a novel and in the film version by Scorsese), and *Jesus Christ Superstar*. In addition, a theological work, William Klassen's *Judas, Betrayer or Friend of Jesus*,[17] is clearly a major influence, as well as the author's personal enthusiasm for the rock group, *Judas Priest*.[18] Not only is Judas a central cultural figure, but the author describes a shift in the treatment of Judas which has quite widespread manifestations and the evidence, therefore, is on his side to some extent, even if the theology is more contested.

Yvonne Sherwood: *A Biblical Text and its Afterlives,*
The Survival of Jonah in Western Culture (2000)

Our final example, Sherwood's *A Biblical Text and its Afterlife, The Survival of Jonah in Western Culture*, is a thorough survey of the exegetical and literary material both within the Christian Mainstream tradition and within the Backwater tradition which begins with Jewish Midrash. She also covers treatment in the visual arts quite extensively. There are, however, three nodal points, in terms of literary and exegetical landmarks, which stand out. These are the *Pirke de Rabbi Eliezer*, Melville's *Moby Dick* (inevitably)[19] and *Patience* by the *Gawain*-poet. These three

---

17 William Klassen: *Judas, Betrayer or Friend of Jesus?* (London: SCM, 1996).
18 See Paffenroth, op. cit., p. xi.
19 The continuing importance of *Moby Dick* for western culture is illustrated by allusions made to the novel in Harold Bloom's essay billed as 'Harold Bloom on literature for a fading

works, in many ways, support the book's wider argument about the resistance of the Jonah story to closure, about the unconventional theology which persistently emerges from readings which are open to the text itself, and about the story's responsiveness to the chaotic elements in human experience, as well as the text's responsiveness to the techniques of poststructuralist analysis. Sherwood's study could have centred on *Moby Dick* as a response to the Jonah story,[20] but it is much richer for the inclusion of the other material.

I believe that this section of the book has demonstrated the usefulness of the concept of 'nodal points' in illuminating the varying approaches of the fourteen essayists. We may summarise the ways in which they deploy texts which we have identified as nodal points:

1. Levenson, as a rather dated study, offers the prospect of discarded nodal points.

2. The Pritchard volume reveals cultural break-points which pre-date and go beyond the inventiveness of the modern novel.

3. Warner charts nexuses expressive of the deep religious currents of western culture which she herself wants to see abandoned.

4. Quinones is the mapper of literary landmarks which continue to be part of a landscape, irrespective of multiple readings.

5. Haskins uses works of art and literature as nodal points in the service of a feminist critique of a legend which (like Warner) she wishes to discard.

---

empire' but entitled 'Reflections in the Evening Land', published in *The Guardian Review*, 17.12.05.

20 In private correspondence, the author explained that a large amount of material about *Moby Dick* had to be excluded on grounds of space.

6. Cohn creates a map of the nodal points in early scientific writing which were a response to problems over the Genesis account of the Flood and, at the same time, provokes the sense of ignored nodal points in literature and art.

7. Trexler identifies nodal points in the form of critical moments in which the Magi feature as emblems of either social legitimation or of subversion.

8. Stocker outlines the critical stages in the changing faces of a Judith story which is determinedly counter-cultural.

9. Norris demonstrates how Milton's work can in effect be seen as a nodal point for the whole reception-history of the Eden story.

10. Wroe presents an absentee nodal point in the shape of *The Master and Margarita*.

11. Pippin selects an array of flashpoints to illuminate the impact of the biblical Apocalypse on modern western culture.

12. Gaines assembles together fragmentary nodal points in a sort of unofficial reception-history of Jezebel.

13. Paffenroth navigates six or seven nodal points in the service of one particular, 'reformist' agenda.

14. Sherwood demonstrates the remarkable intractability of the Jonah story largely through the prism of three literary and exegetical works.

Finally, as an illustration of the critical significance of the selection of nodal-points, we may briefly consider the case of a reception-history sketched in Boitani's *The Bible and Its Rewritings*, that of the story of Susanna and the Elders.

Boitani was concerned to demonstrate the baroque features of the interaction between the reception-history of the apocryphal book as a resurrection-motif in catacomb art and the development of the martyr-legend of Saint Susanna. Although thoroughly aware of other aspects of the reception-history, he made this his focus. However, the choice of other nodal-points could produce very different accounts of the reception-history of this quasi-biblical story. Concentrating on the Early English poem *Susannah* we would have a reception-history focussed on the lament of the innocent victim.[21] Making early Protestant drama the fulcrum,[22] we would have Susanna as an icon of faith, even as a proto-feminist. Concentrating on Renaissance painting, we would find the story inseparable from the history of *voyeurism* in art.[23] In this context, the urtext becomes a key example of 'the silencing of women within the stories of men'.[24] If Handel's oratorio *Susanna* were treated as the chief nodal-point, we would have an entrée into the reception-history of the urtext in the eighteenth-century and an interesting scene of conflation with the story of Solomon.[25] Treating James Bridie's play *Susannah and the Elders* as the end-point, we would have a story celebrating modern sexual liberation.[26]

---

21   See David C. Fowler: *The Bible in Early English Literature* (London: Sheldon, 1977), pp. 140–1. Fowler's verdict on *Susannah*: 'not a major poem … but it deserves an honoured place, along with *Jacob and Joseph*, among the contributions of minstrelsy to the biblical tradition'. (Ibid., p. 141.)

22   See Ruth H. Blackburn: *Biblical Drama under the Tudors* (The Hague: Mouton, 1971), pp. 136–41, for a discussion of Thomas Garter's play *Susanna* as an entertaining and edifying example of Protestant drama.

23   See Griselda Pollock: *Differencing the Canon* (Abingdon: Routledge, 1999), pp. 110–15, for a discussion which centres around Artemesia Gentileschi's painting *Susanna and the Elders* as a deviant or resistant work within a tradition of voyeurism which made Susanna and Judith two of its main subjects. For a discussion of the urtext as the narrative embodiment of the male gaze, see Alice Bach: *Women, seduction and betrayal in biblical narrative* (Cambridge: Cambridge University Press, 1997), pp. 65–72.

24   Alice Bach, ibid., p. 65.

25   Handel's oratorios *Susanna* and *Solomon* both app.eared in the same year, 1749. Scholars think it likely that they shared the same librettist. See Ruth Smith: *Handel's Oratorios and Eighteenth-Century Thought* (Cambridge: Cambridge University Press, 1995), pp. 332–4. Smith also points out the librettist's emphasis on the 'deracinated, dispossessed and unconfident' nature of the Israelite society of *Susanna*, 'opp.ressed by Babylonian exile (a circumstance given great prominence in the libretto but not even mentioned in the source).' Ibid., p. 333. The link with Samuel Richardson's novel, *Clarissa*, actually written over the period 1744–48, which Smith calls 'the obvious literary parallel' (ibid., p. 334) could be considered highly germane to the literary reception-history of the Susanna story, since *Clarissa* and *Pamela*, Richardson's earlier novel, are often considered the foundational English novels. See, for example, the entry on Richardson in Margaret Drabble (ed.): *The Oxford Companion to English Literature* (Oxford: Oxford University Press, 1990), pp. 828–9.

26   See Murray Roston: *Biblical Drama in England* (London: Faber, 1968) for a discussion of Bridie's play. 'The stern morality of the Old Testament is replaced by the modern tendency to absolve the guilty on the grounds of irresistible psychological impulse. Susannah has become

Treating Carlisle Floyd's anti-McCarthyite opera *Susannah* as the key hypertext, we would discover a political fable unrelated largely to the feminist emphasis of recent studies of the urtext.[27] The sheer diversity of possible nodal-points suggests that we may have here an urtext and its reception-history which defies the construction of a unified master-narrative.[28]

Conclusion

Refining our perception of nodal-points in the reception-history of biblical stories, we might, therefore, distinguish between urtexts which seem to spawn a multitude of diverse nodal-points (such as Susanna and the Elders, or The Magi), and urtexts which seem to find their main outworking in one major work of art or literature (Jonah). At the same time, the reception-history writer can choose to exploit the availability of multiple nodal-points in the former case in order to pursue a particular master-narrative or a particular interest. In the postmodernist era, where there is a suspicion of claims implying masterful objectivity, there will be more of a licence to indulge in the one-sided selection of nodal-points than might have been the case previously. The reception-history writer, in selecting one or more of the available hypertexts to serve as a nodal-point or as successive nodal-points, is merely adding a layer to the process of rewriting.

---

more reprehensible for titillating the old men's passions than they for succumbing to them.' (Ibid., p. 283.)

27   See Matthew Boyden: *The Rough Guide to Opera* (London: Rough Guides, 2002), p. 636: 'Floyd saw in the tale of Susannah a reflection of American life in the 1950s, when anticommunist paranoia was turning decent people into informers and malicious gossips'.

28   In an essay reviewing Boitani's original article on the Susanna story, Harold Fisch suggests that one reason for the absence of a Jewish reception-history of Susanna is that the story is itself a midrash on a text from the Song of Solomon: 'I am the tulip of Sharon, the lily of the valleys. Like the lily among thorns, so is my love among the daughters'. (Song 2:1–2). See Harold Fisch: 'Susanna as Parable: A Response to Piero Boitani' in Ellen Spolsky (ed.): *The Judgement of Susanna, Authority and Witness* (Atlanta: Scholars Press, 1996), pp. 35–42.

Chapter 12

A COMPARISON WITH THE RECEPTION-
HISTORIES OF ULYSSES, OVID AND *THE TEMPEST*

The purpose of this chapter is to make a comparison between our fourteen *biblical* reception-histories and three reception-histories of non-biblical material. The three examples chosen are W.B. Stanford's *The Ulysses Theme*, Sarah Anne Brown's *The Metamorphoses of Ovid, From Ovid to Chaucer*, and the collection of essays edited by Peter Hulme and William H. Sherman, *'The Tempest' and Its Travels*.[1] We will endeavour to find out whether similar processes of literary or iconographic appropriation can be identified and also to explore the extent to which the biblical reception-histories seem to have features which are absent from the non-biblical. It will be particularly interesting to discover the outworking of such similarities and differences where the same literary or visual artist has produced works in both fields.

We begin with W.B. Stanford's groundbreaking study of 1954, *The Ulysses Theme*.[2] Stanford speculated about a pre-Homeric Ulysses, but his primary enterprise was to trace the reception-history of the twin narratives of Ulysses found in the *Iliad* and the *Odyssey*, noticing the contrast between the candour of the hero in the first epic and his deceitfulness and wiliness in the second. Believing in the common Homeric authorship of both epics, Stanford saw these different characterisations as indicative of the capacity of Ulysses (in Homer's presentation)

---

1   The Stanford work has been selected because it was a pioneering contribution to the genre of the reception-history of a mythic story, at least within British literary studies. The other two simply represent a sample of the diversity of reception-history surveys now available.

2   W.B. Stanford: *The Ulysses Theme* (Oxford: Blackwell, 1954/ new ed. 1968).

to adapt his behaviour to circumstances, 'controlling his unusual versatility and flexibility in an uneasy environment ... like an Irish chieftain at the court of Elizabeth I or the Jewish hero of Joyce's *Ulysses* at Dublin High School'.[3]

The latter allusion anticipates Stanford's concept of the Ulysses tradition as an organic entity, something which emerges from the study as a whole, as it proceeds from the ups and downs in the reputation of Ulysses in classical times, through various landmarks in English and European literature to the modern pinnacles which the author identifies in Joyce's *Ulysses* and in Kazantzakis's *Odyssey*. It is this sense of the Ulysses tradition as a total entity which is probably Stanford's most significant contribution to literary studies.

Stanford finds the portrait of Ulysses in Virgil's *Aenid* Book Two responsible for the blackening of the hero's character 'for some fifteen hundred years in the western tradition', on the basis of a failure to distinguish between what the poet said *in propria persona* and what his characters Aeneas and Sinon said.[4] Thus Ulysses develops a proverbial character, rather, we might surmise, in the way that Job became Patient Job in western culture.

The author makes a clear distinction between treatments of the Ulysses theme which merely use it as a peg to hang extraneous ideas on and those which constitute a serious engagement with the figure of Ulysses. The former category would include sporadic Christian attempts to allegorise Ulysses, as well as more casual references to the name.

Stanford is very alert to the sense of a cumulative tradition, with Joyce, for example, building on the portraits of Ulysses found in Dante, Shakespeare and Tennyson. He also distinguishes between two divergent strands which he describes as 'centripetal' and 'centrifugal', relying on contrasting pictures of Ulysses as the insistently homeward-bound traveller, the reluctant exile, and Ulysses as

---

3   Ibid., p. 14.
4   Ibid., p. 137.

the anarchic, Romantic spirit, unable to settle.[5] What was particularly radical in Stanford's approach in 1954 was his readiness to read the tradition backwards as well as forwards, understanding Shakespeare's treatment of Ulysses in *Troilus and Cressida*, in the light of Joyce, as well as the revived interest in Homer in his day. The phrase he uses here is 'Seen in the full perspective of the Ulysses myth',[6] denoting an almost postmodern detachment from historical sequentiality, though perhaps it would be more accurate to describe Stanford as envisioning the Ulysses theme as a rolling river, carrying within it material which only fully emerges downstream.

Amongst the highlights of Stanford's survey of what he calls 'the vernacular tradition'[7] are the contrast he draws between Shakespeare's 'comprehensive humanism'[8] and the austere, Senecan attitude and style of the French tragedians; the use of Ulysses as a pawn in Calvinist and post-Tridentine Catholic propaganda; the genius of Girandoux's Ulysses; Du Bellay's Ulysses sonnet as the encapsulation of authentic Ulyssean yearning for escape from exile to the *douceur* of a rustic homeland; Dante and Ulysses as anarchist; Vico and the depersonalisation of Ulysses into a political principle; Charles Lamb's *Adventures of Ulysses* as evidence of the reaction against scientism and renewed interest in the fabulous (Joyce's childhood reading of Lamb was a major influence on him); Calderson's remarkably successful Christian Ulysses; Hauptmann and the madness of Ulysses; the cheating and immoral Ulysses of Giono; Eyvind Johnson's expansive novel of Ulysses's return, *Strandernas Svall* (contrasted with the terseness of Homer); Tennyson's *Ulysses* as a development of Dante's doomed hero; Pascoli's Odysseus (the first revival of the name in the 'vernacular tradition') as the poetic triumph of nihilism; d'Annunzio's Ulysses as a fascist hero. Finally, in Chapter 15, Stanford

---

5   See ibid., p. 181.
6   Ibid., p. 169.
7   Ibid., p. 159.
8   Ibid., p. 171.

278

celebrates 'The Re-Integrated Hero' of Joyce's Dublin-bound Ulysses and the ambitiously multi-religious *Odyssey* of Kazantzakis, described by Stanford as 'an apocryphal, Gnostic gospel'.[9] Joyce and Kazantzakis here represent the outworking respectively of the twin themes of Ulysses as the unwilling wanderer and Ulysses as the non-Homeric incurable wanderer.

In his concluding pages, Stanford hails the Ulysses theme as the most dynamic and versatile of European myths. It is rivalled only by Faust and Don Juan, both of which seem to be developments of divergent themes within the Ulysses tradition itself.[10] He goes on to argue that heroic figures 'like Ulysses', far from being the passive subjects of literary treatment, 'retain a dynamism and momentum of their own', causing writers like Goethe and Tennyson to engage with them in a way productive of a 'mutually energising power'.[11] A footnote directs the reader tentatively towards the Jungian theory of archetypes.[12]

Comparing *The Ulysses Theme* with our fourteen biblical reception-histories, we need to remember that Stanford's work is itself the 'archetypal' or, at least, foundational text for what we now conceive of as literary reception-history, even if our fourteen authors seem to be too far down the line to need to acknowledge the influence of his work. It is notable that the treatment of Ulysses in the visual arts was an afterthought for Stanford, appearing as an appendix in the second edition of his study.

The most important resemblances seem to be as follows:

1. Stanford's own construction of a synoptic Homeric tradition, with a primitive oral stage understood to underpin the whole. This, for his part, brings his work into line with the biblical studies of the time.

---

9   Ibid., p. 224.
10   Ibid., p. 246.
11   Ibid., p. 246.
12   Ibid., pp. 279–80, note 8.

2. The tendency for a generalised folkloric figure to develop, adrift from the informing literary sources. The equivalents in our study would include Eve as a seductress, Cain as a wanderer, the Patient Job, Jonah as a comic figure, Mary Magdalene as a penitent whore, and even the unread Book of Revelation as a symbolic entity.

3. The dichotomising of divergent strands within the tradition. The equivalents in our study would be the multiple roles of the Virgin Mary in Warner; Paffenroth's demonic and humanised Judases; the demonic and regenerate Cains; Judith as heroine and temptress.

4. The sense of the tradition as an organic entity. This is most evident in the upbeat accounts of Quinones and Trexler of their subjects and, in a dismissive way, in Warner's conclusion that the once-glorious Virgin Mary myth cannot be resuscitated in the age of feminism but stands or falls (for her emphatically 'falls') as a whole.

5. The use of the theme in religious and political propaganda. Here, Stocker's Judith seems the most obvious equivalent.

6. The tendency in the modern period for increasingly expansive novelistic treatments. Here there are equivalents in most of our fourteen studies, apart from Warner.

7. The sense that minor works can pick up a cultural shift which may only later be picked up by a 'major' writer or artist. Here we might find, as equivalents, Unamuno's reading of Byron (if we consider Byron 'minor' by comparison); or the outworking of numerous, less successful works, in the Judas of Kazantzakis and Scorsese.

8. The equivalent of the 'mutually energising power' which Stanford detects in the interface between hero and author (citing specifically Goethe and Tennyson) might be Harold Bloom's 'anxiety of influence' in more recent literary-critical terms or Alter's more optimistic sense of later authors engaging creatively

with earlier works. In terms of our fourteen biblical reception-histories, the equivalents might be Trexler's sense of the Magi awaiting moments of socio-cultural need; the development of the Sheba tradition in the *Kebra Nagast* (as described in Pritchard); Byron's Cain, as well as the Cain of Melville, Conrad and Unamuno (as discussed in Quinones); and the obsession of Wilkie Collins with the figure of Mary Magdalene, noted by Haskins.

Addressing the question of what features are present in our collection of biblical reception-histories and absent from Stanford's *The Ulysses Theme*, the most obvious difference is the absence of religious charge in most of the works explored by Stanford. In fact, amongst the major works he discusses, only Calderon's play and Kazantzakis's *Odyssey* have an overtly religious theme. By the same token, two of his major, 'universal' writers, Shakespeare and Joyce, are precisely those who famously avoided the direct treatment of biblical themes.

Stanford's subject also differs from our biblical reception-histories in that there is no duality of dogmatic or doctrinal exegesis versus imaginative interpretation in his field. Nor is there the sense of some historical touchstone which might validate or invalidate a treatment of the theme. The term 'apocryphal' would have no place in the study of the Ulysses myth. If we acknowledge that Eve, Cain, Job, and Jonah have in modern times been recognized as fictional entities, they still belong to a tradition which formerly treated them as historical and are part of a wider construct (the Bible) which is highly dependent on notions of historicity. For Stanford, historical veracity only matters in such things as the historical background to the Trojan War, making his subject more akin to an overtly fictional character, like Spartacus, set against a (historical) biblical background.

Whilst Homer's texts are in many ways the yardstick for later treatments of Ulysses, Stanford hints that the theme is independent of Homer and later treatments may even surpass Homer. But his most significant achievement in *The*

Ulysses Theme is to give the sense of a cumulative tradition, which allows one author to build on the work of another, and of elements in the tradition which disappear and resurface in line with cultural shifts. There is a quasi-biblical nuance to this, which makes all the more ironic his designation of Kazantzakis's *Odyssey* as a 'an apocryphal, Gnostic gospel', remembering that this is the one example in his study in which the figure of Jesus makes an appearance. The sense of Biblical Religion and Classical Mythology as polarities is deeply embedded in our thinking, or certainly it was in 1954.

There is a considerable gap between the intellectual world of Stanford and that of Sarah Anne Brown's *The Metamorphosis of Ovid, from Chaucer to Ted Hughes* (1999).[13] Admittedly, Brown is dealing with the reception-history of a luxuriant poem, containing many stories, rather than the epic story of one hero. But this difference is less important than the postmodernist revolution which has demoted authorial intention and raised the status of the text or textuality as a quasi-autonomous force. If Stanford's authors engaged with a myth which had a momentum of its own, Brown's authors wrestle with a text which is highly self-reflexive and suggestive of its own constructedness. Ovid, himself, repeatedly draws attention, as Brown notes, to the fictiveness of his own writing. Added to these qualities, Ovid's text has seeped through one later text into another, as in Ariel's song in Shakespeare's *The Tempest*, which is present in T.S. Eliot's *The Wasteland* and then in Jorie Graham's *Flood*. 'Graham is not merely reading Ovid refracted through Shakespeare and Eliot as discrete Ovidian voices; she is reading him through Eliot reading Shakespeare reading Ovid.'[14]

Brown discusses Chaucer's *House of Fame* as a prime point of entry for the influence of Ovid over English literature, together with Spenser's *Faerie Queene,*

---

13   Sarah Anne Brown: *The Metamorphoses of Ovid, From Chaucer to Ted Hughes* (London: Duckworth, 1999).

14   Ibid., p. 14.

Shakespeare's *The Tempest* and *A Midsummer Night's Dream*, the works of Marvell, Milton, Keats, Beddoes, Browning, Eliot, Joyce and Virginia Woolf.

She uses the term 'embedded Ovidianism'[15] to describe the absorption of Ovid as a semi-autonomous phenomenon in poets like Keats who, unlike Spenser or Milton, was not a classicist. Part of her argument is that Ovidianism is so pervasive in English literature after Chaucer that, even when Ovid falls severely out of fashion (as in the nineteenth-century), his influence can still be traced. Ovid's *Metamorphoses* likewise can be found influencing the sculpture of Bernini who, in turn, transmits the effect to other artists. Within Ovid's own oeuvre, the *Metamorphoses* can itself be read in part as a reception of his earlier work, *Tristia*.[16]

Chaucer in his *House of Fame* not only uses thematic material taken over from the *Metamorphoses* but is influenced by that work in his very selective use of Trojan War material, with its eccentric attention to minor episodes anticipating Tom Stoppard's approach to Hamlet. Retelling Virgil's story of Dido in the *Iliad*, he exploits his audience's familiarity with the story in his very partial retelling of it. Chaucer is influenced by his reading of the *Metamorphoses* to reject the medieval theory of authorship, with its very respectful attitude to 'authorities'.[17]

Spenser, in turn, sees the skill of the artist as comparable with that of the shapeshifting gods in the *Metamorphoses*. His *Faerie Queene* constantly draws attention to its own artifice and plays on the difficulty of distinguishing art from nature. The unstable world of the *Metamorphoses* influences Shakespeare, most visibly in *A Midsummer Night's Dream*, where the device of a play within a play displays the fictive character of the work. Shakespeare insists, however, on making the story of Pyramus and Thisbe part of the comedy here, the tragedy surfacing only in *Romeo and Juliet*. In *The Tempest*, Ovid's influence is oblique, manifesting

---

15   Ibid., p. 11.
16   Ibid., p. 20.
17   Ibid., pp. 26–9.

itself in 'his fondness for calling attention to the fictive nature of his writing, his manipulation of readers' expectations, the identifications he makes between himself and the creators in the *Metamorphoses*, whether gods or artists, and the blurring of boundaries between what is real and unreal'.[18]

The poetry of Andrew Marvell is examined and found to be exceptionally in tune with the *Metamorphoses*. In fact, Brown finds that this is the blockage in Marvell: 'Whereas tensions and disjunctions between Ovid and his imitators drive the tradition forwards, uncovering new layers of meaning in the *Metamorphoses*, the perfect equilibrium between Ovid and Marvell only produces inertia. In just one important aspect is Marvell unovidian; he fails to metamorphose his source'[19]

Milton is shown borrowing heavily from Ovid in Book One of *Paradise Lost*, which depends upon the unusually serious section of the *Metamorphoses* dealing with the creation of mankind. When Eve looks at her own reflection, Narcissus-like, Echo is the absent presence. Milton's populous heaven comes from the *Metamorphoses*, as does his Satanic Council, the Pandaemonium. He borrows from Ovid's flood story and finds models for Adam and Eve in Pyrrha and Decalion. Milton's doctrine of grace allows his characters to go further than those in Ovid, allowing them finally to escape divine wrath. But his elision of Eve with Pomona implies the surrender of the Genesis plot to that of Pomona's seduction by Verumnus (or Satan in *Paradise Lost*).[20]

Later, Brown discusses the 'absent presence' of the *Metamorphoses* in Keats's *Ode on a Grecian Urn*, where Ovid's tale of Apollo and Daphne is a concealed subtext.[21] She finds Browning an Ovidian in spite of himself and Beddoes's *Pygmalion* a vital, though misogynist, link in the transmission of its eponymous theme.[22]

---

18   Ibid., p. 70.
19   Ibid., p. 99.
20   Ibid., pp. 101–22.
21   Ibid., pp. 141–53.
22   Ibid., pp. 155–79.

Pygmalion features as an element in James Joyce's *The Dubliners* where, in the story *The Dead*, Gabriel Conroy becomes 'an inverse Pygmalion', turning Gretta's feelings to stone. Similarly, Gerty MacDowell in *Ulysses* is an ambiguous Galatea, given autonomy only to behave as a sentimental heroine of romantic fiction.[23]

Brown finds, in Virginia Woolf's *Orlando*, the merging of two different subtexts from the *Metamorphoses*, the stories respectively of Daphne and Apollo and Salamacis and Hermaphrodite. Daphne's story is 'reinvented as an emblem of complementary harmony between the sexes',[24] as Wolf follows earlier writers in reading the legend against the grain. Orlando is transformed into a woman, emphasising the continuity, though not identity, between the male and female states. According to Brown, 'Orlando's spontaneous sex change is as fantastic as Woolf's reinvention of Daphne's fate as a positive experience; the novel is a space for play which, like the wood of *A Midsummer Night's Dream*, we can only visit for a few short hours'.[25]

The points of resemblance between *The Metamorphosis of Ovid* and our fourteen biblical reception-histories seem to be as follows:

1. Ovid's style and tenor are shown to be as influential as his content. The overall *gravitas* displayed both by our fourteen authors and by many of their discussed writers and artists can be said to echo the biblical grand style, particularly as channelled through the Received Text.

2. Marvell's close affinity with Ovid may invite consideration of which *biblical* rewriters are exceptionally close to the style and ethos of their urtexts in the received translation. Brown's point about Marvell as a case of excessive compatibility underlines the sense that new meaning is generated through the convergence of hitherto disparate traditions or semiotic currents.

---

23   Ibid., p. 191.
24   Ibid., p. 205.
25   Ibid., p. 215.

3. Brown's close dissection of Milton's *Paradise Lost* text to suggest his partial capitulation to a contrarian picture of Eve and Satan resembles the argument that Byron finally is overridden by the biblical text of Genesis 4.

4. Joyce's involvement with the Pygmalion theme over a long period may be said to resemble Wilkie Collins's fascination with the Mary Magdalene story or Unamuno's lifelong interest in the story of Cain and Abel.

5. The conflation of Ovidian tales found in Chaucer and Woolf parallels an important feature of biblical reception-history.

6. The transmission of Ovidian influence via the visual arts (Bernini and Velasquez) and its interaction with literature reminds one of M.D. Anderson's study of the interaction between the mystery plays and medieval stained glass art.[26]

7. Woolf's invoking of the *Metamorphoses* to support her prose experiment in *Orlando* seems to be a likely influence on Angela Carter's magic-realist novel *The Passion of the New Eve* which we have considered in the context of Norris's work.

8. The unveiling of Ovidian influence even in authors documented as repudiating Ovid offers the for consideration the question of whether authors overtly hostile to the Bible, like Frost, can be said sometimes to transmit its values in some sense willy-nilly.

The differences between Brown's study and our fourteen biblical reception-histories largely revolve around their respective subjects. Broadly speaking, the latter are concerned with the re-imaging of a text which is inherently didactic and norm-establishing; the former with the influence of a text which is shown by Brown to be fundamentally destabilising and subversive. Like Homer, Ovid belongs to the

---

26   M.D. Anderson: *Drama and Imagery in English Medieval Churches* (Cambridge: Cambridge University Press, 1963).

pagan world of revisited classical antiquity, which from the Renaissance onwards oscillates between being the analogue of and the counterpoint to biblical culture. Unlike Homer, Ovid, seen through the eyes of Brown, appears to be the ancient analogue of Derridean post-modernism.

Brown has little cause to defend or criticize Ovid and his rewriters in the context of a feminist critique (the exception being Beddoes) or, indeed, a postcolonial critique, since Ovid is inferred to be beyond or outside those areas and his thoroughgoing ironic stance seems to align him with his own rewriters.

Our third work is *'The Tempest' and Its Travels* (2000), a collection of essays edited by Peter Hulme and William H. Sherman.[27] There is no attempt here to chart a full reception-history of Shakespeare's play but, instead, we find a series of scholarly forays into episodes in that history. The editors in their Preface observe the shift in recent decades in favour of treating Caliban as the centre of attention, rather than Prospero. Caliban, they argue, is the only minor character in Shakespeare to break free from the original text and become a widely available cultural entity.[28] They find *The Tempest*, a play 'itself about usurpation and force', a very ready vehicle for appropriation and reinvention.[29] Like Auerbach discussing the Genesis text, they notice the large number of blanks in the play, unanswered questions, which we are invited to fill in.[30]

Barbara Mowat discusses *The Tempest* as an exemplary case of intertextuality,[31] with its echoes of the *Aeneid,* Ovid's *Metamorphoses,* and Florio's translation of Montaigne's *Of the Caniballes,* and the storms in Virgil, the *Odyssey,* and the *Argonautica* of Appolonius of Rhodes. She notes the disparity in vividness in

---

27   Peter Hulme and William H. Sherman (eds.): *'The Tempest' and Its Travels* (London: Reaktion Books, 2000).

28   Presumably they discount Falstaff on account of his appearance as the major character in *The Merry Wives of Windsor.*

29   Ibid., p. xii.

30   Eric Auerbach: *Mimesis* (Princeton NJ: Princeton University Press, 1973).

31   In Hulme and Sherman, ibid., pp. 27–36.

Shakespeare's time between literary and documentary accounts of storms. Joseph Roach sees the Tempest in the play less as an event than a destination in the age of vicarious tourism, when the theatre stood in for actual travel: 'Generally speaking, Eden serves as an unbeatably popular destination for the vicarious tourist'. He sees Prospero's speech at the end of the masque in Act IV Scene I as 'a valediction to the magical powers of art prior to the systematic commercialisation of leisure and the rise of the scenic stage'.[32]

Donna Hamilton outlines the importance of the *Aeneid* as a source of cultural codes in the early seventeenth-century with *The Tempest* relying on it as its 'operating system'.[33] Roland Greene discusses the play's use of the tropes provided by insularity and encounter to deal with the alterity of the cultural encounter with Indians, Africans, Jews and Moors. Islands reveal the reality as 'built, imported and contingent'.[34] For Greene, the greatest legacy of *The Tempest* is the works it has spawned, including the great reinventions found in Rodo's *Ariel*, Retamar's *Caliban*, and Césaire's *Une Tempête*.[35]

In an editorial section,[36] we find mentioned G. Wilson Knight's view of *The Tempest* as the summation of all Shakespeare's previous plays (we may find a variant of this in the proclivity of some of our fourteen reception-history writers to claim 'their' biblical story as the key to the whole Bible).

The bulk of the rest of the volume is taken up with *The Tempest* in the context of postcolonial readings, both the play itself in relation to Elizabethan concepts of 'The New World', and the rewritings which are such a marked feature of modern Caribbean and other South American literature. Peter Hulme discusses the work of George Lamming and his influence on the playwrights Roberto Retamar and

---

32   Ibid., p. 70.
33   Ibid., p. 119.
34   Ibid., p. 142.
35   Ibid., p. 145.
36   Ibid., p. 174.

Aimé Césaire.[37] Lamming's essay on *The Tempest* in *The Pleasures of Exile* views the whole play from the perspective of Caliban, emphasing his background as a slave from the 'middle passage'. The essay, which has become a *locus classicus* for postcolonial studies, calls for a dialogue between English society and the Caribbean community which has yet to begin.[38]

Lucy Rix explores Césaire's *Une Tempête* as an exercise in de-essentialising the construction of race, with Césaire himself usurping the part of Shakespeare; Prospero displaced largely by a new character, who randomly distributes the actors' parts and invokes the storm; the intrusion of the Caribbean god, Eshu, into the western pantheon, and Ferdinand acting the role of slave and Stephano and Trinculo as kings and generals. We are directed to the use of Ariel and Caliban as persistent motifs in Latin American culture and politics.[39]

The volume's final essay is a new look by David Dabydeen at Hogarth's painting of circa 1735, *A Scene from The Tempest*,[40] which places the monstrous figure of Caliban in command of the tableau, in line with the painter's mastery of 'the degraded form.'[41] We find an ambivalent Miranda who seems strangely seduced by the hairy figure.

The following points arising from *'The Tempest' and Its Travels* seem pertinent to our study:

1. The reorientation of the play in modern times, to make Caliban the central figure, provides a context for the impulse to rescue minor biblical figures from obscurity. We might see Wroe's Pilate and Paffenroth's Judas partly in this light.

---

37   Ibid., pp. 220–35.
38   Ibid., p. 228.
39   Ibid., pp. 236–49.
40   Ibid., pp. 257–62.
41   Ibid., p. 258.

2. If we extend this sense to the attempt to reassemble the ethnic components of a story, then clearly Gaines's Jezebel would fit into the picture.

3. The sense that *The Tempest*'s openness to reinterpretation is a product of its own rootedness in intertextuality (Ovid, Virgil, etc.) may lead us to consider that the availability of the biblical stories for appropriation and rewriting is a function of their own multiplicity of underlying sources.

4. The idea of *The Tempest* as a vehicle for vicarious travel may remind us of the exotic locations of our biblical stories (Eden, Sheba, Nineveh or the Holy Land as a generic entity) which, assimilated for literary consumption, may attract similar connotations; something perhaps parodied in the novels of Michel Tournier. At the same time, exotic locations may serve the trope of alterity, which would be an advantage to a rewritten biblical story aiming to invoke transcendence.

5. G. Wilson Knight's plea to make this disorientating play the key to all Shakespeare's previous output, whilst an extreme position, might be a useful tool in 'defamiliarising' his work, just as the claims made for their respective biblical stories by Quinones, Sherwood, Stocker and Norris might help invigorate the overall view of the biblical corpus.

6. The postcolonial Caliban has obvious resonance for the reception-history of biblical stories, particularly those of the Queen of Sheba and the Journey of the Magi.

7. The revisiting of Hogarth's painting, hitherto dismissed as run-of-the-mill, suggests that reception-history often has the capacity to harbour hidden masterworks, or at least works which depend on cultural upheavals for their significance to be revealed.

8. The intrusion of the Caribbean god, Eshu, into the world of *The Tempest* (in Césaire's *Une Tempête*) is a reminder of the close connection between the biblical God and the inscription of reality in western literature as a whole.

A similar reminder is implicit in Gaines's gesture towards advocacy of the Canaanite religion of Jezebel.

Where *'The Tempest' and Its Travels* occupies distinctly different territory from our fourteen biblical reception-histories is in its concentration on the twin topics of Elizabethan theatre and the literary representation of the New World; and obviously in the character of its urtext, *The Tempest* itself, as a Shakespearean play rather than a sacred text. It is noteworthy that none of the authors in this volume seem impelled to discuss the rewritten biblical content of *The Tempest*, seen by Steven Marx as an intertext for the Apocalypse.[42]

Conclusion

In summary, we can observe some strong resemblances between our fourteen biblical reception-histories and the three specimen non-biblical case studies, as well as sharp differences which may be ascribed to the status of the biblical urtexts as opposed to that of secular literature. We also find, as we would expect, a number of literary authors in common. What is probably most important is the discussion of common processes, whether those associated by our various authors with folkloric patterns of transmission, the poetic assimilation of source material, the conditions for the rise of the novel, the impact of gender studies or postcolonial studies; or what may seem more speculative theories about the survival and adaptability of stories.

Our next chapter will take this discussion further, particularly in relation to the topic of resisting and enforcing closure.

---

42 See Stephen Marx: *Shakespeare and the Bible* (Oxford: Oxford University Press, 2000), pp. 125–46.

Chapter 13

CLOSURE, NON-CLOSURE, IDEOLOGIES AND CANONS

Throughout this book we have had to deal with the impact of the reception-history writer's master-narrative both on the selection of material (rewritten biblical stories as hypertexts) and on the interpretation of that material. In Chapter 8, we were compelled to draw a broad distinction between 'Committed Stances' and 'Objective Stances'. In this chapter we will look further at the influence of postmodernist theories on the master-narratives of our fourteen authors and at how we might independently apply some postmodernist insights both to the fourteen reception-histories themselves and to the major hypertexts we have discussed.

George Aichele as a Model Postmodernist

George Aichele's *Jesus Framed* provides a useful summary of the postmodernist school of Derrida and Barthes.[1] Texts are inchoate without interpretation. All readings are ideological and all readings 'misread' the text. Writerly texts are more resistant to ideological assimilation than readerly texts.[2] Counter-readings are generated by the oppressed who have to 'steal' the text; dominant readings belong to the oppressor. Closure is brought about by naturalising the text. The Transcendent Signified is a chimera. There is no essential message from writer to reader. Intertextuality denotes the endless play of meaning or clash of competing

---

1   George Aichele: *Jesus Framed* (London: Routledge, 1996).
2   Although Aichele ascribes something like this formula to Barthes, it does seem that Barthes's own view is rather more complex. See below, note 9.

292

ideologies. In the case of the Gospel of Mark (the main subject of *Jesus Framed*), the story of the empty tomb presents the reader with a fantastic escape from referential meaning, but the other canonical gospels use the resurrection stories to reassure the reader and disarm the problematic of the crucifixion. Aichele himself uses the intertext of the story of the insect from Kafka's *Metamorphosis* to elucidate the empty tomb story.

Aichele states that Barthes parcels together the myths of historical objectivity, individualism, nationalism, capitalism, colonialism and patriarchy, as all part of bourgeois ideology.[3]

Seen in this light, several of our biblical reception-histories could be said to borrow the clothes of postmodernism in the service of a finally ideological and therefore bourgeois reading of their subject-matter. This would place them on the same side of the fence as more conservative theological constructions of biblical texts and opposed to those readings which resist all forms of closure or see the text as subversive of all fixed certainties. This would then leave us with the task of distinguishing, both amongst the biblical urtexts and amongst the rewritten biblical stories, between those examples which could be perceived as writerly and those we might designate as readerly. At the same time, those reception-histories which seem to eschew both the ideological overdetermination of meaning and the language of postmodernism might still have to be inspected for evidences of surrender to a complacent theology of the status quo, or simply a 'theology of reading'.

The full-strength Nietzschian postmodernism which Aichele offers here is such a complete and itself closed hermeneutical system that it might seem to repel any mediating position. Yet we can surely recognize the validity of intertextuality as a way of describing the way texts build on other texts (or can be brought into relationship by the reader). It is also easy to acknowledge the force of a distinction between writerly and readerly texts, since we habitually make distinctions, however fluid, between

3   Ibid., Chapter 7.

great literature and populist fiction. We can also notice the competition between ideologies (stated or implicit) without accepting the banishment of the transcendent to a vanishing point completely beyond human experience.

The Opposite Camp

As a reminder of the conservative position on rewritten scripture which lies at the opposite pole from the postmodernist writings of George Aichele, and which offers its own account of the modern appetite for discovering apocryphal biblical texts, we turn now to an attack on the veneration of the non-canonical in Philip Jenkins's *Hidden Gospels, How the Search for Jesus Lost Its way.*[4]

Jenkins sees the whole popular and academic interest in non-canonical gospels as the product of postmodernist rejection of canons, promoted by careerist scholars who have a vested interested in claiming the pre-eminence of texts like the *Gospel of Thomas* and the *Gospel of Mary* and in advocating early dates for them. For him, these texts are not without historical value, but they tell no more about 'the world of Jesus' than the 1880 novel *Ben-Hur*, which 'tells us much about the world-view of nineteenth-century American Christians and antiquarians, but nothing of original value about the first-century events which it describes'.

For Jenkins, the pursuit of the non-canonical is part of a wider cultural rejection of Christian orthodoxy, inflamed by media presentation of the Dead Sea Scrolls and driven by an élite who see themselves as the first to rediscover Gnosticism since antiquity. He sets all this in the context of the critical role played by Christianity in North America, where 'the public is likely to feel that new gospels are simply too important to be left to scholars'. (It is interesting that Jenkins sees Robert Graves's

---

4   Philip. Jenkins: *Hidden Gospels, How the Search for Jesus Lost Its Way* (New York: Oxford University Press, 2001).

294

King Jesus as a sort of jumping of the gun in the context of the discovery of the Nag Hammadi texts.)

Jenkins's book is valuable as a presentation of the conservative rejoinder to some of the currents examined in this book. But it ignores nuanced alternatives to the views which it projects onto the opposition. For example: Is it not possible to place *King Jesus* in a dialogue with the orthodox portrayal of Jesus and to find in *Ben-Hur* (as Larry Kreitzer does[5]) something theologically insightful, rather than to set them both in polarised opposition to a pristine Christianity embedded in a tightly-defined time-capsule? Can theology not be found in material outside the biblical canon? In any case, is the biblical canon really such an impervious entity as Jenkins implies? What about the history of translation and of interpretation? The drift of our reading of our reception-history material so far would suggest that these questions are unavoidable. Nevertheless, *Hidden Gospels* is valuable both as a description of the popular and media-driven reception of unearthed apocryphal material[6] and as a record of a strongly held Evangelical-Christian view of the status of post-biblical texts. It also accentuates the need to explore notions of canonical closure at greater length.

Closure and Non-Closure

During the course of this study both the biblical canon and the more elusive literary canon have been background factors. It may, at this stage, be useful to examine more closely their importance in relation to the notions of closure and openness. Clearly, the biblical canon expresses itself through the making available of our biblical urtexts as designated sacred stories, existing in relation to the construct

---

5   Larry Kreitzer: *The New Testament in Fiction and Film* (Sheffield: Sheffield Academic Press, 1993), pp. 44–66.

6   The popular image of apocryphal material may be greatly influenced by reports of the literal 'unearthing' of texts at Qumran and Nag-Hammadi in the late 1940s, although it is also the case that many other apocryphal texts, such as the Infancy Gospels, survived in European libraries, awaiting metaphorical unearthing.

of a totality of such sacred stories, termed 'The Bible'. More locally, each story actually exists in a closer relationship with specific other stories (Sheba with the Magi; Judas or Pilate with the Wandering Jew) which may have developed through the processes of reception-history, or because of some direct literary or thematic dependence (the Flight into Egypt and the Moses story.) The biblical canon assumes the process of translation from one language to another to be a seamless one and that therefore there is an uncomplicated equivalence between the Passion story in New Testament Greek, Latin, Tudor English and modern English. Following Aichele, we could add that a similar equivalence is generally assumed between the 'intrinsic' Passion story in the gospels and the story as dramatised in the York mystery play or changed about by Kazantzakis.

Apocryphal books, like Judith, exist in a relationship of peripherality or even contest with the biblical canon, but still share some of the religious charge of the canonical material. At times (as Stocker shows), they are treated as fully biblical in status. At other times, they help define the boundary between 'true' and 'untrue'. In recent times they even enjoy a sort of favoured underdog status or gain from the hermeneutics of suspicion.

The literary canon, like the musical canon, is a more flexible entity, allowing authors and works to rise and fall in status. Nevertheless, a consistent, large central core (Chaucer, Shakespeare, Milton, Dickens, Joyce) persists and, in our previous pages, we have sometimes shared in the tendency to give extra weight to 'major' writers rather than 'minor'. Literary theorists often stress the qualities of originality and strangeness as typical of the 'great' works. When it comes to literary retellings of biblical stories, such alterity may, however, be generated by the convergence of different semiotic codes as much as the presence of 'genius', though we should not ignore Harold Bloom's ideas about strong readings.[7] (Although forged as a description of the response of writers to

---

7   The classic formulation is to be found in Harold Bloom: *A Map of Misreading* (New York: Oxford University Press, 1975).

previous secular literary masterpieces, Bloom's 'misreadings' may be suggestive in the context of radical rewritings of biblical stories.)

One of the most substantial sites of confluence in our study is the Garden of Eden story as handled directly by Milton, indirectly by Byron, and then in reaction to Milton by Mary Shelley and others of the modern and postmodern periods.[8] To see these works and the post-Byronic Cain and Abel tradition as examples of strong re-readings or misreadings occasioned by the meeting of both canons, biblical and literary, seems a very apt description.

'Writerly' and 'Readerly' Revisited

We mentioned above Aichele's notion that writerly texts resist closure, whereas readerly texts tend to enforce it.[9] Elsewhere, we have discussed ambiguity as a feature of seminal literary works. Thus Quinones invites us to enjoy the ambiguity of Conrad's *The Secret Sharer* and deplore the formulaic writing of Wouk's *The Caine Mutiny*. At the same time, we have found hidden subversive qualities in the reputedly formulaic romantic novel of du Maurier, *Rebecca*. We may suspect that part of the difference here lies in the 'reading' approach rather than in the intrinsic nature of the text, something reinforced in that other section of Aichele's argument which insists that texts are nothing before interpretation. Perhaps we should talk in terms of the tendency of some texts to attract open-ended readings and the tendency of others to invite ideological or

---

8   The reaction may be said to have set in already with Dryden. For a discussion of Dryden's 'opera' *The State of Innocence and Fall of Man* as a diminution of Milton's vision, see C.A. Patrides: *The Grand Design of God, The literary form of the Christian view of history* (London: Routledge and Kegan Paul, 1972), pp. 125–6.

9   I am conscious, from a reading of *S/Z* and *From Work to Text*, that Barthes offers something more complex than a simple *readerly/writerly* binary opp.osition in his effort to show the intertextual character of all writing. However, the distinction, as filtered through Aichele, serves our purpose. Barthes could also be said to dichotomise *text* and *work*, with *text* (*'La texte'*) as the locus of a rich diversity of connotation and *work* (*'l'oeuvre'*) as the commodified literary product.

sentimental readings. In relation to our fourteen reception-history writers, we should have to refine this distinction to take account of the rejection of a strong literary text, D.H. Lawrence's *The Man Who Died*, by a strong feminist reading of the encompassing tradition (Haskins) and the equally insistent dismissal of a weak literary text, *Jezebel the Jeep*, by a feminist reading of more mixed strength.

An Overview of the Fourteen Reception-Histories

Before we return to the key examples of rewritten biblical stories within our study, it might be useful to chart the position of our fourteen frame narratives in relation to the notions of closure and resistance to closure. The following list, following the chronological order of publication, sets out to assign all fourteen to the categories of 'closure' or 'non-closure', according to whether our previous study suggests the author has closed the urtext or the reception-history to future interpretative possibilities or left it open to interpretation:

Author	Biblical Urtext	Closed/Open
Levenson (1972)	Job	Open
Pritchard (1974)	Sheba	Open
Warner (1976)	Virgin Mary	Closed
Quinones (1991)	Cain and Abel	Open
Haskins (1993)	Mary Magdalene	Closed
Cohn (1996)	Noah's Flood	Closed
Trexler (1997)	The Magi	Open
Stocker (1998)	Judith	Open
Norris (1998)	Eve	Open
Wroe (1999)	Pilate	Closed
Gaines (1999)	Jezebel	Open
Pippin (1999)	Apocalyse	Closed
Sherwood (2000)	Jonah	Open
Paffenroth (2001)	Judas	Open/Closed

Looking at this list, ideological closure seems to be the correct description for Warner, Haskins and Pippin as feminist rejecters of their respective texts. Cohn treats Noah's Flood as a largely spent story, seeing its fate as wrapped up with the early scientific creation debate; a sort of historicist ideological closure. Wroe finally rejects Pilate as part of a valediction to the gospel story as a whole, a secularist ideological closure. Paffenroth is not a secularist, but his narrative implies that there is little vitality left in the story of Judas, now disembodied from the theme of betrayal and domesticated.

The ideological or interpretative openness of the others takes the form of awaiting a new age of faith (Levenson); anticipating the revival of a feminist deity (Gaines); an academic, social-historical perspective (Pritchard and Trexler); a literary and philosophical sense of the potentialities of the urtext story and its reception-history (Quinones, Stocker, Norris and Sherwood.)

An Overview of the Rewritten Biblical Stories

We now turn to some of the key rewritten biblical stories which we have examined in previous chapters, including examples not discussed by our fourteen reception-history writers. The most satisfactory approach, from the point of view of 'grading' literary or artistic rewritings of biblical stories, may be to take further the ideas explored in Chapters 5 and 6 about what we might almost call 'signals of transcendence' in rewritten biblical stories. We can bear in mind here the strictures of the postmodernists about acknowledging the ideological character of all readings, without submitting to their own seemingly ideological exclusion of the transcendent, which threatens its own form of closure.

To help recapture in a summarised form the conclusions reached in Chapters 5 and 6 about the hermeneutical value of the major texts explored, there follows another list:

Work	Hermeneutical Value
David Maine's *Flood*	Counterposes the divine voice with a non-Patriarchal account of the Flood.
Byron's *Cain*	Dramatising the unfeeling cosmos.
Melville's *Billy Budd*	Militarism dethroned.
Conrad's *The Secret Sharer*	Ambiguity enthroned.
Unamuno's *El Otro*	Consciousness means knowing we are dreaming.
Milton's *Paradise Lost*	Milton's 'Mahlerian' approach to reality and argument against political dehumanisation.
Cather's *The Professor's House* and Hemingway's *Garden of Eden*	Eden breaks into a modern realistic narrative to relativise the present.
Kazantzakis's *The Last Temptation*	Ambivalence purged by the dream sequence.
Tournier's *Gemini*	Relativising homophobia.
Tournier's *The Four Kings*	A multi-cultural approach to the Magi.
Joyce's *Ulysses*	Biblical material persisting in an otherwise 'flat' universe.
Roth's *Job*	Judaism persisting in a hostile culture.
Macdonald's *Lilith*	The supernatural re-envisioned.
Du Maurier's *Rebecca*	Nudging patriarchy by celebrating a lost Paradise.
Steinbeck's *East of Eden*	The Biblical Vision lives with Modern Commerce.
Collins's *Jezebel's Daughter*	Wickedness (largely) unredeemed.
Collins's *New Magdalene* and *No Name*	Stereotypes confronted.
Moseley's *Judith*	Stereotypes (temporarily) overcome by Authenticity.
Rice and Lloyd-Webber *Jesus Christ Superstar*	An experiment in playing with the gospel story.
Bulgakov's *The Master and Margarita*	Affirming fiction as a radicalising medium/ Relativising totalitarianism.
Mary Shelley's *Frankenstein*	Industrialised science dethroned.
Mary Shelley's *The Last Man*	Affirming *The Apocalypse* outside of Patriarchal discourse.

Even from this very sparse summary, it will be evident that the hermeneutical achievement of many of these works is connected with the retelling of a biblical story in the context of resistance to an oppressive ideology. We may go on to observe that the openness of the works to the transcendent, the numinous, or just the magical, seems to be the source of their vitality and their ability to relativise the oppressive force, whether this is patriarchy, power-politics, anti-semitism, homophobia, stereotyped behaviour, communist totalitarianism, the flatness of the secular, commercialised world, or the destructiveness of unbridled capitalism.

Apart from *The Last Man*, which is hermeneutical closure on an epic scale, none of these works presents itself as the last word on the biblical story which it reworks. Instead, we find that the invocation of the biblical story is associated with the impinging of a widened sense of reality. It is possible that the reflexiveness and versatility of the biblical urtext and its reception-history lies behind this vigour. Many of the authors betray a consciousness, some sketchy and some detailed, of the hermeneutical tradition or the reception-history which lies behind their own entry into the project of rewriting a biblical story. Milton is acutely aware of the rabbinic midrashic background as well as the Christian exegetical tradition affecting the reception of the Genesis story. Mary Shelley and others rework Milton. Kazantzakis seems to be aware of the D.H. Lawrence story, *The Man Who Died*, as well as the Christian tradition. D.H. Lawrence is very aware of the use of the Apocalypse in chapel preaching, as well as the work of R.H. Charles. Unamuno twice reworks Byron's *Cain.* Joyce seems to be acquainted, more or less, with all previous writing. Tournier knows the esoteric history of the Magi. In a sense, the tradition expresses itself through these authors and, in doing so, engages with the closures offered by contemporary ideologies.

The summaries given above, needless to say, should not be read as closures on the meaning of each text. We have already demonstrated the multivalency of many of these works. But it seems fair to claim that the above readings enjoy a critical consensus as valid interpretations, whatever the range of other possible readings. If the countering-of-ideological-closure can be agreed to be a common theme, this in itself is not a form of closure.

'Valid' and 'Invalid' Rewritings

The question of whether certain readings can be ruled out as invalid is of a different order. Having abandoned authorial intention as a means of delimiting the range of meaning and with the new historicism directed at highlighting submerged contexts (such as the insight that, for the Elizabethan audiences of *Hamlet*, madness was the product of 'the internalisation of disobedience'[10]) rather than authorising historically authentic limitations to meaning, the exclusion of possible meanings becomes a subject either of aesthetic judgement or of doctrinal pronouncement. *The Caine Mutiny* may be rated as a poor piece of literature, because of its use of formulaic conventions and unattractive chauvinism, but it is only excluded from serious consideration because other works (like *Billy Budd*) are more resonant with the depths of human experience and more sophisticated as artistry. These other works, therefore, form a sort of informal, excluding canon. Doctrinal exclusion (as in the initial reaction of the churches to *The Last Temptation of Christ*, the Scorsese film[11]) is related to judgements made about compatibility with the ecclesiastical canon of biblical books, such as the four canonical gospels in the case of that film.

The Last Temptation of Christ is a convenient index of the problem of exclusion, since it is capable of supporting a range of interpretations, like the novel on which it is based (in its time the cause of Greek Orthodox ecclesiastical censure of its

---

10   See Karin S. Coddon: *'Such Strange Desygns':*Madness, Subjectivity, Treason in *Hamlet* and Elizabethan Culture, essay in Susanne L Wofford (ed.): *William Shakespeare: Hamlet* (Boston and New York: Bedford Books, 1994), pp. 380–400.

11   See Chapter 5, p. 154.

author). It has attracted an aura of scandal which seems out of proportion to the actual content of the film.[12] It has also been hailed by cinema critics as one of the greatest achievements of its producer. We are bound, therefore, to reassert that, as a rewritten biblical story, it does not supplant the urtext, and that, if intertextuality is a two-way street, *The Last Temptation of Christ* (or the novel *The Last Temptation*) can equally be read in the light of (say) St Mark's Gospel as the other way round. Indeed, a reader might choose to treat Bunyan's *Pilgrim's Progress* as an intertext for *The Last Temptation*, for that matter.

We might say, therefore, that *The Last Temptation* is invalid if passed off as a sort of verbatim equivalent of the narrative in Mark (ignoring the complexities facing even 'direct' linguistic translations), but perfectly valid as *a* reading, amongst many others, of the Passion story, considered as the outcome of traditional readings of the canonical gospels. It is a response, an interpretation, but in no sense the thing in itself or the equivalent of the thing in itself. It has been a significant part of the discovery of this book that the generation of meaning in the rewriting of biblical stories is precisely dependent on a clear distinction between the urtext (with its canonically sanctioned charge of sacredness) and what is written in response to it. As we saw with Marvell's use of Ovid's *Metamorphoses*, too close an identity between the urtext and its reception can, in any case, defuse the creation of meaning.

Rewritings may be said to be more or less hospitable to their urtexts. Melville's *Moby Dick* is clearly less hospitable to the religious orthodoxy, or indeed simply theism, which has sponsored Jonah as a constituent of the biblical canon, than Milton's *Paradise Lost* or Roth's *Job*. On the other hand, Jonah itself, as Sherwood

---

12 Scorsese himself recounts his lifelong respect for more conventional biblical film epics such as *The Robe* and Passolini's *The Gospel According to St Matthew*. What impressed him about the Jesus of Kazantzakis's novel *The Last Temptation*, however, was that 'this was a Jesus you could sit down with, have dinner or a drink with'. See David Thompson and Ian Christie (eds): *Scorsese on Scorsese* (London: Faber, revised edition 1996), pp. 116–45. The quotation is from p. 117.

demonstrates, sits uneasily with Deuteronomic and other religious orthodoxy, a subversive, even defiant departure from the comforting deity of conventional religion. In that sense, *Moby Dick* responds to a latent anarchy in the urtext, though pushing it much further than anything that can be described as religious faith. Nevertheless, we can still read *Moby Dick* in the light of Jonah, rather than the other way round. To satisfy the postmodernists, we would no doubt have to say that we can choose to read *Moby Dick* in the light of theistic readings of Jonah.

Reading Against the Grain

At times there may be a very thin line between readings of a text 'against the grain' and readings which must be regarded just as rejections of the text. Pippin seems so concerned to root out the patriarchy in the Apocalypse that she seems blind to its central concerns about human suffering and genocidal obliteration. She has changed the whole agenda, like a health-and-safety officer censuring Shakespeare's *Macbeth*. Similarly, *Skinny Legs And All* as a novel seems to rule out the possibility of a female villain in its approach to the figure of Jezebel. On the other hand, Frost's *A Masque of Reason*, though in its burlesque a misfit with the sombre tone of the Book of Job and a failure to find the right register even as a farce, still points back to the biblical text as its point of departure.

Some readings 'against the grain,' equally, like the poor and begging medieval kings mentioned in Trexler's study of the Magi, have the capacity to revivify the tradition by inscribing a social critique which chimes with other biblical themes. The treatment of the story of the Passion as a rock-opera staged in the desert in the film *Jesus Christ Superstar* allows a final differentiation between Jesus and the other members of the cast (who drive away safely in their bus at the end) which is highly resonant with the gospel theme of the divinity of Christ.

Conclusion

In conclusion, this study suggests that, within the specific field of biblical reception-history expressed through the medium of rewritten biblical stories, the term 'closure' is appropriate for those treatments which effectively close down reference back to the urtext; and the term 'non-closure' is appropriate for those treatments which do point back to the urtext, despite (or often by means of) radical changes to the plot or to the style.

The interface between the biblical canon, seen as a fenced-off area of sacred stories, and the more fluid sense of a literary canon, seen as a collection of works displaying 'strangeness' of various kinds (or simply as a collection of works which have attracted rewritings), is the site of convergence between two sorts of 'writerly' text (to use postmodernist terminology). There can be readings in turn of the product of this convergence which respect the intractability or alterity of the work. Equally, there can be readings which submit to what Northrop Frye calls 'human anxiety structures' and seek to turn the work into a 'readerly' text, making it unchallenging (Judas as a regular family man), or which seek to hi-jack the work in the service of an extraneous ideology. Therefore, to adapt the language of Roland Barthes to our specific purposes in this book, we will say that writerly readings enhance our awareness of the text's richness, whereas readerly readings efface the text and replace it with something else.

In this distinction between 'writerly readings' and 'readerly readings' we have a tool which is capable of being applied equally to reception-histories of biblical stories and to the material which they discuss. In terms of the thinking of Levinas, it is a tool which can be used to free the biblical urtext and its most significant rewritings from captivity to any reading, 'ideological' or otherwise, which threatens to suppress their alterity.

Chapter 14

CONCLUSIONS:
THE HERMENEUTICAL VALUE OF LITERARY
RECEPTION-HISTORIES

Over the course of this study we have engaged with the extremes of religious scepticism and with bold attempts to reassert or reframe religious discourse. We have met at least two authors, Dante and Milton, who dared to believe that they were personally writing under divine inspiration and, indeed, extending the range of Scripture.[1] We have met others for whom the rewriting of biblical stories was a compulsion generated either out of a fascination, or a quarrel, with the original text. Our fourteen reception-history writers themselves all display a sort of compulsive interest in their chosen subjects, whether the stance of their respective master-narratives is supportive of theism or not.

The purpose of this closing chapter will be to assess the hermeneutical value of the material we have explored, both at the level of the written-up reception-histories themselves and at the level of the works they discuss. We will bear in mind Rowland Sherrill's distinction between religious discourse as authoritative pronouncement and imaginative literary discourse as expressive of a hypothetical version of reality.[2] We will also recall Harold Fisch's reminder that, in the case of rewritten biblical stories, the urtext still remains the urtext and that later versions remain in a condition of dialogue with it,[3] as well as the postmodern sense, found in Stanley Fish and other postmodernists, that the approach of the *reader* of any

---

1   See Chapter 5, p. 148.
2   See Chapter 7, p. 211.
3   See Chapter 3, pp. 108–109.

text is all-important and that therefore it is precisely the *reader* who allows or disallows a moral or even a theistic reading of any text.[4]

Two important factors in the whole field we have surveyed are firstly the sense that the biblical text constantly invites rewriting through its lacunae and aporia: this is a process that occurs already within the Bible itself. Secondly, there is the sense that reception-history is cumulative, sometimes making it difficult even to read the biblical urtext without the overlaying provided by the tradition. There is, therefore, a sort of reciprocal relationship between the inviting biblical text and the responding tradition. We have also noticed that a creative artist like Blake or Byron can initiate a decisive shift in the reception-history, which others follow not so much by imitation as by reaction or outright misreading.

We have observed the varied ways in which rewritten biblical stories deal with myths and themes which are extraneous to the biblical urtext, such as the Oedipus story; or conflate one biblical story with another. In the modern period, rewritings reflect the pressure of multicultural viewpoints, as well as the influence of non-theistic and nihilistic thinking. These are all forms of 'dialogue' between the sacred text and post-biblical culture.

We have seen how the inherent ambiguity or multivalency of literary texts, as well as works of visual art, defeats the idea that biblical stories are in any simple way re-presented in such works. But we have also noted how this same multivalency defends the reception-history of a biblical story from the master-narrative of ideologues. There are always alternative readings of a given literary text or picture.[5] At the same time, if, as Northrop Frye argues, the Bible itself is 'a violently partisan book,'[6] it is absorbing to examine the effects of ideologies in conflict, as when the

---

4   See Stanley Fish: *Is There A Text In This Class?* (London and Cambridge Mass: Harvard University Press, 1980).

5   For a further discussion of contradictory readings of rewritten biblical stories, see my article 'Against the Grain and With the Grain' in *Theology*, November/December 2008.

6   See Chapter 3, p. 97.

monovocal world of the Deuteronomist meets modern pluralism or the unveiling of its own suppressed voices. When Warner and Haskins read 'against the grain' of much of the material in their respective reception-histories, or when Gaines uses a modern novel to reverse the drift of the Jezebel tradition, we experience a reading which is equivalent to the 'strong reading' of the Deuteronomist.

The evidential value of the gathered reception-history of a biblical story may be described in terms of the added light it throws on an ancient sacred text, though in doctrinally conservative hands this approach may prove to be very selective. But it can also be described more generally as answering to the quest for documentary material indicating the actual responses which the text has generated over time, irrespective of the religious utility of these responses. Sometimes the reception-history seems to have a sort of autonomy, as when the Book of Jonah erupts in *Moby Dick* or (to take a non-biblical example) when Shakespeare's *The Tempest* is found driving post-colonial Caribbean literature.

Staying with the reception-history of Jonah, we have noted Yvonne Sherwood's distinction between the Mainstream and the Backwater traditions, where she celebrates the playful and exploratory character of the midrashic approach to the text, in contrast to the overbearing influence of orthodox Christian readings This would seem to be a tool which could be fruitfully applied to much of the material in our other reception-histories. One thinks particularly of anarchic tendencies in the tradition of the Magi, the modern novels about Judas or Jezebel, the complexities of the Judith reception-history revealed by Margaret Stocker and the reception-history of Job in and beyond Levenson's study. Perhaps the rather ideologically-driven narratives of Warner, Haskins and Pippin would gain from an injection of this perspective, having recourse to the wealth of fantastic literature available in the reception-histories of the Virgin Mary, Mary Magdalene and the Apocalypse.

The sheer quality of material discussed in the fourteen reception-histories ought to refute the sense that we are dealing with the history of the blunting of the text

308

(*pace* Lyle Jeffries[7]), except in the sense that religiously orthodox readings of the urtext are frequently challenged. But we are obliged to consider, from a theological perspective, exactly what emerges which is of positive value. Or, to put it another way, to what extent does the religious sense of The Other prevail over the topic of the Other as the pathological side of culture? We shall now review the evidence of Chapters 4–7 in the light of this question.

It is clear from our discussion of Steiner that there can be no conclusive demonstration that transcendence has a referent outside language. We are in the realms of the choice Leibniz proposes between meaning and no-meaning, or Steiner's own 'leap out of nothingness'. However, the 'as if ' wager on transcendence deserves to be given the same weight as the 'as if' wager on nihilism which is so often the default position of modern discourse about reality, since neither position can finally disprove the other. Within the 'transcendence' camp there is a need, nevertheless, to distinguish between credulity and a sense of The Other which is inflected by all the objections raised by reflection on such key issues as the Holocaust, the crisis of patriarchy, the critiques of post-colonialism and of economic consumerism. In many ways, reception-history is particularly fitted to deliver such a refining of the sense of the Transcendent Other, since it is the history of our culture's dialogue with its own sacred texts.

Steiner's perception that the biblical stories have a double life as pillars of doctrine and as symbols of a more diffuse sense of transcendence is important here, since it is this duality which enables the dialogue to take place. Without the doctrinal background, we would lose (for example) the frisson of Marina Warner's dismissal of the Virgin Mary traditions or the struggles of Victorian and modern novelists with the figure of Mary Magdalene. Without the diffuse sense of transcendence, the story of the Garden of Eden or of Cain and Abel would be confined to the barracks of religious discourse, rather than acting as pivotal points for literature.

---

7   See Chapter 1, p. 21.

309

We have found a sense of the Transcendent Other in some major works of
rewritten scripture, including *Paradise Lost, Moby Dick, No Name, Frankenstein,
The Last Man, Lilith, The Secret Sharer, The Master and Margarita, El Otro, The
Four Kings* and Nicholas Moseley's *Judith*. We have found the biblical urtext in
dialogue with problematising viewpoints in the phenomenon of the rediscovered
Gnostic texts, in various modern treatments of Job, in *East of Eden, Billy Budd,
The Robber Bride, Skinny Legs and All, The Last Temptation,* and *Jesus Christ
Superstar*, as well as Tina Pippin's one-sided account of horror in the Apocalypse.
The multivalency or ambiguity of these (mainly) literary works does not debar
them from being read in either of the above ways, that is either as vehicles of a
sense of transcendence or as texts which problematise the biblical story. Nor can
totalising discourses in written-up reception-histories (such as Warner or Wroe)
prevent us from reading the texts they discuss in variant ways.

We have seen reception-history also as partly the record of the biblical urtext's
contest with competing classical myths, cultural stereotypes, and political usurping.
It is a contest won, for example, when Judith appears on both sides of the
Protestant/Catholic divide after the Reformation or lost, for example, when Eve is
merged with the figure of Pandora. None of these victories or defeats is permanent,
of course, and the contest continues as long as the competing stories remain
significant for human discourse. It is possible to regard the treatment of biblical
stories as a barometer of the cultural standing of the Bible, as Erich Gruen does
when he records the mixture of surrender to and defiance of Hellenistic forms in
Jewish rewritings of the Genesis stories in the early Diaspora,[8] or (in the context
of our study) as Wroe does in associating the demise of the Pilate legend with
decline in belief in the supernatural. The Pritchard volume, read in conjunction
with Said's *Orientalism*, effectively records the movement of the reception-history

8   Erich S. Gruen: *Heritage and Hellenism: The Reinvention of Jewish Tradition* (Berkeley and
     Los Angeles: University of California Press, 1998).

of Sheba from hermeneutical strangeness through colonialist abuse and on to a more progressive, and even radical,[9] form of imaginative appropriation.

Our overview of the fourteen reception-histories themselves has highlighted the implications of treating one literary text as the controlling text for a host of others or of treating one text in the reception-history as pivotal. Quinones justifies his account of Byron's *Cain* as central to subsequent rewritings of the Cain and Abel story largely in terms of documented literary influence, whereas Gaines seems to take *Skinny Legs and All*, a very late treatment of her theme, as the starting-point for her rehabilitation of Jezebel. Such approaches invite the writing of alternative accounts, centred on alternative texts, such as the Wakefield *Mactacio Abel* in the first case, or *Jezebel's Daughter* in the second case.

More importantly still, we have seen that ideological master-narratives such as feminism (Warner, Haskins) or even secularism (Wroe), in a postmodern context, license other, alternative readings of the underlying material, if only in reaction to their partisan approach. Nicholas Boyle's 'Catholic' reading of secular literature is justified in terms of a meeting-point between Levinas's ethical hermeneutics and the open-endedness (multivalency) of most literary texts. Equally, our location of the Transcendent Other in a wide range of rewritten biblical stories (including *The Master and Margarita*, a text significant for Wroe's account) suggests the possibility of alternative master-narratives for all of our fourteen reception-histories, including those which are more neutral in tone than those of the ideologues.

The fact that *any* reception-history is compelled to be selective, by virtue of the sheer abundance of available material, adds to the need to emphasise that no single account can be considered definitive. In this way, a written-up reception-history shares in the provisional status of an imaginative literary text, as a 'hypothetical version of

---

9   We see the rudiments of a radically feminist and postcolonialist Sheba firstly in Reardon's work of art, *She-Bah*, and secondly in the comments of Elisabeth Schüssler Fiorenza, quoted in Chapter 11, p. 262.

reality', even though we may have good grounds for critiquing any given account as more or less plausible on the grounds of literary-historical or textual evidence. In analysing the structures of the fourteen studies, we have also noticed the influence of extraneous programmes, including the use of biblical origins/reception-history as a duality and the imposition of master-narratives derived not just from feminism (Warner, Haskins, Gaines) but from secularism (Wroe) and scientific progressivism (Cohn). It has been apparent that some extraneous programmes (such as Trexler's political sociology) are more hospitable or friendly towards the reception-history material than others. At the other extreme, a highly selective approach to reception-history (Pippin) can be used to condemn the entire tradition.

We have found the distinction between readerly and writerly texts, associated with the name of Roland Barthes,[10] quite useful, in that it highlights the difference between texts which conform to the domesticating habits of the reader and those which defy such habits in order to exhibit 'strangeness'. From a theological perspective, such strangeness can be an entry-point for religious transcendence; but we must acknowledge that, for much literary-critical discourse, religious transcendence is only a metaphor or trope for the human sublime. Ontological issues, once again, go beyond the terms of the discussion. At that level, we can only note George Steiner's association of the death of God with the destruction of reference.[11] However, it should be added that a *theological* reading of the phenomenon of alterity in literature would, as we have argued, build on the philosophy of Emmanuel Levinas, for whom the recognition of alterity in literature is at once an ethical and an ontological concern.

The distinction between readings which enforce closure and readings which avoid closure seems to be a valuable tool for categorising our reception-histories. The enforcing of closure, we have seen, is typical of the ideological readings and

---

10   See Chapter 13, pp. 291 and 296–7.
11   George Steiner: *Real Presences* (London: University of Chicago Press, 1998/1991), p. 93.

is epitomised by the use of a valedictory master-narrative, of the kind we find in Warner, Haskins, Wroe, Pippin and probably Cohn. Those readings which avoid closure (Pritchard, Trexler, Quinones, Stocker and Sherwood particularly) are also those which are detached from any particular ideological reading, whether because of scholarly distancing (Pritchard, Trexler) or because of literary interest (Quinones) or because of the discovery of an anti-ideological bias in the whole tradition (Stocker and Sherwood).

It is noteworthy that our non-biblical reception-histories evince no signs of enforced closure.

Beyond the purview of the reception-histories *qua* reception-histories, we have further argued that many of our major examples of rewritten biblical stories are actually driven by resistance to an oppressive ideology, whether that be patriarchy, power politics, homophobia, anti-semitism, psychological stereotyping, communist totalitarianism, the flatness of secularism or the destructiveness of unrestrained capitalism. These outstanding texts tend to be part of a literary canon, which means that in our field we are dealing with the meeting of two canons: the literary and the religious. This meeting-point has been described in free-market terms by Falck, in his concept of 'Spilt Religion', where the competition between the general canon of literature and the no-longer-privileged canon of the Christian religious stories takes place in a context where all literature has theological resonance.[12]

Intertextuality has been seen as a useful way for describing the relationship of rewritten biblical stories to the biblical urtext, particularly when it is employed to underline the fact that the rewritten version does not supplant the original. It can also be used to invoke the reading of the later text in the light of the urtext or, specifically, of a conventional, pro-theological reading of the urtext (in the case of

---

12 Colin Falck: *Myth, Truth and Literature* (Cambridge: Cambridge University Press, 1989). The relevant section is Chapter 5, 'Spilt Religion'. The term is borrowed from T.E. Hulme, who uses it in a disparaging sense of Romantic literature, unlike Falck.

what is read as a severely contrarian rewriting), rather than the other way round, as we saw with *Moby Dick*. It remains the case, though, that strong rewritings exert a *de facto* influence on readings of the urtext, as is a commonplace in discussions of *Paradise Lost* in relation to the Genesis text.[13]

Apart from the use of ideologically-driven master-narratives to read 'against the grain', as discussed above, we have distinguished between two particular sorts of reading 'against the grain'. These are those which trample over the concerns of the urtext (we have cited Pippin in the case of her reading of the Apocalypse) and those which revivify the urtext (we have cited Trexler's anarchic Magi and *Jesus Christ Superstar*). It is clear that the selection of intertexts is critical in this area as, of course, is the way these intertexts are read.

Finally, we have returned to the readerly/writerly binary description to produce a generalised distinction between readings which enhance our sense of a text's richness and those which efface the text and replace it with something else, usually a simplified ideological reading. Examples here would be Quinones, Stocker and Sherwood as enrichers amongst the reception-history writers or Milton's *Paradise Lost* and Tournier's *The Four Kings* as enrichers amongst the rewritings of scripture. Effacers would include probably Paffenroth and certainly Pippin amongst the reception-history writers and Herman Wouk's *The Caine Mutiny* amongst the rewritings. Richness here, of course, includes the acknowledgement of multivalency and therefore may be equally supportive of readings which are pro-theological or anti-theological or just non-theological. It may also encompass the capacity of a hypertext to *defamiliarise* its hypotext or urtext.[14] However, from

---

13 We noted in Chapter 1 (p. 22) how Julie Sanders argues that it is impossible now to read *Jane Eyre* without a recollection of *The Wide Sargasso Sea*. Julie Sanders: *Adaptation and Appropriation* (Abingdon: Routledge, 2006) is discussed in Appendix C.

14 *Defamiliarisation* , the term associated with the work of the Russian Formalists, is described by David Lodge as 'another word for 'originality'. (David Lodge: *The Art of Fiction* (London: Penguin, 1992), p. 55). Throughout this book we have celebrated works which invoke a sense of strangeness about the urtext.

314

a specifically theological perspective, richness in a piece of literature must be seen as the outworking or product of divinely-gifted language.

Reception-histories of biblical stories have the potential to gather together, for consideration, imaginative encounters between the biblical urtext and perspectives which are emblematic of subsequent cultures. In this they replicate the experience of the reader in following the biblical story against the background of his or her post-biblical life-experience, the reader being (consciously or unconsciously) at the same time the inheritor of the accumulated reception-history of that story. Those who believe that religious disclosures continue to occur outside the limits of biblical history, or that revelation is progressive, will be prepared to find signs of religious transcendence amongst the gathered material. Whilst theology can be found in secular literature generally, rewritten biblical stories offer a special case, since they are unavoidably in dialogue with a text which has been specifically associated in western culture with transcendence.

Contemporary and future creative writers and visual artists will have the advantage of being able to draw on our written-up reception-histories and (one hopes) further examples of the genre when they themselves consider producing 'rewritten' biblical stories. Taking the analogy of performing traditions in music, which are greatly assisted by the existence now of libraries of recorded sound (and picture), we may talk of access to an evolving tradition of interpretation. Some of the interpretations may be regarded as eccentric or wilful by critics but, together, they constitute a totality which *is* the performing tradition. This, in turn, forms the basis not just for historical resumés but for new departures in interpretation.[15]

---

15 To flesh out the analogy, the advent of recorded sound, made available in increasingly sophisticated forms of storage, has permitted comparisons to be made between performing traditions in classical music. So, in the case of the Sibelius symphony-cycle, for example, it is possible for a reviewer to prefer the accounts offered by the conductors Sakari Oramo and Osmo Vänskä when they seem to convey the sense of a constantly evolving Sibelius tradition, as opposed to the version offered by a rival conductor which seems to inhabit a less dialogical world. This approach supports the idea of a performing tradition as a meaning-giving nexus, the platform for innovations in interpretation which are part of a conversation with alternative

Our fourteen examples can be broadly divided into ideological and non-ideological readings, enforcing or resisting closure. The ideological reception-histories mimic the partisan character of the Bible itself, even whilst they often reject the transcendent reference of their material. The non-ideological reception-histories prefer to uphold multivalency, allowing transcendent references to compete freely with alternative readings. The fragmentary nature of biblical stories answers to a modern urge to rewrite the past as a means of legitimising or conferring authenticity on current mental and linguistic structures, according to Stephen Prickett.[16] At the same time, according to Harold Bloom, the western literary tradition as a whole can be understood in terms of the rewriting of previous literature, with the aim of replacing it.[17] If we accept that these two arguments have gained a degree of critical acceptance as valid descriptions of the influences at work in modern imaginative writing, then rewritten biblical stories occupy the territory between the two tendencies, constituting a semiotic hybrid which has the capacity to re-light significance in the reading of the urtext. The fruits of this process are present in the totality of material explored in this book.

Although the rewriting of scripture reaches more dramatic intensity in the modern and postmodern periods, there is plenty of material within Jewish midrashic exegesis, Early and Middle English literature, Sixteenth- and Seventeenth-Century English Literature, and, of course, the Victorian period, as well as European literature and corresponding periods in the visual arts, which is capable of being read in its own right as the rewriting of scripture, rather than merely as the backdrop to more recent developments. Amongst our fourteen reception-history writers, Pritchard, Warner, Trexler, Haskins, Stocker and Sherwood, and, in her

interpretations, both historical and contemporary. (See article by Richard Whitehouse, *International Record Review*, November 2005, p 56.)

16   See Stephen Prickett: *Origins of Narrative: The Romantic Appropriation of the Bible* (Cambridge: Cambridge University Press), 1996, especially Chapter 4.

17   See Harold Bloom: *The Anxiety of Influence* (Oxford: Oxford University Press) 2nd edn., 1997.

own idiosyncratic way, Wroe, are the most alert to the pre-modern material. The conclusion must be, nevertheless, that this is a field which will only be properly cultivated when texts from the pre-modern period become more available to be read as texts-for-now. It may well be that reception-history in the form we have considered it in this book will continue to gain momentum and play its own part in the revival of interest in such texts, especially if they are associated with what we have called the relighting of the biblical story's significance.

In only thirty years the genre we have been considering has emerged and developed. Many of the contributors to the genre have been scarcely aware of each other's work, as though responding to a cultural imperative rather than the example of any school. We must expect that this will change and that, in time, competing accounts of the reception-history of particular biblical stories will appear. When this happens, we will become more sharply aware of the contribution of master-narratives, of the contrast between enforced closure and resistance to closure, and of the possibilities for dialogical models such as Sherwood's Mainstream and Backwater traditions or Stocker's counter-cultural myths. We may also find that quirky rewritings of biblical stories in the aggregate amount to a field of their own in any overview of the reception-history of the Bible.

In turn, all this should offer new avenues for the discussion of the interface between religion and literature, or theology and literature; for the exploration of the Bible's relationship with culture; for biblical commentaries; and for preaching. If Mieke Bal's contention that every reading is a rewriting[18] becomes a commonplace, general readers of the Bible may become more curious about how the central repertoire of biblical stories has been rewritten by the most responsive writers and visual artists of different eras. This will then shift the focus of the production of the genre of reception-histories we have identified from the initiative of the author to

---

18   For example, see Mieke Bal: *Narratology* (Toronto: University of Toronto Press, 2nd edn., 1997), p. 57.

the demand of a new public. The construction of a conceptual framework to handle this output will be important.

More generally, the very availability of the sort of reception-histories of biblical stories examined in this book makes the multivocal richness of the subject-matter inescapable, either because this is what is overtly demonstrated in the work or, sometimes, because the reception-history writer has attempted to apply his or her own ideological strait-jacket to the material, prompting one's awareness of alternative readings.

The creative writer, or the visual artist, as our study has demonstrated, has the capacity very often to release the imaginative potential of the biblical urtext in circumstances quite different from what are assumed to be those of its original production, by rewriting it. Such rewritings can appear to be isolated or rogue entities until they are viewed in the larger context of a reception-history. Our fourteen reception-histories demonstrate, in a few cases by default, what is entailed in marshalling the rewritings in the service of an overview which does justice to the multivalency and the strangeness of both the urtext and its rewritings.

At the same, as a totality, the fourteen studies compel us to remain alert to the theological overtones of Otherness in the material which they discuss and, by extension, in all literature which shares the capacity to challenge the commodification of culture or the diminishing of the range of human discourse.[19] The lasting contribution of this field of enquiry may be to offer more precise co-ordinates for the sense, however fenced-about and qualified, of an ongoing revelation.

---

19   A recent article by Adrienne Rich defines the 'aesthetic' not 'as a privileged and sequestered rendering of human suffering, but as news of an awareness, a resistance, which totalising systems want to quell: art reaching into us for what's still passionate, still unintimidated, still unquenched'. (Adrienne Rich: 'Legislators of the world' in the *Guardian Review*, 18th November 2006, p. 3).

Appendix A

FURTHER EXCURSIONS INTO REWRITING

The three works to be considered here are Mendelssohn's oratorio *Elijah*, the short story *Three Versions of Judas* by Jorge Luis Borges, and Ingmar Bergman's film, *The Seventh Seal*. These works are relevant to the reception-history of the biblical stories of Jezebel, Judas and the Apocalypse respectively. They are not discussed, or even mentioned, by the three authors in our study who deal with the three respective reception-histories, namely Gaines, Paffenroth and Pippin. Given the difficulty of exhaustive treatments of biblical reception-histories, the fact of their exclusion may be less important for us than the light that they throw on the issues raised by our reception-history authors. But these three works also problematize the arguments of the three respective reception-histories which omit to discuss them.

Felix Mendelssohn's *Elijah* appeared in 1846. The work has had a complex afterlife as, on the one hand, the prototype of the English oratorios of Hubert Parry and Edward Elgar, and, on the other, the site of agonised debate within Judaism and Jewish historiography about the consequences of the assimilative tendencies of the German-Jewish community from the late eighteenth-century onwards. Mendelssohn's own conversion to Protestantism has been seen as the epitome of a tragic illusion and placed within 'a teleology in which the Holocaust and the Nazi regime were the fulfilment of an inexorable logic'.[1]

---

1   Leon Botstein: 'Mendelssohn and the Jews', article in *Music Quarterly*, Vol. 82, no 1, Spring 1998, p. 216. Botstein's own point is that the teleology was not app.arent to German Jews prior to the Holocaust. Even in 1937, he notes, an all-Jewish performance of *Elijah* in the Oranienburger Strasse Synagogue in Berlin was construed as 'a Jewish work written by a German Jew affirming the greatness of Judaism'. (Ibid., p. 213).

Whereas in the oratorio, Elijah saves Israel and calls divine destruction upon the heathen nations, in the Germany to which Mendelssohn's national culture was heading, in the light of hindsight, it was Israel which faced annihilation. This certainly casts the apostasy of Ahab and Jezebel in a different light. Indeed, to some ears, the composer's own description of Elijah might sound like the personality profile of a psychotic national leader. In a letter to his friend Julius Schübring, Mendelssohn wrote: 'I imagined Elijah as a real prophet through and through, of the kind we could really do with today: strong, zealous, and yes, even *bad-tempered, angry and brooding – in contrast to the riff-raff whether of the* court or of the people, and indeed at odds with almost the whole world – and yet borne aloft as if on angel's wings'.[2]

Jezebel herself plays a fairly small and rather operatic role in Part Two, proclaiming, 'Hath ye not heard he that prophesied against all Israel?' and finishing an exchange with the Chorus in which she calls upon the Israelites, 'So go ye forth and seize Elijah, for he is worthy to die; slaughter him! Do unto him as he hath done!'[3] In the score she is simply 'The Queen' and it seems significant that the second performance of the oratorio, on 23rd April 1847, rapturously applauded by the audience at the Exeter Hall, was attended by Queen Victoria and Prince Albert with 'almost everybody being in full dress …'[4] The point here, which we will not labour, is that what for Gaines is a misogynist text, can be rewritten for a context which in some respects is a complete rebuttal of the feminist challenge to patriarchy. It is noteworthy that the oratorio does not report the fate of Jezebel or indeed of Ahab, the

2   Quoted in internet article, http: // www.Carmelites.ie/Periodicals/citw2002.3htm. Downloaded 18/05/2006.

3   Mendelssohn: *Elijah, an Oratorio, English Version by W. Bartholomew* (London and New York: Novello, Ewer & Co, 1952, pp. vi and 130–4.

4   From the Journal of Edgar Alfred Bowring, posted on the internet by Duke University Libraries, http: // www.lib.duke.edu/music/bowring.htm

Chorus simply recording that 'mighty kings were overthrown by him (Elijah)'[5] and moving swiftly on to the account of Elijah's translation into heaven.[6]

Borges's *Three Versions of Judas* was part of his collection of short stories, first published as *Artifices* in 1944.[7] Although not mentioned by Paffenroth, there is a paragraph on the work in Hugh Pyper's essay *Modern Gospels of Judas*, where he places it at the extreme wing of anticanonical writing.[8] This is because in the final of the three versions of Judas attributed to the fictional scholar Runeberg, Judas himself becomes the vehicle of the incarnation, God choosing 'an abject existence'[9] to bring himself down to the human level. What this account leaves out is the other two versions. In the first version, Judas, even though a betrayer is strictly superfluous to the economy of the Passion story, makes the personal sacrifice of being the betrayer in response to the mysterious workings of 'the Word' which seeks to encompass the full scope of human life, including its blemishes. In the second version, Runeberg, finding himself condemned by the theologians of his day, rewrites the story again, this time emphasising Judas's treachery as an ascetic act. 'Judas sought hell because joy in the Lord was enough for him .He thought that happiness, like goodness, is a divine attribute, which should not be usurped by men.'[10]

It is the second version, taken further, which leads to the third and most scandalous version, where Runeberg concludes that God's suffering in the Incarnation could not be limited to 'one afternoon on the cross' and therefore should extend to becoming Judas, the fictional theologian having concluded that

---

5   *Elijah*, Ibid., pp. viii and 186–8.

6   Mendelssohn: *Elijah, an Oratorio, English Version by W Bartholomew* (London and New York: Novello, Ewer and Co, 1952), pp. vi and 130–4.

7   The edition we use is Jorge Luis Borges: *Fictions* trans Andrew Hurley (Penguin, London, 2000), where *Three Versions of Judas* app.ears as part of *Artifices*, pp. 132–7.

8   Hugh S. Pyper: *Modern Gospels of Judas, Canon and Betrayal* reprinted in Hugh S. Pyper: *An Unsuitable Book, the Bible as Scandalous Text* (Sheffield: Sheffield Phoenix Press, 2005), pp. 76–88. The reference is to p. 82.

9   Borges, Ibid., p. 136.

10   Ibid., p. 135.

sinlessness and being fully human were mutually incompatible. Although it is possible to read the short story entirely in the light of its final outworking, its title is *Three Versions of Judas* and not *One Version of Judas*. Borges was certainly aware of the writings of Franz Kafka and perhaps also of Soren Kierkegaard, so it seems quite reasonable to find a model for his *Three Versions* in Kakfa's multiple versions of Babel or Kierkegaard's multiple versions of the Akedah.[11] This would lend equal weight to all three versions of Runeberg's story, making them all responses to different aspects of the hermeneutical problems raised by the canonical Judas story. In particular, the first version would be a response to the superfluity of the Judas character; the second version would be a counter-argument in favour of a fleshing-out of Judas as a convincing character-type; the third would be the scandalous rewriting designed to turn the canonical story of the betrayal on its head. Such an interpretation would certainly be compatible with the anarchic, playful, anti-posturing character of most of Borges's literary output.

We have seen how Pippin allows her reading of the Apocalypse to be overdetermined by her account of its influence in the politics and culture of the American Deep South. We now look at Ingmar Bergman's film *The Seventh Seal* as an example of a twentieth-century rewriting of the Apocalypse which neither conforms to Pippin's account of the biblical book as a misogynist text nor accords with ecclesiastical or religious orthodoxy.

The plot of the film has been succinctly summarised by Jorn Donner:

> The Knight Antonius Block returns, after a long crusade, to the Sweden of the fourteenth-century, devastated by the Black Death. He is accompanied by his squire, Jons. On a desolate shore, he engages in a game of chess with Death. The prize for the Knight's victory is to be his life. While the game is in progress, the Knight manages to perform a meaningful act. He saves a couple of travelling jugglers, Jof and Mia, from death. The Knight arrives

---

11   Borges clearly was a voracious reader and certainly read and translated Kafka. See for example Alberto Manguel: *The Art of Reading* (London: Flamingo, 1997), pp. 16–20 and 93.

home and finds his wife. Then enters Death. All present are compelled to join in his dance, while the jugglers look on.[12]

The film can be construed as a confrontation between human delusion and the reality of death, but also as a 'salute to human dignity'.[13] The Knight has deprived his wife of his company for the many years of his delusive spiritual quest away on the Crusades. Yet, in the game of chess with Death, he sacrifices his own life, to deflect Death's attention away from the young couple, Jof and Mia. The flagellants present a picture of human folly before the Last Judgement. Yet the jugglers offer a prospect of creative playfulness and the celebration of human vitality.

Bergman's film, which he probably regarded as his own greatest achievement, began as a one-act play. It seems to have had a strong association with the Cold War threat of nuclear annihilation which was such a feature of the era.[14] Yet, in highlighting the uncomfortable prospect of Death as an inescapable force, it conveys not only a sobering comment on human folly but also the sense of life as a chess game in which it is possible, by guile or determination or sheer strength of character, to bring about events which are not in themselves atrophic. The stark and simple visual images have an impact to which no summary in words can do justice.[15]

Seen as a corrective to Pippin's study, we may say that Bergman's celebrated film asserts the validity of the Book of Revelation's fixation with Death as a universal concern and then attempts to create something life-enhancing from that preoccupation. The female characters in the film vary in character from the

12   Jorn Donner: *The Personal Vision of Ingmar Bergman* (Bloomington & London: Indiana University Press, 1964/1966), p. 139.

13   Donner, Ibid., p. 150.

14   Peter Cowie reports that Bergman told Gunnar Bjornstrand that the atom bomb corresponded to a twentieth-century plague'. See Peter Cowie: *Ingmar Bergman* (London: Martin, Secker & Warburg, 1982), p. 141.

15   'Probably the most parodied film of all time, this nevertheless contains some of the most extraordinary images ever committed to celluloid'. Entry on p. 1076 of John Pym (ed.): *Time Out Film Guide, Eleventh Edition* (London: Penguin, 2003).

324

long-suffering wife of the Knight through to the adulterous wife of the smith Plog but cannot be read as emblems of misogyny. The young jugglers, Jof and Mia, seem to exist in a dimension separate from ideas about patriarchy or female subordination.

Seen as a reading of the biblical book, *The Seventh Seal* is, of course, restricted in its harmonic range.[16] The film, nevertheless, embodies a degree of seriousness about death as a subject for existential concern which sets its apart from almost any other film. In that sense, it upholds the tenor of the urtext of the Apocalypse, even whilst it mocks medieval preaching about Judgement Day, as it does when it portrays a monk haranguing the flagellants and the priest Raval (who inspired the Knight to depart on his crusade) as corrupt.

Conclusion

The three works considered here could have been discussed by the three relevant reception-history writers, Gaines, Paffenroth and Pippin, but were not. They problematize the overall arguments of those authors in that they present themes which the latter underplay.

1. Mendelssohn's *Elijah*, taken as a cultural artefact which is a significant part of the afterlife of I Kings 18 and 19, shows, at the stage of its initial reception in 1847, how, what Gaines labels a misogynist text, could be a supportive component in a culture which was matriarchal (the reign of Queen Victoria). The oratorio's further afterlife as a component in post-Holocaust revulsion at German-Jewish assimilationism during the period 1790–1939 turns Gaines's

---

16 For a panoramic survey of cinematic treatments of the Apocalypse, see Ian Christie: 'Celluloid Apocalypse' in Frances Carey (ed.): *The Apocalypse and the Shape of Things to Come* (London:British Museum Press, 1999), pp. 320–40. Christie argues that the treatment of the Apocalypse is integral to cinematic origins.

validation of Jezebel's syncretism on its head, in one sense, and in another sense makes Gaines's interest in Astarte worship seem frivolous in comparison with the issues at stake in the Nazi period.

2. Borges's *Three Versions of Judas* contradicts Paffenroth's general argument by making the sordid act of betrayal, as an example of human abasement, the basis of its own eccentric 'theology of the Incarnation'. Whereas the drift of Paffenroth's study is to rehabilitate Judas as either the accomplice of Jesus as he engages on the journey to the Passion or as the 'regular guy' who did what anybody would do, Borges's Judas, although he begins as a textual superfluity, ends up as full-blown divine abasement in the least acceptable representation of the human.

3. Bergman's *The Seventh Seal* presents us with the afterlife of the Apocalypse in a Northern European context as opposed to Pippin's world of the American Deep South. The effect of reading Pippin and Bergman as intertexts is to be reminded that the Apocalypse is about the reality of death as an inescapable human experience and that the alternative to 'apocalyptic horror' may simply be the spontaneous life-enhancing act (the Knight protecting Jof and Mia from immediate death) rather than a rejection of the whole symbolic structure of the Apocalypse. Seen as a response to the shadow of the nuclear bomb, Pippin and Bergman might be said to represent respectively the anguish of a pacifist minority in a democratically-elected nuclear state[17] and the helplessness of a neutral non-nuclear European nation.[18]

Our three texts demonstrate the limitations in the master-narratives of Gaines, Paffenroth and Pippin respectively. The reader should perhaps find ways to

---

17 Pippin: *Apocalyptic Bodies*, p. 7: 'While I hold such hope that humans will wake up. and avoid self-destruction (or else I would not be involved in the peace movement), I do not think the Apocalypse desires this end. In my own state, Georgia, there is the manufacture of Trident submarines, the "White Trains", the School for Americas, and Newt Gingrich, to name a few disaster images'.

18 On Bergman and the Bomb, see above Note 13.

entertain their arguments without surrendering to the notion that there is nothing else to be said. As we speculate in the final chapter of this book, the possibility of multiple reception-histories of the same biblical story becoming available in the future could do more justice to the richness of the subject and to the complexity of the afterlives of works like Mendelssohn's *Elijah*, which are themselves part of the afterlife of a biblical urtext.

Appendix B

REVIEW OF MOST: *DOUBTING THOMAS*

Glenn Most, Professor of Greek Philology at Chicago University, has created an interdisciplinary survey of the reception of the passage in John 20 which narrates the doubts of the apostle Thomas concerning the resurrection of Jesus and his demand to touch the nail-holes and wound on his body. The passage is seen as a counterpart to the 'Noli Me Tangere' passage which immediately precedes it in the same chapter, where Mary Magdalene encounters the risen Christ outside the empty tomb.

Most's argument is that virtually all the exegetical history of John 20: 26–28 has been based on the mistaken sense that Thomas actually touches the marks and the wound, whereas the text does not state this and indeed the grammatical construction of the word *apekrithe* ('he answers') indicates that there is no interval between Christ's offer to allow Thomas to place his hand on the marks and in his side and his acclamation of faith, 'My Lord and My God'.

In a review,[1] Frank Kermode praises the erudition of the author of this book, but suggests that it is wayward to dismiss the whole weight of the tradition in favour of one eccentric reading by the obscure twelfth-century theologian, Zigabenus. What perhaps Kermode misses is that, wayward or not, Most's hermeneutical approach gives him a handle on the subject which a more bland or balanced survey might deny.

In that sense, Most has set up a conceit, or a critical tool, which serves the purpose of defamiliarising the subject-matter sufficiently to make the reception-

---

1   Frank Kermode, review, pp. 18–19, in *London Review of Books*, Vol. 28, Number 1, 5th January 2006.

328

history much more open-ended than it would be if it were simply the response to an original text with an agreed meaning.

Most is alert to the lacunary character of all texts, which, following Iser, he says allows for the adaptation and indeed falsification, which permits any text to survive in very different circumstances from those of its original production.[2] He also provides some very salient philosophical observations on human perception and the tendency to trust visual evidence over against that of hearing, which depends invariably on the reliability of persons other than the subject.[3] He avows that his aim is not to offer a definitive account of the meaning of the urtext, but to show the plurality of meanings which it has generated.[4] Later on in his survey, divisions in interpretation almost make it appear as though there were two hermeneutical streams (touch/no touch) from the outset.

The author distinguishes between conventional doubt and what he calls the 'hyperbolic doubt' of the Johannine literary figure, Thomas. He describes this hyperbolic doubt as 'sacrilegious surplus'.[5] For him, the doubt of Thomas is answered not by a tactile experience but by the experience of God recognizing man, following the pattern of the Johannine recognition scenes featuring Nathaniel and Mary Magdalene. Nevertheless, the effect of the narrative is to create the tradition of Doubting Thomas and not Believing Thomas, a testimony to the sacrilegious surplus, and the textual instability of the passage explains the strong charge it exerts in the reception material.

Most classifies apocryphal Thomas material, describing a binary opposition between the non-touching tradition of the Gnostic material and the touching tradition of the rest. There is coverage of the legends connecting St Thomas with

---

2   Most, Ibid., pp. 10–11.
3   Ibid., p. 6.
4   Ibid., p. 7.
5   Ibid., pp. 46–52.

329

India and with the Assumption of the Virgin, and with Salome as a transferred Thomas-figure in the *Gospel of Pseudo-Matthew*, where this second midwife at the birth of Christ doubts the virgin birth and must touch the womb of Mary. He alludes to the reception-history of Doubting Thomas in 'world literature' but, in fact, only offers us a tantalising glimpse of its outworking in the tradition of the doubts of the followers of St Francis of Assisi about his stigmata.

The bulk of the second half of the book is given over, first, to 'Exegetical Reactions', where there is a broad division between Catholic and Counter-Reformation insistence on the spiritual significance of intrusive-touching readings and Protestant avoidance of such readings. There follows a very detailed examination of the iconographic tradition, centred on Caravaggio's *Doubting Thomas*, a painting which is read as the ultimate visual expression of the sacrilegious surplus. The irony, of course, is that a painting can only offer visual evidence rather than tactile evidence. A final short chapter records the cult of the Holy Finger of St Thomas, a relic preserved in the Basilica of Santa Croce in Gerusalemme in Rome. The Afterword concludes that the writer of the Gospel of John has created a character 'with whom all modern readers can identify', since his quasi-scientific quest for proof leads him into all the doubts and inconsistencies which are typical of modernity. 'Thomas stands for us.'[6] In this sense, we are the kin of the Medici, for whom St Thomas represented the cardinal virtue of testing.[7]

Most's text is, naturally, not without its own lacunae and inconsistencies. He acknowledges that there are variant readings of his key iconographic text, the Caravaggio painting,[8] despite the fact that such readings could clearly destabilise his main argument Yet proclaiming the Grimm fairy story *Marienkind* as a radical departure in the reception-history, substituting the overcoming of disobedience

6   Ibid., p. 226.
7   Ibid., p. 188.
8   Ibid., p. 165.

330

('submission') for the overcoming of doubt,[9] he ignores his own earlier recounting of the sense in which the words of Thomas, 'My Lord and My God' in John 20:28 could be read as denoting submission to an emperor[10] and in fact were decidedly so read in the traditions of St Thomas's commission to apostolise India.[11]

Despite this, his survey, selective though it is, can be said to demonstrate the process of Iserian gap-filling which Most discusses. He has useful things to say on the question of identifying variants of a text, where he proposes two rules for deciding whether two texts are related intertextually (relationship to overall theme of the text as a whole and the presence of multiple elements in mutually supporting and cohesive correlations)[12] and on the definition of rhetoric as words commanding a reader's trust.[13] He demonstrates the relevance of the study of visual representation for the study of conflation, epitomised in the similarity of the portrayals of Thomas and Judas in Caravaggio's paintings *Doubting Thomas* and *Arrest in the Garden*.[14]

Although the master-narrative seems at first to be about the divergence of reception-history away from textual facticity, this study actually celebrates the reception of the Doubting Thomas as a rich cultural phenomenon, expressive of changing sensibilities in relation to doubt, to visual perception and to physical touching. Most's discussion of the episode in John 20 as an example of hyperbolic doubt and its spawning of 'sacrilegious surplus' may be suggestive for the impact of other biblical texts in reception-history. He makes no connection between the tradition of Thomas as brother of Jesus (and especially Thomas as a twin) and the theme of Cain and Abel.

---

9   Ibid., p. 118: 'Not only are the characters and the plot different in many obvious ways; more important, the fundamental theological issue is not doubt but rather disobedience'.

10   Ibid., p. 72.

11   Ibid., p. 107.

12   Ibid., pp. 119–20.

13   Ibid., p. 8.

14   Ibid., pp. 212–3.

Appendix C

REVISITING REWRITING. THE RELEVANCE OF JULIE SANDERS: *ADAPTATION AND APPROPRIATION* (2006) TO THIS STUDY

In a review published in 1998 of Jane Smiley's novel *A Thousand Acres*, James A. Schiff noted the surprising neglect of of rewriting as a topic within literary-critical studies.[1] However, Julie Sanders's *Adaptation and Appropriation*[2] has addressed the vacuum, bringing together diverse strands within poststructuralist thinking to argue for a distinction between first-order rewritings ('appropriation') and second-order ('adaptation'). Appropriations exist in a combative relationship with their sourcetext, as in Rhys's novel *The Wide Sargasso Sea*, which sets out to expose the postcolonialist implications of *Mansfield Park*. Adaptations are more conservative, merely setting out to transpose a work from one genre to another or to amplify, as in many film versions of classic Victorian novels.

Sanders catalogues the variety of terms that have been used to distinguish between the sourcetext (or 'parent text' or 'informing text') and its rewriting, including 'pretext and text' and 'hypotext and hypertext'. But she herself prefers the musical analogy of 'theme and variations'. The multiple senses of the word 'after' (chronologically later/in response to/too late to do anything unique) convey the postmodernist approach to retelling.

Other concepts explored include transfocalisation, where the story is told from an alternative point of view (as in *Rosencrantz and Guilderstern are Dead*) and the

---

1   James A. Schiff: 'Contemporary Retellings: *A Thousand Acres* as the latest Lear' (article in *Critique, Studies in Contemporary Literature,* Summer 1998, Vol. 39, No 4), p. 367.

2   Julie Sanders: *Adaptation and Appropriation* (Abingdon: Routledge, 2006).

332

idea of a contemporary work 'writing back' to the original. 'Writing back' tends to describe the postcolonial approach to rewriting, whilst 're-vision' is applied more to feminist rewriting.

Sanders offers a highly valuable tool in her discussion of rewriting as hinging on the interplay between expectation and surprise and in her stringent differentiation between adaptation as a form of conservative allusiveness and appropriation as something implying 'a hostile takeover … opportunities for assault as well as homage'.[3] Marshalling together the observations of Walter Benjamin about the destruction of 'aura' in the modern mass-production of culture, of Kristeva and others about intertextuality, of Homi Bharba about hybridity as a description for the respecting of cultural difference (as opposed to the sterility of cultural synbook), of Powers about the inextricable linkage between describing and altering, and of Mieke Bal to the effect that there can be no neutral re-presentation of a text, this work is a landmark in the study of rewriting as a literary phenomenon.

Possibly Sanders's most radical suggestion from the point of view of our study is that the force of a rewritten text may be such as to turn the tables on the original, making the new version the 'pretext' of the sourcetext. In other words, new readers are led to view the original through the lens of the rewritten version. (We have already noticed earlier versions of this argument in Marina Warner's claims about the colouration of the gospel narratives about Mary by the developed 'Myth and Cult of the Virgin Mary' and in the commonplace observation that *Paradise Lost* can override memories of the Genesis text.)

The rejoinder to this argument is surely that everything depends on the availability to the reader of the sourcetext, called the 'urtext' in our book. Sanders relies on the idea that the rewriting depends on the reader's familiarity with the sourcetext, but seems to allow this sourcetext to exist on a different plane from the particularities of the published text of (say) *Mansfield Park*. It is a sort of

---

3   Ibid., p. 9.

refined 'idea' of *Mansfield Park*, rather like the form of *The Tempest* which lies behind Sibelius's incidental music to Shakespeare's play. Applying this account to literary rewritings of biblical stories, there is no doubt that biblical stories *are* often handled in this way. But they are also read, most characteristically, in a way which cherishes minute attention to the 'original' text and which treats that text as existing in a sort of timeless relationship with the present. (Perhaps George Macdonald as author of *Lilith* captured this sense in describing the biblical world as existing in a sort of parallel universe.) None of this invalidates what Sanders argues about rewriting within general literature, but it may highlight an important difference between the process of reading *A Thousand Acres* as a version of Lear and the process of reading *The Robber Bride* as a version of the biblical Jezebel story. In other words, we would argue, the biblical urtext is more resistant to being eclipsed by the 'hypertext'. Yet, by the same token, the dialogue between the two may be all the stronger for this.

BIBLIOGRAPHY

Achtemeier, Paul J., (ed.), *Harper's Bible Dictionary*, San Francisco: Harper and Row, 1985

Aichele, George, *Jesus Framed*, London: Routledge, 1996

—— and Tina Pippin (eds), *The Monstrous and the Unspeakable, The Bible as Fantastic Literature*, Sheffield: Sheffield Academic Press, 1997

Almond, Philip, *Adam and Eve in Seventeenth-Century Thought*, Cambridge: Cambridge University Press, 1999

Alter, Robert, *Canon and Creativity*, New Haven: Yale University Press, 2000

—— and Frank Kermode (eds), *The Literary Guide to the Bible*, London: Collins, 1987

Amis, Kingsley, *The Alteration*, St Albans: Triad/Panther Books, 1978

Amis, Martin, *The War on Cliché, Essays and Reviews 1971–2000*, London: Jonathan Cape, 2001

Anderson, M.D., *The Imagery of British Churches*, London: Murray, 1955

——, *Drama and Imagery in British Churches*, Cambridge: Cambridge University Press, 1963

Ashe, Geoffrey, *The Virgin*, London: Routledge & Kegan Paul, 1976

Atwood, Margaret, *The Handmaid's Tale*, London: Vintage, 1985/1996

——, *The Robber Bride*, London: Virago, 1994/2003

Auerbach, Eric, *Mimesis: The Representation of Reality in Western Literature* (trans. Willard R. Trask), Princeton NJ: Princeton University Press, 1968

Bach, Alice, *Women, Seduction and Betrayal in Biblical Narrative*, Cambridge: Cambridge University Press, 1997

Bal, Mieke, *Narratology*, Toronto: University of Toronto Press, 2nd edn, 1997

—— (ed), *The Mieke Bal Reader*, Chicago: Chicago University Press, 2006

Balfe, M.W., *Come into the Garden, Maud*, London: W. Paxton, no date.

Bann, Stephen (ed.), *Frankenstein, Creation and Monstrosity*, London: Reaktion Books, 1994

Barthes, Roland, *S/Z* (trans. Richard Miller), Oxford: Blackwell, 1990, original French edn., Paris, 1973

——, 'From Work To Text', in Josué V Harari, *Textual Strategies, Perspectives in Post-Structuralist Criticism*, London: Methuen, 1980

Beal, Timothy K., *Religion and its Monsters*, London: Routledge, 2002

Besserman, Lawrence, *The Legend of Job in the Middle Ages*, Cambridge MA: Harvard University Press, 1979

336

The Bible and Culture Collective, *The Postmodern Bible*, New Haven: Yale University Press, 1995

Blackburn, Ruth H., *Biblical Drama under the Tudors*, The Hague and Paris: Mouton, 1971

Bloom, Harold, *The Anxiety of Influence*, Oxford: Oxford University Press, 1973/1977

————, *A Map of Misreading*, New York: Oxford University Press, 1975/1980

————, *Ruin the Sacred Truths*, Cambridge MA: Harvard University Press, 1989

————, *The Western Canon*, London: Macmillan, 1995

Boitani, Piero, *The Bible and Its Rewritings*, Oxford: Oxford University Press, 1999

Bond, Helen, *Pontius Pilate in History and Interpretation*, Cambridge: Cambridge University Press, 1998

Boss, Sarah Jane, *Empress and Handmaid*, London: Cassell, 2000

Botting, Fred (ed.), *New Casebooks, Frankenstein*, Basingstoke: Palgrave, 2002

Boyden, Matthew, *The Rough Guide to Opera*, London: Rough Guides, 2002

Boyle, Nicholas, *Sacred and Secular Scriptures, A Catholic Approach to Scripture*, London: Darton, Longman and Todd, 2004

Brant, John (ed.), *A Companion to Melville Studies*, New York: Greenwood Press, 1986

Brenner, Athalya and J.W. van Henten, *Recycling Biblical Figures*, Leiden: Deo, 1999

Bridie, James, *Jonah and the Whale*, London: Constable, 1968

Britt, Brian, *Rewriting Moses, The Narrative Eclipse of the Text*, London: T. & T. Clark, 2004

Buchmann, C. and C. Spiegl (eds), *Out of the Garden, Women Writers on the Bible*, London: Continuum, 1995

Brodhead, Richard, (ed.), *New Essays on Moby Dick*, Cambridge: Cambridge University Press, 1986

Brown, Dan, *The Da Vinci Code*, London: Corgi Books, 2004

Brown, David, *Tradition and Imagination*, Oxford: Oxford University Press, 1999

————, *Discipleship and Imagination*, Oxford: Oxford University Press, 2000

Brown, Sarah Annes, *The Metamorphosis of Ovid, from Chaucer to Ted Hughes*, London: Duckworth, 1999

Buber, Martin, *I and Thou* (trans. Walter Kaufmann), Edinburgh: T. & T. Clark, 1970

Budick, Sanford and Wolfgang Iser (eds), *Languages of the Unsayable*, Stanford California: Stanford University Press, 1987

Bufalino, Gesualdo, *The Keeper of the Ruins* (trans. Patrick Creagh), London: HarperCollins, 1994

Bulgakov, Mikail, *The Master and Margarita*, (trans. Michael Glenny), London: Vintage, 2004

Burdon, Christopher, *The Apocalypse in England, Revelation Unravelling, 1700–1834*, London: Macmillan, 1997

Byatt, A.S., *On Histories and Stories, Selected Essays*, London: Chatto and Windus, 2000

Byron, Lord, *The Poetical Works*, Oxford: Oxford University Press, 1961

Cailleteau, Jacques (ed.), *La Tenture de l'Apocalypse d'Angers*, Nantes: Inventaire Generale, 1987

Carey, Francis, *The Apocalypse and the Shape of Things to Come*, London: British Museum Press, 1999

Carrithers Jr, Gale H. and James D. Hardy, *Milton and the Hermeneutic Journey*, Louisina: Louisina State University Press, 1994

Carroll, Robert (ed.), *Text as Pretext*, Sheffield: Sheffield Academic Press, 1992

Carter, Angela, *The Passion of the New Eve*, London: Virago, 1982/2003

Cather, Willa, *The Professor's House*, New York: Vintage, 1990

Chambers, E.K., *The Medieval Stage*, Oxford: Oxford University Press, 1903

Chester, Michael A., *Divine Pathos and Human Being: The Theology of Abraham Joshua Heschel*, London: Valentine Mitchell, 2005

Childs, Brevard, *Biblical Theology in Crisis*, Philadelphia: Westminster Press, 1970

———, *Exodus: A Commentary*, London: SCM Press, 1974

Cohn, Norman, *Noah's Flood, the Genesis Story in Western Thought*, New Haven and London: Yale University Press, 1996

Coleman, Edward D. and Isaiah Sheffer, *The Bible in English Drama: A Survey of Recent Major Plays*, New York: New York Public Library & Ktav Publishing House, 1968

Collins, Wilkie, *The New Magdalene*, Doylestown, Penn: Wildside Press, no date. Original publication London, 1873

———, *Jezebel's Daughter*, Doylestown, Penn: Wildside Press, no date. Original publication London, 1880

———, *No Name* London: Penguin, 1994

Colmer, John, *E.M. Forster, A Personal Voice*, London: Routledge & Kegan Paul, 1975

Corns, Thomas N. (ed.), *A Companion to Milton*, Oxford: Blackwell, 2001/3

Cowie, Peter, *Ingmar Bergman*, London: Martin Secker & Warburg, 1982

Cox, J.M. (ed.), *Robert Frost, A Collection of Critical Essays*, New Jersey: Spectrum, 1962

Curtis, J.A.E., *Bulgakov's Last Decade, the Writer as Hero*, Cambridge: Cambridge University Press, 1997

338

Daniell, David, *The Interpreter's House, A Critical Assessment of the Work of John Buchan*, London: Nelson, 1975
——— *The Bible in English*, New Haven: Yale University Press, 2003
Danielson, Dennis (ed.), *The Cambridge Companion to Milton*, Cambridge: Cambridge University Press, 1999
Davis, Colin, *Michel Tournier, Philosophy and Fiction*, Oxford: Clarendon Press, 1988
Derrida, Jacques, *Of Grammatology* (trans. G.V. Spivak), Baltimore and London: John Hopkins University Press, 1976
——— *Positions*, London: Athlone, 1981
Dever, William and J. Edward Wright (eds), *The Echoes of Many Texts, Reflections on Jewish and Christian Traditions*, Atlanta: Scholars Press, 1997
Didron, A.N., *Christian Iconography* (trans. E J Millington), New York: Frederick Ungar, 1851
Diller, Hans-Jürgen, *The Middle English Mystery Play*, Cambridge: Cambridge University Press, 1992
Dillistone, F.W., *The Novelist and the Passion Story*, London: Collins, 1960
Doane, A.N., *The Saxon Genesis*, Madison and London: University of Wisconsin Press, 1991
Donner, Jorn, *The Personal Vision of Ingmar Bergman*, Bloomington and London: Indiana University Press, 1964/1966
Donoghue, Denis, *Adam's Curse, Reflections on Religion and Literature*, Indiana: University of Notre Dame Press, 2001
Dryden, Edgar A., *Nathaniel Hawthorne, The Poetics of Enchantment*, Ithaca and London: Cornell University Press, 1977
Edwards, Mark, *John*, Oxford: Blackwell, 2004
Elliott, J.K., *The Apocryphal New Testament*, Oxford: Oxford University Press, 1993/1999
Elton, Ben, *This Other Eden*, London: Black Swan, 1993
Erdnest-Vulcan, Daphne, *The Strange Short Fiction of Joseph Conrad*, Oxford: Oxford University Press, 1999
Evans, J.M., *Paradise Lost and the Genesis Tradition*, Oxford: Oxford University Press, 1968
Exum, J. Cheryl and Stephen D. Moore (eds), *Biblical Studies/Cultural Studies, the Third Sheffield Colloquium*, Sheffield: Sheffield Academic Press, 1998
——— (ed.), *Retellings: The Bible in Literature, Music, Art and Film*, Leiden: Brill, 2007
Eysenck, Michael W. and Mark T. Keane, *Cognitive Psychology*, Hove and New York: Psychology Press, 2005
Falck, Colin, *Myth, Truth and Literature*, Cambridge: Cambridge University Press, 1989

Fenton, J.C., *The Gospel of Matthew*, London: Penguin, 1974

Fisch, Audrey A., Anne K. Mellor and Esther H. Schor (eds), *The Other Mary Shelley, Beyond Frankenstein*, Oxford, Oxford University Press: 1993

Fisch, Harold, *New Stories for Old*, London: Macmillan, 1998

———, *The Biblical Presence in Shakespeare, Milton and Blake*, Oxford: Oxford University Press, 1999

Fish, Stanley, *Is There A Text In This Class? The Authority of Interpretive Communities*, Cambridge MA: Harvard University Press, 1980

Flaubert, Gustav, *The Temptation of St Anthony* (trans. Lafcadio Hearn), New York: The Modern Library, 2001

———, *Three Tales* (trans. Roger Waterhouse), London: Penguin, 2005

Fowler, David C., *The Bible in Early English Literature*, London: Sheldon Press, 1977

———, *The Bible in Middle English Literature*, London and Seattle: University of Washington Press, 1984

Frontain, Raymond-Jean and Jan Wojcik, *The David Myth in Western Literature*, Indiana: Purdue University Press, 1980

Frost, Robert, *Selected Poems*, London: Penguin, 1973

Frye, Northrop, *The Great Code, the Bible and Literature*, London: Routledge & Kegan Paul, 1982

Gaines, Janet Howe, *Music in the Old Bones, Jezebel through the Ages*, Carbondale and Edmundsville: Southern Illinois University Press, 1999

Gallagher, Philip J., *Milton, the Bible and Misogyny*, Columbia: University Missouri Press, 1990

Gearon, Liam (ed.), *English Literature, Theology and the Curriculum*, London: Cassell, 1999

Gerin, Winifred, *Elizabeth Gaskell*, Oxford: Oxford University Press, 1980

Getlein, Frank and Dorothy, *Christianity in Modern Art*, Milwaukee: Bruce Publishing, 1961

Gill, Richard, *Happy Rural Seat, The English Country House in Literature and Imagination*, New Haven and London: Yale University Press, 1972

Ginzberg, Louis, *The Legends of the Jews*, Philadelphia: The Jewish Publication Society of America, 1938/1966, seven volumes.

Glatzer, Nahum (ed.), *The Dimensions of Job*, New York: Schocken Books, 1969

Goldsmith, Stephen, *Unbuilding Jerusalem, Apocalyptic and Romantic Representation*, Ithaca, New York: Cornell University Press, 1993

Goslee, David, *Tennyson's Character, 'Strange Faces, Other Minds'*, Iowa City: University of Iowa, 1989

Greenaway, Peter van, *Judas!*, London: Panther, 1976

Gruen, Eric S., *Heritage and Hellenism: The Reinvention of Jewish Tradition*, Berkeley and Los Angeles: University of California Press, 1998

Hamilton, William, *Melville and the Gods*, California: Scholars Press, 1985

Harrison, F., *The Painted Glass of York*, London: SPCK, 1927

Haskins, Susan, *Mary Magdalene*, London: HarperCollins, 1993

Hawthorn, Jeremy, *A Glossary of Contemporary Literary Theory*, London: Arnold, 2000/2003

Hemingway, Ernest, *The Garden of Eden*, New York: Scribner, 2003

Henn, T.R., *The Bible as Literature*, London: Lutterworth, 1970

Hill, Christopher, *The English Bible and the Seventeenth-Century Revolution*, London: Penguin, 1993

Hirst, Wolf Z., *Byron, the Bible and Religion*, Newark: University of Delaware Press, 1991

Howells, Coral Ann, *Margaret Atwood*, Basingstoke: Palgrave, 1996; new edn. 2005

Hulme, Peter and William H. Sherman (eds), *'The Tempest' and Its Travels*, London: Reaktion Books, 2000

Jack, Alison, *Texts Reading Texts, Sacred and Secular*, Sheffield: Sheffield University Press, 1999

Jackson, Rosemary, *Fantasy, The Literature of Subversion*, London: Methuen, 1981

Jacobson, Howard, *The Very Model of a Man*, London: Penguin, 1993

Jacoff, Rachel (ed.), *The Cambridge Companion to Dante*, Cambridge: Cambridge University Press, 1993

James, M.R., *The Apocalypse in Art*, London: The British Academy, 1931

Jameson, Anna Bronwell, *Legends of the Madonna*, London: Longman, Brown, Green and Longmans, 1852

Jasper, David, *A Short Introduction to Hermeneutics*, Louisville, Kentucky: Westminster John Knox Press, 2004

———, *The Sacred Desert: Religion, Literature, Art and Culture*, Oxford: Blackwell, 2004

Jeffrey, David Lyle (ed.), *A Dictionary of Biblical Tradition in English Literature*, Grand Rapids, Michigan: Eerdmans, 1992

———, *The People of the Book,* New York: Eerdmans, 1996

Jeffries, A. Norman and K.W.G. Cross, *In Excited Reverie*, New York: St Martin's Press, 1965

Jenkins, Philip, *Hidden Gospels, How the Search for Jesus Lost Its Way*, New York: Oxford University Press, 2001

Jobling, David, Tina Pippin, Ronald Schleifer (eds), *The Postmodern Bible Reader*, Oxford: Blackwell, 2001

Josipovici, Gabriel, *The Book of God, A Response to the Bible*, New Haven: Yale University Press, 1988

Jung, Carl, *Answer to Job* (trans. R.F.C. Hull), London: Routledge & Kegan Paul, 1963

Kafka, Franz, *The Complete Short Stories* (various trans.; ed. Nahum H Glatzer), London: Minerva, 1992

Kasser, Rodolphe, and Marvin Meyer and Gregor Wurst (eds), *The Gospel of Judas*, Washington DC: National Geographic Society, 2006

Katz, David S., *God's Last Words, Reading the English Bible from the Reformation to Fundamentalism*, New Haven: Yale University Press, 2004

Kazantzakis, Nikos, *The Last Temptation*, London: Faber & Faber, 1975

Kelley, Margot Ann, *Gloria Naylor's Early Novels*, Gainesville, Florida: University Press of Florida, 1999

Kermode, Frank, *The Genesis of Secrecy*, Cambridge MA: Harvard University Press, 1979

Klassen, William, *Judas: Betrayer or Friend of Jesus*, London: SCM Press, 1996

Kreitzer, Larry, *Gospel Images in Fiction and Film*, London: Sheffield Academic Press, 2002

———, *The New Testament in Fiction and Film*, Sheffield: Sheffield Academic Press, 1993

Kristeva, Julia, *The Kristeva Reader* (ed. Toril Moi), Oxford: Blackwell, 1986

Kugel, James L., *The Bible As It Was*, Cambridge MA: Belknap/Harvard, 1997

Labriola, Albert C. and J.W. Smeltz (trans./commentary), *The Bible of the Poor: Biblia Pauperum*, Pittsburgh PA: Duquesne University Press, 1990

Lamming, E.R., *As In Eden*, London: Faber and Faber, 2005/2006

Lawrence, D.H., *Apocalypse*, London: Penguin, 1974

———, *Love Among the Haystacks and Other Stories*, London: Penguin, 1960

Lee, A. Robert (ed.), *Herman Melville: Reassessments*, London: Vista, 1984

Lee, Hermione, *Willa Cather: A Life Saved Up*, London: Virago, 1997

Levenson, J.D., *The Book of Job in Its Time and in the Twentieth Century*, Cambridge MA: Harvard University Press, 1972

Levine, Robert S. (ed.), *The Cambridge Companion to Herman Melville*, Cambridge: Cambridge University Press, 1998/1999

Lewis, Jon, *The New American Cinema*, Durham and London: Duke University Press, 1998

Lewis, J.P., *A Study of the Interpretation of Noah and the Flood in Jewish and Christian Literature*, Leiden: E.J. Brill, 1968

Linafelt, Tod (ed.), *Strange Fire: Reading the Bible after the Holocaust*, Sheffield: Sheffield Academic Press, 2000

Liptzin, Sol, *Biblical Themes in World Literature*, Hoboken NJ: Ktav Publishing, 1985

Lodge, David, *The Art of Fiction*, London: Penguin, 1992

342

Lüdemann, Gerd, *The Unholy in Scripture* (trans. John Bowden), London: SCM Press, 1996

Maccoby, Hyam, *Judas Iscariot and the Myth of Jewish Evil*, New York: Free Press, 1992

MacDonald, Dennis (ed.), *Mimesis and Intertextuality in Antiquity and Christianity*, Harisburg PA: Trinity Press, 2001

Macdonald, George, *Lilith*, Grand Rapids MI: Eerdmans, 2000

Mackenzie, Norman and Jeanne, *The Time Traveller: the life of H G Wells*, London: Weidenfeld and Nicolson, 1973

Maine, David, *The Flood: A Novel*, London: Canongate, 2004

———, *Fallen*, Edinburgh: Canongate, 2006

Mâle, Emile, *Religious Art in France: the Twelfth Century* (trans. Marthiel Mathews), Princeton NJ: Princeton University Press, 1978

Manguel, Alberto, *The Art of Reading*, London: Flamingo, 1997

Marini, Paola and Gianni Peretti, *Castelvecchio Museum*, Venice: Marsilio Editori, 2003

Marsh, Clive and Gaye Ortiz (eds), *Explorations in Theology and Film*, Oxford: Blackwell, 1997

Martz, Louis L., *The Poetry of Meditation*, New Haven: Yale University Press, 1962

Marx, Stephen, *Shakespeare and the Bible*, Oxford: Oxford University Press, 2000

Maurier, Daphne du, *Rebecca*, London: Virago, 2003

May, John R., *Toward a New Earth: apocalypse in the American novel*, Notre Dame, Indiana: University of Notre Dame Press, 1972

Meer, Frederick van der, *Apocalypse: Visions from the Book of Revelation*, London: Thames & Hudson, 1978

Melville, Hermann, *Billy Budd: Sailor and Other Stories*, London: Penguin, 1985

———, *Moby Dick*, London: Penguin, 2003

Merry, Bruce, *Anatomy of the Spy Thriller*, Dublin: Gill and Macmillan, 1977

Millington, Richard H. (ed.), *The Cambridge Companion to Nathaniel Hawthorne*, Cambridge: Cambridge University Press, 2004

Moltmann, Jürgen, *The Crucified God* (trans. R.A. Wilson and John Bowden), London: SCM Press, 1974

Moseley, Nicholas, *Judith*, London: Minerva, 1992; revised from the 1986 edition

Most, Glen, *Doubting Thomas*, Cambridge MA: Harvard University Press, 2005

Moyise, Steve (ed.), *Studies in the Book of Revelation*, Edinburgh: T. & T. Clark, 2001

Muir, Lynette R., *The Biblical Drama of Medieval Europe*, Cambridge: Cambridge University Press, 1995

Murdoch, Brian, *Adam's Grace: Fall and Redemption in Medieval Literature*, Woodbridge: D.S. Brewer, 2000

Naylor, Gloria, *Bailey's Café*, New York: Vintage, 1993

Norris, Pamela, *The Story of Eve*, London: Picador, 1998

Norton, David, *A History of the Bible as Literature*, Cambridge: Cambridge University Press, 1993

Oberman, Heiki A., *The Roots of Anti-Semitism in the Age of Renaissance and Reformation*, Philadelphia: Fortess Press, 1984

O'Connor, Flannery, *Mystery and Manners: Occasional Prose* (Sally and Robert Fitzgerald, eds), New York: Farrar; Straus & Giroux, 1970

———, *A Good Man is Hard to Find*; (Frederick Asals, ed.), New Brunswick NJ: Rutgers University Press, 1993

Otto, Rudolf, *The Idea of the Holy* (trans. John W. Harvey), London: Oxford University Press/Milford, 1936

Paffenroth, Kim, *Judas: Images of the Lost Disciple*, Louisville: Westminster John Knox Press, 2001

Paley, Morton D., *Apocalypse and Millennium in English Poetry*, Oxford: Oxford University Press, 1999

———, *The Traveller in the Evening, The Last Works of William Blake*, Oxford: Oxford University Press, 2003

Panas, Henryk, *The Gospel According to Judas* (trans. Marc E. Heine), London: Hutchinson, 1977

Parkin, Jay, *Steinbeck, A Biography*, London: Heinemann, 1994

Patai, Raphael, Francis Lee Utley and Dov Noy (eds), *Studies in Biblical and Jewish Folklore*, Bloomington: Indiana University Press, 1960

Patrides, C.A., *The Grand Design of God*, London: Routledge and Kegan Paul, 1972

Peach, Linden, *Angela Carter*, London: Macmillan, 1998

Pelikan, Jaroslav, *Jesus Through the Centuries*, London and New Haven: Yale University Press, 1985

Petit, Susan, *Michel Tournier's Metaphysical Fictions*, Amsterdam, Philadelphia: John Benjamins Publishing Co, 1991

Pickett, Lyn (ed.), *Wilkie Collins, Contemporary Critical Essays*, London: Macmillan, 1998

Pippin, Tina, *Apocalyptic Bodies, the Biblical End of the World in Text and Image*, London: Routledge, 1999

Polhemus, Robert, *Lot's Daughters*, Stanford CA: Stanford University Press, 2005

Porter, Stanley E. and Brook R. Pearson (eds), *Christian-Jewish Relations Through the Centuries*, Sheffield: Sheffield Academic Press, 2000

Prickett, Stephen, *Victorian Fantasy*, Cambridge: Cambridge University Press, 1979
———, *Origins of Narrative, the Romantic Appropriation of the Bible*, Cambridge: Cambridge University Press, 1996
Prior, Sandra Pierson, *The Fayre Formez of the Pearl Poet*, East Lansing, Michigan: Michigan State University Press, 1996
Pritchard, James, *Solomon and Sheba*, London: Phaidon, 1974
Prothero, Raymond E. (Lord Ernle), *The Psalms in Human Life*, London: John Murray, 1903
Pym, John (ed.), *Time Out Film Guide, Eleventh Edition*, London: Penguin, 2003
Pyper, Hugh S., *An Unsuitable Book, the Bible as Scandalous Text*, Sheffield: Sheffield Phoenix Press, 2005
Quinones, Ricardo, *The Changes of Cain*, Princeton NJ: Princeton University Press, 1991
Rabkin, Eric, *The Fantastic in Literature*, Princeton NJ: Princeton University Press, 1976
Rad, Gerhard von, *Genesis, A Commentary* (trans. John H. Marks), London: SCM Press, 1963
Ranelagh, E.L., *The Past We Share*, London: Quartet, 1979
Rayner, William, *The Knifeman*, New York: William Morrow & Co, 1969
Reber, Arthur S. and Emily S. Reber (eds), *Penguin Dictionary of Psychology*, London: Penguin, 2001
Rezzaori, Gregor von, *The Death of My Brother Abel* (trans. Joachim Neugroschel), London: Picador, 1986
Roberts, Michèle, *Wild Girl*, London: Minerva, 1991
———, *The Book of Mrs Noah*, London: Vintage, 1999
Robertson Jr, D.W. and Bernard F. Huppe, *Piers Plowman and Scriptural Tradition*, Princeton NJ: Princeton University Press, 1951
Robson, W.W., *The Definition of Literature and other Essays*, Cambridge: Cambridge University Press, 1982
Rohde, Joachim, *Rediscovering the Teaching of the Evangelists* (trans. Dorothea M Barton), London: SCM Press, 1968
Roston, Murray, *Biblical Drama in England*, London: Faber, 1968
Roth, Joseph, *Job, the Story of a Simple Man* (trans. Dorothy Thompson), London: Granta, 2000
———, *The Radetsky March* (trans. Michael Hofmann), London: Granta, 2003
Rudolph, Kurt, *Gnosis, the Nature and History of Gnosticism*, Edinburgh: T. & T. Clark, 1983
Said, Edward, *Orientalism*, London: Penguin, 2003
Sanders, Julie, *Adaptation and Appropriation*, Abingdon: Routledge, 2006

Saramago, José, *The Gospel According to Jesus Christ* (trans. Giovanni Pontiero), London: HarperCollins, 1993

Sawyer, Deborah F., *God, Gender and the Bible*, London: Routledge, 2002

Sawyer, John F., *The Fifth Gospel, Isaiah in the History of Christianity*, Cambridge: Cambridge University Press, 1996

Schaberg, Jane, *The Resurrection of Mary Magdalene, Legends, Apocrypha and Christian Testament*, London: Continuum, 2002

Schneidau, Herbert, *Waking Giants, The Presence of the Past in Modernism*, Oxford: Oxford University Press, 1991

Schotroff, Luise Silvia Schroer, Marie-Theres Wacker (eds), *Feminist Interpretation, The Bible in Women's Perspective*, Minneapolis: Fortess Press, 1998

Schüssler-Fiorenza, Elisabeth (ed.), *Search the Scriptures*, New York: The Crossroad Publishing Company, 1993

Schwarz, Daniel R. (ed.), *Joseph Conrad, the Secret Sharer*, Boston: Bedford Books, 1997

Schwarz, Regina, *The Curse of Cain*, Chicago: University of Chicago Press, 1997

Scott, Nathan A. and Ronald A. Sharp, *Reading George Steiner*, Baltimore: John Hopkins Press, 1994

Shapiro, James, *Oberammergau*, London: Little Brown, 2000

Shatto, Susan (ed.), *Tennyson's Maud, a Definitive Edition*, London: Athlone Press, 1986

Shaw, Philip, *The Sublime*, Abingdon: Routledge, 2006

Shelley, Mary, *Frankenstein*, London: Penguin Books, 1994

———, *The Last Man*, Oxford: Oxford University Press, 1994/1998

Sherwood, Yvonne, *A Biblical Text and Its Afterlives: the Survival of Jonah in Western Culture*, Cambridge: Cambridge University Press, 2000

Shuger, Debora, *The Renaissance Bible*, Berkeley and Los Angeles: University of California, 1998

Smith, Eric, *Some Versions of the Fall*, London: Croom Helm, 1973

Spark, Muriel, *The Only Problem*, London: The Bodley Head, 1984

Spiegl, Shalom, *The Last Trial*, New York: Schocken Books, 1969

Spolsky, Ellen (ed.), *The Judgement of Susanna, Authority and Witness*, Atlanta: Scholars Press, 1996

Stanford, W.B., *The Ulysses Theme*, Oxford: Blackwell, 1954/new edn. 1968

Steiner, George, *Real Presences*, Chicago: Chicago University Press, 1998/1991

———, *No Passion Spent, Essays 1978–1996*, London: Faber & Faber, 1996

Stocker, Margarita, *Judith, Sexual Warrior: Women and Power in Western Culture*, New Haven and London: Yale University Press, 1998

Stott, Rebecca (ed.), *Tennyson*, London: Longman, 1996

Stone, Michael E. and T.A. Bergren, *Biblical Figures Outside the Bible*, Harrisburg: Trinity Press, 1998

346

Tennyson, Alfred Lord, *Poems*, London: Henry Froude, 1904

Tennyson, Hallam (ed.), *Studies in Tennyson*, London: Macmillan, 1981

Tharpe, J.A.C. (ed.), *Frost Centennial Essays II and III*, Jackson, Mississippi: University of Mississippi Press, 1978

Thompson, David and Ian Christie, *Scorsese on Scorsese*, London: Faber, 1996

Tournier, Michel, *The Ogre* (trans. Barbara Bray), New York: Doubleday, 1972

————, *Gemini* (trans. Anne Carter), London: Minerva, 1989

————, *The Wind Spirit, an Autobiography* (trans. Arthur Goldhammer), London: Collins, 1989

————, *The Four Wise Men* (trans. Ralph Manheim), Baltimore: John Hopkins University Press, 1997

Trend, Michael, *The Music Makers, The English Musical Renaissance from Elgar to Britten*, London: Weidenfeld & Nicolson, 1985

Trexler, Richard C., *The Journey of the Magi*, Princeton: Princeton University Press, 1997

Unamuno, Miguel de, *Ficciones* (trans. Anthony Kerrigan), Princeton NJ: Princeton University Press, 1976

————, *Novela/Nivola* (trans. Anthony Kerrigan), Princeton NJ: Princeton University Press, 1976

Voragine, Jacobus de, *The Golden Legend* (trans. William Granger Ryan), Princeton NJ: Princeton University Press, 1993

Warner, Marina, *Alone of All Her Sex*, London: Weidenfeld & Nicolson, 1976

————, *The Beast and the Blonde*, London: Vintage, 1995

————, *Monuments and Maidens*, Berkeley: University of California Press, 2000

Washington, Harold C., Susan Lochrie, Graham and Pamela Thimmes (eds), *Escaping Eden, New Feminist Perspectives on the Bible*, Sheffield: Sheffield Academic Press, 1998

Waugh, David, *Geography, an Integrated Approach*, Edinburgh: Nelson, 1990

Wells, H.G., *The Undying Fire*, London: Macmillan, 1912

Whitt, Margaret Earley, *Understanding Gloria Naylor*, Columbia, South Carolina: University of South Carolina Press, 1999

Wimsatt, Jr., William K., *The Verbal Icon, Studies in the Meaning of Poetry*, Lexington: Kentucky University Press, 1954

Wolff, Robert Lee, *The Golden Key, A Study of The Fiction of George Macdonald*, New Haven: Yale University Press, 1961

Wollstonecraft, Mary, *Maria, or The Wrongs of Woman*, New York: W.W. Norton & Company, 1975. First published London, 1778

Woolf, Rosemary, *The English Mystery Play*, London: Routledge & Kegan Paul, 1972

Wright, Andrew, *Blake's Job, A Commentary*, Oxford: Oxford University Press, 1972

Wright, T.R., *D.H. Lawrence and the Bible*, Cambridge: Cambridge University Press, 2002

Wroe, Ann, *Pilate, the Biography of an Invented Man*, London: Jonathan Cape, 1999

Ziolkowski, Theodore, *Fictional Transfigurations of Jesus*, Princeton NJ: Princeton University Press, 1971

———, *Disenchanted Images*, Princeton, NJ: Princeton University Press, 1977

INDEX

Moseley, Nicholas 58, 59, 167, 177–9, 193, 266, 309
Judith 1, 8, 9, 19, 32, 54–59, 136, 137, 139, 167, 177–9, 193, 197, 198, 218, 224, 231, 235, 241, 249, 266, 272, 273, 279, 295, 307, 309
Most, Glen 91, 327–30
Doubting Thomas 91, 327–30

N

Naylor, Gloria 129, 167, 181, 182, 193
Noah 1, 9, 20, 49–51, 146, 231, 239, 253, 265, 298
Norris, Pamela 1, 8, 49, 60–3, 138, 139, 140, 144, 147, 149, 150, 169, 171, 192, 201, 204, 205, 221, 222, 229, 231, 232, 233, 236, 237, 249, 253, 259, 267, 272, 285, 289, 298

O

O'Connor, Flannery 70, 73–4, 141, 227, 268
Otto, Rudolf 72, 111, 196
Ovid 236, 237, 275, 281, 282, 283, 284, 285, 286, 289, 302

P

Paffenroth, Kim 1, 9, 23, 24, 49, 86–91, 143, 153, 184, 186, 193, 223, 230, 231, 232, 233, 243, 249, 254, 255, 270, 272,

279, 288, 298, 313, 319, 321, 324, 325
Paley, Morton 41, 175
Pelikan, Jaroslav 24
Petrarch 180, 181
Pilate, Pontius 1, 7, 9, 24, 42, 63–6, 89, 139, 161, 162, 163, 164, 225, 226, 229, 241, 242, 243, 249, 254, 267–8, 288, 295, 298, 309
Pippin, Tina 1, 9, 69–76, 140, 141, 186, 189, 190, 191, 193, 196, 226, 227, 230, 232, 240, 243, 249, 250, 255, 268–9, 272, 298, 303, 307, 309, 311, 312, 313, 319, 322, 323, 324, 325
Postmodern Bible 17, 18, 196
Prickett, Stephen 117, 133, 135, 139, 169, 315
Pritchard, James B. 1, 30–5, 126, 208, 221, 222, 228, 231, 232, 240, 248, 252, 256, 261–2, 271, 280, 298, 309, 312, 315
Prothero, Roland 3

Q

Queen of Sheba 1, 30, 31, 32, 33, 34, 35, 126, 127, 136, 159, 177, 197, 198, 201, 204, 208, 218, 240, 261, 262, 280, 289, 295, 310
Quinones, Ricardo ii, 1, 8, 39–4, 49, 130, 131, 144, 151, 154, 156, 172, 175, 212, 213, 214, 222, 223, 228, 232, 233, 237, 239, 248, 252, 263–4, 271, 279, 280, 289, 296, 298, 310, 312, 313

R

Rabkin, Eric 49, 349
Rayner, William 89, 143, 167, 184–5, 193, 270
   The Knifeman 89, 143, 167, 184, 193, 270
Robbins, Tom 68, 70, 140, 227, 268, 269
   Skinny Legs and All 68, 70, 73, 140, 227, 268, 269, 309, 310
Roberts, Michèle 48, 133, 134, 253, 265
Roston, Murray 6, 273
Roth, Joseph 25, 100, 109, 119, 124, 125, 145, 156–8, 165, 251, 260, 261, 302, 349
   Job, the Story of a Simple Man 25, 100, 109, 119, 124, 145, 156, 165, 260, 261, 302

S

Said, Edward 197, 204, 208, 309
Sanders, Julie 20, 115, 219, 313, 331–3
Saramago, José 24, 160
Sawyer, John F. 19, 49
Schneidau, Herbert 14, 198, 199, 203, 209, 239
Scorsese, Martin 154, 270, 279, 301, 302
Shakespeare, William 19, 88, 95, 97, 100, 120, 164, 174, 181, 260, 269, 276, 277, 280, 281, 282, 286, 287, 288, 289, 295, 303, 307, 333
Shelley, Mary 61, 62, 75, 76, 130, 136, 138, 139, 141, 167, 186, 187–9, 200, 201, 202, 203, 204, 211, 217, 218, 219, 251, 252, 259, 267, 296, 300
   Frankenstein 61, 62, 130, 138, 139, 201, 202, 203, 204, 211, 217, 219, 251, 252, 259, 267, 309
   The Last Man 76, 130, 167, 186, 187–9, 300, 309
Sherwood, Yvonne ii, v, 1, 9, 76–86, 124, 141, 142, 143, 167, 197, 209, 210, 211, 227, 228, 229, 231, 232, 241, 250, 252, 256, 259, 270–1, 272, 289, 298, 302, 307, 312, 313, 315, 316
Shuger, Debora 47
Smith, Eric 6
Solomon and Sheba 1, 30, 31, 32, 33, 34, 261, 262
Southwell, Robert v, 167, 180–2, 193
Spiegl, Shalom 6
Stanford, W.B. 3, 5, 275–8, 279, 280, 281
Steinbeck, John 40, 41, 43, 167, 175–6, 192
   East of Eden 43, 167, 175–6, 192, 309
Steiner, George ii, 4, 72, 93, 95, 112–17, 137, 198, 308, 311
Sterne, Laurence 16
Stocker, Margarita 1, 8, 54–9, 84, 136, 137, 138, 139, 177, 178, 193, 198, 223, 224, 228, 231, 232, 235, 241, 244, 245, 249, 250, 252, 253, 266, 272, 279, 289, 295, 298, 307, 312, 313, 315, 316
Susannah 273, 274

Anthony C. Swindell

Dr. Anthony C. Swindell is the Rector of St. Saviour, Jersey, Channel Islands. He has studied at Cambridge University and holds a Ph.D. from the University of Leeds, England.